A Brit's Guide
to
rlando
and
Walt Disney World

2002

★

Simon Veness

foulsham

The Publishing House, Bennetts Close, Cippenham, Berkshire, SL1 5AP, England

ISBN 0-572-02744-3

Text copyright © 2002 Simon Veness

Series title, format, logo and layout design copyright © 2002 W. Foulsham & Co. Ltd

Other books in this series:
A Brit's Guide to Las Vegas and the West 2002, Karen Marchbank, 0-572-02746-X
Choosing A Cruise, Simon Veness, 0-572-02738-9
A Brit's Guide to New York 2002, Karen Marchbank, 0-572-02741-9

DEDICATION

To my wife, Karen, without whose non-stop support and assistance this book would never have become a reality.

IN MEMORIAM

This edition is also dedicated to Sylvia Murray, from Ontario, Canada, one of my fellow Moderators on the website wdwinfo.com, who lost her brave battle with cancer on June 7, 2001, leaving a young son, Nick. She served as an inspiration to many and will be remembered as one of the people who helped bring the magic of Disney to life for others. We miss you, Sylvia.

SPECIAL THANKS

Special thanks for this edition go to: Virgin Holidays, The Walt Disney Company, Alamo Rent A Car, Universal Orlando, Orlando Convention and Visitors Bureau, Kissimmee Convention and Visitors Bureau, St Petersburg/Clearwater Area Convention & Visitors Bureau, Daytona Beach Area Convention & Visitors Bureau, Disney's Animal Kingdom Lodge, Hard Rock Hotel, Grand Theme Hotels, Country Inn & Suites by Carlson, and Airwave Communications.

My sincere thanks also go to all the hard-working people at Foulsham who help to bring my work to life every year.

Printed in Malaysia

Contents

8. Off The Beaten Track

(or, When You're All Theme-Parked Out). A taste of the real Florida – Winter Park, Aquatic Wonders Boat Tours, Boggy Creek Airboats and Parasail, Orange Blossom Balloons, Everglades and the Bahamas, Flying Tigers Warbird Restoration Museum and Warbird Adventures, Green Meadows Petting Farm, Disney and Cruising, Seminole County, Forever Florida, Disney's Wilderness Preserve, The Beaches – St Pete's/Clearwater, Cocoa Beach & Daytona, Sports, including golf, fishing, water sports, horse riding, spectator sports and Disney's Wide World of Sports™, Motorsport.

9. Orlando by Night

(or, Burning the Candle at Both Ends). Downtown Disney, Pointe*Orlando, Universal's CityWalk, Downtown Orlando, Disney Shows, Arabian Nights, Pirate's Dinner Adventure, Mark II Dinner Theater, Medieval Times, Sleuth's, night-clubs, live music, discos, bars.

10. Eating Out

(or, Watching the Americans at Their National Sport). Full guide to local-style eating and drinking, rundown of the fast-food outlets, best family restaurants, American diners and speciality restaurants.

11. Shopping

(or, How to Send Your Credit Card into Meltdown). Your duty-free allowances, full guide to the main tourist shopping complexes, discount outlets, malls and speciality shops.

12. Going Home

(or, Where Did the Last Two Weeks Go?). Avoiding last-minute snags, full guide to Orlando International and Orlando/Sanford Airports and their facilities for the journey home.

13. Your Holiday Planner

Examples of how to plan for a two-week holiday, with a Five-Day Disney Hopper Plus Pass and Seven-Day Pass, and blank forms for your holiday!

Foreword

It's another bright new year in the story of the world's most exciting holiday destination and you are in pole position to prepare for and look forward to all the fun that lies in store. Whether you are a first timer to the Sunshine State of Florida (and, if so, what kept you?), or one of the many repeat visitors (and one of our regular readers – we know who you are!), I would like to extend a hearty Brit's Guide welcome to the next best thing to actually being in Orlando.

Things continue to develop at an amazing pace in this tourist wonderland and, while it now seems a long time since I sat down to draft the first edition of this book, it is only eight years. In that time, the pace of development has been quite staggering and it is no wonder so many millions flock back here time after time. This latest edition (the seventh) of the UK's best-selling guidebook continues to present a huge challenge in keeping up to date with it all, as the three principal areas that comprise this vast holiday resort (the counties of Orange, Osceola and Seminole) remain vigorously engaged in making things newer, bigger and better almost by the day. It can be an exhausting task, but I'm not going to pretend it isn't also great fun.

*Looking ahead to 2002, the Walt Disney World Resort should be bursting with a very special 'birthday' tribute to the man who made it all possible, Walt himself, in their **100 Years of Magic celebration**. New parades, rides and shows have been liberally sprinkled through all four parks, with Disney-MGM Studios at the heart of the festivities. And, having had my own sneak preview of what's in store, I can safely say it should be another thoroughly memorable year in the kingdom of the Mouse! Of course, the rest of Orlando will not be left out, and Universal Orlando continues to develop their action-packed site with another fabulous hotel resort, Loews Royal Pacific. International Drive is again a hive of development, the Kissimmee area should now benefit from several years of construction and roadworks as part of their BeautiVacation project, and the city of Orlando itself also demonstrates a growing ability to catch the eye.*

However, despite all these attempts to keep us dazed and confused in the name of having fun, the Brit's Guide remains dedicated to providing the most informed and user-friendly travel service you can find, especially if used in conjunction with our friends at the website www.wdwinfo (see below), by far the best Internet resource on all things Disney out there. I like to think this book is researched and written with a real tourist's eye for detail and value, including all the information you really need to know, not just what the brochures want you to believe. It aims to give you a good idea of what to expect and (most importantly) how to plan and budget for it, as well as being a useful companion while you are there.

Most significantly, you will get the inside track on how to have the best holiday you can, at the best price and with the least fuss. Prepare to be amazed (and exhausted!) by what's in store, but don't say I didn't tell you so. Now, excuse me while I put my feet up for a while … have a nice day now. Simon Veness *(e-mail me at simonveness.orlando1@virgin.net or join me at www.wdwinfo.co.uk)*

1 Introduction
(or, Welcome to the Holiday of a Lifetime)

Welcome to the most exciting holiday experience in the world, bar none, guaranteed. This area of central Florida we call Orlando is a vast conglomeration of adventure rides, thrills, fun and fantasy the like of which exists nowhere else, and we are not talking just about the *Walt Disney World Resort in Florida* here.

First off, you need to be aware of the bewilderingly extensive and complex nature of most of what lies in wait in this tourist wonderland. Disney remains the leading attraction in town, but there is a strong supporting cast, of which Universal Orlando and Sea World are outstanding examples.

There is something to suit all tastes and ages – young or old, families, couples or singles – but it exacts a high physical toll. You'll walk a lot, queue a lot and probably eat a lot. You will have a fabulous time, but you'll end up exhausted as well. It is not so much a holiday as an exercise in military planning.

Eight theme parks

In simple terms, there are now eight major theme parks which are generally reckoned to be essential holiday fare, and at least one of those will require two days to make you feel it has been well and truly done. Add on a day at one of the water fun parks, a trip to see some of the wildlife or other more 'natural' attractions, and the lure of the nearby Kennedy Space Center, and you're talking at least 11 days of pure adventure-mania. Then mix in the night-time attractions of *Downtown Disney*, Universal's CityWalk and a host of dinner shows, and you get an idea of the awesome scale of the entertainment on offer. Even given two weeks, something has to give – just make sure it isn't your patience/ pocket/sanity!

So, how do we innocents abroad, many of us making our first visit to the good ol' USA, get full value from what is still, without doubt, a truly magical holiday?

There is no set answer of course, but there are some pretty solid guidelines to steer you in the right direction and help avoid some of the more obvious pitfalls. Central to most of them is *planning*. At the back of this guide there is a useful 'calendar' to fill in and use as a ready reference guide. Don't be inflexible, but be aware of the time demands of the main parks, and give yourself a few quiet days by the pool or at one of the smaller attractions to recover your strength.

Also, be aware of the vast scale and complexity of this wonderland, and try to take in as much of the clever detail and breadth of imagination on offer, especially in *Walt Disney World Resort in Florida*.

Orlando

Orlando itself is a relatively small but bright young city which has been taken over to the immediate south-west by the *Walt Disney World Resort in Florida*, to give it its full title, which opened with the *Magic Kingdom Park* in 1971 and has encouraged a massive tourist expansion ever since. New attractions are being added all the time and the city is periodically in danger of being swamped by this vast out-pouring of rampant commercialism and aggressive tourist marketing. However, there is still a genuine concern for the environment, and the development should not get out of hand, at least in the near future (although it is easy to imagine it already has in some parts).

The tourist area generally known as Orlando actually consists of three counties. Orange County is the home of the city of Orlando, but much of *Walt Disney World Resort in Florida* is in Osceola County, with Kissimmee its main town. Seminole County, home of Sanford Airport, is immediately to the north of Orange County.

The local population numbers slightly above 1.6 million, of which some 160,000 are actively employed in the tourist business, but, in 2000, some 42 million people decided on Orlando as the place for their holiday, spending in excess of $18 billion in central Florida! Britain accounts for more than a third of all foreign visitors to Orlando, and in 2000 that was around 1.4 million of us. Those figures represent a near 100 per cent increase in the last 10 years, with the international airport seeing its traffic boom from eight million passengers in 1983 to a massive 30.82 million just 17 years later. In addition, the full Orlando area boasts more than 103,000 hotel rooms and 3,500 places to eat.

Walt Disney World Resort Florida

This actually consists of four distinct, separate theme parks, 21 speciality hotel resorts, a camping ground, three water parks, a state-of-the-art spectator sports complex, five 18-hole golf courses, four mini-golf courses and a huge shopping and entertainment complex (*Downtown Disney*). It covers 47 square miles (almost 31,000 acres). Alton Towers and Thorpe Park would comfortably fit into one of its car parks. Indeed, Alton Towers, Britain's biggest theme park, is 60 times smaller than *Walt Disney World Resort in Florida*. Disney's most-frequented park, the *Magic Kingdom*, has a single-day record attendance in the region of 92,000 – Thorpe Park in Surrey (500 acres) peaks at around 15,000. The Disney organisation does things with the most style, but the others have caught on fast and they are all creating new amenities almost as fast as they can think of them.

Intriguingly, only around half of Disney's massive site is currently developed, leaving plenty of room for new accommodation and attractions, while even the existing parks have potential for an extra ride or two, and there are several major projects on the drawing board. They maintain an extremely high customer service ethic and are always looking at ways to refresh the existing attractions. Their 15-month *100 Years of Magic* celebration was due to open on 1 October 2001 (see What's New in 2002), adding still more novelty and freshness to the overall experience.

Here's a quick rundown of what's on offer.

The Magic Kingdom Park: this is the essential Disney, including the fantasy of all its wonderful animated films, the adventure of the Wild

FLORIDA

How far from Orlando to . . .

Bradenton	130 miles	Miami	220 miles
Clearwater	110 miles	Naples	230 miles
Cocoa Beach	40 miles	Sarasota	140 miles
Daytona	60 miles	Silver Springs	80 miles
Fort Lauderdale	205 miles	St Augustine	120 miles
Fort Myers	190 miles	St Petersburg	105 miles
Jacksonville	155 miles	Tampa	75 miles
Key West	375 miles	Venice	160 miles

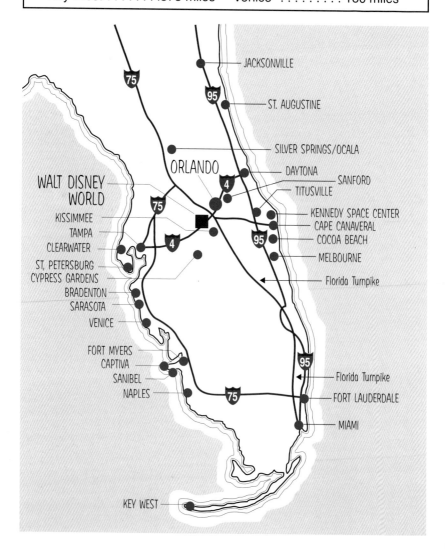

100 Years of Magic Parade

West and African jungles, and the excitement of some classy thrill rides like Space Mountain, a huge indoor roller-coaster, and the ExtraTERRORestrial Alien Encounter.

Epcot: this is Disney's look at the world of tomorrow through the gates of Future World, plus a potted journey around our planet in World Showcase. It's more educational than adventurous, but still possesses some memorable rides, including Test Track and Universe of Energy, and some great places to eat.

Disney-MGM Studios: here you can ride the movies in style, meeting up with Star Wars, the Muppets and Indiana Jones, drop into the fearsome Tower of Terror or the thrilling new Rock 'n Roller Coaster and learn how films are really made.

Disney's Animal Kingdom Theme Park: billed as 'a new species of theme park': this delivers another contrasting and hugely entertaining scenario. With cleverly realistic animal habitats, including a 100-acre safari savannah, captivating shows and several terrific rides, it offers a change of pace from the other parks.

Disney's Typhoon Lagoon Water Park: bring your swimming costume and spend a lazy day splashing down water slides and learning to surf in the world's biggest man-made lagoon.

Disney's River Country Water Park: more watery fun 'n games, with some great slides and the accent on nature.

Disney's Blizzard Beach Water Park: this is the big brother of all the water parks, with a massive spread of rides and slides in a 'snowy' environment.

Disney's Wide World of Sports Complex: offers the chance to watch world-class events like tennis, baseball, basketball, athletics, volleyball and many others.

Downtown Disney: incorporates **Pleasure Island, Marketplace** and the **West Side** of themed restaurants, a cinema complex, the *DisneyQuest* arcade of interactive games, Virgin Megastore and world-famous Cirque du Soleil circus company. New Year's Eve is the Pleasure Island theme, with a choice of eight night-clubs. For *Walt Disney World Resort in Florida* hotels, see Chapter 4, while their picture-perfect **Wedding Pavilion** features in many brochures for the chance to get married in fairytale style.

Most people buy one of the multi-day passes which allow you to move between the various parks on the same day, while all grant unlimited access to *Walt Disney World Resort's*

Life-size pinball at DisneyQuest

transport system of monorails, buses and ferries (always get your hand stamped if you leave one park but intend to return). Make no mistake, you can't walk between the parks, and trying to do more than one in a day in any depth is a recipe for disaster. The choice of tickets for Disney in particular is becoming bewildering, and the addition of 7- and 10-day passes hasn't helped. Here are the main choices at the ticket booths: **1-day tickets**, giving access to one of the four main parks; **4-Day Park Hopper**, providing 4 days at the main parks, with multiple parks on the same day; **5-Day Park Hopper**, 5 main park days, with multiple same-day visits; **5-Day Park Hopper Plus**, 5 days at the four parks, with multiple same-day visits, plus 2 visits to any of Blizzard Beach, Typhoon Lagoon, River Country, Pleasure Island and Wide World of Sports™ (excluding special events at WWoS); **6-Day Park Hopper Plus**, 6 days at the main parks, plus 3 of the options above; and the **7-Day Park Hopper Plus**, a week at the main parks, plus 4 of the options. All multi-day passes give savings on 1-day tickets, and unused days never expire (so can be saved for any time in the future). In the UK, you can buy the 5- and 7-Day Park Hopper Plus through tour operators, ticket brokers and *Disney Stores*, while the special **World Pass** is available ONLY over here, giving 10 days' entry to the four main parks, water parks, Pleasure Island, Disney Quest and Wide World of Sports (excluding special events), plus a FREE character breakfast. The World Pass expires 21 days after its first use. Guests at *Walt Disney World Resort* hotels can also buy **Ultimate Park Hopper** tickets, giving entry to all the parks, Pleasure Island, Wide World of Sports AND DisneyQuest for the length of your stay, plus a choice of one extra item, such as a character breakfast or *Epcot* guided tour. Price varies according to how long you stay. For stays in excess of two weeks, it is worth considering the **Annual Pass** or **Premium Annual Pass**, which add more value (you can check the Ticket Prices section of www.wdwinfo.co.uk for the latest info).

When it comes to Universal Orlando (see page 13), SeaWorld and Busch Gardens, the choice is a little simpler. Again, you have **1-day Tickets**, but it works out cheaper to buy a **2-** or **3-Day Ticket**, giving access to Universal Studios, Islands of Adventure, Wet 'n Wild water park and the clubs of CityWalk. There is also a clubs-only pass ($7.95 plus tax) or a clubs-plus-film ticket ($11.95) as CityWalk also boasts a 20-screen Cineplex. Even better value are the 2-week **Orlando FlexTickets**. The 4-Park Ticket gives admission to USF, IoA, SeaWorld and Wet 'n Wild, while the 5-Park Ticket is also good for Busch Gardens, and both are valid for 14 days from first use.

With price hikes every year, it is worth shopping around for tickets and buying as soon as possible. **Tour operators** tend to be ABOVE gate price for the convenience of being able to pre-book and budget for all your main costs in one go. If you do want to pre-book, I recommend the **Keith Prowse** agency (02890 232425, or see your travel agent) as

BRIT TIP: Be wary of travel agent pressure to buy too many tickets. You may well find you can't fit everything in, plus, for some attractions, you can often buy cheaper in Orlando, even from the tour operators' reps.

GETTING AROUND ORLANDO

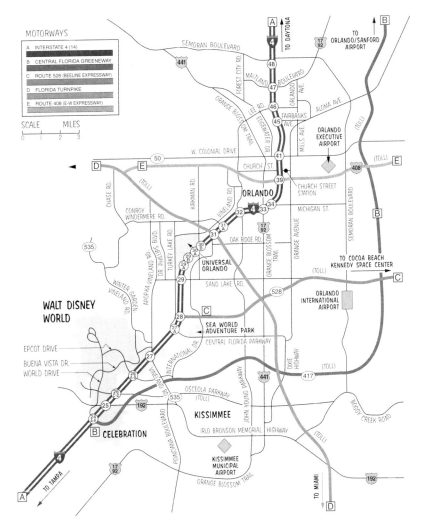

one of the best for competitive prices AND pre-booking convenience, while they do several one-off tickets, excursions and 2-day trips specially for the UK market. They also supply the actual tickets as opposed to a voucher which you have to exchange at the ticket booths.

You can also look up Dreams Unlimited Travel and their online TicketRes service for some good discounts and special offers (www.dreamsunlimitedtravel.com/ticketres).

A first word of warning: you don't want to try to do *Walt Disney World Resort* in one chunk. Apart from ending up with serious theme park indigestion, you'll probably also hit one of the parks on a busy day (check the Busy Day Guide on page 280). The *Magic Kingdom* Park and

KEY TO ORLANDO – MAIN ATTRACTIONS

A1	Disney's Animal Kingdom Theme Park
A	Magic Kingdom Park
B	Epcot
C	Disney-MGM Studios
D	Universal Orlando
E	SeaWorld Adventure Park
F	Busch Gardens
G	Kennedy Space Center
H	US Astronaut Hall of Fame
I	Splendid China
J	Cypress Gardens
K	Silver Springs
L	Gatorland
M	Disney's Typhoon Lagoon Water Park
N	Disney's Blizzard Beach Water Park
O	Disney's River Country Water Park
P	Water Mania
Q	Wet 'n Wild
R	Discovery Cove by SeaWorld
S	Holy Land Experience
T	Ripley's Believe It or Not
U	Guinness World of Records/Titanic
V	Orange County History Center
W	Downtown Disney
X	Green Meadows Petting Farm
Y	Fantasy of Flight

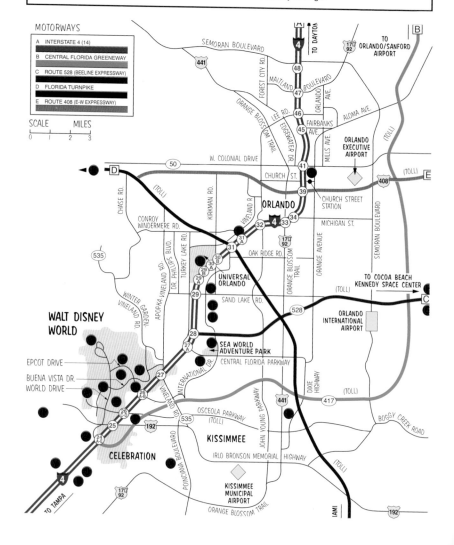

Jungle Cruise at Silver Springs

Epcot can be particularly exhausting (especially with children), and you'll need a quiet day afterwards.

The others

If *Walt Disney World Resort in Florida* is what you think Orlando is all about, you'll be in for a pleasant surprise when you read this round-up of some of the other attractions on offer. **Universal Orlando** is the newest resort development that aims to rival Disney with its choice of two theme parks, water park, entertainment district and series of speciality hotels. **Universal Studios:** this features the state-of-the-art simulator ride Back to the Future, the mind-boggling Terminator 2 attraction, Jaws, Kongfrontation, Earthquake, Woody Woodpecker's Kid Zone and the Men in Black ride. **Islands of Adventure:** new in 1999, Universal's second park is a superb blend of thrill rides, family attractions, shows and awesome, eye-catching design, with some of the most technologically advanced hardware in the world. **SeaWorld:** don't be put off thinking it's just another dolphin show, this is *the* place for the creatures of the deep, with killer whales being the main attraction, a bright, refreshing atmosphere and a pleasingly serious ecological approach, plus the five-star thrill rides Journey to Atlantis and Kraken. SeaWorld also has an exclusive new neighbour, **Discovery Cove**, that offers the chance to swim with dolphins, among other things. **Busch Gardens:** the sister park to SeaWorld, here it's creatures of the land, with the highlights being the new Rhino Rally ride, Myombe Reserve, a close-up look at the endangered Central African highland gorillas, and the Edge of Africa safari experience. A real treat, plus a number of brain-numbing roller-coasters and other rides. **Cypress Gardens:** a chance to slow down and take in the more scenic attractions of beautiful gardens, water-skiing shows and animal encounters. **Kennedy Space Center:** the dramatically upgraded home of space exploration. **Silver Springs:** a close look at Florida nature via jeep and boat safaris through real swampland, with several alligator displays. **Splendid China:** a novel alternative attraction, a 5,000-mile journey through China with miniaturised reproductions of

Montu at Busch Gardens

features like the Great Wall and the Terracotta Warriors, plus live shows, acrobats, dancers, great shopping and food. **Fantasy of Flight:** this

> BRIT TIP: The humidity levels – up to 100 per cent – and fierce daily rainstorms in summer take a lot of visitors by surprise, so take a lightweight, rainproof jacket or buy one of the cheap plastic ponchos available in local shops.

aviation museum experience has the world's largest private collection of vintage aircraft, plus fighter-plane simulators.

So that's a good taste of what's on offer, the next question is when to go? Florida's weather does vary a fair bit, from bright but cool winter days in November, December and January, with the odd drizzly spell, to furiously hot and humid summers punctuated by tropical downpours.

The most pleasant option is to go in between the two extremes, i.e., in spring or autumn. You will also avoid the worst of the crowds. However, as most families are governed by school holidays, July to September remain the most popular months for Brit visitors, and so there will also be some advice on how to get one jump ahead of the high-season crush.

And now to business. Hopefully, we've whetted your appetite for the excitement in store. It's big, brash and fun, but above all it's American, and that means everything is exceedingly well organised, with a tendency towards the raucous rather than the reserved. It's clean, well maintained and very anxious to please: Floridians generally are an affable bunch, but they take affability to new heights in the main theme parks, where staff are almost

painfully keen to make sure you 'have a nice day'.

Also close to every American's heart is the custom of tipping. With the exception of petrol pump attendants and fast-food restaurant servers, just about everyone who offers you any sort of service in hotels, bars, restaurants, buses, taxis, airports and other public amenities will expect a tip. In bars, restaurants and taxis, 15 per cent of the bill is the usual going rate while porters will expect $1 per bag. Brits are notoriously forgetful of this little habit but, as all service industry workers are automatically taxed on the assumption of receiving 15 per cent in tips, you will be doing a major service to the local economy if you remember those few extra dollars each time.

It is also useful to know dollar travellers' cheques can be used as cash, so it is not necessary (as well as not being advisable) to carry large amounts of cash around. **Take note that all Orlando prices, both where indicated in this book and on every price-tag you see, do not include the 6–7 per cent Florida Sales Tax. There is also a 4–5 per cent Resort Tax on hotel rooms.**

The use of credit cards is nearly essential as they are accepted everywhere, are easy to carry and use and provide an extra degree of buying security. In some cases, notably car hire, you can't operate without your flexible friend, so don't

> BRIT TIP:
> Tipping Guide
>
> | Bill | Suggested Tip |
> |------|---------------|
> | $15 | $2.25 |
> | $20 | $3.00 |
> | $25 | $3.75 |
> | $30 | $4.50 |
> | $40 | $6.00 |
> | $50 | $7.50 |

leave your Visa or Mastercard at home!

Holiday visitors to America do not need a visa providing they hold a valid British passport showing they are a British Citizen (and which does not expire before the end of your holiday). Instead, all you do is fill in a green visa waiver form (usually handed out on your flight or when you check in) and hand it in with your passport to the US immigration official who checks you through first thing after landing. However, British Subjects do need a visa (£30), and you should apply at least a month in advance to the US Embassy.

In England, Scotland and Wales write to the Visa Office, US Embassy, 5 Upper Grosvenor Street, London, W1A 2JB (0891 200 290).

In Northern Ireland write to US Consulate General, 3 Queens House, Belfast, BT1 6EQ.

Alternatively, call 0991 500 590 (£1.50/minute) for more detailed visa advice, or log on to their web site at www.usembassy.org.uk.

What's new in 2002

Walt Disney World Resort in Florida will be the focus of a splendid-looking celebration from October 2001 to December 2002. **100 Years of Magic** is a multi-dimensional look at the life and creativity of Walt Disney himself, who would have been 100 on 5 December 2001. It features a new parade in each park, several new attractions – including an exhibit all about Walt the man – and interactive kiosks explaining the Disney magic, as well as a host of special effects and a 122ft Sorcerer Mickey hat to act as the main icon and new focus of *Disney-MGM Studios. Disney's Animal Kingdom* park is due to unveil a whole new area of Dinoland, **Chester & Hester's Dino-Rama!**, which includes two new rides and a carnival-style amusement arcade. Elsewhere in the World, Disney are due to open the first segment of their **Pop Century resort,** the second of their massive, more budget-orientated value hotels. When complete, it will offer 5,760 rooms in colourful blocks representing different decades of the 1900s. Universal Orlando should unveil their third resort hotel with the summer debut of **Loews Royal Pacific**, which will follow in the impressive footsteps of the Portofino Bay and Hard Rock hotels. This completes the major Universal development on this site, but the company still owns more than 1,000 acres adjacent to International Drive and there are, as yet, no firm plans for this land, although at least one more theme park, several hotels and a golf course are thought to be in their grand design.

International Drive continues to thrive and develop as an entity in its own right, with three significant new elements. The **Festival Bay** shopping and entertainment complex should finally be taking shape, while a **Midway Magic** of games, rides and go-karts has grown up just south of Wet 'n Wild. The **Masters of Magic Show** on International Drive is the latest addition to the area's wide-ranging attraction choice, a twice-nightly 90-minute Las Vegas-style illusion extravaganza.

One of the biggest openings will be that of the **Opryland Hotel** on 02-02-02 (at 02:02, of course!). Possibly the most dramatic and ambitious resort in Florida to date, this will be an unmistakable 1,400-room colossus, covered by *4 acres* of glass, and with a strong Florida theme and décor.

Two other new hotels in 2002 will be the 732-room **Omni Orlando Resort**, in the new golf-orientated development of Champions Gate (just south of *Walt Disney World*

Resort in Florida) and an 800-suite hotel by the **Sierra Land Group** on International Drive.

For shopping, the **Mall at Millenia** (just off I4 north of Universal Orlando) promises to take the retail experience really up-market, with an elaborate 200-shop spread highlighted by the three great American department stores of Bloomingdale's and Macy's (the first in Florida), followed by Neiman-Marcus early in 2003. **Orlando Fashion Square Mall** by Orlando Executive Airport should also have more to offer with a 200,000sq ft expansion.

Finally, away from the theme parks, the **Downtown Orlando** area is undergoing something of a regeneration. While much of the rebuilding is for office and business use, the addition of some smart new hotels, shops and the free Lymmo bus system is adding to the picture all the time and making it a highly enjoyable city in its own right. I believe a major new theatre is also in the pipeline, which will put Orlando firmly on the cultural map as a performing arts centre (although it already has much to recommend it).

As ever, there will be announcements that beat our deadline, so don't forget to check out www.wdwinfo.co.uk for all the latest information.

Plan your visit

The next few chapters will help you plan your days and tell you everything you need to know to make your holiday perfect. Draw up a rough itinerary, and then fine-tune it with the help of www.wdwinfo.co.uk.

Now read on and enjoy . . .

Disney's Animal Kingdom Theme Park

© Disney

Planning and Practicalities

(or, How to Almost Do It All and Live to Tell the Tale)

There is one simple rule once you have decided Orlando is the place for you. Sit down (preferably with this book) and PLAN what you want to do very carefully. This is not the type of holiday you can take in a freewheeling, carefree 'make it up as you go along' manner. Frustration and exhaustion lie in wait for all those who do not have at least a basic plan.

So this is what you do. First of all work out WHEN you want to go, then decide WHERE in the vast resort is the best place for you. Then consider WHAT sort of holiday you are looking for, WHO you want to entrust your holiday with and finally HOW much you want to try to do.

When to go

If you are looking to avoid the worst of the crowds, the best periods to choose are October to December (but not the week of the Thanksgiving holiday in November or the Christmas to New Year period), early January (after New Year, and avoiding the President's Day holiday in February) to two weeks before Easter, and April (after Easter) to the end of May. Orlando gets down to some serious tourist business from Memorial Day (the last Monday in May, the official start of the summer season) to Labor Day (the first Monday in September and the last holiday of summer), peaking on the Fourth of July, a huge national holiday. The Easter holidays are similarly uncomfortable (although the weather is better), but easily the busiest is the Christmas period, starting the week before 25 December and lasting until 2 January. It is not unknown for some of the theme parks to close their gates to new arrivals as their massive car parks become full by mid-morning.

The months offering the best combination of comfortable weather and smaller crowds are February and early March (pre-Easter) and October, but never let wet weather

BRIT TIP: Thanksgiving is always the fourth Thursday in November; George Washington's birthday, or President's Day, is the third Monday in February. Try to avoid those weeks!

The Touchdown Hotel at Disney's All-Star Sports Resort

© Disney

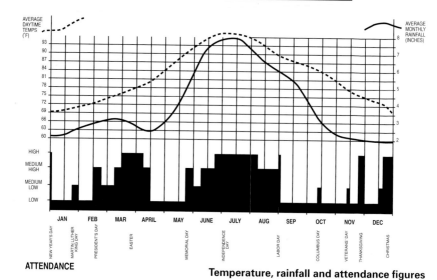

Temperature, rainfall and attendance figures

put you off. Few of the main attractions are affected by rain (although the roller-coasters and water rides will close if lightning threatens), and you will be one jump ahead if you have remembered to bring a waterproof jacket as the crowds noticeably thin out when it gets wet. In any event, all the parks sell cheap, plastic ponchos (although they are even cheaper at Wal-Mart or other supermarkets). In the colder months, take a few lightweight but warm layers for early-morning queues, then, when it warms up later in the day, peel off and leave them in the lockers that are provided in all the parks. And, when it's too hot, take advantage of the air-conditioned facilities (of which there are many) during the warmest parts of the day, although you may also find the indoor facilities can be chilly.

Where to stay

The choice of where to stay is equally important, especially if you have a family who will demand the extra amenities of swimming pools and games rooms. Having the use of a swimming pool is also a major plus for relaxing at the end of a busy day. Inevitably, there is a huge choice of accommodation areas and prices. As a guide, there are four main areas that make up the greater Orlando tourist conglomeration.

Walt Disney World Resort in Florida: some of the most sophisticated, convenient and fun places to stay are to be found in *Walt Disney World Resort in Florida's* hotels sprinkled around its main attractions. The same imagination that has gone into the creation of the theme parks has been at work on the likes of *Disney's Polynesian Resort* and *Disney's Animal Kingdom Lodge.* They all feature free, regular transport to all of the attractions and guests get extra perks like early admission to theme parks on selected days, your own resort ID card (so you can charge meals and souvenirs to your room, and have your gifts delivered to the hotel), free parking and being able to book in advance for restaurants and shows in the parks, while Disney characters pop up for meals at some of them. Many resorts also have great kids' clubs and baby-sitting services. The drawbacks here

2

are, with the exception of *Disney's All-Star Resorts* and the new *Pop Century*, the *Walt Disney World in Florida* hotels are among the most expensive in Orlando, especially to eat in, and you still have a fair drive to get to attractions like Universal Orlando and the Kennedy Space Center. For a one-week holiday it takes some beating, though.

Lake Buena Vista: is a loosely defined area around some pretty lakes to the eastern fringes of *Walt Disney World Resort in Florida* and along Interstate 4 that again features some of the more up-market hotels. It also has the convenience of being handy for all the *Walt Disney World in Florida* parks, with most hotels offering free transport, and excellent leisure and shopping facilities. It tends to be a bit pricey, but its proximity to Interstate 4 makes it convenient for much of Orlando.

International Drive: this ribbon development lies midway between *Walt Disney World Resort in Florida* and downtown Orlando and is therefore an excellent central location. Running parallel to Interstate 4, it is about 15–20 minutes drive from the main theme parks, while it is also a well-developed tourist area in its own right, with some great shopping, restaurants and attractions like Wet 'n Wild, Ripley's Believe It Or Not, WonderWorks and Skull Kingdom. The downside is it does get congested and occasionally hazardous with tourist traffic in peak periods and you have to make a slightly earlier Disney start in the morning. But it does represent good value for money and possesses a rarity in Orlando in that you can go for a long stroll along real pavement. A sub-district off I-Drive is now the Universal area of Kirkman Road and Major Boulevard, which is developing new hotels all the time.

Kissimmee: budget holiday-makers can be found in their greatest numbers along the tourist sprawl of Highway 192, an almost unbroken 12-mile strip of hotels, motels, restaurants and shops. It offers some of the best economy accommodation in the area and is handy for *Walt Disney World Resort in Florida's* attractions, although it gives you the longest journey to Universal Orlando and downtown Orlando. A car is most advisable here, although the scheduled completion of the BeautiVacation project (and the end, thankfully, of the choking roadworks) to enhance the heavily built-up stretch of 192 from Route 535 as far west as Splendid China, with pavements, landscaping, bus shelters, benches and water fountains, means this should now be a much-improved location.

Split holidays

It is fair to say you can't really go far wrong no matter what you're seeking from your holiday, as long as you plan well. The Atlantic coast and some great beaches are only an hour's drive away to the east, the magnificent Florida Everglades are little more than 3–4 hours to the south, and there are more wonderful beaches and pleasant coast roads to the west. There are great shopping opportunities almost everywhere, while Orlando is also home to some stunning golf courses, and there are plenty of opportunities either to play or watch tennis, baseball and basketball. A common choice nowadays is to split the holiday by having a week or two in Orlando as well as a week elsewhere in Florida like the Gulf Coast or Florida Keys. The main tour companies offer a huge variety of packages, with cruise-and-stay options increasingly popular.

If you can afford the time (and the expense), the best combination is to have two weeks in Orlando itself and then a week relaxing on one of Florida's many fabulous beaches. A

Ron Jon's Resort

2-week, half-and-half split is a popular choice, but can tend to make your week in Orlando especially hectic, unless you pick your additional week on the Atlantic coast at somewhere like Cocoa Beach. This resort, near to Cape Canaveral and the Kennedy Space Center, is only an hour from Orlando and offers the choice of being able to return to Disney for the day. A few companies offer a good 10-day Orlando and 4-day coast split. Fly-drives obviously offer the greatest flexibility of doing Orlando and seeing something else of Florida, but again there is a lot to tempt you in just two weeks and you may find it better to book a one-centre package that includes a car as well as your accommodation so you can still travel around but avoid too much packing and unpacking.

The Rock Hotel at Disney's All-Star Music Resort

© Disney

Travel companies

There is some serious competition for your hard-earned holiday money and, in the last couple of years, the travel companies have worked hard to keep the cost of an Orlando holiday down, making it excellent value for money, whether you fly-drive, book your own flights or just take a package.

Shop around to get the best value for your holiday £, but I recommend making sure your package is booked with an ABTA agent for holiday security should anything go wrong. At the last count, there were more than 80 tour operators offering holidays to Florida, and here is a rundown of the biggest and best.

Virgin Holidays: the biggest operator to MCO (that's Orlando Airport in travel-agent-speak), Virgin also have the biggest and most exhausting brochure. They

Kids have fun on Virgin flights

offer the largest variety of combinations, including Miami, the Keys, New York, Toronto, Chicago, the Bahamas, Mexico, eight Caribbean islands and some tempting cruises, as well as the Florida coasts. A strong selling point is Virgin's non-stop scheduled service to Orlando (from Manchester as well as Gatwick) with award-winning in-flight entertainment, free drinks and special kids' meals and games. They have a veritable army of well-briefed

Orlando's downtown

reps in Orlando and a good, all-round choice of accommodation in the different areas, and are popular for fly-drives, flying into Orlando and out from Miami. Flight up-grades to their Premium Economy (extra leg-room and bigger seats) or the wonderful Upper Class service are available and the Virgin service throughout is impeccable. You can pre-book seats (on 01293 747205) and even check in the day before your flight at Gatwick. Orlando is also an increasingly popular choice as a wedding venue, and Virgin have their own wedding co-ordinators for ceremonies in *Walt Disney World Resort in Florida* or elsewhere in Florida. For golf, tennis and scuba-diving enthusiasts there are also activity packages. Other bonuses include single-parent discounts, extra help for passengers with disabilities, 'kids eat free' deals at selected hotels and some excellent non-driver packages, including an Attraction Pass for 10 round-trip journeys to any of the main attractions or shopping malls. Virgin also have a unique return flight check-in service at *Downtown Disney*, open from 8.30am–1pm on your

final day so you can get rid of your suitcases and make good use of the time. You can visit their Internet site on www.virginholidays.com or call 0870 000 0870 for a brochure.
Airline: Virgin Atlantic.
Airport: Orlando International.
   Travel City: the UK's largest independent direct-sell Florida specialist, with more than 130,000 customers in 2001, they offer a wide range of holidays at ultra-competitive prices, including fly-drives, one and two-centre holidays, private pool villas and Caribbean cruises. A sharp reservations team have excellent local knowledge and can advise you on where to stay, what to do and the latest 'what's new' information. You can also pre-book flight seats (for a small fee), airport hotel and parking. Flights are either on their own charter airline ATA, other major charter airlines or scheduled flights. They have a double baggage allowance offer (£10/person or £25 for a family of four) where you can increase your allowance from the normal 20kg to 40kg when you book an ATA flight. Travel City also have a dedicated arrivals centre at Orlando-Sanford Airport and a welcome centre at the Lake Buena Vista Factory Shops which is open 7 days a week. Travel City can be found on Teletext page 222, or you can book direct on 08709 909 127 or 08707 428 081.
Airline: ATA (American TransAir).
Airport: Orlando-Sanford Airport.

BRIT TIP: Virgin are the company I fly with most often on Orlando research trips – out of choice.

Azure waters and pure white sands at Castaway Cay with a DisneyCruise.

Thomson: another of the largest, mass-market operators, Thomson have an excellent reputation in Orlando, where they have a large team of reps and Service Centres on I-Drive, and offer six departure airports (including Birmingham, Newcastle and Glasgow). You can now pre-book your flight seats in advance for a small charge, and they also feature great in-flight entertainment. Thomson price their packages very competitively for the family market, with special children's fares and bonuses like 'kids eat free' and 'extra value' hotels, while they offer a decent selection of coastal resorts for two-centre holidays and an increasing number of private villas. They also organise wedding packages (from £639) at Cypress Gardens, Cypress Grove, Leu Gardens or the Gulf Coast. Flight up-grades cost £60 (for extra leg room) and £120 (for their Premium service, with wider seats, complimentary drinks, choice of meals and priority boarding). Check out www.thomson-holidays.com for their website.
Airline: Britannia.
Airport: Orlando International.

Airtours: also in the leading group who take around 100,000 British tourists to Orlando every year, they fly mainly non-stop from nine UK airports, with good in-flight entertainment and fun-packs for kids. For £20/person seats can be pre-booked in the family areas. They offer a highly recommended Premiair Gold comfort up-grade (extra leg-room, free bar, pre-selected menu, late UK check-in) for £149 or £179/person (see below). Airtours has some novel 10- and 11-night packages (from Manchester, Gatwick and Glasgow only) to offer a more flexible choice and are the only operator to offer a 15-seater mini-van. New for 2002 is an Airtours service desk at the huge McDonald's on International Drive

and Sand Lake Road (with special meal deals!). They also have some imaginative 2-centre combinations, including a new holiday providing a week at a *Walt Disney World Resort in Florida* hotel and a week at a Universal Orlando resort, plus Florida Keys, Las Vegas, New Orleans, Florida coasts and cruises with Carnival. Villa accommodations are now a prominent part of their programme, with good quality pool-homes on offer throughout Florida. Airtours make a feature of their fly-drive packages, with a range of 'Drive and Stay' holidays which offer a wide choice to the Florida sun-seeker, especially return visitors. In keeping with their new flexible-price approach, you can now book different options, from the top-of-the-range *Holiday Plus* (including pre-booked flight seating, 60-minute latest check-in, in-flight refreshment, choice of meal, pre-departure pack, 25kg luggage allowance and a reduced price Premiair Gold up-grade – £149), *Economy Holidays* (90-minute check-in, 20kg luggage allowance and Premiair Gold up-grade option – £179), *Sundeal Holidays* (the no-frills option, with accommodation assigned on arrival, a two-hour latest check-in, only 15kg luggage allowance and no optional up-grades or in-flight meal – it costs £15 extra) to pure *Flight Only* (as Sundeals, but no accommodation). For a brochure, call 01235 824428 or visit their website at www.airtours.co.uk.
Airline: Airtours International.
Airport: Orlando-Sanford.

First Choice: a comprehensive flight programme uses eight UK airports (including Glasgow, Newcastle and Cardiff, but not always non-stop), plus a Classic Premium up-grade (extra leg-room and in-flight services, plus special check-in facilities) for £139 and pre-bookable seats on their smart in-house airline (£14/adult and

£5/child). They offer an extended choice of twin-centre holidays, including an imaginative International Drive-Disney resort split (tip: do I-Drive first!), a range of Florida beach options (including coach transfers for non-drivers) and golf and diving facilities at selected hotels. First Choice have a family-friendly touch offering hotels with themed kids suites, price reductions, low-start prices and 'kids eat free' deals, plus villas and apartments (with their own reps) that can work out better value for large groups.
Airlines: Air 2000, Airtours International.
Airports: Orlando-Sanford.

Three other First Choice brands also sell Florida – **First Choice Villas**, for a solely villa-based holiday, **Eclipse**, a direct-sell operator, and **Unijet** (see below). Their website is also worth checking out, www.firstchoice.co.uk, and you can request a brochure on 020 8880 8155.

Unijet: although bought out in 1998 by First Choice, Unijet continue to operate in their own right, flying from eight UK airports. Unijet pride themselves on their value-for-money family packages (including 'kids eat free' hotel deals) and offer an increasing number of holiday homes as well as hotels, which are great value for larger families or groups. They feature six of *Walt Disney World Resort in Florida's* big hotels, from the budget options to the top of the range, and an expanded range of two-centre and tailor-made holidays (including some popular Caribbean cruises). You can also question their Florida resort team or pre-book excursions on floridainfo@unijet.com. Unijet's well-run wedding service offers Cypress Gardens and Leu Gardens, as well as *Disney's Wedding Pavilion*. Call 0500 767767 for a brochure or visit www.unijet.com.
Airlines: Air 2000, Airtours

International, JMC and Britannia.
Airports: Orlando-Sanford and Orlando International (Britannia).

British Airways Holidays: another company to benefit from their direct, scheduled air service (kids' activity packs, etc), British Airways Holidays offer great flexibility, with almost any duration and combination possible. Beach add-ons, cruises, twin centres - for example with Turks & Caicos, Cayman Islands, The Bahamas, Antigua and Barbados – and an extensive selection of quality but great value private homes are all on offer. They also fly to Miami and Tampa to open up plenty of fly-drive and multi-centre possibilities, hence BAH are popular with the many repeat visitors to Florida. Call 0870 2424 243 for a brochure or visit www.baholidays.co.uk.
Airline: British Airways.
Airport: Orlando International.

British Airways Holidays also has a joint venture business with **Thomas Cook Holidays**, with the latter geared primarily to the more regular packages aimed at first and second-time visitors. Cook's 2002 programme expands it's *Walt Disney World Resort in Florida* portfolio with the addition of the new Pop Century Resort and a revamped holiday homes selection, with townhouses sleeping six leading in at as little as £57 per night. They offer flights with Virgin or a new daily service with Continental (via Newark, New York) from Gatwick, Birmingham, Glasgow, Manchester and Stansted.
Airlines: Virgin Atlantic, Continental (via New York).
Airport: Orlando International.

Jetsave: Florida specialists Jetsave put the accent on flexibility, with a wide range of just about everything for your Orlando holiday. For accommodation, you have the full selection of motels, hotels (especially the kid-friendly variety), resorts, apartments and holiday homes (or

Great shopping at Pointe*Orlando

villas, as we would call them), and simple, accurate star ratings for each property. The Jetsave High Flyers Club (01235 824324) is also worth joining for a few little extras. You can fly (with connecting flights in some cases) from any of 23 UK airports into one of eight Florida gateways, fly any day, stay for any duration and up-grade to extra leg-room seats, business or even first class (expensive, though). Twin-centre options (which can be split any way for a fortnight) feature a good range of Florida beaches, plus New Orleans, Caribbean and various cruises. Check their fine website on www.jetsave.co.uk.

Airlines: Britannia, Virgin Atlantic, British Airways.
Airport: Orlando International.

Cosmos: although better known for European holidays, their Orlando operation is very well organised with one of the most readable brochures, catering mainly for the family market and offering a full range of accommodation. They feature hotels, villas and apartments, and promise even more options in 2001, including Universal's fabulous new hotels, new cruises, and an increased selection of villas with pools (including top-of-the-range executive homes). Their 'Dream Weddings' feature includes balloons, Cypress Gardens and even a sunset yacht cruise, as well as Disney's Wedding specialities. Kids' prices

lead in at £149 with free entrance at a choice of six attractions for under 13s (including Water Mania, WonderWorks and Pirates Cove mini-golf) and under 12s eat free at many hotels. Call Cosmos on 0161 476 5678 or log on to their website at www.cosmos-holidays.co.uk.
Airlines: Monarch (Premium Cabin up-grade £110), Airtours International, Air 2000, Britannia.
Airports: Orlando-Sanford. *Stop press: Cosmos will be discontinuing their Florida programme in 2002.*

JMC: Part of Thomas Cook, this firm continues to build on a reputation for being one of the most quality-conscious mass-market operations. Free kids' passes to a few of the smaller attractions, free kids' meals (under 12s), some all-inclusive accommodation and a wide choice of quite select villas are all JMC features, while they also offer many Disney properties and a good range of twin-centre choices, including Cancun (Mexico) and the Bahamas. New features include pre-planned Fly Tours, cruise-and-stay holidays, and Vehicle Not Vital properties for those not wanting to drive, with the chosen accommodation within easy reach of shops, bars and restaurants and with good transport to the attractions. There are some 'all-in' deals that include your attraction tickets and free transport. Their wedding packages (from £419) are another stand-out, with seven locations, including Winter Park and Cypress Gardens. Disney weddings are also available, with prices starting from £1399. Flights are from eight UK airports and – praise be for a charter operator! – there are FREE pre-allocated seats.
Airlines: JMC Airline, Air 2000, Airtours International.
Airport: Orlando-Sanford.

Kuoni: as in all their holidays, Kuoni offer the up-market version of Orlando, with some of the best hotels, a strong tie-up with *Walt*

Disney World Resort in Florida, a comprehensive wedding and honeymoon service and a new Price Watch guarantee (money back if you find an identical holiday for less). They have an extensive range of twin-centre options, including the Florida Keys, Boca Raton and Marco Island, and some excellent executive holiday homes. The average price reflects the more exclusive nature of many of their packages (plus their flexible, tailor-made choice facility), but there are some big child reductions, 'kids eat free' hotels, and Kuoni use only scheduled airlines. Call 087007 458664 for a brochure, 01306 742222 to book or look up their website at www.kuoni.co.uk.
Airlines: Virgin Atlantic, United (via Washington) and British Airways.
Airport: Orlando International or Miami Airport.
   Funway Holidays: this is the sister company of America's largest tour operator and a leading specialist in holidays to the US, hence they offer a tailor-made service to match Orlando with any other option, making for total flexibility of choice from no less than 22 UK airports. Their private homes are a big feature of the Florida programme, but they also serve up some terrific-value deals, especially with low children's prices, if you book early, making them consistently among the best prices for a family of four. They also use only scheduled airlines. A wide range of two-centre options include the Gulf Coast, Miami and the Keys, plus cruises to the Bahamas and Caribbean from Miami. Other extras include 'kids eat free' hotels, free kids' clubs, free hotel nights at certain times and free shuttles at selected hotels for non-drivers. Look them up at www.funwayholidays.co.uk or call 020 8466 0222 for a brochure.

Airlines: various scheduled, including Virgin, BA and Continental.
   Airport: Orlando International.
   Style Holidays: one of the UK's top self-catering specialists (and a Thomas Cook-owned company), they offer a huge selection of private-pool homes and hotel suites, with accommodation from 2-, 3- and 4-bed homes up to luxurious 5- and 6-bed varieties, as well as the usual range of hotel and Disney resort options. All properties are in named, well-described situations so that the location, facilities and size can be matched to needs. Their comprehensive Florida brochure has an excellent variety of Gulf Coast villas (all of which can be combined with Orlando), while they maintain a high standard of in-resort service. Transfers can be arranged for non-drivers (£15 per person each way) and they offer the full range of pre-bookable attraction tickets. For bookings and brochures, call 0870 444 4404 or 0870 444 4414, or check out www.style-holidays.co.uk. Brochures can be ordered by e-mail, brochures@style-holidays.co.uk.
   Airlines: JMC.
   Airport: Orlando-Sanford.

Islands of Adventure

Walt Disney Travel Company: Disney's own travel operation comes with the full Mouse Ears style. A sharp, informative brochure is backed up by expert reservations consultants and every *Walt Disney World* resort is featured, as well as a handful of non-Disney hotels and holiday homes, plus a series of mid-range and up-market twin-centre options in the likes of St Petersburg and Marco Island, making for a broad range of choice. The detail is good, with character-branded ticket wallets and luggage tags, autograph books for the kids and an information book, plus, in 2002, children staying at most Disney resorts will receive a refillable mug for free fizzy drinks throughout their stay. *Walt Disney World Resort in Florida* guests get an Unlimited Park Hopper ticket included while non-Disney guests get a Disney 5-Day Park Hopper Plus. Car rental is, uniquely, with National, which adds to the all-round quality of service, while there is a free airport transfer for those not wishing to drive straight away. A new upgrade choice, Disney's Adventure Magic, offers special dining, merchandise and recreation options (such as golf, boating and VIP viewing of parades and fireworks) at a cost of £139 per person (aged 3 and older) for 7 nights. As with all things Disney, you tend to pay top dollar, but you are assured of great service and invaluable extras like exclusive welcome meetings actually in the *Magic Kingdom* Park and 'children eat free' deals at selected hotels. For a brochure, call 0870 2424 910 or visit www.disneyworld.co.uk.
Airlines: Britannia, British Airways (for a supplement).
Airport: Orlando International.
There are plenty of other options worth checking out, including:
Trailfinders (highly recommended by several readers; 020 7937 5400, or www.trailfinders.com), **USAirtours**

(0345 353353), **Travel 4** (0541 550066), **Travelbag** (01420 88380), **Transolar Holidays** (0151 630 3737), **Totally Florida** (by Mercury Travel, 0870 8870060), **Premier Holidays** (01223 516688), **Key To America** (01784 248777), and **Destination USA** (020 7253 2000).
Flightbookers (020 7757 2000, or www.ebookers.com) and the **Flight Centre** (08708 999888) feature keen flight-only services. Scanning Teletext (page 222) will often reveal many special deals on full packages or flights alone. The pages of www.expedia.co.uk are also worth looking up.
Finally, for those looking to book an independent package, but wanting help with Disney accommodation, meal reservations, etc, the excellent **Dreams Unlimited Travel** internet service is a must. Check out their website at www.dreamsunlimitedtravel.com for the essential information on this excellent no-cost service which can save you time, money and hassle. They also feature other Orlando hotels on their DreamsRes on-line booking service and a discount ticket agency, TicketRes, on the same site.
The important thing is to establish a plan of what you want to do, then get a selection of brochures and compare the prices and attractions of each one.

What to see when

Once you arrive, the temptation is to head for the nearest theme park, then the next, and so on. Hold on! If there is such a thing as theme park indigestion, that's the best recipe for it. Some days at the parks are busier than others; it is simply not possible to cover more than one a day, and it may be inadvisable to attempt two of the main parks on successive days. So here's what you do.
With the aid of the Holiday Planner on pages 274–80, make a

note of all the attractions you want to try to see and pencil them in over the duration of your holiday.

The most sensible strategy is to plan around the eight 'must-see' parks of *The Magic Kingdom* Park, *Epcot, Disney-MGM Studios, Disney's Animal Kingdom* Theme Park, Universal Studios Florida and the Islands of Adventure theme park, SeaWorld and Busch Gardens. If you have only a week, consider dropping Busch Gardens (it's furthest away from Orlando and doesn't have quite the same magical appeal as the others) and concentrate on the Disney parks and Universal Studios, with SeaWorld as an extra if it fits into your plan. Science fact and fiction addicts will be hard-pressed not to include the Kennedy Space Center, but it will probably bore small children.

As a basic rule, the *Magic Kingdom* Park is the biggest hit with children, and families often find it requires two days. The same can be said of *Epcot,* but there are fewer rides to amuse small children and the emphasis is as much on education as entertainment, although it all has Disney's slick, easily digestible coating. Only the most fleet of foot, given the benefit of a relatively crowd-free period, will be able to negotiate *Epcot* successfully in a day. *Disney's Animal Kingdom* Theme Park is also a little short on attractions for the youngest kids (unless they really love their animals, as mine do), but it still requires nearly all of its 8am–6pm opening hours. *Disney-MGM Studios* – home of the new 100 Years of Magic celebration – is a 9–5 park (where you can usually fit in all the attractions in a day), while SeaWorld needs rather longer and Universal Studios Florida can be a 2-day park when Orlando is at its busiest. Islands of Adventure will almost certainly keep everyone, except possibly the under-5 age group, busy

all day, too. Busch Gardens, extremely popular with British families, is another full-day affair, especially as it is 75–90 minutes' drive away to Tampa in the south-west, but an early start to the Kennedy Space Center (an hour's drive to the east coast) will mean you can be back in your hotel swimming pool by tea-time, confident you have fully enjoyed One Small Step For Man. All the attractions are detailed in Chapters 5–8, so try to get an idea of the time requirements of them all before you pick up your pencil.

Smaller attractions

Of the other, smaller-scale attractions, the nature park of Silver Springs is a full day out as it also involves a near 2-hour drive to get there, but everything else can be fitted around your Big Eight Itinerary. The water parks are all a good way to spend a relaxing afternoon, while Cypress Gardens is another quieter place to while away half a day or so. There are also a number of smaller-scale attractions in Orlando which will probably keep the children amused for several hours (and often after the theme parks have closed). Gatorland is a unique look at some of Florida's oldest inhabitants and is a good combination with a ride at Boggy Creek Airboats. Ripley's Believe It Or Not museum and WonderWorks interactive house of fun are both good family centres for several hours. Add in the terrific haunted house attraction Skull Kingdom, the Guinness World Records Experience and *Titanic* exhibitions at The Mercado, and the more old-fashioned lure of go-karts and other fairground-type rides at Fun Spot (all of them on the I-Drive corridor), and you have a full day of alternative fun and frolics. Aviation fans must not miss a trip to Fantasy of Flight (further down I4) or the Flying

Life in the fast lane!

Tigers Warbird Air Museum in Kissimmee for a novel experience.

DisneyQuest, another part of the *Downtown Disney* set-up, is a hugely imaginative interactive 'arcade' that guarantees up to half a day's fun (especially for older children). Each main tourist area is also well served with imaginative mini-golf courses that will happily absorb any excess energy for an hour or so from those who haven't been exhausted!

Evenings

Then, of course, there is the evening entertainment, with a similarly wide choice of extravagant fun-seeking. By far the best, and a must for at least one evening each, are *Downtown Disney Pleasure Island* at *Walt Disney World Resort in Florida*, Universal's new CityWalk and the fast-developing Pointe*Orlando area. All will keep you fully entertained until the early hours. Another popular source of fun are the various dinner shows: a 2–3 hour cabaret based on themes like medieval knights, pirates, Arabian Nights and murder mysteries that all include a hearty meal. Then there are the huge variety of night-clubs and bars, many offering live music. See Chapter 9 for the full details.

What to do when

There are a couple of handy general guidelines for avoiding the worst of the tourist hordes, even in high season. The vast majority of fun-seekers in town are American, and they tend to arrive at the weekends, get settled in their hotels, and then head for the main theme parks, i.e. *Walt Disney World Resort in Florida*, first. That means Mondays and Tuesdays are generally bad times for the *Magic Kingdom* Park and *Epcot*. Additional busy times are created by Disney's *early entry days* or Surprise Mornings at three of their parks. These allow *Walt Disney World* hotel guests in an hour before official opening time and mean the parks stay especially busy on those days. If you are NOT staying in a Disney property and can't take advantage of *Early Entry*, these are best avoided: Sunday, *Disney-MGM Studios;* Monday, *Magic Kingdom* Park; Tuesday, *Epcot;* Wednesday, *Disney-MGM Studios;* Thursday, *Magic Kingdom* Park; Friday, *Epcot;* Saturday, *Magic Kingdom* Park. *Disney's Animal Kingdom* tends to be busiest on Monday, Tuesday and Wednesday and is a tough park to get round when it's crowded. The popular water parks of *Blizzard Beach*, *Typhoon Lagoon* and *River Country* hit high tide at the weekend, and Thursday and Friday in summer.

At Universal Orlando, the picture is still evolving after the opening of their Islands of Adventure park. However, the weekends definitely see above-average crowds, while Universal Studios also tends to be busier on Thursdays and Fridays and

IoA on Mondays and Tuesdays.

If *Walt Disney World Resort in Florida* is humming in the early part of the week, that makes it a good time to visit SeaWorld, Busch Gardens, Cypress Gardens, Silver Springs or the Kennedy Space Center. Wet 'n Wild and Water Mania are best avoided at the weekends when the locals come out to play (see also page 280, Busy Day Guide).

> BRIT TIP: If your hotel is not far from the park take a couple of hours out to return for a siesta or a swim. Have your hand stamped for re-entry when you leave (your car park ticket will also be valid all day), and then enjoy the evening entertainment back at the park, which is often the most spectacular part of the day.

Making sure you get the most out of your days at the main theme parks is another art form, and there are a number of practical policies to pursue. The official opening times are all well publicised and don't vary much between 9 and 9.30am. However, apart from the obvious advantage of arriving early to try to get at the head of the queues (and you will encounter some SERIOUS queues, or lines as the Americans call them), the parks may well open earlier than scheduled if the crowds build up quickly before the official hour. So, you can get a step ahead of the masses by arriving at least 30 minutes before the expected opening time, or an hour early during the main holiday periods. Apart from anything else, you will be better placed to park in the vast, wide open spaces of the public car parks and

catch the tram to the main gates (anything up to half a mile away!).

Once you've put yourself in pole position, don't waste time on the shops, scenery and other frippery which will lure the unprepared first-timer. Instead, head straight for some of the main rides and get a few big-time thrills under your belt before the main hordes arrive. You will quickly work out where the most popular attractions are as the majority of the other early birds will be similarly prepared and will flock in the appropriate direction. Use Chapters 5 and 6 to help you plan your individual park strategies.

As another general rule, you can also benefit from doing the opposite of what the masses do after the initial rush has subsided.

Pace yourself

A word of warning: the *Walt Disney World Resort in Florida* parks, notably the *Magic Kingdom* Park, stay open late in the evening during the main holiday periods, occasionally until midnight, and that can make for a long day for young children. Therefore it is important to pace yourself, especially if you have been one of the first through the gates. There are plenty of opportunities to take time-outs and have a drink or bite to eat, and you can take advantage of the American propensity to take meal-times seriously by avoiding lunchtime (12 noon–2pm) and dinnertime (5.30–7pm). So, after you've had a couple of hours of real adventure-mania, it pays to take an early lunch (i.e. before midday), plunge back into the hectic thrill of it all for another 3 hours or so, have another snack-sized meal in mid-afternoon and then return to the main rides, as the parks tend to quieten down a little in late afternoon.

Finally, a word about shopping in Orlando – it's world class. Your battle plan should also include at least a half-day to visit one of the spectacular shopping malls, as well as some of the discount outlets and speciality centres like Old Town in Kissimmee, Orlando Premium Outlets, the Mercado and the Pointe*Orlando on I-Drive.

Clothing and comfort

The most important part of your whole holiday wardrobe is your footwear. You are going to spend a lot of time on your feet, even during the off-peak periods. The smallest of the parks covers 'only' 100 acres, but that is irrelevant to the amount of time you will spend queuing. Don't decide to break in those new sandals or trainers. Comfortable, well-worn shoes or trainers are essential. Otherwise, you need dress only as the climate dictates. T-shirts and shorts are quite acceptable in all of the parks (but swimwear is not acceptable away from pool areas) and most restaurants and other eating establishments will happily accept informal dress.

BRIT TIP: Don't pack a lot of smart or semi-formal clothing – you really won't need it in hot, informal Florida.

If, after a long day, you feel the need for a change of clothes or a sweater for the evening, use the handy lockers which all the theme parks provide. All the main parks are also well equipped with pushchairs (or strollers) for a small charge, and baby services are freely located at regular intervals.

It is absolutely *vital* to use high-factor sun creams at all times, even during the winter months when the sun may not feel that strong but can

still burn. Nothing is guaranteed to make you feel uncomfortable for several weeks like severe sunburn. Orlando has a sub-tropical climate and requires higher-factor sun creams than even a holiday in the Mediterranean. Use sun blocks on sensitive areas like your nose and ears, and splash on the after-sun cream liberally at the end of the day. Local skincare products are widely available and usually inexpensive (especially at Wal-Mart or K-Mart stores).

BRIT TIP: The summer is mosquito time. Buy a spray-on insect repellent. Alternatively, try Avon's Skin So Soft which works wonders at keeping the bugs at bay.

Don't forget a waterproof sun cream if you are swimming. Wear a hat if you are out theme park-ing in the hottest parts of the day, and try to avoid alcohol, coffee and fizzy drinks until the evening as they will all make you dehydrated and susceptible to heatstroke. You will need to increase your fluid intake *significantly* during the summer months in Orlando, but stick to still soft drinks (try Gatorade, a squash-like energy drink) or water.

Should you require medical treatment, whether it be for sunburn or other first aid, consult your tour company's information about local hospitals and surgeries. In the event of a medical, or other, emergency, dial 911 as you would 999 in Britain.

It cannot be over-stressed that you should have comprehensive travel and health insurance for any trip to America as there is NO National Health Service and ANY form of medical treatment will need to be paid for – and is usually expensive. Keep all the receipts and reclaim on your return home.

Emergency out-patients departments can be found with Centra Care at Florida Hospital Medical Center (in four locations: 12125 South Apopka-Vineland Road, near the Crossroads at Lake Buena Vista; 7848 West Irlo Bronson Memorial Highway, near Splendid China; 6001 Vineland Road, near Universal Studios; and 1462 West Oakridge Road, near Florida Mall) and Sand Lake Hospital on 9400 Turkey Lake Road, while the East Coast Medical Network (407 648 5252) and House Med Inc (407 239 1195) both make hotel 'house calls' 24 hours a day. House Med also operates MediClinic, a walk-in facility on 2901 Parkway Boulevard, Kissimmee, open daily 9am–9pm, and Orlando Regional Healthcare System (operators of Sand Lake Hospital) have Walk-In Medical Care centres on International Drive (407 351 3035 and 239 6679) open 8am–8pm. The two largest chemists (drug stores) are Eckerd Drugs at 908 Lee Road and Walgreens at 6201 I-Drive (both open 24 hours).

Travel insurance

Having said you should not travel without good insurance, you should also not pay over the odds for it. Tour operators are notoriously expensive or may imply you need to buy their insurance policy when you don't. In all cases make sure your policy covers you in the USA for: **medical cover** of at least £2 million; **personal liability** up to £2 million (though this won't cover driving abroad; you would still need Supplementary Liability Insurance with your car-hire firm); **cancellation** or **curtailment** cover up to £3,000; **personal property** cover up to £1,500 (but check on expensive items, as most policies limit single articles to £250); **cash** and

document cover, including your passport and tickets; and finally that the policy gives you a 24-hour **emergency helpline**. If you go bungee jumping or even horse riding, check your policy includes **dangerous sports cover**.

Shop around at reputable dealers like **American Express** (0800 700 737), **AA** (0191 235 6513), **Bradford & Bingley** (0800 435642), **Club Direct** (0800 0744 558), **Columbus** (0207 375 0011), **Direct Travel** (01903 812345), **GA Direct** (0800 121007), **Options** (0870 848 0870), **Premier Direct** (0990 133218), **Primary Direct** (0870 444 3434), **Thomas Cook** (0845 600 5454), **Travel Insurance Direct** (0990 168113), **Worldcover Direct** (0800 365121) and **Worldwide Travel Insurance** (01892 833338).

Florida with children

I am often asked what I think is the right age to take children to Orlando, and there is no set answer, I'm afraid. Some toddlers take to it instantly, while some 6- or 7-year-olds are left rather bemused. Quite often, the best attractions for young children are the hotel swimming pool or the tram-ride to a park's front gates! Some love the Disney characters at first sight, while others find their sheer size quite frightening. There is simply no predicting how they will react, but I do know my oldest boy (then 4½)

> BRIT TIP: Don't tell the kids they are going on holiday until you arrive at the airport. It guarantees a good night's rest beforehand and is worth it for the look on their faces when they realise! – Reader *Fiona Chapman*

loved just about every second of his first experience (apart from the fireworks – see below) and still talks about much of it (especially the monorail!). Yes, a 3-year-old may not remember much of it, but they will have fun and provide YOU with some great memories and photos/video.

And here are some top tips for travelling with youngsters – with thanks to the folks at wdwinfo.co.uk for chipping in! (there are additional tips in the theme parks chapters):

The flight: Try to look calm (even if you don't feel it) and relaxed. Small children will pick up on any anxieties and make them worse! Pack a bag with plenty of little bits for them (comics, sweets, colouring books, small surprise toys, etc.) and keep vital 'extras' like Calpol (in sachets, if possible), change of clothes, small first aid kit (plasters, antiseptic cream, baby wipes), sunglasses, hat and sunscreen in your hand luggage.

If they are fussy with their food, you may want to take a bottle of their favourite squash. Ribena is unheard of in the States, for example.

Once you're there: take things slow and let your children dictate

BRIT TIP: Push-chairs are essential, even if your children are a year or two out of them. The distances involved around the parks wear kids out quickly, and a pushchair can save a lot of discomfort (for dads especially!). You can take your own, hire them at the parks or even buy one there at a local supermarket for around £10.

what pace you go at, to a large extent. The heat, in particular, can make for angsty children in no time flat, so take time-outs for drinks, splash zones or attractions with air-conditioning. Remember to carry your small first-aid kit with you. Things like baby wipes always come in handy, and it is a good idea to take spare clothes with you, which you can then leave in the handy lockers at all the main theme parks.

In the sun: carry sun-cream and sunblock at all times and use it frequently, in queues, on buses, etc. A children's After Sun cream is also a good idea. And please ensure you all drink a lot of water or non-fizzy drinks. Tiredness is often a result of mild dehydration.

BRIT TIP: If you have a fridge in your hotel or holiday home, put drink cartons in the freezer overnight and they will be cool for much of the next day in your back-pack.

Eating out: look for the 'kids eat free' deals in many places, as they can apply to children up to 12 at times, and take advantage of the many buffet options (see Chapter 10, Eating Out) to fill the family up or for picky eaters. 'Many restaurants do Meals To Go if you want a quiet meal in your own accommodation without the worry of the kids playing up!' Lisag, wdwinfo.co.uk. Try to let your children get used to the (size of the) characters before you take them to one of the many fabulous Disney character meal opportunities (my oldest can't get enough of them!).

Having fun: try to involve your children in some of the decision-making and be prepared to go with the flow if they find something unexpected they like (the many

BRIT TIP: 'Don't have food panics if your child will eat only pancakes and/or chicken nuggets every day for two weeks. It won't kill them and it takes much of the worry out of theme park meal-times.' Mindy, wdwinfo.co.uk

squirt fountains and splash zones in the main parks are an example – swimsuits and/or a change of clothes are definitely a good idea!). The Orlando rule of 'You Can't Do It All' applies especially with children, so just make the most of what you do all enjoy together. And beware the evening fireworks at parks like *Magic Kingdom* Park and *Epcot* – they are very loud, and young children can get quite distressed (my oldest had to be taken out of *Epcot* in a hurry!). The resort hotels around the *Magic Kingdom* Park all offer safer ways to view the fireworks – at a distance!

Travellers with disabilities

The parks pay close attention to the needs of holiday-makers with disabilities. There are few rides that cannot cater for them, while wheelchair availability and access is almost always good. All Disney hotels have rooms accessible for guests with disabilities – call 407 939 7807 or visit www.disneyworld.com – while they also publish a *Guidebook for Disabled Guests* (as do Universal), available in all three main parks. Life-jackets are always on hand at the water parks, and there are special tape cassettes for blind visitors.

Disabled drivers should take their orange car badge with them as this is honoured in the US and there are designated parking areas at all theme parks. For more local assistance,

Walker Medical & Mobility Products specialise in three-wheeled electric scooters and wheelchair rentals, with free delivery and pick-up even from holiday homes. Call 407 331 9500 for more info. **Rainbow Wheels**, (see their website at www.rainbowwheels.com), are another specialist company who rent full-size or mini vans equipped for wheelchair users. Call them on 407 365 8813.

Reader Les Willans confirms: Orlando is superb when it comes to accessibility for wheelchair users like myself, but Americans often use quite offensive language, such as the term 'handicapped', when referring to the disabled.

Measurements

American clothes sizes are smaller, hence a US size 12 dress is a UK size 14, or an American jacket sized 42 is really a 44. Shoes are the opposite: a US 10 should fit a British size 9 foot. Their measuring system is also still imperial and NOT metric.

BRIT TIP: if you shop at any Wal-Mart store in America, you can return any faulty or mis-size goods to your local Asda for a refund, provided you keep your receipts.

American-speak

Another thing to watch out for are words or phrases that have a different meaning across the Atlantic. For instance, when Americans say the first floor, they mean the ground floor, the second floor is really the first, and so on. (NB: NEVER ask for a packet of fags. Fag is a crude, slang term for homosexual, hence you will get some VERY funny looks.) See overleaf:

American	English	American	English
Check or Tab	Bill	Lines	Queues, so 'Stand in line' not 'Queue up')
Restroom	Public toilet		
Bathroom	Private toilet		
Eggs 'over easy'	Eggs fried both sides but soft	Elevator	Lift
		Underpass	Subway
Eggs 'over hard'	Eggs fried both sides but hard!	Subway	Underground
		Mailbox	Postbox
Eggs 'sunny side up'	Eggs fried on just one side (soft)	Faucet	Tap
		Collect call	Reverse charge phone call
French fries	Chips		
Chips	Crisps	Gas	Petrol
Cookie	Biscuit	Gas pedal	Accelerator
Grits	Porridge-like breakfast dish made out of ground, boiled corn	Trunk	Car boot
		Hood	Car bonnet
		Fender	Car bumper
		Antenna	Aerial
		Windshield	Windscreen
Biscuit	Savoury scone	Stickshift	Manual transmission
Hash browns	Grated, fried potato (delicious!)		
		Trailer	Caravan
Jelly	Jam	Freeway	Motorway
Silverware or place-setting	Cutlery	Divided highway	Dual carriageway
		Denver boot	Wheel clamp
Liquor	Spirits	Turn-out	Lay-by
Seltzer	Soda water	No standing	No parking OR stopping
Shot	Measure		
Liquor store	Off-licence	Parking lot	Car park
Broiled	Grilled	Semi	Articulated truck
Grilled	Flame-grilled	Ramp	Slip-road
Sub	Torpedo roll	Intersection	Junction
Shrimp	King prawn	Construction	Roadworks
Sherbet	Sorbet	Yield	Give way
Eggplant	Aubergine	Purse	Handbag
Appetiser	Starter	Fanny pack	Bumbag
Entree	Main course	Pants	Trousers
To go	Take-away (as in food)	Undershirt	Vest
		Vest	Waistcoat
Candy	Sweets	Pantyhose	Tights
Drug store	Chemist	Sneakers	Trainers
Bandaid	Plaster	Shorts	Underpants
Movie theater	Cinema	Facecloth	Flannel
Sidewalk	Pavement	Quarter	25 cents
Pavement	Roadway	Dime	10 cents
Bill	Note (as in $5 note)	Nickel	5 cents
		Penny	1 cent
Crib	Cot	Downtown	The city or town centre (not the run-down part!)
Cot or rollaway	Fold-up bed		
Diaper	Nappy		
Stroller	Pushchair	A/C	Air-conditioning

Wedding bells

Florida is increasingly sought after by couples looking to tie the knot (some 20,000 couples a year at the last count), and Orlando offers a terrific range of wedding services, from ceremony co-ordinators, photography and flowers to a wonderfully scenic range of venues like Cypress Gardens, Winter Park and Leu Gardens, plus more unusual venues like the pit-lane of the Richard Petty Driving Experience at *Walt Disney World Resort in Florida* or even at 145mph around the speedway itself! **Walt Disney World's Wedding Pavilion** offers true fairytale romance, with the backdrop of Cinderella Castle and Seven Seas Lagoon. You can opt for traditional elegance in this Victorian setting with up to 260 guests or the full Disney experience, arriving in Cinderella's glass coach and with Mickey and Minnie among the guests. Disney's wedding organisers can tailor-make the occasion for individual requirements (407 828 3400). Universal have a wedding service based on their beautiful Portofino Bay Hotel. Call 407 503 1120 for their wedding specialist.

All the main **tour operators** feature wedding options and co-ordinated services, and offer ceremonies as varied as aboard a hot air balloon or helicopter (Virgin), Caledesi Island beach (Airtours and Jetsave) or luxury yacht (Cosmos). Prices vary from £349 (Chapel of Love – Airtours) to £1,399 (Disney Pavilion – Unijet).

You can also **do it yourself** by calling at the Osceola County Administrative Building, 17 South Vernon Street, Room 231-A, Kissimmee 8.30am–4.30pm Mon–Fri (407 847 1424). Both parties must be present to apply for the marriage licence, which costs $88.50 (in cash) and is valid for 60 days, while the ceremony (equivalent to a British register office) can be performed at the same time for an extra $20. Passports and birth certificates are required and, after acquiring a marriage licence, a couple can get married anywhere in Florida. The County's Marriage Department can also supply names of public notaries to conduct the ceremony if you want to get married elsewhere, like one of the more picturesque resort hotels, which are usually amenable to providing the venue. For more information, you can call the Orlando/Orange County Convention & Visitors' Bureau for an information pack (407 363 5872).

Safety First

While crime is not a serious issue in Central Florida, this is still big-city America and you need to keep your wits about you. This is not the time to leave your common sense at home.

The area has its own Tourist Oriented Policing Service (or TOPS), centred on International Drive, with more than 70 officers patrolling purely the main tourist areas, arranging crime prevention seminars with local hotels and generally ensuring Orlando takes good care of its visitors. You will often see the local police in these areas out on mountain bikes, and they are a polite, helpful bunch should you need assistance or directions. Tourism is such a vital part of the local economy the authorities cannot afford not to be seen to be taking an active role against crime, hence the area has a highly safety-conscious attitude.

Having said all that it would be foolish to behave as if the villainous element did not exist and therefore there are a number of guidelines which all visitors to America in general, and Orlando in particular, should follow. Put simply, it is just a matter of being sensible.

© Disney

The Disney Wedding Pavilion

For example, just as it would be inadvisable to walk around the darker corners of London late at night alone, so it would in parts of Florida.

Emergencies

General: in an emergency of any kind, for police, fire department or ambulance, dial 911 (9-911 from your hotel room). It is a good idea to make sure your children are aware of this number, while for smaller-scale crises (mislaid tickets or passports, rescheduled flights, etc.) your

> BRIT TIP: A handy idea for your journey over is to use a business address rather than your home address on all your luggage. It is less conspicuous and safer should any item be stolen or misplaced.

holiday company should have an emergency contact number in the hotel reception. If you are travelling independently and run into passport or other problems that require the assistance of the British Consulate in Orlando, their office is located in Sun Bank Towers, 200 South Orange Avenue, with walk-in visitors' hours 9.30am–noon and 2–4pm, or phone 9.30am–4pm on 407 426 7855.

Medical: here's a bulletin from an informed British source who works with American paramedics – if you are taking regular prescription drugs, check with your doctor or pharmacist to see if they have a different name in the US. Many do (adrenaline is known as epinephrine) and it is worth finding out and carrying the drug with both names in case of an emergency. (Many thanks to Valerie Mulcare-Tivey for this advice.) Another reader points out the American term for Paracetamol is Acetaminophen.

Hotels

While in your hotel, motel or guest house, you should always use door peepholes and security chains whenever someone knocks at the door. DON'T open the doors to strangers without asking for identification, and check with the hotel desk if you are still not sure.

> BRIT TIP: If your room has already been cleaned before you go out for the day, hang the 'Do Not Disturb' sign on the door.

It is stating the obvious, but keep your room doors and windows locked at all times and always use deadlocks and security chains. It is still surprising how many people simply forget basic precautions when they are on holiday (the local police never cease to be amazed at how many people do leave their common sense behind when they leave home!). Always take your cash, credit cards, valuables and car keys when you go out, and don't leave the door open at any time, even if you are just popping down the corridor to the ice machine. And make a point of asking hotels about their safety precautions when you make a reservation. Do they have electronic card-locks (which can't be duplicated) and do they have their own security staff?

Don't be afraid to ask reception staff for safety pointers in the surrounding areas or if you are travelling somewhere you are not totally sure about. Safety is a major issue for the Central Florida Hotel/Motel Association, so hotel staff are usually well briefed to be helpful in this area. Using a bumbag (the Americans call them fanny packs!) is a better bet than a shoulder or handbag.

> **BRIT TIP:** If you want to be extra safety-conscious, you can hire mobile phones, pagers and even two-way radios from as little as $20 a week from Airwave Communications, tel 407 843 1166.

Nothing is guaranteed to get the local police shaking their heads in disbelief and disgust than the tourist who goes round looking like an obvious tourist. The map over the steering wheel is one obvious giveaway, but other no-nos are wearing large amounts of jewellery, carrying masses of photographic equipment or flashing wads of cash around. The biggest single giveaway of all is leaving your camera or camcorder on a front seat of the car.

Finally, and this is VERY strong police advice, in the unlikely event of being confronted by an assailant, DO NOT resist or 'have a go', as it more often than not will result in making the situation more serious.

Money

Following on from the advice about bumbags, it is inadvisable and unnecessary to carry large amounts of cash with you. US travellers' cheques are accepted almost

> **BRIT TIP:** Be forewarned all American banknotes are EXACTLY the same green colour and size. It is only the picture of the president and the denomination in each corner that change.

everywhere as cash and can be readily replaced if lost or stolen, as can credit cards, which are another widespread form of currency. Visa, Mastercard and American Express are almost universally accepted. The Sun Bank in Disney's *Magic Kingdom* and Epcot is open 7 days a week should you need extra help with any financial transactions. It is also worth separating the larger notes from the smaller ones in your wallet to avoid flashing all your money in public view. Losing £200 worth of travellers' cheques shouldn't ruin

Cypress Gardens

your holiday – but losing £200 in cash might.

Most hotels will offer the use of safes and deposit boxes for your valuables, and many rooms now come equipped with mini-safes in which it is a good idea to leave your passports, return tickets, cameras etc., when you don't need them. Always keep your valuables out of sight, whether in the hotel room or the car. Use the car boot if you leave a jacket or camera.

Driving

Car crime is one of the biggest forms of criminal activity in America and has led to some of the most lurid headlines, especially in the Miami area a few years back. Once again, it pays to make a number of basic safety checks before you set off anywhere. The first thing is to be SURE of the car's controls before you drive out of the hire company's car park. Which button is the air-conditioning, which side of the steering wheel are the indicators and where are the windscreen wipers? Check BEFORE you leave! Also, make sure you know your route in advance, even if it is only a case of memorising the road numbers. Most of the car-hire companies now give good directional instructions on how to get to your hotel from their car park so read them before you set off.

Just about the main item on the list of local police Dos and Don'ts is to use your map BEFORE you set off – trying to drive with the map over the steering wheel is just asking for an accident, let alone marking you out as an obvious tourist.

Check that the petrol tank is full and never let it get near empty. Running out of 'gas' in an unfamiliar area holds obvious hazards. If you stray off your pre-determined route, stick to well-lit areas and stop to ask directions only from official businesses like hotels and garages or

better still, a police car or station. Always try to park close to your destination where there are plenty of street lights and DO NOT get out if there are any suspicious characters lurking around. Always keep your doors and windows closed (if it's hot, you've got air-conditioning, remember?), and don't hesitate to lock the doors from the inside if you feel threatened (larger cars have doors that lock automatically as you drive off). And, please, don't forget to lock the doors when you leave the car. Not many rental cars have central locking, so it is important to double-check.

> **BRIT TIP:** American freeways, highways and expressways (with the exception of the Florida Turnpike) do not have service stations, so if you need petrol you will have to get off the motorway (although not very far in most cases).

Miami crooks had developed the habit of trying to get cars to stop by trying to look official or deliberately bumping into obvious hire cars from behind. The easily identified hire car plates have now been phased out, but still NEVER stop for a non-official request. Go instead to the nearest garage or police station, and always insist on identification before unlocking your car and getting out of it for an official. It is comforting to know that a unique aspect of driving in Orlando is that none of the main tourist areas have any sort of no-go areas to be avoided. The nearest is the portion of the Orange Blossom Trail south of downtown Orlando. This houses a selection of strip clubs and 'adult bars' that are not particularly attractive and can be downright seedy at night.

Should you require any further information on being safe in Orlando, contact the Community Affairs office of the Orange County Police on 407 836 3720.

Know before you go

You can contact these organisations for advance information. Florida Tourism (www.flausa.com) have an info line on 09001 600555 (60p/minute) that lists all Florida destinations and gives other consumer lines in the UK, while they have a free information pack if you call 01737 644882. The Orlando Tourism Bureau in London has a 24-hour information line on 0800 092 2352, on which you can request their free *Destination Imagination* information pack or check out www.orlandoinfo.com/uk. The Orlando/Kissimmee information line is 09001 600 220 (calls 60p per min). You can also look up the Kissimmee Convention & Visitors Bureau on www.floridakiss.com.

When you arrive in the area, it is also worth checking out Orlando's ONLY official **Visitor Center** at 8723 International Drive (407 363 5872) for discounted attraction tickets, free brochures and accommodation advice and free information pamphlets and maps. The Kissimmee **Visitor Center** is at the eastern end of the Highway 192 tourist drag (407 847 5000 or 1-800 327 9159 in the States) and they have a toll-free accommodation line in the US of 1-800 333 KISS.

Of course, THE Internet site for all things Orlando and Disney is the information and fun-packed **www.wdwinfo.co.uk** (and

www.wdwinfo.com), to which I also contribute. The creation and maintenance of this independent site is a truly mind-boggling feat. It is a huge achievement, with its complete range of theme park info (right down to rides under refurbishment, park hours and ride height requirements), news, weather, facts, figures and tips, plus discount offers throughout Orlando, discussion boards and a chat forum. For up-to-the-minute advice and assistance, there is no better Internet resource. And don't overlook the websites at www.usfinfo.com and www.swoinfo.com for the full picture.

Of course, the official sites aren't bad either, with Disney's the pick of the bunch: www.disneyworld.co.uk (check opening hours, parades and book tickets on-line). Then there is www.universalorlando.com, plus www.seaworld.com and www.buschgardens.com. The local newspaper is also worth checking out (especially for their Calendar pages of what's on), find their website at www.orlandosentinel.com.

There are then a plethora of unofficial and fan websites, like www.wdwig.com (especially for their restaurant section), www.wdwmagic.com (great for Disney trivia and rumours), www.arkstar.com/dreamfinder (for more insider info; creator Arlen Miller also runs auctions of Disney collectibles and an e-mail Disney news service if you e-mail him at dsnyana@kua.net), www.wdisneyw.co.uk and www.orlandorocks.com (for all theme park addicts).

Right, that's enough planning for now, on to the real thing …

3

Driving and Car Hire

(or, The Secret of Getting Around on Interstate 4)

For the vast majority, introduction to Orlando proper comes immediately after clearing the airport via the potentially bewildering complexity of the local road systems in a newly acquired hire car. Yet driving here is a lot more simple and, on the whole, enjoyable than driving in the UK. In particular, anyone used to the M25 should find Orlando's motorways a lot less pressured.

Before you get to your hire car, however, a quick note about Orlando International Airport and the new Orlando-Sanford Airport, which is primarily a British charter flight gateway 30 miles to the north of Orlando. There is a full breakdown of how both airports work in Chapter 12, but you need to be aware of a couple of quirks on arrival.

Orlando International is one of the most modern and enjoyable airports you will encounter, but it does have a bewildering double baggage collection system. You disembark at one of four satellite

> BRIT TIP: Make sure you follow the correct instructions to collect your hire car. There are several different desks for each of the main hire companies and, if you do not check in at the right one, you will waste a lot of time.

terminals and have to collect your luggage immediately, then put it on another baggage carousel that takes it to the main terminal while you

---

I-Ride trolley

BRIT TIP: Alamo are also a Brit's Guide partner company and can offer our readers a special rate with this book. They are my car rental company of choice – quick and efficient service. *See inside front cover for details.*

ride the passenger shuttle. Once in the main terminal you will be on Level Three and need to descend to Level Two for baggage reclaim. There are porters here to help you tote your luggage down to Level One for car pick-up (please remember a tip, usually $1 per bag), while the trolleys need $1 in change to operate. Taxis and limos are also found on Level One. Several tour operators – notably Virgin Holidays – now have help desks here, too. The public bus system, Lynx (see below), operates from the A side of Level One, in spaces A32–34.

The Big Four hire companies who all have check-in desks at the airport are Dollar, National, Budget and Avis and all offer the most comprehensive hire services, if rather lacking in the personal touch. (You can save time if you are using one of these four by going straight to their desk BEFORE collecting your luggage, completing the paperwork and then returning to the baggage hall for your luggage, thus beating the worst of the queues). However, there is also a telephone desk at Level One connecting you to one of another **19** hire companies who often work out better value (notably Alamo Rent A Car).

A quick call brings their bus to pick you up and take you to their nearby depot, which also gives you a look at the surrounding roads before you have to drive on them. Hertz

and Avis are the biggest companies in the US, but Dollar and Alamo are the tops for tourist business. Dollar include Thomson, Airtours, Virgin, Style Holidays, Travel City, Cosmos, First Choice and jmc in their typical packages, while Alamo are the main clients for Unijet, Funway, Jetlife, Jetsave, Kuoni, British Airways Holidays and Thomas Cook Holidays, among others. Alamo's international tour centre, a 10-minute bus ride from the airport, features no less than 52 terminals, plus desks for the tour operator reps (handy for any paperwork wrangles), a changing area and a childcare area.

Orlando without a car

Although being mobile is advisable, it is possible to survive without a car. Be aware, though, that few of the attractions are within walking distance of anywhere and taxis can be expensive. If you decide not to drive, your best base is either *Walt Disney World Resort in Florida* (free transport throughout, but harder to get to the rest of Orlando) or International Drive for its location, good pavements (or 'sidewalks') and the great I-Ride Trolley. Many hotels also have free shuttles to the main parks (notably in Kissimmee) or a regular mini-bus service for a small charge.

There are basically 3 different routes for your transport. The

International Drive at night

reliable, cheap, but slightly plodding **Lynx bus system** covers much of Metro Orlando. Their website is at www.golynx.com and their information line is on 407 841 8240. Ask for a copy of their excellent System Map, which shows all their routes (or 'Links') and the main attractions. Worth noting are **Link 42** from the International Airport to I-Drive, **Links 56** and **50**, respectively from Kissimmee and the I-Drive area to *Walt Disney World Resort in Florida*, and **Link 4** from Kissimmee to downtown Orlando. A new service now covers western Highway 192 in Kissimmee for the first time, from Osceola Square Mall all the way west past Splendid China to Secret Lake Drive and the Sleep Inn – look for **Link 55**. They are only $1 a ride (plus 10c for any transfers) or $10 for a weekly pass (children 6 and under go free with a full-fare passenger). They average a bus every 30 minutes in the main areas, every 15 minutes from 6–9am and 3.30–6.30pm. Remember to have the right change (including any transfers). All buses are wheelchair accessible. Look for the pink paw-print signs that are the Lynx bus stops.

The International Drive area also has the great value **I-Ride trolley**, which operates along a six-mile stretch from Belz at the top, to SeaWorld via Westwood Boulevard and Sea Harbor Drive (the Gold Line) and three miles from the Orange County Convention Centre up to the junction of I-Drive and Kirkman Road via Universal Boulevard (the Green Line). Two new routes were due to start in October 2001, the Blue Line, from SeaWorld down to the new Orlando Premium Outlets shopping centre via Westwood Boulevard, and the Red Line, from Belz up to the Universal Orlando area, via Kirkman and Major Boulevard (look up www.iridetrolley.com or call 407 354

5656). Running every day, 7am–11.30pm at roughly 15-minute intervals, it costs 75c per trip (25c for seniors) – please have the right change – or you can buy Unlimited Ride passes for 1, 3, 5, 7 or 14 days at $2, $3, $5, $7 or $14. If you need to transfer between routes, ask for a transfer coupon when you board (transfers are free with Unlimited Ride passes). Kids 12 and under go free with an adult, and all trolleys have hydraulic lifts for wheelchairs. Passes are sold at most hotel service desks and visitor centres.

There is also a coach service ($5/person) to Busch Gardens in Tampa, with five departures daily between 8am and 10.15am from SeaWorld and the I-Drive area, called The **Busch Shuttle Express**. It's free if you have Busch tickets in advance (included in the 5-Park Orlando FlexTicket). For more details, see Busch Gardens section on page 160.

After public transport, there is a raft of well-organised firms who offer **shuttle services** to the attractions for a set fee and excursions to places like Kennedy Space Center and Busch Gardens that pick up at the hotels.

The main firms are Mears (www.mears-net.com, tel 407 839 1570), Transtar (www.transtar1.com, tel 407 856 7777) and Coach USA (www.coachusa.com, tel 407 826 9999). Mears offer the most comprehensive service, from limousines to coaches, and typical round-trip shuttle fares would be: Airport–*Walt Disney World*, $27/person ($19/child); Airport–International Drive, $23/person ($16/child); Airport–Highway 192 in Kissimmee $27–39/person ($19–30/child); *Walt Disney World*–Universal Orlando, $12/person; International Drive–*Walt Disney World*, $12/person; International Drive or *Walt Disney World*–Kennedy Space Center,

$19/person. Mears also offer a SuperPass service of 3/4/5/6/7 days of unlimited service to and from the main area attractions (including airport transfers) from I-Drive or *Walt Disney World* for $58/$69/$80/$91/$102.

> **BRIT TIP:** The boot size on American cars tends to be smaller than the British equivalent. And you will not get 7 people PLUS their luggage in a 7-seater van!

The excellent **Tiffany Town Car** services (www.tiffanytowncar.com) also come highly recommended for airport transfers and feature a 30-minute grocery stop if you are self-catering. Then there are the excursion services offered by the likes of Gray Line (www.grayline.com, 303 433 9800), International Drivers (tel 407 352 5151 and on www.swimdolphins.com), and Keith Prowse (see page 10). Finally, for groups of 4 or 5, taxis can be a convenient occasional option. The journey from the International Airport to I-Drive would cost $40, plus tip (about $9 each for 5), $10 from I-Drive to Universal Orlando and $20 from I-Drive to *Walt Disney World Resort in Florida*. Try Central Florida Taxi on 407 851 7523 (freephone 1-800 441 3276 in Florida) or Yellow Cab Co on 407 422 4561.

The car

Ultimately, having a car is the key to being in charge of your holiday, and on a weekly basis it tends to work out quite reasonable price-wise, too.

Weekly rates can be as low as $100 for the smallest size of car (an **Economy**, usually a Fiesta-sized hatchback; next up is the

Subcompact, an Escort-sized car; the **Compact**, a small family saloon like an Orion; the **Midsize** is a more spacious four-door, five-seater like a Vectra; and the **Fullsize** would be a large-style executive car like a Granada, and you can get larger still).

But beware these low starting rates. There are a number of insurances, taxes and surcharges which are pretty much essential, and these can easily take the final weekly rate to $280 or more. However, all the big rental companies now offer all-inclusive rates which do away with the 'hidden extras', and which can work out significantly cheaper if booked in advance in the UK. Rates can be as low as £159 a week, and you also benefit from easier processing at the Orlando end, making the whole business quicker. To book, call **Alamo** (see inside front cover for our special readers' offer) or **Dollar** on 0800 252897. Or you could try **Avis** (0990 900 500); **Budget** (0880 181181); **Thrifty** (0990 168 238); **Hertz** (0990 906090); **National** (0345 222525); or **Suncars** (0990 005566).

> **BRIT TIP:** Be firm with the hire company check-in clerk as some can be pushy to try to get you to take extras, like car up-grades, you don't need.

Once again, the scale of the car-hire operation is huge, and, with upwards of 300 tourists arriving at a time, it can be a pretty formidable business getting everyone off and running. The currently widespread practice of British holiday companies offering free car hire with their packages does not mean it won't cost you anything. It is only the *rental* cost which is free and you will still be expected to pay the insurance,

I•RIDE Trolley Service Routes

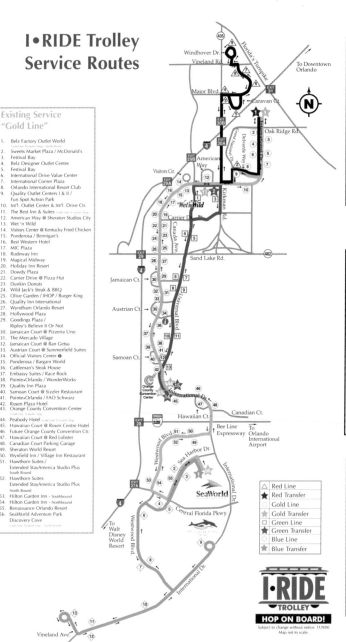

Existing Service "Gold Line"

1. Belz Factory Outlet World
   Gold Line Transfer Stop - Eastbound
2. Sweets Market Plaza / McDonald's
3. Festival Bay
4. Belz Designer Outlet Centre
5. Festival Bay
6. International Drive Value Center
7. International Corner Plaza
8. Orlando International Resort Club
9. Quality Outlet Centers I & II /
   Fun Spot Action Park
10. Int'l. Outlet Center & Int'l. Drive Ctr.
11. The Best Inn & Suites *Gold Line Transfer Stop*
12. American Way @ Sheraton Studios City
13. Wet 'n Wild
14. Visitors Center @ Kentucky Fried Chicken
15. Ponderosa / Bennigan's
16. Best Western Hotel
17. MIC Plaza
18. Rodeway Inn
19. Magical Midway
20. Holiday Inn Resort
21. Dowdy Plaza
22. Carrier Drive @ Pizza Hut
23. Dunkin Donuts
24. Wild Jack's Steak & BBQ
25. Olive Garden / IHOP / Burger King
26. Quality Inn International
27. Wyndham Orlando Resort
28. Hollywood Plaza
29. Goodings Plaza /
    Ripley's Believe It Or Not
30. Jamaican Court @ Pizzeria Uno
31. The Mercado Village
32. Jamaican Court @ Ran Getsu
33. Austrian Court @ Summerfield Suites
34. Official Visitors Center ❶
35. Ponderosa / Bargain World
36. Cattleman's Steak House
37. Embassy Suites / Race Rock
38. Pointe•Orlando / WonderWorks
39. Quality Inn Plaza
40. Samoan Court @ Sizzler Restaurant
41. Pointe•Orlando / FAO Schwarz
42. Rosen Plaza Hotel
43. Orange County Convention Center
    Gold Line Transfer Stop
44. Peabody Hotel *Gold Line Transfer Stop*
45. Hawaiian Court @ Rosen Centre Hotel
46. Future Orange County Convention Ctr.
47. Hawaiian Court @ Red Lobster
48. Canadian Court Parking Garage
49. Sheraton World Resort
50. Wynfield Inn / Village Inn Restaurant
51. Hawthorn Suites /
    Extended StayAmerica Studio Plus
    South Bound
52. Hawthorn Suites
    Extended StayAmerica Studio Plus
    North Bound
53. Hilton Garden Inn - Southbound
54. Hilton Garden Inn - Northbound
55. Renaissance Orlando Resort
56. SeaWorld Adventure Park
    Discovery Cove
    Gold Line Transfer Stop - Northbound

Existing Service "Green Line" Universal Blvd.

1. Wet 'n Wild /
   Clarion Hotel Universal
2. Best Inn & Suites
   Green Line Transfer Stop
3. Hampton Inn / Perkins
   Howard Johnson
4. Republic Square / MidPoint Plaza
5. Hampton Inn / Country Inn & Suites
6. Holiday Inn @ Mercado Village
   South Bound
7. Holiday Inn @ Mercado Village
   North Bound
8. La Quinta Inn & Suites - South Bound
9. La Quinta Inn & Suites - North Bound
10. Spring Hill Inn - South Bound
11. Spring Hill Inn - North Bound
12. Pointe•Orlando - South Bound
13. Pointe•Orlando - North Bound
14. Orange County Convention Center
    Green Line Transfer Stop - North Bound
15. Peabody Hotel
    Green Line Transfer Stop - North Bound

"Red Line" Major Blvd. Proposed Service End of Year 2001

1. Belz Factory Outlet World
   Red Line Transfer Stop - North Bound
2. Fun Spot Action Park
   International Festival Shopping Center
3. TGI Fridays
   Holiday Inn
   Mystery Fun House
4. Radisson Twin Towers
5. Days Inn
   Cracker Barrel
6. Delta Court of Flags
7. Ramada Inn
   Suburban Lodge
   Red Roof Inn
   Sleep Inn
8. Studio Plus Suites
   Best Western
   Universal Shopping Plaza
9. Wingate Inn
   Wellesley Inn
   Hampton Inn

"Blue Line" S. International Dr. Service End of Year 2001

1. SeaWorld *Blue Line Transfer Stop - South Bound*
2. Renaissance Hotel - South Bound
3. Renaissance Hotel - North Bound
4. Marriott Horizons Resort
5. Hilton Grand Vacations
6. Marriott Horizons Resort
   Marriott Cypress Harbor
7. Ramada Inn - South Bound
8. Ramada Inn - North Bound
9. Quality Inn Parc Corniche
   International Golf Club
10. Holiday Inn Crowne Plaza
11. Oasis Lakes
12. Vistana Vacation Villages
13. Premium Outlet Mall

Legend:
△ Red Line
★ Red Transfer
○ Gold Line
◉ Gold Transfer
□ Green Line
★ Green Transfer
◇ Blue Line
◈ Blue Transfer

I•RIDE TROLLEY
HOP ON BOARD!
Subject to change without notice. 11/9/00.
Map not to scale.

BRIT TIP: You probably won't be able to take the keys out of the ignition unless you put the car in 'Park' first. This sometimes causes much consternation!

taxes and other extras BEFORE you can drive the car away (which makes the all-inclusive packages even more attractive). Having a credit card is essential, and there are two main kinds of insurance, the most important being the Loss or Collision Damage Waiver, LDW or CDW. This currently costs around $19 a day and covers you for any damage to your hire car. You can manage without it, but the hire company will then insist on a huge deposit in the order of $1,500 on your credit card, and that could wipe out your credit limit in one go (and you are also liable for ANY damage).

You will also be offered Supplemental Liability Insurance or Extended Protection at around $12 a day. This covers you against being sued for astronomical amounts by any court-happy American you may happen to bump into (not strictly essential, but good for your peace of mind). Drivers under 25 have to pay an extra $10–20 per day, while all drivers must be at least 21. Other additional costs (which all mount up over a two-week holiday) include local and Florida state taxes which can add another $6 a day to your final bill, Airport Access Fee at $4 per day and then there's petrol (or gas, in America), although this is still appreciably cheaper than ours in the UK. Ask to return the tank full yourself, as this will also save a few $s on their fill-up option.

For those on a tight budget or happy to take the DIY route, you can cut costs by using travel insurance specialists like Extra Sure (tel 020 7480 6871), whose Americasure policy offers both LDW and SLI at £5/day. You may still need to leave a credit card imprint with the hire firm, but they should accept these insurances and save you money (but do still check in advance).

Drivers also please note: you may feel the effects of jet-lag for a day or two after arrival, but this can be reduced avoiding alcohol and coffee in-flight and instead drinking plenty of water.

Most soon find driving is a pleasure rather than a pain, mainly because nearly all hire cars here are

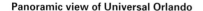

Panoramic view of Universal Orlando

automatics and rarely more than a year old. And, because speed limits are lower than we're used to at home (and rigidly enforced), you won't often be rushed into taking the wrong turn. Keep your foot on the brake when you are stationary as automatics tend to creep forward, and always put the automatic gear lever in 'P' (for Park) after turning off the engine.

Controls

All cars are fitted with air-conditioning, which is essential during spring, summer and autumn. The button to turn it on will be marked A/C, Air, or will just be a snowflake symbol. (Handy hint: to make it work, you also have to switch on the car's fan!) Don't be alarmed by a small pool of liquid under your car in summer – it's condensation off the A/C unit.

Power steering is also common on many hire cars, so be gentle around corners until you get the feel of it. Larger cars also have cruise control which lets you set the desired speed and take your foot off the accelerator (or gas pedal, in American-speak). There will be two buttons on the steering wheel, one to switch the cruise control on, the other which you push to set the desired speed. To take the car off cruise control either press the first button again or simply touch the brake. The handbrake may also be different. Some cars have an extra foot pedal to the left of the

BRIT TIP: The Beeline Expressway (528) and Greeneway (417) are both toll roads, so it's handy to have some change. Toll booths are reluctant to change more than $20 notes.

brake, and you need to push this to engage the handbrake. There will then be a tab just above it which you pull to release it, or a second push on the pedal if there is no tab. The car probably won't start unless the gear lever is in 'P', which can be confusing at first. To put the car in 'D' for Drive, you also have to depress the main brake pedal. D1 and D2 are extra gears for steep hills (none in Florida!). Few cars have central locking, so make sure you lock ALL the doors.

Getting around

Your car-hire company should provide you with a basic map of Orlando plus directions to your hotel. Insist these are provided as all the hire companies make a big point of this in their literature. Try to familiarise yourself with the main roads of the area in advance and learn to navigate by the road numbers (it's much easier than names, and the directional signs mainly use the numbers) and the exit numbers of the main roads.

When you drive out of the **International Airport** (or the hire company's off-airport depot) don't look for signs to 'Orlando' – the airport's new signage should be a big help here. The main tourist areas are all south and west of the city proper, so follow the appropriate signs for your hotel. For the International Drive area you want the Beeline Expressway (usually just listed as Route 528) all the way west until it crosses International Drive just north of SeaWorld. The main hotel area of I-Drive (as it is known locally) is to the north, so keep right at the exit. For western Kissimmee and *Walt Disney World Resort*, go south out of the airport and take the Central Florida Greeneway (Route 417) all the way west until it intersects with State Route 536 at

Exit 6 (for Animal Kingdom resorts, stay on until Exit 3 and take Osceola Parkway). You can then follow 536 straight across into *Walt Disney World Resort in Florida* or take the Interstate 4 west for one junction until it hits the main Kissimmee Routeway, Highway 192 (or the Irlo Bronson Memorial Highway). For eastern Kissimmee, come off Route 417 at Exit 11 with the Orange Blossom Trail (Highway 441), and going south brings you into Highway 192 at the other end of the main tourist drag.

> BRIT TIP: Watch out for one small hiccup on the Greeneway heading south. Just after Junction 34 it appears to split into two where it meets Highway 408. Stay in the RIGHT lane to keep on the south-bound motorway.

Leaving **Orlando-Sanford Airport** is also a straightforward affair, boosted by the airport's simple design. Dollar and Alamo have made a big impression here with their British-dedicated operations. There is no off-airport shuttle to your car to slow you down, just a quick walk from the airport's baggage reclaim hall to the car-hire office. But please remember to have your paperwork and especially your driving licence with you or you WILL find yourself either delayed or refused a car altogether (in the case of forgetting your licence).

It may be much further to the north and involve more driving time, but you usually save time overall. You leave the airport on East Lake Mary Boulevard and quickly hit the junction with the Central Florida Greeneway (Highway 417) on which

you head south. The slip-road on to this toll motorway is just under the fly-over on your LEFT, and you will need about $4.50 in total to reach Kissimmee or *Walt Disney World Resort in Florida* or $3.75 to reach International Drive (via the Beeline Expressway, Route 528).

You can avoid the tolls by staying on Lake Mary Boulevard for 4 miles until you hit Interstate 4, but you will may well hit the 4–6pm snarl-up through the city centre. The Greeneway is an excellent, easy-driving introduction to Orlando roads, even if it does cost a few dollars.

For radio traffic news and reports, tune to 1680AM.

Signs and road names

It's best to be aware of a few other potential pitfalls. First, the system of signposting and road-naming can be confusing. For instance, you cannot fail to find the main attractions, but retracing your steps back to the hotel afterwards can prove tricky because they often take you out of the parks a different way. (Disney is notoriously poor at sign-posting to help find your way out. A good tip is to get a copy of their Transportation Guide/Map from Guest Services at any park and use it to help navigate.) Here, it is vital to learn the main road numbers (and directions, either east-west or north-south) around the attractions so you know where you are heading, and if you want I4 east or west or 192 as you exit *Epcot* or *Disney-MGM Studios*. Also, exits off the Interstate and other main roads can be on EITHER side of the carriageway, not just on the right. This potential worry is offset by the fact you can overtake in ANY lane on multi-lane highways, not just the outside ones. Therefore, you can happily sit in the middle lane and let the rest of the world go by until you see your exit. However, you don't get much advance notice of turn-offs. You get the sign and then the exit in quick succession. But, once again, the speeds at which you are travelling tend to minimise the dangers of missing your turn-off. It is handy if your front-seat passenger acts as navigator, though.

Orlando has yet to come up with a comprehensive tourist map of its streets and the maps supplied by the car-rental companies tend to be simplified. It helps that none of the main attractions is off the beaten track, but the support of your navigator can be useful.

BRIT TIP: The Osceola Parkway toll road which runs parallel to Highway 192 is a much handier route in to *Walt Disney World* from much of Kissimmee and costs only $1.50. Use Sherberth Road for Disney access from west 192, especially if they are any lingering roadworks.

Around town, and in the main tourist areas, you will come across another method of confusing the unwary in the way road names are displayed. At every junction you will see a road name hung underneath the traffic lights suspended ABOVE the road. This road name is NOT the road you are on, but the one you are CROSSING. Once again there is no advance notification of each junction and the road names can be difficult to read as you approach them, especially at night, so keep your speed down if you think you are close to your turn-off so you can get in the correct lane. If you do miss a turning, nearly all the roads are arranged in a simple grid system

so it is usually easy to work your way back. Occasionally, you will meet a crossroads where no right of way is obvious. This is a 4-way stop, and the priority goes in order of arrival, so when it's your turn you just indicate and pull out slowly (America doesn't have many roundabouts, so this is the closest you will get to one).

As mentioned, some major highways are also toll roads, so have some change handy in varying amounts from 25 cents to $1. They all give change (in the GREEN lanes), but you will get through much quicker if you have the correct money (in the BLUE lanes). On minor exits of Osceola Parkway and the Greeneway, there are auto-toll machines *only*, so try to keep some loose change in your car.

As well as the obvious difference of driving on the 'wrong' side of the road (a particular hazard in car parks), there are also several differences in procedure. The most frequent British errors occur at traffic lights (which are hung above the road, not on posts – easy to miss occasionally).

At a red light it is still possible to turn RIGHT, providing there is no traffic coming from the left and no pedestrians crossing, unless otherwise specified (signs will occasionally indicate 'no turn on red'). Turning left at the lights, you have the right of way with a green ARROW, but you have to give way to traffic from the other direction on a SOLID green light.

The majority of accidents involving overseas visitors take place on left turns, so take extra care here. There is also no amber light from red to green, but there IS an amber light from green to red. A flashing amber light at a junction means proceed but watch for traffic joining the carriageway, while a flashing red light indicates it is okay to turn if the carriageway is clear.

Restrictions

Speed limits are always well marked with black numbering on white signs and, again, the police are pretty hot on speeding and on-the-spot fines are steep. Limits vary from 55 to 70mph on the Interstates (and can change frequently), where there is also a 40mph minimum speed, to just 15 or 20mph in some built-up areas.

Flashing orange lights suspended over the road indicate a school zone so proceed with caution, while school buses cannot be overtaken in either direction when they are unloading and have their hazard lights on. U-turns are forbidden in built-up areas and where a solid line runs down the middle of the road. It is illegal to park within 10ft of a fire hydrant or a lowered kerb, and never park in front of a yellow-painted kerb – they are stopping points for emergency vehicles and you will be towed away. Never park on a kerb, either. Seat belts are compulsory for all front-seat passengers, while child seats must be used for under 4s and can be hired from the car companies at around $5 a day (better still, bring your own). Children of 4 or 5 must either use a seat belt, whether sitting in the front or back, or have a child seat fitted.

Additionally, you must put your lights on in the rain, and you must park bonnet first. Reverse parking is frowned upon because number plates are often found only on the rear of cars and patrolling police cars like to be able to read them without the officers having to stop and walk round the car. If you park parallel to the kerb you must be facing in the direction of the traffic. Disabled drivers should note their orange disabled badge IS recognised in Florida for parking in the well-provided disabled parking spaces.

Finally, don't drink and drive. Florida has strict laws, with penalties of up to 6 months in prison for first-time offenders. The legal blood-alcohol limit is lower than in Britain, so it is safer not to drink at all if you are driving. It is also illegal to carry open containers of alcohol in the car itself.

> **BRIT TIP:** The Kissimmee-St Cloud tourist information office on east Highway 192 has the best free map of the area, clearly indicating all the main routes and attractions.

Attention AA members – here comes a bonus for you. Not only is your membership recognised by the equivalent AAA in the States, but you also benefit from several special deals, including area maps and ticket and hotel discounts. The Florida AAA centre is situated in Heathrow, north of Orlando, just off junction 50 of I4 (turn left on Lake Mary Boulevard, then first right on to International Parkway and the AAA is half a mile down on the left). For details (and savings like $5.75 off SeaWorld tickets, 10% off Universal Orlando tickets and meals, and special hotel rates) call the info number on the back of your AA card and ask for their USA pack, which gives you a special AAA card and their entitlements. It is even worth joining the AA (about £40) for the AAA discounts, which could add up to several hundred dollars if you take full advantage of them. Call 0870 544 4444.

Downtown Orlando

Accidents

In the unlikely event of having an accident, no matter how minor, the police must be contacted before the cars can be moved (except on the busy I4). Car-hire firms will insist on a full police report for the insurance paperwork. In the case of a breakdown, there should be an emergency number for the hire company among their essential literature, or, if you are on a major highway, raise the bonnet of your car to indicate a problem and wait for one of the frequent police patrol cars to stop for you (or, if you have a mobile phone, dial *FHP). Remember, also, always to carry your driving licence and your hire agreement forms with you in case you are stopped by the police. Should you be pulled over, remain in your car with your hands on the wheel and be polite to the officer. Once they learn you are British, you *may* just get away with a ticking-off for a minor offence!

Key routes

As already mentioned, the main route through Orlando is **Interstate 4** (or I4), a 4-, 6- or 8-lane motorway linking the two coasts. Interstates are always indicated on blue shield-shaped signs. For most of its length, I4 travels east-west, but, around Orlando, it swings north-south, although directions are still given east (for north) or west (for south). All main motorways are prefixed I, the even numbers generally going east-west and the odd numbers north-south. Federal Highways are the next grade down and are all numbered with black numerals on white shields, while state roads are known as Routeways (black numbers on white circular or oblong signs). All the attractions of *Walt Disney World Resort in Florida*, plus those of SeaWorld and Universal Orlando are well signposted from I4. Cypress Gardens is a 45-minute drive from central Orlando (south) west on I4 and Highway 27, while Busch Gardens is 75 minutes down I4 to Tampa. The Kennedy Space Center is a good hour's drive along the Beeline Expressway (Route 528) which intersects I4 at junction 28.

NB: Florida Department of Transportation will begin re-numbering ALL the Interstate junctions in early 2002 to a new mile-based system. However, the existing numbers will remain in use alongside the new ones, until summer 2004.

International Drive is the second key local roadway, linking as it does a 12-mile ribbon of hotels, shops, restaurants and attractions like Wet 'n Wild, the Mercado Shopping Center, The Pointe, Skull Kingdom, Guinness World Records Experience, WonderWorks and Belz Factory Outlet shopping malls. (Be aware that International Drive South, from Highway 192 north to Route 535, is NOT the main stretch, although they will, ultimately, link up.) From I4, take junctions 27A, 28, 29 or 30A travelling (north) east, or 30B, 29A or 28 travelling (south) west. To the north, International Drive runs into Oakridge Road and then the South Orange Blossom Trail, which leads into downtown Orlando (junctions 38-41 off I4). I-Drive is also bisected by Sand Lake Road and runs away into Epcot Drive, via Route 536, to the south, which is another handy way to the attractions of *Walt Disney World Resort in Florida*. It is a major tourist centre in its own right and makes an excellent base from which to operate, especially to the south of Sand Lake Road, near the Mercado Shopping Center, where you have the benefit of proper pavement. It's a 20-minute drive to Disney and 10 minutes from Universal. However, I-Drive can be congested at peak times, especially around Sand Lake Road, so use I4 for north-south journeys. Universal Boulevard, a recent I-Drive link to Universal Orlando, is also less congested.

The other main tourist area is the town of **Kissimmee** to the south of Orlando and the south-east of *Walt Disney World Resort in Florida*. It's an attraction in its own right, being the home of Water Mania, the Old Town shopping complex, Gatorland, Green Meadows Petting Farm and the Medieval Times and Arabian Nights dinner shows, plus more hotels and restaurants. It is all grouped along a 19-mile stretch of Highway 192 (The Irlo Bronson Memorial Highway), which intersects I4 at junction 25B, and is not much more than 10 minutes from *Walt Disney World Resort in Florida*, 20 from SeaWorld and 25 from Universal Studios. The downtown area of Kissimmee is off Main Street, Broadway and Emmett Street and is, for once, ideal for walking.

A handy addition to **Highway 192** are the series of Markers along the stretch from Splendid China (Number 4) to just past Medieval Times (Number 15). These highly visible numbered signs are good locators of many hotels, restaurants and attractions on local maps.

Fuel

Finally, a quick word about re-fuelling your car at an American gas station. You will often have a choice of attendant or self-serve. You do not tip the attendant but you do pay a slightly higher price to cover the service. Most gas stations will also require you to pay in advance at night, i.e. before filling the car, and will require the exact amount in cash or your credit card. Some pumps also allow you to pay by credit card without having to go in to the cashier's office. The American gallon is smaller (by about a fifth) than the British version. Always use unleaded fuel and, to make American petrol pumps work, you must first lift the lever underneath the pump nozzle. RaceTrac petrol stations are usually the cheapest locally (even for soft drinks and cigarettes), although they don't take credit cards.

Local maps

The best and most up-to-date free maps are the bright orange *Welcome Guide-Map* (also full of discount coupons), available in the main tourist areas, and the pull-out map inside the *Kissimmee-St Cloud Visitors' Guide* (from the official Visitor Center on east Highway 192, tel 407 847 5000). AA members are well catered for (see page 49), but the best paid-for maps are the *Trakker* series, with four products covering Orlando: the Pocket Map ($3.25) is almost as detailed as the AAA ones, while the City Slicker (a laminated fold-out of the main areas, $5.95) is useful in the car, and the Orlando/Walt Disney Popout Map is a handy theme park reference guide. They also do a full Orlando Atlas ($16.95), and Trakker Maps are found in all good bookshops in central Florida. You can contact them (and order maps) via www.trakkermaps.com or phone 305 255 4485 in Florida.

Mobile phones and two-way radios are often handy for Orlando holidays and another Brit's Guide partner provides a truly excellent service here. **Airwave Communications** are pioneering a state-of-the-art Nextel radio/phone/wireless (with Internet access), which has built-in direct lines for things like taxis, dinner bookings, babysitters, doctors and film processing. Amazingly, this service is *free*, but it must be pre-booked on 407 843 1166 or e-mail Airwave@cfl.rr.com

Now, on to your accommodation ...

4 Accommodation

(or, Making Sense of American Hotels, Motels and Condos)

To list all the various hotels, motels, holiday homes, guesthouses, condominiums, campsites and other forms of accommodation available in the Orlando area would fill a book, so it is not the intention here to attempt a comprehensive guide. The metropolitan Orlando area can boast the second highest concentration of hotels anywhere in the world and more are being built all the time, with the number of rooms now in excess of 103,000. Therefore, the following detail is intended only as a general guide to the bigger, better or budget types.

Hotels

The first thing to be aware of is that American hotels, particularly in the largest tourist areas like this, tend towards the motel type, even among some of the bigger and more expensive 'hotels'. This doesn't mean you will be short-changed as far as facilities and service are concerned, but you won't necessarily be located in one main, internal building. The chances are your room will be in one of several blocks arranged around the other facilities such as the swimming pool, restaurant, etc. As well as the difference in style, this means it is important to be security-conscious in matters like ensuring the room is locked and checking the ID of anyone who knocks at the door (although it is not something to be

worried about). The size of rooms rarely alters, even between two and four-star accommodation. It is generally the extra amenities and service which give a hotel extra star rating, not the size of the rooms themselves. A standard room usually features two double beds and will comfortably accommodate a family of four.

BRIT TIP: Few hotels have got round to providing hair-dryers as standard, although they can often be ordered from the front desk. If you bring your own, you will need a US plug adaptor (with two flat pins). Their voltage is also different, 110–120 AC, as opposed to our 220, so your hair-dryer/electric razor will work rather sluggishly.

The other feature of motel-type accommodation which frequently takes British visitors by surprise is the lack of a restaurant in many cases. This is because the American hotel scene operates purely on a room-only basis – meals are always extra, and hence dining facilities are not always provided. This means you may have to get out of your hotel/motel and drive to the nearest restaurant (of which there are a multitude – see Chapter 10) just for breakfast. Check the brochure carefully to see what dining facilities the hotels provide if this would be a concern.

As a general rule, hotels in Orlando are big, clean, efficient and great value for money. Another standard feature is the abundance of soft-drink and ice machines, with ice buckets in all the rooms (although you may find you are paying over the odds for a can of Coke, or whatever, from the machine at the end of your corridor).

All types of accommodation will also be fully air-conditioned and, when it is really hot, you will have to live with the drone of the A/C unit at night. DON'T turn off the air-conditioning when you go out, even when it is cool in the morning because, by the time you return, the chances are your room will have turned into an oven.

Note also that the most expensive place to make a telephone call from is your hotel room! Nearly every hotel adds on a 45–70 per cent surcharge (Disney resorts add a $15 'connection fee') to every call (you can also be charged for a call even if no one answers if it rings five or more times). A better way to make your calls is to buy a local phonecard, which even the holiday companies now sell, and use a normal payphone. To call Britain from the USA, dial 011 44, then drop the first 0 from your area code.

Remember also that hotel prices (both in this book and in Orlando) are always per *room* and not per *person*. They will be cheaper out of the main holiday periods, but prices are still likely to vary from month to month, with special deals offered from time to time. Always ask for rates if you book independently and check if any special rates apply during your visit (don't be afraid to ask for their 'best rate' at off-peak times which can be lower than any

published rate). There can also be an additional charge ($5–$15 per person) for more than two adults sharing the same room. It often pays to book in advance because Orlando's popularity as a convention centre means it is busy much of the time.

If you've just arrived and are still looking for accommodation, head for one of the two official Visitor Centers in the area, one on International Drive just south of the Mercado Center (on the corner of Austrian Court and open every day 8am–7pm) and the other on the eastern stretch of Highway 192 in Kissimmee (open 8am–5pm), where they keep an updated list of all the hotels and their rates, with brochures on the latest special deals.

Alternatively, if you are comfortable with the auction-type websites like www.priceline.com, you can pick up the occasional bargain.

However, for genuinely good deals, and all with accommodation that is regularly checked for cleanliness and service, I recommend the online service of Dreams Unlimited Travel, find them at: www.dreamsunlimitedtravel.com/ dreamsRes

The lobby of Disney's Wilderness Lodge

© Disney

The full-service tourist centres of **Know Before You Go** (407 396 5400 or 1-800 749 1993, or online at www.knowbeforeugo.com) and **Vacation Works** (407 396 1844 or 1-800 396 1883, web site at www.vacationworks.com) also deal in discounted accommodation as well as attraction tickets.

We place hotels, motels and holiday homes in four price bands to give you a rough ready reckoner, although bear in mind no price is set in stone. These bands are:

$	=	up to $45 per night
$$	=	$46–$90
$$$	=	$91–$150
$$$$	=	$151–plus

BRIT TIP: Buy your soft drinks at the supermarket, and a neat polystyrene cooler for about $4 that you can fill with ice from your hotel ice machine to keep your drinks cold.

Also, there is no widely accepted star rating system for American hotels, so, bearing in mind there is little difference in the size of rooms (usually quite generous, with two double beds, TV and full en-suite facilities) we have our own C grades, based on the number of facilities and extra creature comforts. Hence, a CCCCC grading will include the highest level of hotel facilities and service, while a CC or C will be the more basic motel-type.

Resort hotels for Walt Disney World in Florida

In keeping with the rest of this guide, a review of Orlando's hotels starts with *Walt Disney World Resort in Florida*. With the convenience of being almost on the doorstep of the main attractions, and linked by an excellent free transport system of monorail, buses and boats, Disney's hotels, holiday homes and campsites are all magnificently appointed and maintained. They range from the futuristic appeal of *Disney's Contemporary Resort* (the monorail travels right through the main building) to the oversized fun of *Disney's All-Star Resorts*, and their landscaping, imagination and attention to detail are as good as the Theme Parks themselves. In all, there are more than 25,000 rooms throughout the 47 square miles of *Walt Disney World Resort in Florida*, while the 780-acre *Disney's Fort Wilderness Resort & Campground* has 1,192 sites. However, all this grandiose accommodation comes at a price. A standard room at *Disney's Grand Floridian Resort & Spa* can cost $479 a night in high season (the suites can top $2,000!) and even the more modest *Disney's Caribbean Beach Resort* can be more than $150 a night. Eating out in the hotels and resorts is not cheap, and you will only find limited fast-food outlets along I-Drive and Highway 192.

However, there is a budget choice for holiday-makers in the shape of *Disney's All-Star Sports, Music and Movies Resorts*. This means the convenience of being so close to some of Orlando's biggest attractions has been opened up to a lot more holiday budgets, and it is worth a lot, especially in high season when the surrounding roads are packed.

Staying with The Mouse is one of the great thrills, for the style, service and the extras involved. The 21

BRIT TIP: It is usual in American hotels to tip the housemaid by leaving $1/adult each day before your room is made up.

resorts offer a superb array of facilities, and children especially love being a part of Disney full time. Here are the benefits: **Resort ID card**, every guest can ask for a 'charge' card with which to charge almost all your food, gifts and services in *Walt Disney World Resort in Florida* to your room account, plus have any purchases shipped to your room. **Early entry:** every day, one of the parks is open to resort guests an hour early. These are known as EE

BRIT TIP: For the smoothest entry to *Walt Disney World Resort in Florida* from Highway 192, take Seralago Boulevard opposite the Holiday Inn Hotel & Suites next to Old Town, turn left on to a non-toll stretch of Osceola Parkway and follow the signs to your chosen park.

days (see page 28). **Free parking:** with your ID card, there is no charge for your car at any of the parks. **Free transport:** forget the car and use the monorail-bus-boat network to get around. **Dining priority:** guests can make Priority Seating arrangements for all restaurants, shows and special events between 60 and 120 days in advance (two years in the case of dinner shows). Call 407 939 3463. NB: A Priority Seating (or PS, as it is known) is not strictly a reservation but a guarantee of the first available table when you turn up. **Priority golf:** the best tee times are reserved for *Walt Disney World Resort in Florida* guests and can be booked 90 days in advance on 407 939 4653. **Children's services:** all resorts have in-room or group baby-sitting (subject to availability; you can book

in advance on 407 827 5444) and the eight Deluxe resorts have supervised activity centers and dinner clubs (around $7 per child per hour), usually open until midnight.

E Nights: periodically, resort guests get the chance to buy a $12 ticket for an extra three hours doing the main rides at one of the parks after official closing time (great value). **Mickey on call:** okay it's a bit twee, but what better way to wake up than with an alarm call from the Mouse himself?

Around the **Magic Kingdom** Resort area you will find four of the grandest properties. The 15-storey **Disney's Contemporary Resort** boasts 1,050 rooms, a cavernous foyer, shops, restaurants, lounges, a real sandy beach, a marina, two swimming pools, six tennis courts, an electronic games centre and a health club – and magnificent views, especially from the superb, hotel-top California Grill restaurant (try to arrange a Priority Seating to coincide with the park's fireworks). Don't miss **Chef Mickey's** for a breakfast or dinner buffet with all your favourite characters. There is also the Mouseketeer Club for 4–12s. As with all resort accommodation, rooms are large, scrupulously clean and well furnished. $$$$+, CCCCC.

Disney's Polynesian Resort is a South Seas tropical fantasy brought to life with ultra-modern sophistication and comfort. Beautiful sandy beaches, lush vegetation and architecture disguise the fact 853 rooms can be found here, built in film-set wooden longhouse style and

BRIT TIP: Dine in wonderful South Seas style at the 'Ohana restaurant, but don't ask for the salt – unless you want to spark an amazing reaction!

End Zone Food Court at Disney's All Stars Sports Resort

all with balconies and wonderful views. There are excellent eating opportunities, plus canoe rentals, a beautiful new pool area (a big hit with kids), a games room, shops and children's playground. The Neverland Club caters for 4–12s (5pm– midnight). $$$$+, CCCCC.

Disney's Wilderness Lodge Resort, opened in 1994, is one of the most picturesque places to stay. It is an imposing re-creation of a National Park lodge in amazing detail, down to the hot stream running through the massive wooden balcony-lined atrium lobby and out into the gardens, past the swimming pool (with hot and cold spas) and ending in the resort's own Old Faithful geyser, erupting every hour! It offers authentic backwoods charm with true luxury but is connected to the *Magic Kingdom* Park by boat and bus only. It also has two full-service restaurants: the outstanding **Artist's Point** and the **Whispering Canyon Café** (for a lively breakfast and huge all-you-can-eat buffets), a snack bar and a pool bar. The Cubs Den is for 4–12s (4.30pm–midnight). $$$$, CCCCC.
The Villas at Wilderness Lodge are a recent development of 136

studio and one and two-bedroom villas. Facilities include fully-equipped kitchens, living room space, private balconies and whirlpool baths. There is also a quiet pool area, spa and health club.

Disney's Grand Floridian Resort & Spa completes the quartet of *Magic Kingdom* Resort area hotels, a hugely elaborate mock Victorian mansion with 900 rooms, an impressive domed and towered foyer and staff in Edwardian dress. The rooms are luxurious, hence the mega price range, and it is worth a look even if you are staying somewhere else. It also has six restaurants, including *Walt Disney World Resort in Florida's* top-of-the-range **Victoria and Albert's** (where their set, six-course dinner with wine will set you back more than $110 per

> **BRIT TIP:** *Disney's Grand Floridian, Contemporary* and *Polynesian Resorts* are situated on the monorail, the best system for getting into the *Magic Kingdom* Park and *Epcot*.

KEY TO
WALT DISNEY WORLD
AND LAKE BUENA VISTA
ACCOMMODATIONS

1 Disney's Contemporary Resort
2 Disney's Polynesian Resort
3 Disney's Wilderness Lodge
4 Disney's Grand Floridian Lodge And Spa
5 Walt Disney World Swan
6 Walt Disney World Dolphin
7 Disney's Caribbean Beach Resort
8 Disney's Yacht Club Resort
9 Disney's Beach Club Resort
10 Disney's Boardwalk
11 Disney's All-Star Resorts
12 Disney's Port Orleans Resort (French Quarter)
13 Disney's Port Orleans Resort (Riverside)
14 Disney's Coronado Springs Resort
15 The Villas At The Disney Institute
16 Disney's Old Key West Resort
17 Disney's Fort Wilderness Resort & Campground
18 Disney's Animal Kingdom Lodge
19 Disney's Pop Century Resort (open Spring 2002)
20 Hilton At Walt Disney World
21 The Grosvenor
22 Wyndham Palace Resort & Span
23 Doubletree Guest Suites Resort
24 Best Western At Walt Disney World
25 Hotel Royal Plaza
26 Courtyard By Marriott
27 Hyatt Regency Grand Cypress
28 Marriott's Orlando World Center
29 Embassy Suites Resort Lake Buena Vista
30 Radisson Inn Lake Buena Vista
31 Sierra Suites Hotel
32 Buena Vista Suites
33 Summerfield Suites At Lake Buena Vista
34 Vistana Resort
35 Sheraton Safari Resort
36 Holiday Inn Sunspree Resort
37 Marriott Village
38 Holiday Inn Family Suites
39 Opryland Hotel (open February 2002)

MAGIC KINGDOM PARK®

BAY LAKE

DISNEY'S RIVER COUNTRY WATER PARK

DISNEY'S FORT WILDERNESS RESORT

SEVEN SEAS LAGOON

MONORAIL

TICKET & TRANSPORTATION CENTER

CAR PARK

WALT DISNEY WORLD SPEEDWAY

TOLL PLAZA

WORLD DRIVE

DISNEY'S ANIMAL KINGDOM THEME PARK

DISNEY'S BLIZZARD BEACH WATER PARK

CAR PARK

TO HIGHWAY 192

SHERBERTH RD.

EPCOT DRIVE

VISTA BOULEVARD

GOLF VIEW DR.

CAR PARK

CAR PARK

EPCOT

WORLD SHOWCASE LAGOON

DISNEY-MGM STUDIOS

VICTORY WAY

DISNEY'S WIDE WORLD OF SPORT COMPLEX

OSCEOLA PARKWAY

CAYMAN WAY

SEABREEZE DR.

BUENA VISTA DR.

CAR PARK

BONNET CREEK PARKWAY

MAPLE DR.

COMMUNITY DR.

SASSAGOULA CIRCLE

BUENE VISTA DR.

LAKE BUENA VISTA

HOTEL PLAZA BLVD

DOWNTOWN DISNEY

DISNEY'S TYPHOON LAGOON WATER PARK

LAKE AVENUE

PALM PARKWAY

WINTER GARDEN-VINELAND RD.

VINELAND RD.

(27)

4

26 A-B

26 C-D

WORLD CENTER PARKWAY

SOUTH INTERNATIONAL DRIVE

TO INTERNATIONAL DRIVE

(TOLL)

TO KISSIMMEE

TO HIGHWAY 192

person) and the chic seafood-orientated **Narcoossee's**, with its excellent view over Seven Seas Lagoon and the nightly Electrical Water Pageant, four bars and a comprehensive array of sporting and relaxation facilities. A wonderful new pool area – complete with water-slide – was also taking shape in summer 2001. The Mouseketeer Club caters for 4–12s (7am–midnight), and the **1900 Park Fare** restaurant is one of the most popular for character meals. $$$$+, CCCCC.

Epcot Resort area

The *Epcot* resort area features six hotels, including arguably the best value properties of them all. The unmistakable *Walt Disney World Resort in Florida* **Swan** and **Dolphin** hotels are perfectly situated to be within walking distance of the *Epcot* and *Disney-MGM Studios* parks, the Boardwalk entertainment district and the Fantasia Gardens mini-golf courses. The 'entertainment architecture' style is fun and quite extensive, they have the full range of resort benefits, facilities and style, yet they are privately run and so come up a little cheaper than Disney's other deluxe hotels. The Swan features a 45ft statue atop the hotel, which boasts 758 large rooms (including 55 suites), while the Dolphin (1,509 rooms, with 136 suites) is crowned by two even bigger dolphin-fish statues. The duo effectively make up one mega-resort, with no less than 17 restaurants, four tennis courts, three pools (one, an amazing grotto pool with hidden alcoves and water-slide), a kids' pool and a white-sand beach, two health clubs, bike and paddle boat rentals, a great range of shops, video arcade and the Camp Dolphin centre for kids 4–12 (1–4.30pm, 6–11pm, $12/hour). Even for non-guests, the Italian restaurant **Palio's** (the Swan)

and **Shula's Steak House** (Dolphin) are worth seeking out. **The Coral Café** also features Disney character breakfasts, and some of their little touches for children are immensely thoughtful. And, at night, the whole resort looks just magnificent. Check out www.swandolphin.com for even more detail on these perfectly-situated gems. Transport is by boat (to *Epcot* and *Disney-MGM Studios*) and bus. $$$$, CCCCC (tel 407 934 3000).

The 45-acre **Disney's BoardWalk Inn and Villas** resort is the most extravagant property in *Walt Disney World*, featuring a 378-room Inn, 532 villas, four themed restaurants, a TV sports club and two night-clubs, plus an impressive array of unique shops, sports facilities and a huge, free-form swimming pool with a 200ft water slide, all situated on a re-created semi-circular boardwalk around Crescent Lake. The overall effect is stunningly pretty, and the attention to detail in the rooms is quite breathtaking. Outstanding features are the summer-cottage style villas, Mediterranean restaurant **Spoodles** (for arguably the best buffet breakfasts in Orlando) and the **Big River Grille & Brewing Works** for a magnificent array of beers. Top of the range is the expensive but magnificent seafood restaurant, the **Flying Fish**. Even if you are not staying here, it is a delightful resort to visit for a meal, the night-life (especially **Jellyrolls** piano bar and

BRIT TIP: While the Yacht and Beach Club are firmly in the Deluxe bracket, you can still visit to sample Beaches & Cream Soda Shop for arguably the best burgers in *Walt Disney World Resort in Florida*.

the ESPN Sports Club) or just a wander along the boardwalk. The Harbor Club caters for 4–12s (4pm–midnight). $$$$+, CCCCC.

Disney's Caribbean Beach Resort boasts some 2,112 rooms, with the accent on moderate price and value for money. The rooms tend to be a little plainer (although they still comfortably house a family of four), but the restaurants, bars and outdoor activities (including a lakeside recreation area with themed waterfalls and slides) are still a big hit with children. The six counter-service outlets in the food court at Port Royale (the hub of this pretty resort) can get busy in the morning, and the Trinidad South and Barbados 'islands' are a fair walk from the centre, but it is an action-packed resort with some imaginative touches, like Parrot Cay Island with its tropical birds and kids' play area. Transportation from the five Caribbean 'islands' that make up the resort to the theme parks is purely by bus. $$$, CCCC.

Going up-market again, the refined, almost intimate, **Disney's Yacht Club** has 635 rooms designed with nautical themes, all set around an ornamental lake. For a hearty breakfast, the Yacht Club Galley (one of three restaurants and two bars) offers some of the best fare in *Walt Disney World Resort in Florida*. Sister hotel **Disney's Beach Club** completes the *Epcot* line-up. With 580 spacious rooms set along a man-made white-sand beach, it's like a tropical island paradise. You can go boating or catch a water-shuttle service to *Epcot*, while other theme park transportation is provided by bus. Water fun is provided for both Yacht and Beach Club resorts at the shared Stormalong Bay, a magnificent 2½-acre recreation area with water slides and a sandy-floored lagoon. The Sand Castle Club caters for 4–12s (4.30pm–midnight). Both $$$$+, CCCCC.

Disney's Animal Kingdom Resort area

Disney's All-Star Resorts are Disney's first serious venture into capturing a big share of the budget hotel market. Here, for just $77–$109 a night year-round, you can stay in one of the five sports-themed blocks (Surfing, Basketball, Tennis, Baseball and American Football) centred around a massive food court, two swimming pools, a games arcade and shops; the music-themed version (Jazz, Rock, Broadway, Calypso and Country); or the Movies complex (Mighty Ducks, 101 Dalmatians, Fantasia, Love Bug and Toy Story). The latter is possibly the most imaginative, with its Fantasia pool and kids' play areas, and the most popular blocks are Toy Story and 101 Dalmatians (both of which are non-smoking only). All three centres, which have a total of 5,760 rooms, have pool bars, shops, laundry facilities, video games rooms and a pizza delivery service, and, while their bright, almost garish decor lacks the refined touches of other resorts, and rooms are smaller than their higher-priced counterparts, they are well designed for budget-conscious families who still want to enjoy all the *Walt Disney World Resort in Florida* conveniences. Transport to the parks is provided by bus. $$–$$$, CCC. There is also the bonus (if that's the right word!) of a large **McDonald's** (one of only two in *Walt Disney World Resort in Florida*) at the entrance to the All-Star complex.

Disney's Coronado Springs Resort is possibly the best value of the moderate resorts (Caribbean Beach and Port Orleans) and is also the newest. With slightly more in the way of facilities for its 1,967 rooms spread throughout its 136 acres (four pools, including the beautiful – and massive – Lost City of Cibola feature pool, with water-

© Disney

Disney's Animal Kingdom Lodge

slide, jacuzzi and kids' pool/play area, pool bar and grill, two games arcades, a boating marina, bike rentals, restaurant, food court and convenience store, lounge bar, gift shop, beauty salon and health club, business centre, and two guest launderettes) and a wonderfully scenic Mexican/Spanish architecture theme in three 'villages' (Casitas, Ranchos and Cabanas), Coronado is an often-overlooked treasure. Check out the **Maya Grill** and its new Latino cuisine style for a memorable meal, the lovely one-mile walk around the 15-acre central lagoon, and the main pool's changing facilities, which mean you can have checked out of your room but still take advantage of the pool area before your flight home. Coronado is also only five minutes from Disney's Animal Kingdom and is well served by Disney's bus network. $$$, CCCC.

Disney's Animal Kingdom Lodge opened in April 2001 and is a truly stunning example of architectural artistry. The basic premise is it is a private game lodge

© Disney.

The lobby at Disney's Animal Kingdom Lodge

on the edge of a 33-acre animal-filled savannah, which many of the rooms overlook. The all-encompassing African theming – from the decor, to the shopping, cuisine, restaurant styling and even the musky, wood-laced smells – is almost overwhelming, and the effect of being able to open your curtains to a vista full of giraffes and zebras is immense. And all that wonderful creativity comes before you consider the actual amenities of this 1,293-room deluxe resort – two restaurants, a cafeteria, a bar, an elaborately-themed 'watering-hole' main pool (with water-slide) and kids' pool, a massage and fitness centre, a large gift shop, children's play area and a four-storey atrium lobby that makes you gasp. Main restaurant **Jiko** (see also Chapter 10, Eating Out) is spectacular enough, but then there is the buffet-style **Boma**, a 'marketplace' restaurant featuring African dishes from an exhibition wood-burning grill and rotisserie for both breakfast and dinner. Quite awesome. Indeed, the lavishness and detail of the design are unmatched anywhere I have seen to date, and that's on top of the magnificent animal savannahs, inhabited by more than 200 mammals and birds. Guides are on hand to tell guests all about the animals and their habitats, while children can listen to African folklore stories around the outdoor firepit or become junior safari researchers while mum and dad do some wine-tasting (the hotel boasts the largest collection of South African wines in America) or take a hotel tour detailing the wealth of art and architecture on display. Rooms range from standard doubles (with the same slightly dated layout of the moderate resorts) to one- and two-bedroom suites, some with bunk beds for the kids. Simba's Cubhouse is for the 4–12s (4.40pm–midnight), and Disney transport is by bus. My

one quibble is some of the in-resort prices (in the bar and gift-shop, for example) are a bit steep, but it is worth staying here, even only for a night, to experience an exercise in majesterial hotel design. $$$$, CCCCC.

Disney's Pop Century Resort is due to open the first stage of another 5,760-room value resort, like All Stars, in Spring 2002. Its theme is the decades of the 1900s, hence there will be 10 different blocks with giant icons – like yo-yos, Rubik's cubes and juke-boxes – and period phrases or sayings that will either make you laugh out loud or cringe! The overall effect and amenities will be similar to the All Stars, with six pools sprinkled through the 235-acre complex (still with some Disney character theming), while the whole resort will be split in two around a lake, with the 1900s–40s on one side (due to be completed by mid-2003) and the 1950s–90s (the first section to be completed) on the other. The two halves will have their own reception area (with large-screen TV showing Disney films to keep the kids amused during check-in), shops, food court, cafe and pool bar, plus laundry facilities and a room pizza delivery service. It adds significantly

Disney's Pop Century Resort

© Disney

to Disney's more budget-orientated offerings and, like the All Stars, will have its own dedicated bus service to the parks. $$-$$$, CCC.

Downtown Disney Resort area

The other main accommodation centre within *Walt Disney World* is the area surrounding *Downtown Disney*. Here you will find: **Disney's Port Orleans Resort**, a two-part complex (formerly the two distinct resorts of Port Orleans and Dixie Landings) split into the 2,048-room *Riverside* area – with a steamboat as a reception area, a wonderful cotton mill-style food court, a full-service Cajun-themed restaurant and an old-fashioned general store (i.e. gift shop) – and the 1,008-room *French*

BRIT TIP: To make a reservation at any *Walt Disney World* resort, call 407 934 7639. For information, don't forget www.disneyworld.co.uk and the best bookings service, www.dreamsunlimited.com

Quarter, which has the **Sassagoula Floatworks** and **Food Factory** court, two bars, a games room and shopping arcade.

The Riverside boasts Ol' Man Island, a magnificent 3½-acre playground, incorporating swimming pool, kids' area and a fishing hole, while the French Quarter has Doubloon Lagoon. Kids will especially enjoy the Mardi Gras dragon slide and alligator fountains, as well as their own play area. The eye-catching landscaping and architecture vary from rustic Bayou backwoods to turn-of-the-century New Orleans. Transportation for

both sections is provided by bus. $$$-$$$$, CCCC.

Disney's Old Key West Resort is partly a holiday ownership scheme of five-star proportions, but the one, two or grand three-bed studios in a magnificent Key West setting can also be rented on a nightly basis ($$$$+, CCCC) when not in use by club members. Facilities include swimming pools, tennis courts, games room, shops and fitness centre.

Finally, right next door to *Downtown Disney* are the **Villas at the Disney Institute**, a selection of extremely well-appointed bungalows (sleeping up to five), treehouse villas (for six) and townhouses (sleeping four or six), the latter with daily housekeeping. The excellent **Seasons Dining Room** is also here, along with six pools, four tennis courts, fitness facilities, beauty salon and spa, jogging trails, nature walks and bike paths. The peaceful woodland setting is a long way from the hustle and bustle of the big resorts, but the Villas still cater well for children, with a playground and Camp Disney fun as well as educational programmes (7–15-year-olds). $$$$+, CCCC.

Camping Disney Style

Disney's Fort Wilderness Resort & Campground, on Bay Lake, opposite the *Magic Kingdom*, offers an impressive array of camping facilities and chalet-style homes that can house up to six. Two 'trading posts' supply fresh groceries, while there are two bars and cafés and a range of on-site activities, including the thrice-nightly Hoop-Dee-Doo Musical Revue, campfire programme, films, sports, games and a prime position from which to view the nightly Electrical Water Pageant. Buses and boats link the campsites with other *Walt Disney World* areas. $-$$$$, CCC.

Disney Hotel Plaza

In addition to the official *Walt Disney World* hotels, there are another seven 'guest' hotels inside *Walt Disney World Resort in Florida* itself at the **Disney Hotel Plaza** on the doorstep of *Downtown Disney*. These benefit from a free bus service to the attractions and guaranteed admission to the theme parks, and you can make reservations for shows and restaurants before the public, but they are almost all more expensive than similar hotels outside *Walt Disney World*. Top of the list (for service, mod cons and price) is the 10-storey, 814-room **Hilton** in the *Walt Disney World Resort in Florida* (which benefits from being on the Surprise Mornings system for entry to the theme parks an hour early, tel 407 827 4000, $$$$+, CCCC). Also fairly expensive are the **Grosvenor Resort** (626 sumptuously appointed rooms, exceptional service, colonial décor, and also with the bonus of early entry to the Disney parks on the Surprise Mornings, $$$–$$$$, CCCC, 407 828 4444), **Wyndham Palace Resort & Spa** (a bustling, 27-storey cluster offering 1,014 rooms, many with a grandstand view of *Epcot*'s Spaceship Earth, plus a European-style spa, three heated pools, tennis courts, a marina with boat rentals and the superb **Arthur's 27** restaurant with stunning views from the top floor, tel 407 827 2727, $$$$, CCCC) and the contemporary **Doubletree Guest Suites** (229 family-sized suites offering every conceivable in-room convenience and great kids' facilities, tel 407 934 1000, $$$$, CCCC). More modest ($$$, CCC) are the Caribbean-themed **Best Western Lake Buena Vista** (325 rooms, good views over the Marketplace, in-room coffee-makers, two restaurants, cocktail lounge and night-club, tel 407 828 2424), and the **Courtyard by Marriott** (323 rooms in a 14-storey tower and six-storey annex featuring glass-walled lifts, three pools, wonderful gardens and the early entry Surprise Mornings for the parks, tel 407 828 8888, $$$, CCC). Finally, the lovely **Hotel Royal Plaza**, with a pleasant, welcoming aspect, 372 wonderfully spacious and well-equipped rooms and 22 suites, a neat, full-service diner-restaurant and relaxing lounge bar, a landscaped pool area, four tennis courts, a health club and a Disney gift shop. Like all the hotels in the Boulevard, it is well positioned for a stroll to *Downtown Disney*'s attractions and features free bus transport and guaranteed access to the parks, plus preferred tee times at all five Disney golf courses ($$$, CCCC, tel 407 828 2828).

You can book your holiday through **The Walt Disney Travel Company** on 0870 2424 900 or contact your local travel agent.

As you move further away from *Walt Disney World Resort in Florida* the prices tend to moderate. Here's a round-up.

Lake Buena Vista

You can still spend a small fortune, however, at the **Hyatt Regency Grand Cypress**, reckoned to be Orlando's top hotel. This 1,500-acre resort offers three nine-hole and one 18-hole golf course (all designed by Jack Nicklaus), a swimming pool with waterfalls and slide, 21-acre boating lake, tennis complex, health club and equestrian centre. Rates START around $200, but the 750 rooms and suites are magnificently appointed and the resort is wonderfully picturesque (it also has five restaurants, three lounges and a pool-side bar), tel 407 239 1234, $$$$+, CCCCC.

Nearby is **Orlando World Center Marriott** (www.orlando.com/owcm)

KEY TO INTERNATIONAL DRIVE ACCOMMODATIONS

1 Peabody Orlando
2 Wyndham Orlando Resort
3 Renaissance Orlando Resort
4 Sheraton Studio City
5 Delta Orlando Resort
6 Days Inn Lakeside
7 Holiday Inn Express
8 Quality Inn International
9 Quality Inn Plaza
10 Embassy Suites Jamaica Court
11 Howard Johnson Plaza
12 Howard Johnson Inn
13 Rosen Plaza Hotel
14 Las Palmas Hotel
15 Enclave Suites
16 Quality Suites At Parc Corniche
17 Wynfield Inn

18 Summerfield Suites Hotel
19 Comfort Suites
20 The Doubletree Castle
21 Rosen Centre Hotel
22 Hawthorn Suites
23 Holiday Inn & Suites At Universal
24 Best Western Plaza
25 Embassy Suites I-Drive/Conv. Center
26 Radisson Hotel Universal Orlando
27 Portofino Bay Hotel
28 Hard Rock Hotel
29 Amerisuites Conv. Center
30 Sheraton World Resort
31 Sierra Suites
32 Homewood Suites
33 Country Inn & Suites
34 Royal Pacific Resort (open Summer 2002)

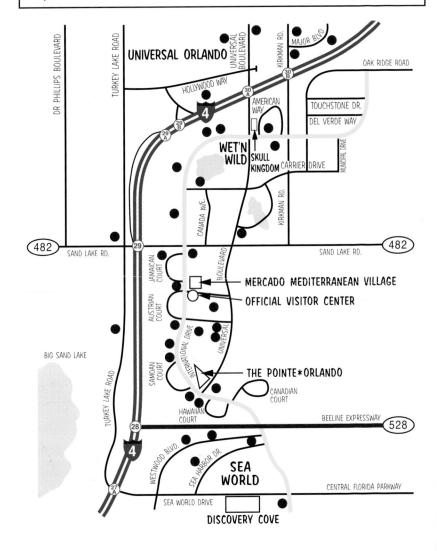

Wyndham Palace Resort

another personal favourite and an impressive landmark as you approach *Walt Disney World*, set as it is in 200 landscaped acres and surrounded by another golf course. An elaborate lobby, Chinese antiques and the sheer size of the hotel (2,003 rooms, including 110 suites, after a recent expansion, seven restaurants, four pools, tennis courts and a health club) put it in the expensive range ($$$$, CCCCC, tel 407 239 4200), but it is very conveniently situated and possesses one of the most picturesque pool areas, complete with waterfalls and palm trees, plus the whizziest glass-fronted lifts anywhere! It does, however, get busy, especially with convention business.

Similarly, but on more budget lines, the **Holiday Inn Sunspree Resort** at Lake Buena Vista (507 rooms, tel 407 239 4500, www.kidsuites.com; $$$, CCCC) is excellent for children's facilities, featuring a highly rated supervised childcare programme, a good range of pools, restaurants and other facilities. All rooms feature mini-kitchenettes. It also features the trademark 'Kidsuites' which offer an attractive novelty for families – a private playhouse/bedroom built into the hotel room, equipped with its own TV, cassette player, video game player, clock, fun phone, table and chairs. They offer a refreshing alternative to normal hotel accommodation, right down to the separate check-in for the youngsters. Sunspree, perfectly situated for Disney and with free transport, also boasts a 2,100sq ft Cyber Arcade, with access to the Internet and other high-tech elements, while it has the extra option of 50 two-room suites for more family comfort. Kids 12 and under eat free.

A novel choice is the African-themed **Sheraton Safari Hotel**, which boasts the Python water slide, heated pool and kids' pool, with free transport to Disney parks and kids eat free with parents at Casablanca's restaurant. Rooms are well equipped, with hair-dryers, coffee-makers and ironing boards, and all within walking distance of the Crossroads shopping centre, a good selection of neighbouring shops and restaurants and close to *Downtown Disney* Marketplace (tel 407 239 0444, www.sheratonsafari.com; $$$, CCC½). There are 489 rooms, including 96 huge suites, all with an exotic safari theme, and the breakfast buffet at **Casablanca's** (highly recommended) is worth checking out. With its great location and

Sheraton Safari Hotel

expansive style, the Sheraton Safari is an ideal mid-range family choice.

Some of the big hotel chains also have one or two of their smartest properties in this area, notably the **Radisson Inn Lake Buena Vista** (200 rooms, tel 407 239 8400; $$$, CCC) and the recently refurbished **Doubletree Club Hotel** (246 rooms, tel 407 239 4646; $$$, CCC½).

There are some excellent suites hotels here (see also under Suites and Holiday Homes, page 74), such as the **Embassy Suites Resort Lake Buena Vista** ($$$$, CCCC), the **Sierra Suites Hotel Lake Buena Vista** ($$$, CCC) and the extensive **Buena Vista Suites** ($$$, CCC½), which all offer great value for larger families.

Kissimmee

Moving out along Highway 192 (the Irlo Bronson Memorial Highway) into Kissimmee, you will find the biggest choice of budget accommodation in the area. Facilities generally vary little and what you see is what you get. All the big hotel chains can be found along this great tourist sprawl, and rates can be as low as $25 per room off-peak, or $35 for a room with a kitchenette (what the Americans call an 'efficiency'). Be prepared to shop around for a good rate (discounts may be available at off-peak times), especially if you cruise along Highway 192 where so many hotels advertise their rates on large neon signs. As a general rule, prices drop

> BRIT TIP: When booking one of the chain hotels, make sure you have its full address – it is easy to end up at the wrong Holiday Inn or Howard Johnson!

the further you go from *Walt Disney World*. Don't be afraid to ask to see inside rooms before you settle on your holiday base (some of the smaller motels can be pretty ordinary, to say the least).

Chains

Among the leading chains are **Best Western** (all with pools, family orientated but large, in the budget $–$$ range), **Days Inn** (rather characterless and some without restaurants, but the newer properties are still good value – $$ in most cases – and convenient, with some rooms available with kitchenettes), **EconoLodge** (see under Best Western, but slightly more expensive), **Howard Johnson** (also a bit dearer, but with more spacious rooms and some with free continental breakfast), **Quality Inn** (sound, popular chain, and in $–$$ range), **Ramada** (rates can vary more widely between hotels in the $$–$$$ range, some offer free continental breakfast) and **TraveLodge** (another identikit group, but also on the budget $–$$ side). The **Fairfield Inns** are the budget version of the impressive Marriott chain (in the $$ range). The **Holiday Inn** chain varies so widely in both price ($$–$$$) and service, I have picked out only those most worthy of note.

Doubletree hotels and suites are another up-market chain with excellent facilities, as are the **Radisson** group (both in the $$$ range). The Marriott chain has three other family-friendly brands, the **Residence Inn by Marriott**, **SpringHill Suites** and **Courtyard by Marriott** (both $$$). Their smart new Lake Buena Vista complex at the junction of I4 and Route 535 features a Fairfield Inn, Courtyard and Springhill Suites (www.marriott-village.com), with 24-hour gated security, free Disney transport and some great shared facilities.

The recently renovated **Renaissance World Gate Hotel** (577 rooms, tel 407 496 1400; $$$, CCCC) has been a big hit since it changed from the Doubletree Orlando Resort, with its oversized rooms, excellent facilities and pleasingly good service.

In pure budget territory, the motel-type **Inns of America, Knights Inn, Motel 6, Comfort Inn** and **Super 8 Motel** brands all deliver a basic $ service, but the **Hampton Inn** and **Red Roof** groups seem to manage a more quality-conscious approach in the same price category. The **La Quinta Inn and Suites** series, in the $$–$$$ range, has half a dozen well-equipped new properties in the area, notably two on International Drive.

Independent organisations

In addition, there are literally dozens of smaller, independent outfits who offer special rates from time to time in order to compete with the big boys. Look out in particular for offers of 'kids eat free' as this can save you quite a bit. Of the non-chain operators, the **Casa Rosa Hotel** offers simple, relatively peaceful Mediterranean-style hospitality (on west Highway 192, tel 407 396 1060, $–$$$, CC). The **Park Inn International** (same location, tel 407 396 1376) also has one of the better lake-front locations to go with its budget rates ($–$$, CCC); some rooms have kitchenettes.

For pure budget price, the **Magic Castle Inn and Suites Maingate** take some beating with their range of amenities – free continental breakfast, free Disney transport, fridges in all rooms, kids' playground, guest laundry and picnic area (107 rooms and 15 suites, tel 407 396 2212 or 1-800 446 5669, $–$$, CC½).

A firm personal choice is the **Holiday Inn Hotel and Suites Maingate East**, which also boasts Kidsuite rooms and Camp Holiday children's programmes, making it an outstanding family resort. Good attention to detail (hair-dryers, coffee-makers, microwaves and fridges even in standard rooms), free Disney transport and its proximity next door to Old Town make for great flexibility and value for money (614 rooms and 110 suites, tel 407 396 4488, $$–$$$, CCC½). Children get their own check-in area too, which is a neat touch, and under-13s

> BRIT TIP: Hotels designated Maingate East or Maingate West should be close to Disney's main entrance on Highway 192, although it is wise to check.

eat free, as they do at the smart **Holiday Inn Maingate West**, with its tropical courtyard, free-form heated pool and kiddie pool (287 rooms, tel 407 396 1100, $$, CCC). The **Holiday Inn Nikki Bird Resort**, just west of Disney's Highway 192 entrance, is another good family location with its 23-acre tropical setting, three pools, basketball and volleyball courts and children's entertainment (529 rooms, tel 407 396 7300, $$, CCC). **Angel's Diner**, the hotel's standout restaurant, offers some fabulous breakfast and dinner buffets.

The **Four Points Hotel by Sheraton Lakeside** on west Highway 192, is surprisingly good value (and has a great reputation with its guests) for a big-name group, especially with three pools, tennis courts, kids' playgrounds, mini-golf, paddleboats and two restaurants. Kids 10 and under eat breakfast and dinner free with

KEY TO HIGHWAY 192 ACCOMMODATIONS

1. Orlando World Center Marriott
2. Buena Vista Suites
3. Caribe Royale Resort Suites
4. Radisson Resort Parkway
5. Renaissance World Gate Hotel
6. Casa Rosa Hotel
7. Park Inn International
8. Magic Castle Inn & Suites Maingate
9. Holiday Inn Hotel & Suites Maingate East
10. Holiday Inn Maingate West
11. Holiday Inn Nikki Bird Resort
12. Four Points Hotel by Sheraton Lakeside
13. Celebration Hotel
14. Opryland Hotel (February 2002)
15. Comfort Suites Maingate
16. Tropical Palms Funsuites
17. Holiday Inn Family Suites
18. Orange Lake Resort
19. Villages at Mango Key
20. Ron Jon's Resort
21. Wonderland Inn
22. Comfort Suites Resort Maingate East
23. Hampton Inn Maingate West
24. Buenaventura Lakes

Celebration Hotel

paying adults and there is free Disney transport (651 rooms, tel 407 396 2222, $$–$$$, CCC½).

Slightly off the beaten track but with extra charm is the **Celebration Hotel** in the Disney-inspired town of Celebration. Just off Highway 192, the Central Florida Greeneway and I4, this unique hotel is still well-situated, yet offers a small-town America style. With only 115 rooms in its 1920s wood-frame design, the Celebration has a classy ambience a long way from the usual tourist hurly-burly. Rooms come in a choice of attic-like Retreat, Traditional (with either one king or two queen-size beds), Studio (with separate seating area) or two-room Suite and are all beautifully furnished. Lovely artwork, hardwood floors, unhurried, courteous staff and a good array of facilities – pool, jacuzzi and fitness centre, plus superb **Plantation Restaurant** (for buffet breakfast and new-Florida cuisine dinners Tue-Sat) and bar – mark this out as a real gem. It is also within a short stroll of the town's boutique shops, restaurants and peaceful walks. A shuttle service to the theme parks is also offered (for a small fee). For couples after a quieter or more romantic retreat, this member of the Grand Theme Hotels group (with the Sheraton Safari, Doubletree Castle, Sheraton Studio City and new Westin Grand Bohemian), is an ideal choice (tel 407 566 6000, or see their website at www.celebrationhotel.com; $$$$, CCC).

The newest – and possibly most dramatic – property in the area is the 1,400-room **Opryland Hotel**, due to open in February 2002. A cross between a convention centre and a vast turn-of-the-century Florida mansion, it will feature four acres of indoor gardens and landscaped waters under a glass dome. Three intricately-themed areas bear witness to a creativity of Disneyesque proportions, and the resort should offer just about every creature comfort you can think of, with an array of restaurants (from fine dining to food court style), an adults-only pool, family activity pool and beach (with water-slides), a full-service spa, children's day care centre and a wide selection of shops. Standard rooms promise some of the most smart and spacious accommodation in the area, while there is also a hotel-within-a-hotel as the central Emerald Tower will feature an even more up-market room choice, with some huge suites. It is the internal architecture, though, which promises to mark this hotel out as arguably the most ambitious in Florida to date. One area is built and landscaped like the Florida Everglades, complete with native plants and trees, another

The Peabody Orlando

copies the old world charm of St Augustine – complete with replica Spanish Fort! – while the third aims to reproduce the style and eclecticism of Key West, with a mock-up marina and sailboat. There will also be elaborate artwork, water features and live entertainment. And all this takes place under a massive glass roof with the benefit of climate control. I think you will need to see it to believe it, while some of the restaurants should be quite superb. It is also well situated, on the junction of South International Drive and Osceola Parkway (tel 407 239 4800, or visit their website at www.oprylandhotels.com/florida; $$$$, CCCCC).

International Drive

Further away from *Walt Disney World Resort in Florida*, but handy for Universal Orlando, SeaWorld and closer to downtown Orlando is the final main tourist area. For overall location and value for money,

BRIT TIP: For an attraction with a difference, don't miss the Peabody's twice-daily Duck March, which sees their trademark ducks take up residence 11am–4pm in the huge lobby fountain. It's a fascinating sight and a great place for afternoon tea. Just sit and watch them roll out the red carpet for the resident mallards!

I-Drive is hard to beat. It is more thoughtfully laid out, some attractions are within walking distance, and it is a good base for non-drivers.

Top of the range for quality is the **Peabody Orlando**, a luxurious, 891-room tower block, including an Olympic-size pool, health club, four tennis courts and some of the best restaurants in Orlando, notably the gourmet cuisine of **Dux** and the amazing **B-Line Diner** (see Eating Out, Chapter 10). Service is superb and the whole style is a cut above normal tourist fare. Check out the **Royal Duck Palace** if you don't believe me. However, rates are suitably impressive ($$$$+, CCCCC) and the convention business can make it a hectic proposition (tel 407 352 4000, www.peabodyorlando.com). The hotel has also begun a massive expansion project to add 1,000 rooms in a 42-storey tower block (the tallest in central Florida), plus more restaurants, shops and a spa.

The recently refurbished (at a cost of some $53m) **Wyndham Orlando Resort** (1,052 rooms, tel 407 351 2420, www.wyndham.com; $$$, CCCC) is similarly extravagant but with less of the price tag. It boasts a formidable line-up of facilities – three swimming pools, a full service restaurant and bar, a deli and an ice cream shop, two pool bars, a pool restaurant, tennis courts, a kids' club and game arcade, and even a health club with a gym, saunas, steam room and massage therapy – in its beautifully landscaped grounds and is well situated at the junction of I-Drive and Sand Lake Road. Rooms are all spacious and scrupulously clean, and there is the choice of deluxe kings, deluxe doubles and family fun suites. The whole resort is spread out over 42 acres, which takes some getting around, but it represents one of the best all-round hotels for the money.

Going upscale again, the magnificently appointed **Renaissance Orlando Resort** (on Sea Harbor Drive, 778 rooms, tel 407 351 5555, $$$, CCCCC), claims the world's largest atrium lobby and boasts some equally enormous rooms and suites, an Olympic-size pool, tennis courts, fitness centre including sauna and steam room and special kids' play areas and activities. The Renaissance also has some magnificent restaurants (all with children's menus), including the seafood-themed **Atlantis**, the Asian cuisine of **Haifeng** and a stupendous Sunday buffet. All the rooms have recently been renovated and the fixtures and fittings are of a high standard, while they now have a 24-hour health club and a self-serve laundry. As the closest hotel to SeaWorld, the Renaissance also offers some great packages in conjunction with the park and its sister, Discovery Cove. Well worth checking out (also on their website www.renaissancehotels.com).

On slightly more budget lines but still in a grand style, the remodelled 21-storey **Sheraton Studio City Hotel** (formerly Universal Tower) is an I-Drive landmark at the entrance to Universal Orlando and features a full art deco film-theme design, from the shower curtains and mirrors to the large-scale architecture and landscaping. Facilities include a heated outdoor pool and a paddling pool, games room, fitness room, **Starlight Grille** restaurant and free shuttle service to Universal, Wet 'n Wild (within walking distance) and SeaWorld. The clever 1950s film styling is truly startling and even the staff add to the theme, which makes you feel like you are 'on set'. Check out www.sheratonstudiocity.com for more details. All rooms have hair-dryers, coffee-makers and Nintendo games (302 rooms, tel 497 321 2100, $$$, CCCC).

The **Quality Inn International** (728 rooms, in the heart of I-Drive, kids under 12 eat free, tel 407 996 1600, $$, CCC), and **Quality Inn Plaza** (a massive 1,020 rooms in multiple blocks with multiple pools and another 'kids eat free'

restaurant, tel 407 345 8585, $–$$, CCC), are both firmly in budget territory but make for excellent bases in this area.

Another I-Drive landmark (next door to the Mercado) is the **Doubletree Castle Hotel**, a nine-storey fantasy modelled on Cinderella's castle at the *Magic Kingdom*. It features tower and turret rooms, a grand outdoor heated pool, hot tub, pool bar and grill, fitness centre, gift shop and a kids' play area. Rooms are immaculately furnished and there is a free shuttle to *Walt Disney World*, SeaWorld and Universal (216 rooms, tel 407 345 1511, $$$–$$$$, CCCC).

The other eye-catching property on I-Drive is the **Rosen Centre Hotel**, the third largest hotel in Orlando, right next to the Beeline Expressway. It caters primarily for the convention trade (it is right next door to the massive Convention Center), but also offers excellent tourist facilities with its 1,334 rooms and 80 suites. It features a huge swimming grotto, an exercise centre, tennis courts, two top-quality restaurants (including the seafood-based **Everglades**) and two bars (tel 407 354 9840; $$$, CCCC).

Universal Orlando

With the expansion of Universal as a major resort destination has come the development of the locale around it on Kirkman Road and Major Boulevard. It is highlighted by Universal's own resort hotels, and these are easily some of the best in the area. The **Portofino Bay Hotel** is the jewel in the crown, a splendid re-creation of the famous Italian port and a stunning resort in its own right, with every possible facility and a little bit more. The elaborate porticos, the genuine *trompe l'oeil* (false 3-D) painting, the lovely harbourside piazza and the faithful

Sheraton Studio lobby

ornamentation of the waterfront make it one of the most memorable settings of any hotel in Florida, and the 750 rooms are all impeccably appointed, with lashings of Italian style. The standard rooms are truly deluxe, with huge beds (and proper duvets, a first for an Orlando hotel), spacious bathrooms, mini-bar and coffee facilities, ironing board and hair-dryer, while the exclusive Villa rooms feature butler service, fax facility, CD and video players and separate showers, plus their own private pool area. There are also 18 elaborate Kids' Suites for extra family fun, with separate themed rooms that include TV, Sony Playstation, CD player and play area. The resort facilities are equally breathtaking – a Roman aquaduct-style pool with waterslide, a completely enclosed kids' play area and wading pool, a separate quiet pool, jacuzzis, a full (if expensive) health spa, business centre, gift shops (check out Galleria Portofino

Rosen Center

for some magnificent artwork and jewellery) and video games room. There is also the Campo Portofino activity centre for kids 4–14, from 5–11.30pm every day ($45 for the first child and $35 for each additional child). For wining and dining, the Portofino boasts seven restaurants and lounges, including **Mama Della's** a wonderfully authentic Italian family dining experience, an aromatic **Deli**, a pizzeria and gelateria. All in all, it is a spectacular choice. $$$$+, CCCCC.

New in 2001 was the **Hard Rock Hotel**, very possibly the 'coolest' hotel in Orlando. This is the home of rock chic (it is actually themed as a former rock star's home that has been converted into a hotel!), 650

Italian Piazza at Portofino Bay Hotel

rooms and suites in the architectural style of a California mission, with public areas decorated with pieces from the Hard Rock group's extensive collection of rock 'n roll memorabilia. High ceilings, wooden beams, marble floors and eclectic artwork make for a unique genre of décor that is both eye-catching and elegant, while the rock star theme is maintained through most of the public areas, from the black-suited foyer staff to the music that plays fairly constantly (not to everyone's taste, but those who like it will just love it). The 14-acre site includes three bars (the ultra-cool Velvet Bar, Lobby Lounge and Beach Club poolside bar and grill), two

Hard Rock Hotel

restaurants (the full-service **Sunset Grill** and the five-star, dinner-only **Palm Restaurant**), a fitness centre, Hard Rock gift shop (with live TV links to other HR Cafes around the world), Camp Lil' Rock (for the 4–14s, like Campo Portofino) and games room. The pool area which is the hotel's focus is just terrific, with a large, free-form pool and 240ft water-slide, two Jacuzzis, a sand beach and volleyball court, shuffleboard, and life-size chess and checkers. There is even a sound system *under water* in the pool! The rooms (including 14 kids' suites) are another standout feature, big, modish, beautifully furnished in the hotel's trademark cool chic style and wonderfully comfortable, they feature a radio/CD player (and you get a free Hard Rock CD when you check in), mini-bar, coffee maker, in-room safe and either a king-size or two queen-size beds. It all adds up to another awesome package from the Universal designers. $$$$, CCCC. A third hotel, the **Royal Pacific Resort**, is scheduled for summer 2002, adding a tropical South Seas touch at more moderate price.

Finally, all Universal resort guests benefit from a number of exclusive privileges: resort ID card (for buying food, merchandise and other items through Universal Orlando), free water taxi transport; priority seating at most restaurants (just show your room key card); package delivery to your room; the chance to buy a special Length of Stay pass (for unlimited access to the parks while you are at the resort); and, most importantly, **Universal Express** no-wait access to virtually all the rides all day (just by showing your room key card and admission ticket). For all Universal hotels, tel 407 224 7117 (or see their website at www.universalorlando.com).

The choice around Universal is also growing. There are recent examples of the budget **Days Inn, Hampton Inn, TraveLodge** and **Country Inn** chains, plus the **Extended Stay America** group (good, clean efficiency studios, but few other amenities), but there are also two excellent mid-range properties.

The **Radisson Hotel Universal Orlando** is a twin-tower, 742-room complex, recently refurbished to provide a smart resort with spacious, tropical-themed rooms, a large pool, kids' playground and jacuzzi, pool bar, video games room, hair salon,

Westin Grand Bohemian

4

gym and sauna, plus a sports bar, full-service restaurant and food court. It also offers a free shuttle to Universal (right across the road), SeaWorld and Wet 'n Wild (tel 407 351 1000; $$, CCC). The **Holiday Inn Hotel & Suites** is a similar proposition, with 256 rooms and 134 one- and two-bedroom suites for great flexibility, a large heated outdoor pool and on-site TGI Friday's restaurant (tel 407 351 3333, $$–$$$, CCC).

As a final word on new hotels, the **Westin Grand Bohemian** adds a true touch of class to the downtown area. Part of the quality-conscious Grand Theme Hotel group, the hotel features an early twentieth-century Austrian theme, with the accent on fine art, fine dining and fine service. Its 14 storeys make it a major landmark, and it also boasts a sensational restaurant (**The Boheme**), one of the most stylish bars I have encountered anywhere, (the Bosendorfer Lounge), and a 14th-floor concierge suite, plus an in-hotel **Starbucks** coffee lounge, a heated pool, spa and fitness centre. The rooms are superbly appointed and feature high-speed Internet access, mini-bars, radio/CD players and huge interactive TVs, while there are 36 sumptuous suites. All rooms feature the Westin Heavenly Bed, one of the most luxurious sleeping experiences in the known world!

The art collection, both classical and modern, liberally sprinkled through the public rooms – notably a $250,000 Imperial Grand Bosendorfer piano – is more reminiscent of an art gallery than a hotel, and, while it is predominantly a business person's hotel, the Grand Bohemian could well become a tourist attraction in its own right for culture vultures. Call 407 313 9000 for more details ($$$$, CCCC) or www.grandbohemianhotel.com.

Suites and holiday homes

Now, here is a look at a fast-growing area of accommodation in Orlando – suites hotels and holiday homes. These are a valuable way of larger family groups or friends staying together and cutting costs both by doing much of their own cooking and the extra value of sharing. The homes, whether individual houses, collections of houses, resorts or condominiums (holiday apartment blocks), all usually have access to excellent facilities in the form of swimming pools and recreation areas, and are fully equipped with mod cons like microwaves, TVs and washer-dryers. For these, a hire car is just about essential, but the savings for, say, a group of eight staying together are obvious. The following can be only a representative selection.

Basically, the choice is between what the Americans call suites – apartments built in hotel-like blocks around communal facilities but lacking some hotel features like bars, room service and lounges – or out-and-out holiday homes, some in private residential areas and others in estate-type developments, most of which have their own pools and tend to work out slightly cheaper.

Suite things

Suites hotels seek to provide extra value for larger families or groups. Typically, a suites room gives you a living room and mini-kitchen, including microwave, coffee-maker, fridge, cutlery and crockery, while many offer a complimentary continental breakfast (or better). All have swimming pools and grocery stores or snack bars. They vary only in the number of bedrooms and can usually sleep six to ten people.

They include the **Comfort Suites** (on west Highway 192 near Splendid China, tel 407 390 9888, on Turkey

Lake Road, 407 351 5050, adjacent to I4 and International Drive, plus their smart new 198-room development behind Old Town in Kissimmee, which even offers a fitness centre, (tel 407 397 7848, $$–$$$, CCC); the **Tropical Palms Funsuites** (on Holiday Trail, next to Old Town, 407 396 4595, $$–$$$, CCC½) with well-equipped studio and two-bedroom suites; the two-bedroom, two-bath studios of **Enclave Suites** (on Carrier Drive, just off Kirkman Road, $$–$$$, CCC½) where kids eat free with their parents; or the new **AmeriSuites** (on I-Drive, in Lake Buena Vista and by the airport, tel 1-800 833 1516, $$–$$$, CCC), which boast a heated pool, fitness centre, gift shop and a substantial free breakfast.

Family choice

The most remarkable property, though, is the **Holiday Inn Family Suites Resort** at Lake Buena Vista (almost opposite Orlando World Center Marriott, on International Drive South). From the lobby, themed as a turn-of-the-century railway station, through the amazing range of facilities (food court, general store, Club Car casual dining, lounge-bar, toddlers' play area, video games room, fitness centre, mini-golf, swimming pool and elaborate kiddie pool), to the choice of six different one and two-bedroom suites (classic suites, Kidsuites, Sweetheart suites, cinema suites, business suites, and residential suites), here is a dazzling family choice, especially with their Camp Holiday activity programme and separate check-in for kids. The Kidsuites feature a semi-private bedroom with bunk beds (additional fold-out child's sleeper available), TV, video and CD/cassette player, video game system, activity table and

chairs, plus, of course, the private adult king bedroom. The **Club Car Restaurant** has an excellent free buffet breakfast daily, and there is free regular transport to all the Disney parks. The zero-depth-entry water playground with its array of squirty fountains will ensure the young 'uns don't want to go anywhere else! For more info, check out www.hifamilysuites.com or tel 407 387 5437, $$$, CCCC.

Other one-off suites properties worthy of note include the well-appointed **Buena Vista Suites** (tel 407 239 8588, $$$, CCC) and the massively eye-catching **Caribe Royale Resort Suites** (both at the lower end of I-Drive, tel 407 238 8000, $$$$, CCCC½), with their choice of one-bedroom suites and two-bedroom villas, super pool area with water slide and one of the best free breakfast buffets in town. Equally, the **Hawthorn Suites** (three properties in Orlando), **Homewood Suites** (two in Lake Buena Vista and one on I-Drive) and the **Sierra Suites** (Lake Buena Vista and I-Drive) offer a more up-market feel with mid-range pricing ($$–$$$, facilities vary). The two **Summerfield Suites** (on I-Drive, tel 407 352 2400, and LBV, tel 407 238 0777, or www.summerfield-orlando.com) are another fine example, with suites sleeping up to eight, free breakfast, convenience store and fresh, inviting ambience ($$$, CCC).

One of the newest offerings is the **Country Inn & Suites** on Universal Boulevard (also in Lake Buena Vista and Kissimmee). Nicely situated just off the main I-Drive drag, it represents great value with its large, clean rooms, free continental breakfast, local phone calls and Disney transport, plus pool and fitness centre. The 170 standard rooms feature in-room safe, coffee-maker, hair-dryer and iron/ironing board, while the 48 king suites also

Holiday Inn Family Suites

include microwave and fridge. It is little more than a mile from Universal Orlando and half a mile from Wet 'n Wild, yet in a much quieter location than many of the I-Drive hotels (tel 407 313 4200, www.jaytelhotels.com; $$-$$$, CCC)

Holiday resorts

Another accommodation type which combines the best of hotels, suites and private villas are the handful of genuine resort-style complexes, some of which double as timeshare resorts.

These purpose-built resorts are a kind of cross between condominiums and motels, with the advantage of great in-resort facilities. The best of these include the **Orange Lake Resort** (4½ miles west of Maingate on Highway 192, tel 407 239 0000, $$$–$$$$, CCCC), with a mixture of two-bedroom, two-bath villas and suites, golf, watersports and even a cinema,

> BRIT TIP: Staying in a holiday home but need groceries delivered for your arrival or during your stay to save valuable park time? Check out The Pantry Store at their website at www.onvacationgrocery.com or on 407 654 2511 for that free delivery service, seven days a week.

and the **Villages at Mango Key** (on Lindfields Boulevard, 4 miles west of Maingate, tel 407 239 7100, $$$, CCC), a collection of smart, new two- and three-bedroom townhouses, with pool, jacuzzi,

Country Inn and Suites, Universal Boulevard

tennis and volleyball.

Ron Jon's Resort on the western fringe of 192 is a timeshare set-up that often has good-value apartments to rent on a weekly basis. Their newest blocks offer huge two-bedroom flats, with well-equipped kitchens (down to coffee-makers and ice-makers), while the complex itself has two pools plus the Liki Tiki Lagoon mini water park, tennis courts, paddle boats, bikes, pool-side bar and grill and a free continental breakfast Mon–Fri (when timeshare presentations are held). You don't have to attend any timeshare hard-sell, just enjoy the great facilities of this resort, now 'twinned' with the Ron Jon Surf Shop empire, (tel 407 239 5000, $$$, CCCC). Look up www.islandone.com for more details.

Top of the range in this category, though, is the **Vistana Resort** (just off the lower end of I-Drive in Lake Buena Vista, tel 407 239 3100, $$$–$$$$, CCCCC), where facilities include fitness centres with steam and sauna rooms, five pools and 13 tennis courts, to back up their luxurious two-bedroom villas that sleep up to eight.

Holiday homes

There are now dozens of companies offering private homes with pools throughout central Florida, some more reliable than others, so here are just a select few who pass the *Brit's Guide* credibility test. **Welcome Homes USA** have condos, villas and private homes in the Kissimmee area, with some smart properties at a broad range of prices. Their full-size houses (3–5 bedrooms) come with communal or private pools. Homes are only 10 or 15 minutes' drive from *Walt Disney World*, in residential areas, and feature everything from dishwashers to teaspoons (but not hair-dryers). For details, call 407 933 2233

($$–$$$$, CC) for their holiday homes and 407 933 2889 for their well-equipped condo complex, or check out their website at www.welcome-homes.com.

For similar great value and excellent properties **Alexander Holiday Homes** (tel 407 932 3683), also in Kissimmee, manage some 260 properties, from standard condo villas to ultra-luxury large executive homes sleeping up to 10, all with pools and immaculately furnished, within 15 minutes of *Walt Disney World*. From fully fitted kitchens to walk-in wardrobes and private pools, these are a great way to enjoy a bit of Florida freedom. Alexander were the first company of their kind in Orlando, and still offer a friendly, efficient service in keeping with the Sunshine State ($$–$$$, CC). They also boast one of the largest Internet sites in Florida on www.floridasunshine.com, on which nearly all of their properties are featured.

Premier Vacation Homes offer a great range of spacious properties with two to six bedrooms, sleeping up to 14, all in secure residential communities within a 15-minute drive of *Walt Disney World*. The homes are privately owned and have been purchased and furnished as a 'vacation' home, with screened pools, two TVs, fully equipped kitchens (including dishwasher, washer-dryer, microwave and coffee-maker), at least one king or queen bed, and free local phone calls. Maid service can be provided for an additional fee. The Luxury homes (two to four bedrooms) are their standard accommodation, while the Executive homes (three to six bedrooms) are bigger still, with an extra TV, a VCR and a gas barbecue grill (tel 407 396 2401, 0500 892634 in the UK, or see their website at www.premier-vacation-homes.com $$$, CC).

A company I have got to know recently and can recommend whole-heartedly are **Florida Leisure**, British-owned and with great attention to detail. With just 80 homes, from two to a massive six bedrooms, in the Kissimmee area (and most of them barely a year old), they pride themselves on a real personal touch. Many of their properties are in the Executive range, which means the fullest range of amenities in addition to their large, private, screened pools, and often in a secure, gated community. They also feature the invaluable Internet attribute of putting ALL their homes up for viewing, by both photo and video, and what you get in this case is most definitely what you get in this case ($$-$$$$, CCC). Call Nigel or Marion on 407 870 1600 or look up www.floridaleisure.com.

Bed and breakfast

The range of accommodation even includes a few places offering bed and breakfast. However, these are some way removed from a traditional British B&B as they tend to go for a more upscale, almost boutique style. Principle among them is the **Wonderland Inn** in Kissimmee, an 11-room restored Historic Registry property off the beaten track but only 10 minutes from the Highway 192 area. Each room features a delightful, individual touch, and several are designed for singles as well as doubles, plus one honeymoon suite. The attentiveness and service of the dedicated staff are truly wonderful and even the gardens – which include orange trees (fresh-squeezed juice for breakfast, just heavenly!), begonias and jasmine – have an old-fashioned charm light years removed from the hectic tourist whirl elsewhere. The whole renovation cost some $300,000 and it is easy to see why (tel 1-877 847 2477 or visit their website at www.wonderlandinn.com; $$$, CC).

The pretty Lake Eola district downtown also boasts two fine properties. **The Veranda** (tel 407 849 0321, $$$-$$$$, CCC) has 12 intimate, cottage-style rooms, ranging from Queen Studio and King Suites to a lovely honeymoon suite, set in landscaped gardens with a private courtyard, swimming pool and spa area. Breakfast features fresh pastries, seasonal fruits, juices, tea and coffee, and the quiet setting is another bonus (although there are some good restaurants and shops within easy walking distance). The nearby **Eo Inn** is another little gem, a genuine boutique hotel and spa (with a huge range of treatments, from massage to aromatherapy, body-wraps, waxing, facials and pedicures), featuring 17 deluxe rooms, including a startlingly spacious king lake balcony suite. The lush grounds, rooftop terrace and lake vistas make for a truly refreshing alternative to the usual hotel experience. Breakfast is not usually included, but the excellent bakery café **Panera Bread** is part of the complex (tel 407 481 8485, www.eoinn.com; $$$-$$$$, CC).

Babysitting

For folks who want an evening off from parenthood to take advantage of Orlando's night-life, babysitting is a ready option. The two most relied-upon, fully trained and licensed companies are **KinderCare** (also contracted to *Walt Disney World Resort in Florida* and Airtours, tel 407 846 2027) and **Anny's Nannies** (tel 407 826 8949). Both will visit hotels, motels, condos and homes, while KinderCare also organise group events and activities.

Right, that's enough planning and preparation for now, it's time to HIT THE THEME PARKS ... !

The Theme Parks – Disney's Fab Four

(or, Spending the Day with Mickey Mouse and Co.)

By now you should be prepared to deal with the main business of any visit to Orlando: *Walt Disney World Resort in Florida* and the other main theme parks of Universal Orlando, SeaWorld and Busch Gardens.

If you have only a week in the area this is where you should concentrate your attention but even then you may decide Busch Gardens is a bridge too far. If you have less than a week, you should concentrate on seeing as much of *Walt Disney World Resort in Florida* as possible. There is SO much packed into every park and the main tourist areas, even two weeks will scarcely be enough to give first-timers more than an outline picture of central Florida.

BRIT TIP: Beware offers of free tickets for theme parks as they are used as inducements to visit timeshare firms (see below). And never buy a ticket from an unofficial source as it may be stolen or non-transferable.

Firstly, you *can* save money off many attractions if you shop around. Disney tickets are available at *The Disney Stores* in the UK, and through Keith Prowse and most of the tour operators. But try not to buy ALL your tickets in advance as many people still get too many for the time they have there – be sensible.

You will also find **discount coupons** in many of the tourist publications distributed in Orlando, while the **tour operators'** welcome meetings have special deals or packages from time to time. The official **Visitor Center** at 8723 International Drive (in the Gala Center on the corner of Austrian Row, tel 407 363 5871 or www.orlandoinfo.com) also has some good offers which are worth checking out before you buy. It is also possible to pick up free tickets for attending timeshare presentations but I don't recommend it as they can take up half a day of your precious holiday.

BRIT TIP: If you DO want to check out timeshare options, look first at *Disney Vacation Club* for the guaranteed way to secure memorable holidays. Call 407 566 3300 or visit http://disney.go.com

Ratings

All the rides and shows are judged on a unique rating system that splits them into the Thrill Rides and Scenic ones. Thrill rides earn T ratings out of five (hence a TTTTT is as exciting as they get) and scenic rides get A ratings out of five (an AA ride is likely to be over-cute and missable). Obviously it is a matter of opinion to a certain extent, but you

Beauty and the Beast

or AAAAA attraction should not be missed! The latter will have the longest queues and so you should plan your visit around these rides. Some rides are restricted to children over a certain height and are not advisable for people with back, neck or heart problems, or for pregnant women. Where this is the case I have just noted 'Restrictions: 3ft 6in', and so on. Height restrictions (strictly enforced) are based on the average 5 year old being 3ft 6in tall, 6s being 3ft 9in and 9s being 4ft 4in.

Where families have small children, but mum and dad still want to try the ride, you DON'T have to queue twice. When you get to the front of the queue, tell the operator you want to do a 'baby swap'. This means mum can ride while dad looks after junior, and, on her return, dad can ride while mum does the babysitting. Many children also get a thrill from collecting autographs from the various Disney characters they meet, and most shops sell some neat **autograph books** for that purpose.

can be sure a T or A ride is not worth your time, a TT or AA is worth seeing only if there is no queue, a TTT or AAA should be seen if you have time, but you won't miss much if you don't, a TTTT or AAAA ride is a big-time attraction that should be high on your list of things to do, and finally a TTTTT

100 Years of Magic

Magic Kingdom Park

The starting point for any visit has to be the *Magic Kingdom*, the park that best embodies the spirit of delight that *Walt Disney World Resort in Florida* bestows on its visitors. It's the original development that sparked the tourist boom in Orlando back in 1971. In comparative terms, the *Magic Kingdom Park* is similar to *Disneyland Paris*® and *Disneyland Park* in Los Angeles. Outside those, it has no equal as an enchanting and exciting day out for all the family. All Disney employees are also known as Cast Members, and they are almost unfailingly cheerful and keen to help.

I will now attempt to steer you through a typical day at the parks, with a guide to the main rides, shows and places to eat, how to park, how to avoid the worst of the crowds and how much you should expect to pay.

This essential park takes up just 100 of *Walt Disney World Resort in Florida's* near 31,000 acres but attracts almost as many visitors as the rest put together! It has seven

The Magic Kingdom Park at a glance

Location	Off World Drive, Walt Disney World		
Size	100 acres in 7 'lands'		
Hours	9am–7pm off peak; 9am–10pm Washington's birthday, spring school holidays; 9am–11pm high season (Easter, summer holidays, Thanksgiving and Christmas)		
Admission	Under 3, free; 3–9 $38 (one-day ticket), $152 (4-Day Park Hopper), $197 (5-Day Park Hopper Plus); adult (10+) $48, $192, $247.		
Parking	$6		
Lockers	Yes; under Main Street Railroad Station; $5 ($2 refund)		
Pushchairs	$7 and $13 (Stroller Shop to right of main entrance, $1 deposit refunded)		
Wheelchairs	$7 ($1 deposit refunded) or $40 ($10 deposit refunded) (Main Ticket Centre or Stroller Shop)		
Top Attractions	Splash Mountain, Space Mountain, Alien Encounter		
Don't Miss	Share A Dream Come True Parade, SpectroMagic Parade (high season and weekends) and Fantasy in the Sky fireworks		
Hidden Costs	**Meals**	Burger, chips and coke $6.95 Three-course dinner $32 (Cinderella's Table)	
	Kids' meal	$3.25	
	T-shirts	$19–$28	
	Souvenirs	$0.40–$458	
	Sundries	Mickey Mouse Hat (with ears!) $16	

separate 'lands', like slices of a large cake centred on the most famous landmark of all Florida, Cinderella's Castle. There are more than 40 attractions packed in here, not to mention numerous shops and restaurants (although the eating opportunities are less impressive than *Epcot* and *Disney-MGM Studios*).

It's easy to get lost or overwhelmed by it all, especially as it does get so busy (even the fast-food restaurants have serious queues in high season), so study the notes and plan your visit around what most takes your fancy.

> BRIT TIP: If you have pre-paid vouchers for park entrance rather than the actual tickets, you have to exchange them at a ticket booth. Go to the Guest Relations window and you will avoid the queues here.

Another essential note on queuing here is *Disney's FastPass* system. All the main attractions at the parks now have this wonderful service that allows you to roam while you wait for your allotted time to ride. How it works: just insert your main park entrance ticket into the FastPass turnstile (to the side of each attraction entrance) and you get another ticket giving you a period in which to return and do the ride with only a minimal wait. You can hold only one FastPass ticket per 2-hour period, but, if you start by going to one of the FastPass rides, collecting your ticket and returning later, you can by-pass a lot of standing in line. Many people still miss this, but it is absolutely FREE (FastPass rides are also indicated by FP in the text for each attraction).

Location

The *Magic Kingdom* Park is located at the innermost end of the vacation kingdom, with its entrance toll plaza three-quarters of the way along World Drive, the main entrance road off of Highway 192. World Drive runs north-south through *Walt Disney World*, while the Interstate 4 entrance, Epcot Drive, runs basically east-west. Unless you are staying at one of Disney's resort hotels, you will have to pay your $6 parking fee at the toll plaza and that brings you to the car park (or 'parking lot' in American-speak), an enormous stretch of tarmac that can accommodate more than 10,000 cars. The majority arrive between 9.30 and 11.30am, so the car parks can become pretty jammed then, which is another good reason to get here EARLY. If you are not here by 9am during peak periods, you might want to wait until after 1pm, or even later when the park is open late into the evenings (as late as 11pm in high summer and Xmas). Note on your parking ticket exactly what area you are parked in and the row number, e.g. Mickey, Row 30. You will struggle to remember otherwise, and all hire cars look exactly the same!

To give you another idea of the size of the operation, a system of motorised trams carries you from the car park to the Transportation

> BRIT TIP: Reader Roy Williams says: 'We bought a bright, 3-inch plastic ball that we fixed to our car aerial, enabling us to find it easily on our return each time.' You could also leave a familiar, non-valuable item in the window for extra help.

and Ticket Center at the heart of the operation. Unless you already have your ticket (which will save you valuable time), you will have to queue up at the ticket booths here to go any further. Once you have ticket in hand, you pass the booths to either the monorail or ferryboats that will bring you to the doorstep of the *Magic Kingdom* Park itself. Of course, if you are staying on a *Walt Disney World* property, you can catch the monorail directly or one of the buses that make up the free transport system (both the bus and monorail deliver you to the park's front door). If you're at the head of the queue and can get straight on, the monorail (dead ahead of you) is slightly quicker. Otherwise, if you have to queue for the monorail, it is usually better to bear left and take the ferryboats which may be slightly slower but involve less queuing.

BRIT TIP: You can sometimes get to ride up front on the monorail (and get a special 'driver' certificate!) if you ask a Cast Member when you get on to the platform.

One final note, in all the main theme parks you may well find one or two attractions closed for refurbishment to mark the constant process of keeping everything fresh. However, you'll never be short of things to do!

Main Street, USA

Right, we've finally reached the park itself … but not quite. Hopefully you've paid heed to the need to arrive early and you're among the leading hordes aiming to swarm through the main entrance. The published opening times may say

BRIT TIP: Save paying up to three times more for your drinks by bringing your own bottled water in a back-pack to all the parks and use the many drinking fountains for refills.

9am, but the gates to the *Magic Kingdom* Park are likely to open up to 45 minutes before then. This will bring you into **Main Street, USA**, the first of the seven lands. Immediately on your right is **Exposition Hall**, a photographic centre featuring archive film material, a mini cinema showing Disney classics and a series of interactive games, plus some cartoon photo opportunities. On your left is **City Hall**, where you can pick up a park map and daily schedule (if you haven't been given one at the toll plaza) and make reservations for the main restaurants. Ahead of you is **Town Square**, where you can take a one-way ride down Main Street, USA on a horse-drawn bus or fire engine and visit the **Car Barn** mini museum or shop at the **Main Street Gallery** for exclusive Disney collectibles. The Street itself houses some of the best shopping in the *Magic Kingdom* Park (check out the massive Emporium), plus the *Walt Disney World* **Railroad**, the park's Western-themed steam train that runs the full circumference of the park and is one of the better attractions when the queues are long elsewhere. For dining, you have breakfast, lunch and dinner at **Tony's Town Square Restaurant**, specialising in Italian meals, **The Plaza Restaurant** (lunch and dinner, sandwiches, salads and sundaes), **The Crystal Palace** (breakfast, lunch and dinner, buffet-style food with Winnie the Pooh, Tigger and Co.), **Casey's Corner** (hot-dogs, chips

5

MAGIC KINGDOM PARK
ADVENTURELAND
1 Jungle Cruise
2 Swiss Family Treehouse
3 Pirates Of The Caribbean
4 The Enchanted Tiki Room
5 Magic Carpets of Aladdin
FRONTIERLAND
6 Big Thunder Mountain Railroad
7 Country Bear Jamboree
8 Raft To Tom Sawyer Island
9 Splash Mountain
LIBERTY SQUARE
10 The Hall Of Presidents
11 The Haunted Mansion
12 Liberty Belle Riverboat
13 Diamond Horseshoe Saloon Revue
FANTASYLAND
14 Castle Forecourt Stage
15 Legend Of The Lion King
16 Peter Pan's Flight
17 'it's a small world'
18 Snow White's Adventures
19 The Many Adventures Of Winnie The Pooh
20 Mad Tea Party
21 Fantasyland Character Festival
22 Ariel's Grotto
23 Cinderella's Golden Carousel
24 Dumbo The Flying Elephant
TOMORROWLAND
25 Tomorrowland Indy Speedway
26 Space Mountain
27 Galaxy Palace Theater
28 Astro Orbiter
29 The ExtraTERRORestrial Alien Encounter
30 Walt Disney's Carousel Of Progress
31 Tomorrowland Transit Authority
32 Buzz Lightyear's Space Ranger Spin
MICKEY'S TOONTOWN FAIR
33 The Barnstormer At Goofy's Wiseacre Farm
34 Minnie's Country House
35 Mickey's Country House
36 Toontown Hall Of Fame
37 Donald's Boat
TRANSPORT
38 Walt Disney World Railroad Stations
39 Boat Dock
40 Monorail Station
41 Bus Station

MAGIC KINGDOM PARK

and soft drinks), and **Caffe Italiano** (coffee and pastries). **Disney characters** also appear periodically outside Exposition Hall.

Look out for the **Guest Information Board** at the top of Main Street USA (on the left) that gives waiting times for all the attractions through the day.

Unless you are a late arrival, give Main Street no more than a passing glance for the moment and head for the end of the street where you will find the real entrance to the park. This is where you will have to wait for the final opening hour to arrive, the famous 'Rope drop', and you should adopt one of three tactics here, each aimed at doing one or two of the most popular rides before the queues become substantial (an hour for Splash Mountain is not unknown).

One: if you fancy heading straight for the five-star log-flume ride Splash Mountain, keep left in front of the Crystal Palace and the majority of the crowd will head for the same place.

Two: if you have young children who can't wait to ride on Cinderella's Golden Carrousel or the other Fantasyland rides, stay in the middle and head directly through the castle.

Three: if the thrills of the ExtraTERRORestrial Alien Encounter and the indoor roller-coaster Space Mountain appeal to you first, move to the right by the Plaza Restaurant and you'll get straight into Tomorrowland. Now you'll be in pole position for the opening rush to the main attractions (and it *will* be a rush – take care if you're here with small children).

Adventureland

If you head for the first option, to the left (effectively going clockwise around the park – always a good idea), you will enter **Adventureland**. If you're heading for Splash Mountain with the rest of the early queue-beaters, you pass the Swiss Family Treehouse on your left and bear right through an archway (with restrooms on your right) into Frontierland, where you go left and

Mickey opens the SpectroMagic Parade

© Disney

BRIT TIP: If you are determined to get the most from your day, have a good breakfast BEFORE you arrive to give you plenty of energy and save time once the park is open!

Splash Mountain is dead ahead. Stopping in Adventureland, however, these are the attractions you will encounter.

Swiss Family Treehouse: this imitation Banyan tree is a clever replica of the treehouse from Disney's 1960 film *Swiss Family Robinson*. It's a walk-through attraction where the queues (rarely long) move steadily if not quickly, providing a fascinating glimpse of the ultimate treehouse, complete with kitchen, rope bridges and running water! AAA.

Jungle Cruise: it's not so much the scenic, geographically suspect boat ride (where the Nile suddenly becomes the Amazon) that is so amusing here as the patter of your boat's captain, who spins a non-stop yarn about your adventure that features wild animals, tropical plants, hidden temples and sudden waterfalls. Great detail but long queues, so visit either early morning or late afternoon (evening queues are shortest, but you'll miss some of the detail in the dark). AAAA (FP).

Pirates of the Caribbean: one of Disney's most impressive attractions that involves their pioneering work in audio-animatronics, life-size figures that move, talk and, in this instance, lay siege to a Caribbean island! Your underground boat ride takes you through a typical pirate adventure and the wizardry of the special effects is truly amazing. This is worth several rides, although it may be a bit spooky for very young children. Queues are rarely long and almost non-existent late in the day. AAAAA.

The Enchanted Tiki Room: this bird-laden audio-animatronics venture features Iago (from *Aladdin*) and Zazu (*The Lion King*) at the head of a colourful, 16-minute revue that will appeal especially to younger children. Queues are rare here, too. AAA.

BRIT TIP: Both the Pirates and Tiki Room are air-conditioned and offer a cooling break in the heat of the day.

Magic Carpets of Aladdin: here, in a new, Agrabah-themed area styled after the animated film, the latest ride spins you up, down and around as you try to dodge the spitting camel! Your 'flying carpet' tilts as well as levitates, but it is basically simple stuff geared towards younger children. TT (TTTT for under 5s).

Disney characters also turn up outside Pirates of the Caribbean, and the best of the shopping is the **House of Treasure** here and **Agrabah Bazaar**. For food, you have **Aloha Isle**, for yoghurt and ice cream and **Sunshine Tree Terrace** (fruit snacks, yoghurt, tea and coffee).

Frontierland

Passing through Adventureland brings you to the target for many of the early birds. This Western-themed area is one of the busiest and is best avoided from late morning to late afternoon.

Splash Mountain: based on the 1946 classic Disney cartoon *Song of the South*, this is a watery journey into the world of Brer Rabbit, Brer Fox and Brer Bear. The first part is all jolly cartoon scenery and fun with the main characters and a couple of minor downward swoops in your eight-passenger log-boat. The conclusion, a five-storey plummet at 45 degrees into a mist-shrouded pool, will seem like you are falling off the edge of the world! A huge adrenaline rush, but busy almost all day (try it first thing or during one of the parades to avoid the worst of the queues). You will also get VERY wet! Restrictions: 3ft 4in. TTTTT (FP).

Big Thunder Mountain Railroad: when Disney do a roller-coaster they make it one of the classiest, and here it is, a runaway mine train that swoops, tilts and plunges through a mock abandoned mine filled with clever props and scenery. You'll need to ride it at least twice to appreciate all the detail, but again queues are heavy, so go first thing (after Splash Mountain) or late in the day. Restrictions: 3ft 4in. TTTT (FP).

Country Bear Jamboree: now here's a novelty, a 16-minute musical revue presented by audio-animatronic bears! It's great family fun with plenty of novel touches (watch for the talking moose-head). Again, you'll need to beat the crowds by going early morning or early evening. AAAA.

Frontierland Shootin' Arcade: apart from the Penny Arcade in Main Street, USA, this is the only other attraction that costs extra, as you shoot at a series of animated targets. TT.

Tom Sawyer Island: take a raft over to this overgrown playground, with mysterious caves, grottos and mazes, rope bridges and Fort Sam Clemens, where you can fire air guns at passing boats. A good get-away in early afternoon when the crowds are at their highest, while **Aunt Polly's Dockside Inn** is a refuge within a refuge for snacks and soft drinks. TT. Shops here sell cowboy hats, guns and badges as well as Native

American and Mexican handicrafts, while, for food, try **Pecos Bill Café** (salads, sandwiches and burgers) or the **Turkey Leg Wagon** (tempting, smoke-grilled turkey legs).

Liberty Square

Continuing the clockwise tour brings you next to a homage to post-Independence America. A lot of the historical content will go over the heads of British visitors, but it still has some great attractions.

The Diamond Horseshoe Saloon Revue: after all the audio-animatronic gadgetry here's an honest-to-goodness saloon show performed by real people. If you fancy a slapstick song-and-dance routine featuring can-can girls, corny comedy and audience participation, this is for you. Snacks are available before the show. AAA.

> BRIT TIP: When you are faced by more than one queue for an attraction, head for the left-hand one. Almost invariably this will move slightly quicker than that on the right.

Liberty Belle Riverboat: cruise America's 'rivers' on an authentic paddle steamer, be menaced by Indians and thrill to the tales of the Old West. This is also a good ride to take at the busiest times of the day, especially early afternoon. AAA.

The Haunted Mansion: a clever delve into the world of ghost train rides that is neither too scary for kids nor too twee for adults. Not so much a thrill ride as a scenic adventure, hence AAAA (FP). Watch out for the neat touch at the end when your car picks up an extra 'passenger'. Longish queues during the main part of the day, however.

5

Buzz Lightyear's Space Ranger Spin

The Hall of Presidents: this is the attraction that will mean least to us, a two-part show that is first a film about the history of the Constitution and then an audio-animatronic parade of all 43 American presidents. Technically it's impressive, but dull for young children, although it is another air-conditioned haven. AAA. Shopping here includes **Ye Olde Christmas Shoppe** and **The Yankee Trader**, while eating opportunities consist of the full-service **Liberty Tree Tavern** (serving hearty soups, steaks and traditional dishes like meatloaf and pot roast, plus dinner with Mickey and Co.), **Columbia Harbour House** (for counter-service fried chicken or shrimp and chips) and **Sleepy Hollow** (a picnic area serving snacks, fresh fruit and drinks).

Fantasyland

Exiting Liberty Square you walk past Cinderella Castle and come into the spiritual heart of the *Magic Kingdom* Park and the area with which young children are most fascinated. The attractions here are all designed with kids in mind, but some of the shops are quite sophisticated in their wares, while **Cinderella's Royal Table** is a must for a fun family meal.

'it's a small world': this could almost be *Walt Disney World*'s theme ride, a family boat trip through the different continents, each represented by hundreds of dancing, singing audio-animatronic dolls in delightful pageants of set-pieces. It sounds twee, but it actually creates a surprisingly striking effect, accompanied by Disney's annoyingly catchy theme song which younger children adore. Crowds are steady and peak in early afternoon. AAAA.

Dumbo the Flying Elephant: parents hate it but kids love it and all want to do this 2-minute ride on the back of a flying elephant that swoops in best Dumbo style (even if the ears do not flap). Do this one early or expect a long queue. TT (TTTT under 5s).

Mad Tea Party: again the kids will insist you take them in these spinning, oversized tea-cups that have their own 'steering wheel' to add to the whirling effect. Actually, they're just a heavily disguised fairground ride. Again, go early or expect serious crowds. TT (TTTT under 5s).

The Many Adventures of Winnie the Pooh: building on the timeless popularity of Pooh, Tigger and Co. is this family ride offering a

Disney's Agrabah Bazaar

fairly predictable jaunt through Hundred Acre Wood with several notable special effects and another original soundtrack. AAA (AAAAA under 5s) (FP).

Snow White's Adventures: this lively, fast-paced ride tells the cartoon story of Snow White with a few ghost train effects that may scare small children. Good fun, though, for parents and kids. Again, you will need to go early or late (or during the main afternoon parade) to beat the queues. TTT (TTTTT under 5s).

Cinderella's Golden Carrousel: the centrepiece of Fantasyland shouldn't need any more explanation other than it is a vintage carousel ride which kids adore. Long queues during the main part of the day. T (TTT under 5s).

Legend of the Lion King: children also love this cleverly-staged version of the Disney cartoon, using puppets, actors and special effects to tell the story of the lion cub born to be king. It is a bit of a test of endurance, though, as queues are long and then there is a pre-show you have to stand through before taking your seat in the air-conditioned theatre. AAAA.

Peter Pan's Flight: don't be fooled by the long queues at this one, it is a rather tame ride by *Magic Kingdom* standards, although it is still a big hit with kids. Its novel effect of flying up, up and away with Peter Pan quickly wears off, but there is still a lot of clever detail as your 'sailing ship' journeys over London to Neverland. AA (AAAA under 5s) (FP).

In addition to the rides, there are different musical shows daily on the Castle Forecourt Stage in front of the Castle, while the *Sword In The Stone* show is re-enacted several times a day near Cinderella's Carrousel.

Fantasyland Character Festival behind Dumbo allows you to meet some more Disney characters, as does **Ariel's Grotto** (where children frequently get very wet in the squirt ponds!), which draws quite a queue at peak periods. At the **Fairytale Garden**, on the corner of the Castle facing Tomorrowland, youngsters can enjoy *Storytime with Belle.*

Eating opportunities are at **The Pinocchio Village Haus** (salads, burgers and hot-dogs), the **Enchanted Grove** (ice drinks and juices, **Scuttle's Landing** and **Mrs Potts' Cupboard** (for ice creams and sundaes). **Cinderella's Royal Table** is a lovely setting for a meal, be it breakfast, lunch or dinner (but you need to book for all three – 407 939 3463). The majestic hall, waitresses in costume and well-presented food make for a memorable experience, with the food consisting of salads, seafood, roast beef, prime rib and chicken. It's a touch pricey for dinner, though. Shopping is provided by **Tinkerbell's Treasures** and **Sir Mickey's**.

Mickey's Toontown Fair

In the top corner of Fantasyland (just past the Mad Tea Party) is the shrub-lined entrance to **Mickey's Toontown Fair**. It is easy to miss, but it does have its own station on the railroad. Its primary appeal is to children, and they won't want to miss the chance to meet their favourite Disney characters. It is

The Barnstormer at Goofy's Wiseacre Farm

© Disney

exceptionally kid-friendly and well landscaped, and features a huge merchandising area, the **County Bounty** – wallets beware!

Mickey's Country House: here is a walk-through opportunity to see Mickey at home and have your picture taken with him in the Judge's Tent. AAAA (plus TTTTT for the photo opportunity. Just watch those awed young faces!).

Minnie's Country House: this is a chance to view Minnie's home and 'unique memorabilia', all designed in a country and western style. AAA.

Toontown Hall of Fame: here, there are three opportunities to meet a host of other Disney favourites. The Villains Room features the likes of Captain Hook and Jafar, Mickey's Pals lets you meet Goofy, Pluto, Minnie and Co., and Famous Faces introduces characters such as Cinderella, Snow White and Pocahontas. TTTTT (for kids!).

The Barnstormer at Goofy's Wiseacre Farm: this is a mini roller-coaster just for the young 'uns (although possibly a bit too much for the under 5s) and is another masterpiece of design as it swoops through the barn, even if it is a pretty short ride for all the queuing. TTT (TTTT for 5–9s). Restrictions: 3ft.

Donald's Boat: parents beware, your youngsters could get very wet here. If you have encountered the dancing fountains at Epcot between Future World and World Showcase, prepare for more watery delights as this boat-themed fountain spouts off in all sorts of ways. You might want to bring a change of clothes or swimsuit for your offspring. AAAA (under 10s).

Tomorrowland

Continuing down from Fantasyland finally brings you into the last of the seven Lands. It boasts a cartoon-like space-age appearance guaranteed to appeal to youngsters, and has some of the park's more original shops.

Space Mountain: this is one of the three most popular attractions, and its reputation is deserved. It is a fast, tight-turning roller-coaster completely in the dark save for occasional flashes as you whizz through 'the galaxy'. Don't do this after you've just eaten! The only way to beat the almost non-stop crowds here is to go either first thing, late in the day or during one of the parades or the fireworks show. Restrictions: 3ft 8in. TTTTT (FP).

Tomorrowland Indy Speedway: despite the long queues, this is a rather tame ride on supposed race tracks that just putt-putts along on rails with little real steering required. Restrictions: children must be 4ft 4in to drive alone. T (TTTT under 6s).

Astro Orbiter: this is a jazzed-up version of the flying Dumbos in Fantasyland, just a bit faster and higher and on rockets. Large, slow-moving queues are another reason to give this a miss unless you have children. TT (TTTT under 10s).

Walt Disney's Carousel of Progress: this one will surprise, entertain and amuse. It is a 100-year journey through modern technology with audio-animatronics and a revolving theatre that reveals different stages in that development. Its 22-minute duration is rarely threatened by crowds. AAA.

Tomorrowland Transit Authority: a neat 'future transport system', the TTA gives an elevated view of the area, with a glimpse inside Space Mountain, in electro-magnetically powered cars. If the queues are short, which they usually are, give it a go. AAA.

ExtraTERRORestrial Alien Encounter: this draws some HUGE queues (so go early) to its clever, high-tech preamble and scary show: a 'teleportation' demonstration that goes wrong and brings an Alien to life in the middle of the audience. The fear factor adds a new dimension to the park, but it will be too much for most under 9s (and anyone scared of the dark!). Restrictions: 3ft 8in. TTTT.

Buzz Lightyear's Space Ranger Spin: kids will not want to miss this chance to join the great Toy Story character in his battle against the evil Emperor Zurg. Ride into action against the robot army – and shoot them with laser-cannons! A sure-fire family winner, especially as you get to keep score. AAAA (FP)

The **Galaxy Palace Theater** hosts live musical productions featuring Disney characters and talent shows, at various times throughout the day. For food, **Cosmic Ray's Starlight Café** has burgers, chicken and salads, The **Plaza Pavilion** does pizza, subs and salads, **Auntie Gravity's** (ouch!) **Galactic Goodies** serves ice cream and juices and the **Lunching Pad** (double ouch!) at **Rockettower Plaza** offers smoked turkey legs, snacks and drinks.

Having come full circle you are now back at Main Street, USA, and you should return here in early afternoon to avoid the crowds and look at the impressive array of shops, while the Dapper Dans, a strolling barbershop quartet, provide good musical fun.

100 Years of Magic

As part of *Walt Disney World Resort in Florida's* 100 Years of Magic celebration, the *Magic Kingdom* Park will join in with a series of interactive kiosks that invite guests to *Discover The Stories Behind The Magic*, events in Disney history that inspired the creation of the park. Look out for the chance to buy one of the four special **Magical Moments pins** which suddenly light up at key

moments (notably during parades and in the Haunted Mansion!).

The tour de force, however, will be the new **Share A Dream Come True** parade every day at 3pm. This six-part extravaganza, along Main Street and through Frontierland, is designed as a flurry of classic Disney moments frozen inside giant snow globes full of special effects. All the character favourites will be featured, along with a new musical score, plus some lighting tricks along the parade route. Watch out for the chance to be a part of the parade as it will stop at regular intervals to allow characters to select people to dance and play-act with them. The globes themselves will feature some outstanding effects, with Aladdin taking to the air on his flying carpet, the Wicked Queen turning into the evil old hag and snow in the leading globes. I fully expect this to be one of the most dazzling parades Disney have ever staged and a must-see part of 100 Years of Magic.

5

BRIT TIP: Try to sit on the left side of Main Street USA (as you face the Castle) to stay in the shade if it's hot. People start staking out the best spots here up to an hour in advance.

There's more

If you think the park looks good during the day, prepare to be amazed at how wonderful it looks at night when some of the lighting effects are astounding. When the park is open in the evenings (during the main holiday periods and weekends), there is also the twice-nightly **SpectroMagic Parade** (wait for the second one to beat the crowds), a mind-boggling light and sound festival full of glitter and

SpectroMagic Parade

razzamatazz, with the Disney characters at the centre of a multitude of sparkling lights and fibre-optic effects. It's difficult to do it justice in words, so make sure you see it. Evening hours are also highlighted by **Fantasy in the Sky** firework show over the Castle which is sparked off every night in peak periods by Tinkerbell (seeing is believing!).

At Easter and Christmas, the daily parade takes on extra seasonal charm with appearances by the Easter Bunny and Father Christmas.

You can also breakfast with Disney characters at Cinderella's Royal Table ($14.95 for adults, $7.95 for 3–11s; 8-10am, from 7.30am on Mon, Thur and Sat), have dinner with them at the Liberty Tree Tavern ($19.95 and $9.95; 4pm–park close) or visit the Crystal Palace for breakfast ($14.95 and $7.95; 8–10.30am), lunch ($15.95 and $8.25; 11.30am–2.45pm) and dinner ($19.95 and $9.95; 4pm–park close) with Pooh, Tigger and Co. You can book a Disney character meal (from a choice of 19) up to 60 days in advance, on 407 939 3463.

Halloween and Christmas

Two additional annual events in the *Magic Kingdom* Park are **Mickey's Not So Scary Halloween Party** (on selected dates in October) and **Mickey's Very Merry Christmas Party** (late November and December) which provide a separate, party-style ticketed event from 7pm–midnight, with most of the rides open and extra themed fun and games (and snow with the Christmas party!), plus a parade and more fireworks. Tickets cost around $30 and can be booked on 407 939 7671.

If the crowds get too heavy, you

> BRIT TIP: Not many people think to watch the fireworks from Mickey's Toontown Fair, but you get a great view from here.

CAN escape by leaving the park in early afternoon (get a hand-stamp for re-admission and keep your car park ticket which is valid all day) and returning to your hotel for a few hours' rest or a dive into Disney's River Country Water Park, just a short boat ride away.

Finally, one of the park's best-kept 'secrets' is the **Keys to the Kingdom**, a 4/5-hour guided tour of many backstage areas, including the service tunnel under the park, and entertainment production buildings. It costs an extra $58 (including lunch; not available for under 16s). Call 407 939 8687 for details of this, **Disney's Family Magic Tour**, a 2-hour guided adventure that takes you on a search for clues throughout the park, at $25 ($20 for children) or **Disney's Magic Behind Our Steam Trains tour** ($30/person; no under 10s) as you join the crew who prepare the park's steam trains each day.

MAGIC KINGDOM PARK with children

Here is a rough guide to the rides which appeal to different age groups. Obviously, children vary enormously in their likes and dislikes but, as a general rule, you can be fairly sure the following will have most appeal to the ages concerned (also taking into account the height restrictions):

Under 5s
Walt Disney World Railroad, Main Street Vehicles, Jungle Cruise, The Enchanted Tiki Room, Country Bear Jamboree, Liberty Belle Riverboat, 'it's a small world,' Peter Pan's Flight, Legend of the Lion King, Cinderella's Carrousel, Dumbo, Adventures of Winnie The Pooh, Mickey's Country House, Donald's Boat, Tomorrowland Indy Speedway (with a parent), Buzz Lightyear's Space Ranger Spin, Tomorrowland Transit Authority.

5–8s
Walt Disney World Railroad, Pirates of the Caribbean, Jungle Cruise, Swiss Family Treehouse, Magic Carpets of Aladdin, Enchanted Tiki Room, Country Bear Jamboree, Liberty Belle Riverboat, Tom Sawyer Island, Big Thunder Mountain Railroad, Splash Mountain, Haunted Mansion, Legend of the Lion King, Snow White's Scary Adventures, Mad Tea Party, Many Adventures of Winnie The Pooh, Mickey's Country House, Donald's Boat, The Barnstormer, Tomorrowland Indy Speedway (with parent), Tomorrowland Transit Authority, Buzz Lightyear's Space Ranger Spin, Carousel of Progress, Astro Orbiter, Space Mountain (with parental discretion).

9–12s
Pirates of the Caribbean, Big Thunder Mountain Railroad, Splash Mountain, Diamond Horseshoe Saloon Revue, The Haunted Mansion, Mad Tea Party, The Barnstormer, Tomorrowland Indy Speedway (without parent), Buzz Lightyear's Space Ranger Spin, Extra-TERRORestrial Alien Encounter, Carousel of Progress, Astro Orbiter, Space Mountain.

Over 12s
Big Thunder Mountain Railroad, Splash Mountain, Haunted Mansion, ExtraTERRORestrial Alien Encounter, Astro Orbiter, Space Mountain.

Epcot

Amaze and annoy your friends by revealing *Epcot* stands for 'Experimental Prototype Community Of Tomorrow' (or the tourist's version: Every Person Comes Out Tired!), once you have marvelled at the amazing entertainment value of this 260-acre playground. Actually, it is not so much a vision of the future as a look at the world of today, with a strong educational and environmental message which children in particular are quick to pick up on.

At more than twice the size of the *Magic Kingdom* Park, it is more likely to require a 2-day visit (although under 5s might find it less entertaining) and your feet in particular will notice the difference!

Location

Epcot is located on Epcot Drive and the parking fee is again $6 as you drive into its main entrance (there is a separate entrance for guests of *Disney's Yacht* and *Beach Club Resorts, Disney's BoardWalk Inn* and *Villas* and the *Walt Disney World Swan* and *Dolphin* Hotels). It opened in October 1982 and its giant parking lot is big enough for 12,000 vehicles, so again a tram takes you from your car to the main entrance (although if you are staying at a *Walt Disney World* hotel you can catch the monorail or bus service to the front gate). Once you have your ticket, you wait by the turnstiles for the opening moment (often accompanied by a Disney character or two) and are then admitted to the central plaza area, between the two Innoventions centres.

Epcot is divided into two distinct parts arranged in a figure of eight and there are two tactics to avoid the worst of the early morning crowds. The first or lower half of the '8'

consists of **Future World**, six different pavilions arranged around Spaceship Earth (the giant 'golfball' that dominates the *Epcot* skyline) and Innoventions. The second part, or the top of the '8', is **World Showcase**, a potted journey around the world via 11 internationally presented pavilions that feature a taste of their culture, history, shopping, entertainment and cuisine. Once you are through the gates, start by heading for the Future World pavilions to your left (Universe of Energy, Wonders of Life and Test Track) and then continue up into World Showcase. This way you will visit some of the best rides in *Epcot* ahead of the main crowds. Alternatively, if the rides don't appeal quite so much as a visit to such diverse cultures as Japan and Morocco, spend your first couple of hours in the Innoventions centres (which are busy from mid-morning), then head into World Showcase as soon as it opens at 11am and you will be ahead of the crowds for several hours. If you time your journey around the Showcase (which is a full 1½-mile walk) to arrive back in Future World by late afternoon, you will find the worst of the milling throng will have passed through (except for Test Track).

The other thing you will want to do early on is book a table for lunch or dinner at one of the many fine restaurants around World Showcase (Mexico, Morocco, Canada and Japan are all highly recommended). The best reservations go fast, but check in at the Guest Relations office (immediately on the left as you enter the Innoventions Plaza) and they will be able to give you advice and make a Priority Seating booking (never just a reservation at Disney, remember).

Epcot at a glance

Location	Off *Epcot* Drive, *Walt Disney World*
Size	260 acres in Future World and World Showcase
Hours	9am–9pm (Future World), 11am–9pm (World Showcase)
Admission	Under 3, free; 3–9, $38 (one-day ticket), $152 (4-Day Park Hopper), $197 (5-Day Park Hopper Plus); adult (10+) $48, $192, $247.
Parking	$6
Lockers	Yes; to left underneath Spaceship Earth and International Gateway; $5 ($2 refund)
Pushchairs	$7 (to right underneath Spaceship Earth and International Gateway, $1 deposit refunded)
Wheelchairs	$7 ($1 deposit refunded) or $40 ($10 deposit refunded) (same location)
Top Attractions	Test Track, Spaceship Earth, Honey I Shrunk the Audience, Maelstrom,Universe of Energy, American Adventure
Don't Miss	IllumiNations, Tapestry of Dreams parade, live entertainment (including Off Kilter in Canada) and dinner at any of the World Showcase pavilions.
Hidden Costs	**Meals**	Burger, chips and coke $7.54 Three-course dinner $31 (Le Cellier, Canada)
	Kids' meal	$3.25
	T-shirts	$19–$32
	Souvenirs	$0.40–$1,100
	Sundries	Disney character imposed photo $17.95

5

Future World

Here is what you will find in the first part of your Epcot adventure.

Universe of Energy: there is just the one attraction here but it is a stunner as you are taken on a 45-minute show-and-ride in the company of American comedienne Ellen DeGeneres that explores the creation of fuels from the age of dinosaurs to their modern day usages. The film elements convince you that you are in a conventional theatre, but then your seats suddenly rearrange themselves into 96-person solar-powered cars and you are off on a journey through the sights, sounds and even smells of the prehistoric era, with some realistic dinosaurs! Queues are steady but not overwhelming throughout the day from mid-morning. AAAAA.

Wonders of Life: this is one of Future World's most popular pavilions, hence you need to be here either early or late in the day. **Body Wars** is a terrific simulator ride

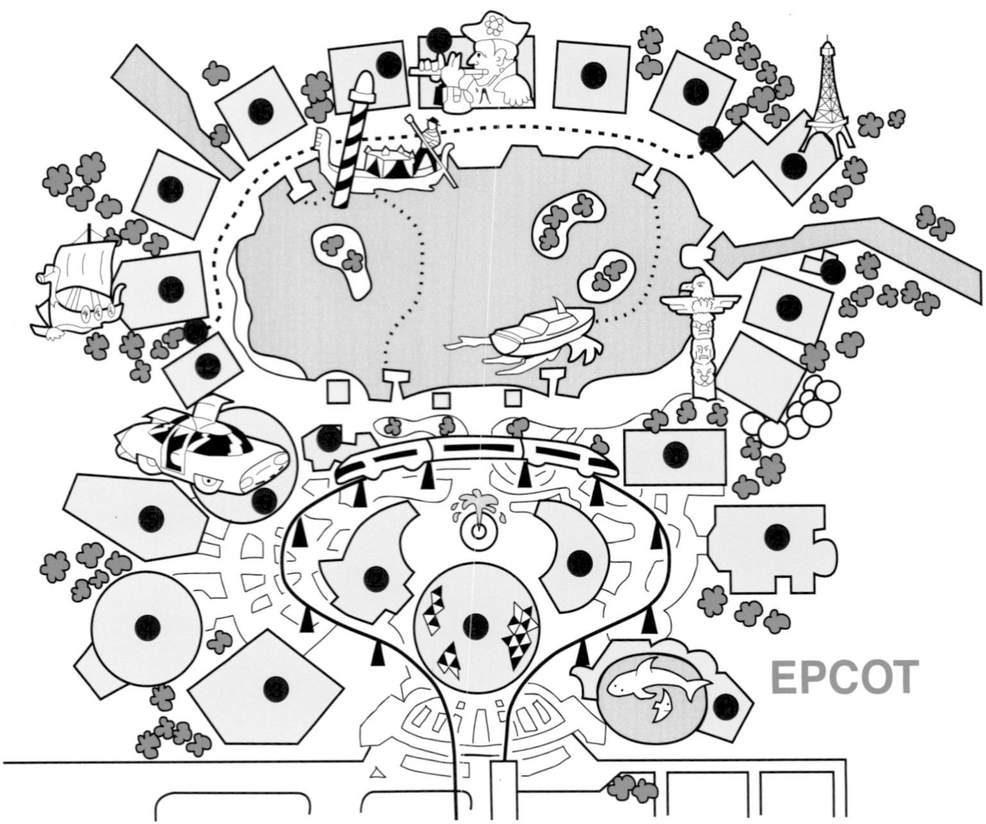

FUTURE WORLD

1 Spaceship Earth
2 Innoventions East
3 Universe Of Energy
4 Wonders Of Life
5 Mission: Space (Opening 2003)
6 Test Track
7 Odyssey Center
8 Imagination!
9 The Land
10 Innoventions West
11 The Living Seas

WORLD SHOWCASE

12 Mexico
13 Norway
14 China
15 Germany
16 Italy
17 The American Adventure
18 Japan
19 Morocco
20 France
21 International Gateway (To Epcot
   Resort Hotels)
22 United Kingdom
23 Canada
24 Tapestry of Dreams parade route

EPCOT

The new icon at Epcot

Mission: Space: the old Horizons pavilion has been pulled down and, in its place, is the construction for Mission: Space, a dramatic new high-tech attraction which will feature a simulated shuttle launch and space travel, among other things. It sounds quite dazzling, but sadly it is not due to open until 2003.

Test Track: the newest ride at *Epcot* is a big production, a 5½-minute whirl along the *Walt Disney World*'s longest and fastest track to date. Test Track starts with a pre-show into the world of General Motors' quality and safety techniques, preparing riders for first-hand experience of vehicle testing. The way the cars whizz around the outside of the building (at up to 60mph) gives you just a glimpse of what's in store. The reality is pretty good, too, as you are taken on a tour of a GM proving ground, including a hill climb test, suspension test (hold on to those fillings!), brake test, environment chamber, barrier test (remember those crash test dummies?) and the steeply banked high-speed finale. For those who manage to regain their breath, there is a post-show area with a multimedia film and the chance to view the latest GM models. There are some interactive driving tests, plus a smart gift store, and it all adds up to an extremely involved exhibit (although a bit technical for youngsters). The

through the human body as in the films Fantastic Voyage or the more recent Inner Space. It is quite a violent adventure, too, hence it is not recommended for people who suffer from motion sickness, anyone with neck or back injuries, or pregnant women. Restrictions: 3ft 4in. TTTT. **Cranium Command** is a hilarious theatre show set in the brain of a 12-year-old boy, showing how he negotiates a typical day. It is both audio-animatronic and film-based. See how many famous TV and film stars you can name in the 'cast'. AAAA. **The Making of Me** is a sensitive film on the creation of human life and will therefore require parental discretion for children as it has its explicit moments, although not without humour. AAA. **The Fitness Fairground**, with hands-on exhibits like exercise bikes, gives you the chance to see just how far all the holiday fun has taken its toll on your body! The **Pure and Simple** restaurant serves breakfast to 11am and then a range of snacks thereafter. Hot tip: this is a good pavilion in which to spend time if you need to cool down!

Test Track in Future World at Epcot

downside is the HUGE queues it attracts, topping two hours at peak times, while the available FastPasses often run out. Head straight here after opening or come back in the evening to keep your queuing to bearable levels. If you are on your own, you can save time by using the Singles Queue here. Restrictions: 3ft 4in. TTTT (TTT for teens) (FP).

The next door **Odyssey Center** offers baby-care and first aid facilities, telephones and restrooms.

Imagination!: The two-part attraction here starts with **Journey Into Your Imagination**, a fairly tame ride through the mock experiments and illusions of the Imagination Institute designed to measure your IQ (Imagination Quotient). Narrated by Eric Idle and featuring a gravity-defying section (seeing is not believing in this case!), it is gentle fun and rarely draws much of a crowd. AAA. (It is also unpopular with fans of the Dreamfinder ride it replaced, and there are strong rumours it will soon be closed to allow for a new concept based on the film Monsters, Inc.). You exit into **Image Works**, an interactive playground of unusual sights and sounds, which will probably amuse children more than adults (although you are also tempted here to part with more money, on various cartoon images and select-your-own CDs).

Come out of the building and turn right for the fabulous 3-D experience of **Honey, I Shrunk The Audience**, as Rick Moranis reprises his hapless inventor character Wayne Szalinski. A neat 8-minute pre-show is the perfect prelude to the fun and games in store. If you have seen Muppet*Vision 3-D at *Disney-MGM Studios* you might have an idea what to expect. Special effects and moving seats add to the entertainment that makes you feel you have been miniaturised. And beware the sneezing dog! AAAAA

(FP). Outside, kids are always fascinated by the Jellyfish and Serpentine Fountains that send water squirting from pond to pond, and there is always one who tries to stand in the way and 'catch' one of the streams of water. Have your cameras and camcorders ready! If you have young children, bringing a change of clothing is advisable.

The Land: this pavilion features four elements that combine to make a highly entertaining but educational experience on food production and nutrition. **Living with the Land** is an informative 14-minute boat ride that is worth the usually long queue. This journey through various types of food production sounds a dull idea, and it may not appeal much to younger children, but adults and school-age kids will sit up and take notice of the three ecological communities, especially the greenhouse finale. AAAA (FP). Having ridden the ride you can also walk the walk on the Behind The Seeds guided tour through the greenhouse complex and learn even more about *Walt Disney World Resort in Florida's* horticultural projects. It takes an hour ($6 for adults, $4 for children), but you have to book up in person at the desk near the Green Thumb Emporium. **Food Rocks**, just to the right as you exit the ride, is easy to overlook, but don't! This musical tribute to nutrition, presented by Food Rappa (what a great name!) and featuring Pita Gabriel (ouch!) is a hilarious 12-minute skit that will amuse kids and adults alike. AAAA. The **Circle of Life** is a 15-minute live-action/animated story that explains environmental concerns, easily digestible for kids. Queues not a problem here, either. AAA.

The **Sunshine Season** food court offers the chance to eat some of Disney's home-grown produce, and there are healthy alternatives to the usual fast food fare, while the

Garden Grill Restaurant is a slowly revolving platform that offers more traditional food, including pasta, seafood and delicious rotisserie chicken. Mickey and friends stage character breakfasts here (8.40–11.10am, from 7.40am Tue and Fri; $8.25 for kids 3–11 and $14.95 for adults), lunch (11.30am–4.20pm; $9.95 and $16.95) and dinner (4.30pm–park close; $9.95 and $18.95), but book early.

The Living Seas: this pavilion does for the sea what The Land Pavilion does for the land. A 7-minute film pre-show leads on to the ride, a 3-minute trip around the man-made 5.7-million-gallon aquarium that takes you to Sea Base Alpha, the main attraction. This two-level development takes visitors through six modules that present stories of undersea exploration and marine life, including a research centre that provides a close-up encounter with the endangered manatee. Crowds build up substantially through the day, so go either early or late. AAA.

The pavilion also includes the highly recommended Coral Reef restaurant that serves magnificent seafood, as well as providing diners with a grandstand view of the massive aquarium. Dinner for two will cost around $60, which isn't cheap, but the food is first class.

Spaceship Earth: this ride spirals up the 18 storeys into the 'golfball', telling the story of communication from early cave drawings to modern satellite technology. This is one of the most popular rides in the park, largely because of its visibility and location, hence you need to do it either first thing or late afternoon when the crowds have moved on from Future World into World Showcase. The highlight is the depiction of Michelangelo's painting of the Sistine Chapel, which will be lost on small kids, but it's an entertaining 15-minute journey all along. AAAA.

As you exit the ride you come into the Global Activity Center, presented by AT&T, with a host of interactive educational exhibits.

Innoventions East and West: These two centres of hands-on exhibits and computer games – subtitled **The Road to Tomorrow** – were revamped for the Millennium celebrations, and include a glimpse of _Walt Disney World Resort in Florida's_ latest investigations into virtual reality entertainment, and other demonstrations of current and future technologies, especially the Internet and computers, by companies like IBM, Xerox, Compaq, Motorola and General Motors. The kids will gravitate to the free **Video Games of Tomorrow** selection presented by Sega and they may take a bit of moving along! Both sides are routed like a journey into the future and will reward the enquiring mind in areas like People At Play and Mouse House Jnr. Worth waiting for are the **Ultimate Home Theater Experience** (West) and the opportunity to send a video e-mail to friends in the **Internet Zone** (East). This latter is also home to the **Mission: Space Launch Center**, which features several hands-on challenges and displays that preview the blockbuster new ride in Future World in 2003.

Musical entertainment is provided periodically in the Innoventions Plaza, along with other innovative live acts. Food outlets include the counter service **Electric Umbrella Restaurant** for lunch and dinner (sandwiches, pizza, burgers and salads) and the **Fountain View Espresso and Bakery** for tea, coffee and pastries. Visit **Ice Station Cool**, presented by Coca-Cola™, for some free product samples and the chance to encounter real snow! You'll also find the huge shopping plaza **Mouse Gear** in Innoventions East, featuring stacks of quality _Epcot_ and Disney souvenirs.

World Showcase

If you found Future World a huge experience, prepare to be amazed also by the more down-to-earth but equally imaginative pavilions around the World Showcase Lagoon. Each features a glimpse of the host country in dramatic settings. Several have either amusing rides or films that show off the tourist features of the countries, while in nearly every case the restaurants offering national fare are some of the best in Orlando.

Mexico: starting at the bottom left of the circular tour of the lagoon and moving clockwise, your first encounter is the spectacular pyramid that houses Mexico. Here you will find the amusing boat ride along **El Rio del Tiempo**, the River of Time, which gives you a potted 9-minute journey through the people and history of the country. Queues here tend to be surprisingly long from mid-morning to late afternoon. AAA. The rest of the pavilion is given over to a range of shops in the **Plaza de los Amigos** that vary from pretty tacky to sophisticated, and the **San Angel Inn**, a dimly-lit and romantic full-service diner offering

---

Honey I Shrunk The Audience

© Disney

traditional and tempting Mexican fare. Outside, on the lagoon, is the **Cantina de San Angel**, a fast-food counter for tacos, chilli and burgers, while, as with all World Showcase pavilions, there is live entertainment and music.

> **BRIT TIP:** The Cantina is a great spot from which to watch the nightly IllumiNations fireworks and laser show, but you need to arrive at least an hour early.

Norway: next up is Norway, which features probably the best of the rides in World Showcase, the Viking-themed **Maelstrom**. This 10-minute longboat journey through the history and scenery of the Scandinavian country features a short waterfall drop and a North Sea storm, and attracts longish queues during the day, so the best tactic is to go soon after World Showcase's 11am opening. TTT. There are periodical Norwegian-themed exhibits in the reconstruction **Stave Church** and twice-daily guided tours (sign up at the Tourism desk). The pavilion also contains a clever reproduction of Oslo's Akershus fortress. **Restaurant Akershus** offers lunch and dinner buffets and the **Kringla Bakeri Og Kafé** serves open sandwiches, pastries and drinks.

China: the spectacular architecture of China is well served by the pavilion's main attraction, the stunning **Wonders of China**, a 20-minute, 360-degree film in the circular Temple of Heaven. Here you are surrounded by the sights and sounds of one of the world's most mysterious countries in a special cinematic production, the technology of which alone will leave you breathless. If you were ever tempted to pay a visit to the country itself, this film will convince you. Queues build up to half an hour during the main part of the day. AAAA. **Land of Many Faces** is an exhibit introducing China's ethnic peoples. Two restaurants, the **Nine Dragons** (table service, decent if unremarkable food) and the **Lotus Blossom Café** (counter service, fairly predictable spring rolls and stir-fries) offer tastes of the Orient, while the **Yong Feng Shangdian Department Store** is a virtual warehouse of Chinese gifts and artefacts. Don't miss the periodic shows of Oriental music and acrobatic acts on the plaza in front of the Temple.

The **Outpost** between China and Germany features hut-style shops and snacks, with entertainment from Africa and the Caribbean.

Germany: this offers more in the way of shopping and eating than entertainment, although you still find strolling players, courtyard musicians and a lively **Biergarten**, with its brass band. It also offers hearty portions of German sausage, sauerkraut and rotisserie chicken. The **Sommerfest** is fast food German-style (bratwurst and strudel), while this pavilion boasts the highest number of shops of any Epcot pavilion, including chocolates, wines, china, crystal, toys and cuckoo clocks.

Italy: similarly, Italy has pretty, authentic architecture (including a superb reproduction of St Mark's Square in Venice), lively music and amusing Italian folk stories, three tempting gift shops (including Perugina chocolates and Armani collectibles), and its restaurant, **L'Originale Alfredo di Roma Ristorante**. It's a touch expensive, but the atmosphere, decor and singing waiters (!) add extra zest to the meals, which include fettucine, chicken, veal and seafood. Expect a three-course meal to cost about $35.

America: at the top of the lagoon and dominating World Showcase is the **American Adventure**, not so much a pavilion as a celebration of the country's history and constitution. A colonial fife and drum band add authentic sounds to the eighteenth-century setting, overlooked by a faithful reproduction of Philadelphia's Liberty Hall. Inside the Hall, you will find the spectacular American Adventure show, a magnificent film and audio-animatronic production lasting half an hour which details the country's struggles and triumphs, its presidents, statesmen and heroes. It's a glossy, patriotic performance, featuring outstanding audio-animatronic effects, and, while some of it will leave foreign visitors fairly cold, it is difficult not to be impressed by the sense of pride and achievement inherent in so much American history. It doesn't pull any

BRIT TIP: Kids, to get the best signatures from your Disney favourites, use a thick pen or pencil, as some characters have trouble writing otherwise!

punches on Native American issues, either. Avoid at midday for the queues. AAAA. Outside, handcarts offer touches of American nostalgia and antiques, while the **Liberty Inn** offers fast-food fare for lunch and dinner. The **America Gardens Theater** facing the lagoon presents musical performances from worldwide artists and Disney characters which vary seasonally.

Japan: next up on the clockwise tour, you will be introduced to typical Japanese gardens and architecture, including the breathtaking Chi Nien Tien, a round building one-half scale reproduction of a temple, some magnificent art exhibits (notably the Bijutsu-kan Gallery), musical shows and dazzling live entertainment. For one of the most entertaining meals in *Epcot*, the **Teppanyaki Dining** rooms and **Tempura Kiku** both offer a full, table-service introduction to Japanese cuisine while **Yakitori House** is the fast-food equivalent and the **Matsu No Ma Lounge** features sushi and cocktails. The restaurants are hosted by Mitsukoshi, as is the superb department store.

Morocco: as you would expect, this is a real shopping experience, with bazaars, alleyways and stalls selling a well-priced array of carpets, leather goods, clothing, brass ornaments, pottery and antiques (seek out that Magic Lamp!). All of the building materials were faithfully imported and hand-built to give Morocco a great degree of authenticity, even by the World Showcase's high standards, and will keep you gazing at its clever detail around the winding alleyways to the **Nejjarine Fountain** and gardens, which can be enjoyed on a guided walking tour. **Restaurant Marrakesh** offers a full Moroccan dining experience, complete with traditional musicians and a belly dancer. It's slightly pricey ($55 for the Moroccan feast for two) but the atmosphere is always lively and entertaining.

France: France is predictably overlooked by a replica Eiffel Tower, but the smart streets, buildings and the sheer cleanliness of it all is a long way removed from modern-day Paris! This is pre-World War One France, with official buskers, comedy street theatre and mime acts adding to the rather dreamy atmosphere. Don't miss **Impressions de France**, another stunning big-film production that serves up all the grandest sights of France to the accompaniment of the

music of Offenbach, Debussy, Saint-Saëns and Satie. Crowds get quite heavy from late morning but it is a stunning performance (although kids might feel left out). AAAA. If you are looking for a gastronomic experience this is also the pavilion, as there are three restaurants, of which **Chefs de France** and **Bistro de Paris** are major discoveries. The former is an award-winning, full-service and therefore expensive establishment featuring top quality cuisine created by French chefs on a daily basis, while the latter offers more intimate bistro dining, still with an individual touch and plenty of style. Alternatively, the **Boulangerie Patisserie** is a sidewalk café offering more modest fare at a more modest price. Shopping is also suitably chic.

United Kingdom: this may be a slight disappointment to British visitors, the least inspired of all 11 international pavilions, and certainly with little to entertain those who have been inside a traditional pub before or shopped for Royal Doulton or Pringle goods. It is partly offset by some good street entertainers and the excellent Beatles tribute band, the British Invasion, but that really is the sum total here. The **Rose and Crown Pub** is fairly authentic, but you can get better fare (steak and kidney pie $13, cottage pie $12 and a pint of Bass, Harp Lager or Guinness for a whopping $5) at these prices. Many rave about the **Harry Ramsden's**

BRIT TIP: The Rose & Crown Dining Room is actually a great place from which to see the nightly IllumiNations fireworks spectacular, especially if you can get a table on the Terrace.

fish and chip shop here, but I'm not over-keen. Other shops are the **Tea Caddy**, the **Magic of Wales**, the **Queen's Table**, **Lords and Ladies** (perfumes, tobacco, family crests) and the **Toy Soldier** (traditional games and toys).

Canada: completing the World Showcase circle, the main features here are **Victoria Gardens**, based on the world-famous Butchart Gardens on Vancouver Island, some spectacular Rocky Mountain scenery, a replica French gothic mansion, the Hôtel du Canada, and another stunning 360-degree film, **O Canada!** As with China and France, this showcases the country's sights and scenery in a terrific, 17-minute advert for the Canadian Tourist Board. It gets busiest from late morning to late afternoon. AAA. Resident band **Off Kilter** are also one of the most entertaining I've seen anywhere. Want to hear rock 'n roll bagpipes? This is the group for you! **Le Cellier Steakhouse** is a modestly priced dining room offering steaks, prime rib, seafood, chicken and several vegetarian dishes for lunch and dinner.

Around World Showcase are also 11 **Kidcot Fun Stop** activity centres, at which children can collect a special 11-point Star Medallion to get stamped at each of the pavilions as they visit them. The Medallion has a pop-out disc centre, the use for which will become apparent at the Tapestry of Dreams parade (see below).

Disney characters also put on a show several times a day at **Showcase Plaza**, just across the bridge from Future World to World Showcase, and take their sight-seeing bus on tour to several locations in World Showcase, so have those autograph books handy!

Planning your visit

If you plan a 2-day visit, it makes sense to spend the first day in World Showcase, arriving early and heading there while most of the rest of the morning crowds linger in Future World, booking your evening meal around 5.30pm, and then lingering around the lagoon for the evening entertainment. For your second visit, try arriving in mid afternoon and then doing Future World in more leisurely fashion than is the case in mid-morning to mid-afternoon. Queues at most of the pavilions are almost non-existent for rides like Universe of Energy, Body Wars and The Land, although Test Track stays busy nearly all day (except for the evening, when everyone is around the lagoon for the firework finale). Make best use of the FastPass system here by grabbing a pass for Test Track early on and then riding Universe of Energy or Body Wars. You CAN do Epcot in a day – if you arrive early, put in some speedy legwork and give some of the detail a miss. But, of all the parks, it is a shame to hurry this one. In the shops (almost 70 in all), try to save your browsing for the busiest times when most people are on the rides. The Innoventions centers are also busiest from mid-morning to mid- afternoon, and crowd-free in the evening.

100 Years of Magic

Epcot's contribution to the 15-month celebration of Walt Disney is, along with the other parks, in the form of the **interactive kiosks** inviting guests to Discover The Stories Behind the Magic and the special **Disney's Magic Moment pins**, which illuminate in spectacular fashion at key moments. However, there is also a twice-daily parade around World Showcase (from Norway to France) which

5

promises to be another show-stopper. **Tapestry of Dreams** is a development of the Tapestry of Nations parade which was such an amazing feature of Disney's Millennium celebrations here. It takes the basic premise of a series of large, elaborate puppet-like figures and rolling percussion units and adds four new floats, known as Dream Catchers, with characters called Dream Spinners. The parade is geared towards children's dreams for the future and is narrated in suitable fashion with magnificent music by Hans Zimmer and British composer Gavin Greenaway (prepare to have your heart-strings severely tugged!). At strategic points, children will be invited to pull out the centre disc of their Star Medallion (from the World Showcase Kidcot centres – see above) and deposit a Magic Dream Wish into the net carried by the Dream Spinners. It sounds an inspired touch and, with the existing elements of this brilliantly coloured street festival, it should be a memorable occasion.

IllumiNations: Reflections of Earth

The day's big finale at *Epcot* received a dramatic revamp for the magnificent Millennium celebrations in 2000 and has been retained for some time to come after it proved such a huge hit. **IllumiNations: Reflections of Earth**, is a firework and special-effect extravaganza awesome even by Disney standards. Again, Greenaway provides original music for a 15-minute performance of vivid brilliance. Some 2,800 firework shells are launched as a celestial backdrop to a series of fire-and-water effects on the World Showcase lagoon. The central icon is a 28ft video globe of Earth that opens in a spectacular climax of choreographed pyrotechnics. Don't

miss it! However, be aware people start staking out the best Lagoon-side spots up to 2 hours in advance.

The ultimate way to view IllumiNations is by private boat on one of three **speciality cruises** from Disney's Boardwalk or Yacht/Beach Club resorts (for non-residents, too). They vary from $120–$275 per boat (holding 4–12 guests) and can be used for special celebrations. The basic cruise costs $120 and the pontoon boat holds up to 12. The level-one cruise adds soda, sandwiches, water and snacks and costs $200 for up to 4 guests and $20 for each additional person. The level-two cruise adds fruit, cheese and dessert, costing $275 for 4 and $35 for each additional guest. Call 407 939 7529 up to 90 days in advance to book. Be aware cruises launch regardless of whether fireworks are taking place at times.

Epcot also has some special behind-the-scenes tours (but not for under-16s). **Dolphins In Depth** ($140, including souvenir video, T-shirt and refreshments) is a 3½-hour delve into the backstage and research areas of the Living Seas pavilion, including a chance to meet the resident dolphins. **Gardens of the World** ($59) is a 3-hour botanical tour of the gardens in *Epcot*, and includes tips for your own garden. **Hidden Treasures** is a 3- ($59) or 5-hour ($90, including lunch and gift) tour of the 11 countries of World Showcase. **Undiscovered Future World** is a 4½-hour journey into the creation of *Epcot*, Walt's vision for the Resort and backstage areas like IllumiNations ($49). **Backstage Magic** ($199) goes behind the scenes of *Epcot*, *Magic Kingdom* Park and *Disney-MGM Studios* on a 7-hour tour into little-seen aspects, like animators at work in Disney-MGM Studios and tunnels below the Magic Kingdom Park. Tours must be booked on 407 939 8687.

Two other *Epcot* specialities are the wonderful **International Flower and Garden Festival** (mid-April to June), and the **Food and Wine Festival** (late October to November), which showcases national and regional cuisines, wines and beers, with the chance to attend grand Winemakers Dinners and Tasting Events, or just sample the inexpensive offerings of more than 20 food booths around World Showcase. In the case of the former, you can really take time out to slow down and smell the roses – and it's free!

EPCOT with children

Here is our rough guide to the rides which appeal to different age groups in this park:

Under 5s
Spaceship Earth, Universe of Energy, Journey Into Your Imagination, The Living Seas, Living with the Land, Circle of Life, El Rio del Tiempo.

5–8s
All the above, plus Body Wars, Cranium Command, Test Track, Innoventions, Honey I Shrunk The Audience (with parental discretion), Image Works, Food Rocks, Maelstrom, The American Adventure.

9–12s
All the above, plus Behind the Seeds tour, Treasures of Morocco tour, Impressions de France, Wonders of China, O Canada!

Over 12s
All the above, plus Land of Many Faces (China), Bijutsu-kan Gallery, Norway guided tours, Off Kilter, British Invasion.

IllumiNations at Epcot

© Disney

Disney-MGM Studios

Welcome to Hollywood! Well, the Walt Disney version of it. When it opened in May 1989, Michael Eisner, Chairman of the Walt Disney Company, insisted it was 'the Hollywood that never was and always will be'. Sounds double Dutch? Don't worry, all will be revealed in your day-long tour of this real-life combination of theme park and working TV and film studio. It's the most common question about *Disney-MGM Studios*, and yes, there really are film and TV productions going on even while you're riding around the park peering into the backstage areas. For 2002, *Disney-MGM Studios* is also the focus of the **100 Years of Magic** celebration, with a number of extra new attractions, and an awesome grand icon – a 12-storey **Sorcerer Mickey hat** at the centre of the park, a gigantic, shimmering symbol of the Disney magic.

Rather bigger than the *Magic Kingdom* Park at 135 acres but substantially smaller than *Epcot*, *Disney-MGM Studios* is a different experience yet again with its combination of rides, spectacular shows (including the unmissable Fantasmic!), street entertainment, film sets and smart gift shops. Like the *Magic Kingdom* Park, the food on offer won't win awards, but some of the restaurants (notably the **Sci-Fi Dine-in Theater** and **50s Prime Time Café**) have superbly imaginative settings to keep everyone amused. *Disney-MGM Studios* also has rather more to keep the attention of smaller children than *Epcot*, but you can still easily see all it has to offer in a day unless the crowds are really heavy.

Location

The entrance arrangements will be fairly familiar if you have already visited any of the other parks. *Disney-MGM Studios* are located on Buena Vista Drive (which runs between World Drive and Epcot Drive) and the parking fee is $6. Look out for the landmark 130ft water tower adorned with Mickey Mouse ears and dubbed – wait for it – the Earffel Tower!

Again, make a note of where you park before you catch your tram to the main gates, where you must wait for the official opening hour. If the queues build up quickly, the gates will again open early, so be ready to jump the gun and get a running start.

Once through the gates you are into Hollywood Boulevard, which is a street of mainly gift shops, and you have to decide which of the main attractions to head for first, as these are the ones where the queues will be heavy nearly all day. Try to ignore the lure of the shops as it is better to browse in the early afternoon when the queues build up at the rides. Incidentally, if you thought *Walt Disney World Resort in Florida* had elevated queuing to an art form in their other two parks, wait until you see the clever ways they are arranged here! Just when you think you have got to the ride itself there is another twist to the queue you hadn't seen or an extra element to the ride which holds you up. The latter are called 'holding pens' and are an ingenious way of making it seem like you are being entertained instead of queuing. Look out for them in particular at the Great Movie Ride, Twilight Zone™ Tower of Terror and Jim Henson's Muppet*Vision 3-D. An up-to-the-minute check on queue times at all the main

Disney-MGM Studios at a glance

Location	Off Buena Vista Drive or World Drive, Walt Disney World
Size	135 acres
Hours	9am–7pm off peak; 9am–10pm high season (Easter, summer holidays, Thanksgiving and Christmas)
Admission	Under 3, free; 3–9, $38 (one-day ticket), $152 (4-Day Park Hopper), $197 (5-Day Park Hopper Plus); adult (10+) $48, $192, $247.
Parking	$6
Lockers	Yes; next to Oscar's Super Service, to right of main entrance; $5 ($2 refundable)
Pushchairs Wheelchairs	$7 (from Oscar's Super Service, $1 deposit refunded) $7 ($1 deposit refunded) or $40 ($10 deposit refunded) (same location)
Top Attractions	Twilight Zone™ Tower of Terror, Rock 'n Roller Coaster, Star Tours, Great Movie Ride, Who Wants To Be A Millionaire – Play It, Voyage of the Little Mermaid, Muppet*Vision 3-D
Don't Miss	Disney Stars and Motor Cars Parade, Indiana Jones™ Stunt Spectacular, Fantasmic!
Hidden Costs	**Meals**	Burger, chips and coke $6.95 Three-course dinner $30 (Brown Derby)
	Kids' meal	$3.25–$4.75
	T-shirts	$19–$32
	Souvenirs	$1.25–$385
	Sundries	Rock 'n Roller Coaster photo $16.95

attractions is kept on a **Guest Information Board** on Hollywood Boulevard, just past its junction with Sunset Boulevard, where you can also book one of the feature restaurants.

Disney-MGM Studios is laid out in rather more confusing fashion than its counterparts, which have neatly packaged 'lands', so you need to consult your map frequently to ensure you're going in the right direction.

The main attractions

Having said that, the opening-gate crowds will all surge in one of four directions which will give you a pretty good idea of where you want to go. By far the 'biggest' attraction in *Disney-MGM Studios* is The **Twilight Zone™ Tower of Terror**, a magnificent haunted hotel ride that culminates in a 13-storey drop in a lift. The queues here build up to two hours at peak periods. Consequently, if the Tower appeals to you, do it first! Head up

DISNEY-MGM STUDIOS

1 Parade Route ... Disney Stars and Motor Cars
2 100 Years of Magic Central
3 Indiana Jones™ Epic Stunt Spectacular!
4 ABC Sound Studio 'Sounds Dangerous'
5 Star Tours
6 Disney's Hunchback Of Notre Dame – A Musical Adventure
7 Jim Henson's Muppet*Vision 3-D
8 Honey, I Shrunk The Kids Movie Set Adventure
9 Catastrophe Canyon On Disney-MGM Studios Backlot Tour
10 Disney-MGM Studios Backlot Tour
11 Backstage Pass Tour
12 The Great Movie Ride
13 Voyage Of The Little Mermaid
14 Who Wants To Be A Millionaire – Play It!
15 The Magic Of Disney Animation
16 The Twilight Zone™ Tower Of Terror
17 'Beauty & The Beast' – Live On Stage
18 Guest Information Board
19 Toy Story Pizza Planet
20 Fantasmic!
21 Rock 'N Roller Coaster Starring Aerosmith
22 Playhouse Disney – Live On Stage
23 Walt Disney: One Man's Dream

DISNEY-MGM STUDIOS

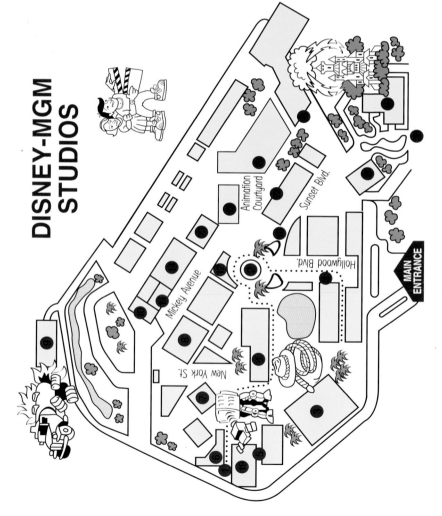

© Disney

5

Sorcerer Mickey's hat for the 100 Years of Magic Celebration

Hollywood Boulevard then turn right into Sunset Boulevard and it is at the end of the street, looming ominously over the park. **Rock 'n Roller Coaster** starring Aerosmith, at the end of Sunset Boulevard on the left, is another huge draw but is also a FastPass ride like Tower of Terror, so you can get a pass for one and ride the other if you head here first.

Star Tours, the great Star Wars™ simulator ride, and **Voyage of the Little Mermaid** are also serious queue-builders and FP attractions. If you are not up for the really big thrills, grab a pass for Mermaid (straight up Hollywood Boulevard, past Sunset, turn right into Animation Courtyard) then head for Star Tours (back across the main square past the Indiana Jones show). Finally, the new **Who Wants To Be A Millionaire – Play It!** attraction is a major success, but has only 10 shows (accommodating 1,600 people a time) a day, hence FastPasses can run out quickly. So, if this appeals to you, head here first (past the Little Mermaid and along Mickey Avenue).

Here's a full rundown of all the current attractions in more detail, working in a clockwise direction.

The Great Movie Ride: this faces you (behind the new hat icon) as you walk in along Hollywood Boulevard and is a good place to start if the crowds are not too serious. An all-star audio-animatronics cast recreate a number of box office smashes, including Jimmy Cagney's *Public Enemy*, Julie Andrews in *Mary Poppins*, Gene Kelly in *Singing in the Rain* and many more masterful set pieces as you ride through on your conducted tour. Small children may find the menace of the Alien too strong, but otherwise it has fairly universal appeal and features some live twists it would be a shame to spoil by revealing. AAAA.

ABC Sound Studio 'Sounds Dangerous': this sound FX special features American comedian Drew Carrey in an instalment of a spoof undercover police show *Sounds Dangerous*. Most of the show is in the dark – which upsets some young children – and is centred on your special headphones as Carrey's stakeout goes wrong. Clever and amusing – if a bit tame for older children – you exit into the Sound Works Studio to try out some well-known sound effects. AAA.

Indiana Jones™ Epic Stunt Spectacular!: consult your park map for the various times during the day when this rip-roaring stunt cavalcade hits the stage. A specially-made movie set creates three different backdrops for Indiana Jones™ stunt men and women to put on a dazzling array of clever stunts, scenes and special effects from the Harrison Ford film epics. Again, there is an audience participation element and some amusing sub-plots I won't reveal. Queues for the near-45-minute show begin to form up to half an hour before showtime so be prepared for a wait here, but the auditorium holds more than 2,000 so everyone usually gets in. TTTT (FP).

Star Tours: anyone remotely amused by the *Star Wars™* films will enjoy just queuing up for one of my personal favourites, a breathtaking 7-minute spin in a Star Speeder. The elaborate walk-in area is full of *Star Wars™* gadgets and gizmos that will take your attention away from the fact you often have to queue for up to an hour. From arguing robots C-3PO and R-2D2 to your robotic 'pilot', everything has a brilliant sense of space travel, and the ride won't disappoint! Restrictions: 3ft 4in, no children under 3. TTTT (plus AAAAA). (FP).

Jim Henson's Muppet*Vision 3-D: the 3-D is crossed out here and 4-D substituted in its place, so be warned some strange things are about to happen! A wonderful 10-minute holding-pen pre-show

takes you in to the Muppet Theater for a 20-minute experience with all of the Muppets, 3-D special effects and more – when Fozzie Bear points his squirty flower at you, prepare to get wet! It's a gem, and children in particular will love it. Queues build up through the main parts of the day, but Disney's queuing expertise makes them seem shorter than they actually are. AAAAA (FP).

Disney's The Hunchback of Notre Dame – A Musical Adventure: this clever 32-minute musical and animated puppetry show highlights the key elements of the Disney film and is staged five times a day in the **Backlot Theater**. It features a wonderfully elaborate stage setting, too. AAA. Have your cameras handy in this area for the Backlot, a collection of clever façades that look like city scenery, which you can wander around on foot. There is also a recreation of **Al's Toy Barn** from the *Toy Story* cartoon, and children can meet Buzz Lightyear, Woody and Jessie here at various times.

Honey, I Shrunk the Kids Movie Set Adventure: this kids' adventure playground gives youngsters the chance to tackle gigantic blades of grass that turn out to be slides, crawl through caves, investigate giant mushrooms and more. However, some may turn round and say 'Yeah. A giant ant. So what?' and head back for the rides. There can be long queues here, too, so arrive early if the kids demand it (and bring plenty of film). TT (TTTT under 9s).

Backstage Pass: the first element of a three-part sequence takes you behind the scenes of Disney film and TV-making. This 25-minute section introduces the Jim Henson creature feature lab (including working models from *101 Dalmatians*), an amusing look at the *Home Improvement* TV show, a glimpse of *Disney-MGM Studios* soundstages and their current productions (plus the new Millionaire attraction) and a full-scale set-up of the world of Cruella De Vil. It is a fascinating tour, but it won't do much for small children and you will find it hard going with pushchairs. AAA.

The Disney-MGM Studios Backlot Tour: part 2, which takes 35 minutes, starts with some more special effects (involving a clever and funny water tank with a mock Pearl Harbor attack!) before you board the special trams for a look at the off-limits part of the Studios. You are introduced to the production backlot, famous 'houses' and props before visiting **Catastrophe Canyon** for a demonstration of special effects that try both to drown you and blow you up! AAA (plus TTTT!).

You exit into part 3, the **American Film Institute Showcase** of costumes and props from recent films.

Who Wants To Be A Millionaire – Play It!: brand new is Disney's version of the hit TV show. Based on the US programme (presented by Regis Philbin rather than our Chris Tarrant), it is still effectively the same show. The great twist is EVERYONE gets to play – all 1,600 members of the audience. Whoever is fastest with the put-them-in-order question starts in the hotseat, and, as you play along, you build up a score, with the top 10 shown on screen at various stages. Then, when a contestant loses out, the person with the highest score in the audience is next up! The hosts do a terrific job of maintaining the TV 'illusion' and there are the usual rules and lifelines which add to the sense of reality here (although you play for Disney points, not money. The points still add up to some great souvenirs and prizes, though). One difference is there can be no Phone A Friend lifeline, for obvious reasons. Instead, you have Phone A

Complete Stranger, where a passer-by is grabbed off the street outside or the Backstage Pass tour (it happened to me, and they put you in the spotlight!). It is addictive fun, and the only drawback is it has become so popular the FastPass tickets run out quickly, so try to get here early in the day. AAAAA (FP).

Walt Disney: One Man's Dream: as part of 100 Years Of Magic, Disney's Imagineers have come up with this new attraction, an interactive show-and-tell chronicle of Walt himself and his accomplishments. From archive school records to a model of the submarine Nautilus from *20,000 Leagues Under The Sea*, the story of the man behind the Mouse is designed to come to vivid life with a number of hands-on elements, especially when the scene moves on to the creation of his theme parks. The homage to the creator of the magic concludes with a preview of Disney's future developments, including new parks in Hong Kong and Tokyo, plus a 10-minute film encapsulating everything Walt achieved and dreamed about. AAAA (expected).

Voyage of the Little Mermaid: this 17-minute live performance is primarily for children who have seen and enjoyed the Disney cartoon. Like Legend of the Lion King in the *Magic Kingdom* Park it brings together live actors, animation and puppetry to recreate the highlights of the film. Parents will still enjoy the special effects, but queues tend to be surprisingly long so go either early or late. Those in the first few

> BRIT TIP: Try to sit at least half-way back in the Mermaid theatre, especially with children, as the stage front is a bit high for little 'uns.

rows may get a little wet. AAA (AAAAA under 9s) (FP).

The Magic of Disney Animation: an amusing and entertaining 40-minute tour through the making of cartoons. It's up to you how you pace the walk-through tour, but don't miss Robin Williams in a special cartoon, Back to Neverland, with Walter Cronkite, and the fascinating view of some of Disney's animators at work. It concludes with a film of some of the highlights of Disney's many animated classics, and you will be amazed at how much you have learned in the course of your tour (although small children might be a bit lost by it all). Queues are rarely serious here, so it's a good one for the afternoon. AAAA.

Playhouse Disney – Live On Stage: straight out of several popular kids' TV series comes this new 20-minute live show with such pre-school favourites as *Bear in the Big Blue House* and *Rolie Polie Olie*, plus others like *Doug* and his Bluffington friends. Much of this can be seen only on cable or satellite TV in the UK, so it is doubtful how much it will mean to the kids it is aimed at, but it should still be a colourful and entertaining offering. AAA (AAAAA under 5s).

The Twilight Zone™ Tower of Terror: the tallest landmark in *Walt Disney World Resort in Florida* (at 199ft) invites you to experience

Hollywood Boulevard

another dimension in this mysterious Hollywood hotel that time forgot. The exterior is intriguing, the interior is fascinating, the ride is scintillating and the queues are mind-blowing! The only unfortunate aspect of this thrilling attraction, which is so much more than just the advertised 13-storey free-fall, is the fact much of the queuing is outside in the sun, and, when it is hot, you are almost melting by the time you reach the air-conditioned, spooky hotel. Typically, just when you think you are through to the ride itself, there is another queue, but the inner detail is so clever you can spend the time inspecting how realistic it all is – before you enter the Twilight Zone itself. You have been warned! Restrictions: 3ft 6in. TTTTT (FP).

Rock 'n Roller Coaster starring Aerosmith: Disney's first big-thrill inverted coaster is a sure-fire draw for the high-energy ride addicts, with a magnificent indoor setting and nerve-jangling ride. It features a clever 3-D film show starring rock group Aerosmith in their recording studio. That preamble leads to the real fun, set to specially recorded tracks from the band themselves and with outrageous speaker systems, as riders climb aboard Cadillac 'cars' for this memorable whizz through a mock Los Angeles setting (watch out for a close encounter with the 'Hollywood' sign!). The high-speed

The unmissable Fantasmic! special effects show at Disney-MGM Studios

launch and inversions ensure an up-to-the-minute coaster experience. Go first thing or expect serious queues. Restrictions: 4ft 4in TTTTT (FP).

> BRIT TIP: Beat the crowds by booking a Fantasmic dinner package when you enter the park (or in advance on 407 939 3463). Just make an early-evening Priority Seating for the Brown Derby or Mama Melrose's, and you get no-wait VIP seating later for the show.

The Twilight Zone™ Tower of Terror

'Beauty and the Beast' – Live on Stage: a live performance of the highlights of this recent Disney classic will entertain the whole family for 20 minutes in the nearby Theater of the Stars. Check the daily schedule for showtimes. AAA.

Fantasmic!: this epic special-effects spectacular is simply not to be missed. Staged every night in a 6,900-seat amphitheatre behind the Tower of Terror™, it features the 'dreams' of Mr M Mouse, portrayed as the Sorcerer's Apprentice, through films such as *Pocahontas*, *The Lion King* and *Snow White*, but hijacked by various Disney villains, leading to a tumultuous battle, with Our Hero emerging triumphant.

The Wicked Witch in Fantasmic!

Dancing waters, shooting comets, animated fountains, swirling stars, balls of fire and more combine in a truly breathtaking presentation – just watch out for the giant, fire-breathing dragon! The 25-minute show begins seating up to 90 minutes in advance and it is advisable to head there at least half an hour beforehand to be sure of a seat (watch out for the splash zones!). AAAAA.

100 Years of Magic

In keeping with the park's focus for the special celebration, an all-new daily parade **Disney Stars and Motor Cars** should now be one of the highlights. The theme is a film premier in 1930s and 40s Hollywood, with a series of genuine vintage cars and clever replicas being used to mount a riotous cavalcade of Disney showbiz favourites. It kicks off with motor-cycle police outriders and goes through some 15 crazily customised cars – including a 1929 Cadillac – that provide the likes of Aladdin, Mary Poppins, Mulan, the Muppets and new films like Atlantis and Monsters Inc with a chance to show off in larger-than-life fashion. Watch out for the Star Wars 'Land Speeder' with a radio-controlled R-2D2 and a special Villains limo that are sure to add bags of fun to the occasion – and the largest parade ever staged in *Disney-MGM Studios*. The lead car will also feature any special guests at the Studios that day or a visiting family or two will be chosen to be the 'stars' instead! AAAAA (expected). Of course, there are also the **interactive kiosks** inviting guests to Discover The Stories Behind the Magic and the special **Disney pins** which promise to give some Magic Moments at various times (notably with the parade).

You can also meet **Disney**

characters along Mickey Avenue and in Washington Square in the Backlot, and be entertained by performing 'actors and actresses' in Hollywood Boulevard.

Food and shops

While the choice of food may not be wide, there is plenty of it and at a

BRIT TIP: I always recommend the Sci-Fi Diner or 50s Prime Time Café to make your main meal a bit different.

reasonable price. The **Hollywood Brown Derby** offers a full-service restaurant in fine Hollywood style (reservations necessary – special Early Evening Value meals 4–6pm), while **Mama Melrose's Ristorante Italiano** is a similar table-service Italian option. The **Sci-Fi Dine-In Theater Restaurant** is a big hit with kids as you dine in a mock drive-in cinema, with cars as your 'table', waitresses on roller-skates and a big film screen showing corny old black-and-white science fiction clips. The **50s Prime Time Café** is another hilarious experience as you sit in mock stage sets from American 50s TV sitcoms and eat meals 'just like Mom used to make'. (The waiters all claim to be your brother and warn you to take your elbows off the table, etc. Hilarious!). Priority seatings are also necessary. The fast-food eateries consist of the **ABC Commissary, Backlot Express, Rosie's All-American Café** or the **Toy Story Pizza Planet & Arcade** for various counter-service options, from sandwiches and salads to pizza, pasta and fajitas. Disney character meals are available at **Hollywood & Vine** for breakfast and lunch ($14.95 and $16.50 for adults, $7.95 and $8.95 for 3–11s; 8.15am–3.30pm, and from 7.30am on Wed and Sun) but you need to book first thing for these (or call 407 939 3463).

There are also 20 gift and speciality shops, six of them along Hollywood Boulevard, which are worth checking out in early afternoon. **Sid Caheunga's One-of-a-Kind** (just to the right of the main entrance gates as you look out) stocks rare movie and TV items, including many celebrity autographs. Try the **Legends of Hollywood** (on Sunset Boulevard) for a rather different range of souvenirs and **It's a Wonderful Shop** (in the Backlot) for Christmas gifts and collectibles. **Keystone**

Clothiers (at the top of Hollywood Boulevard) offer some of the best Disney apparel in any of the parks. All the main rides and film attractions also have their own shops, too.

For a detailed look behind the scenes at Disney animation, the **Inside Animation** tour provides 3 hours of in-depth fascination of this art (not for under 16s) at $59/person. Call 407 939 8687 to book.

At Christmas, don't miss the incredible **Osborne Family Lights**, switched on in the evening in the Backlot Tour area for guests to wander around. Just amazing!

5

DISNEY-MGM STUDIOS with children

Here is our general guide to the rides which appeal to the different age groups in this park (and it is, possibly, the best spread of all):

Under 5s
Playhouse Disney – Live On Stage, Voyage of the Little Mermaid, Beauty and the Beast Live on Stage, Hunchback of Notre Dame Musical Adventure.

5–8s
Voyage of the Little Mermaid, Beauty and the Beast Live On Stage, Honey I Shrunk the Kids Movie Set Adventure, Sounds Dangerous, Muppet*Vision 3-D, Hunchback of Notre Dame Musical Adventure, Disney-MGM Studios Backlot Tour, Backstage Pass, Star Tours (with parental discretion), Fantasmic!

9–12s
Sounds Dangerous, Indiana Jones Epic Stunt Spectacular, Great Movie Ride, Star Tours, Muppet*Vision 3-D, Hunchback of Notre Dame Musical Adventure, Disney-MGM Studios Backlot Tour, The Magic of Disney Animation, Beauty and the Beast Live On Stage, Rock 'n Roller Coaster, Tower of Terror, Fantasmic!

Over 12s
Indiana Jones Epic Stunt Spectacular, Star Tours, Great Movie Ride, Muppet*Vision 3-D, Disney-MGM Studios Backlot Tour, Backstage Pass, Who Wants To Be A Millionaire – Play It!, The Magic of Disney Animation, Rock 'n Roller Coaster, Tower of Terror, Fantasmic!

Disney's Animal Kingdom Theme Park

Disney's newest, smartest and most radical theme park opened its gates for the first time in April 1998, and represents a completely different Disney park experience. With its emphasis on nature and conservation, it largely eschews the non-stop thrills and attractions which mark out the other three parks and instead offers a change of pace, a more peaceful and relaxing motif, as well as Disney's usual seamless entertainment style – plus two decent thrill rides.

The attractions are relatively few, just five out-and-out rides, plus two scenic journeys, two nature trails, five shows (including the hilarious 3-D film It's Tough to Be a Bug! and the full-blown theatre of Festival of the Lion King), an elaborate adventure playground, conservation station and petting zoo, and a Disney character greeting area. It's a far cry from the hustle-bustle of the *Magic Kingdom* Park, and it carries a strong environmental message that aims to create a greater understanding of the world's ecological problems. School-age children should find it quite educational, though under 5s may be a little left out. It is outrageously scenic, notably with the 145ft Tree of Life and the Kilimanjaro Safaris, but it won't overwhelm you with Disney's usual sense of grand style. Rather, it is a chance to experience a part of the world that is both threatened and threatening in a safe, secure manner. It is obviously not the Real Thing, but it does provide a genuine glimpse of some of the world's most majestic areas in a manner that allows ecology and Disney's commercial touch to co-exist happily and meaningfully.

The most conclusive word on Disney's first full-blown animal adventure goes to Professor David Bellamy, who told me: 'This park has been designed and looked after by the best animal welfare people you can think of. Bad zoos are bad news and should be closed down, but good zoos are good news and the only hope for keeping about 500 species of animal alive in the future'. The park does get horribly crowded, however, and the walkways can be very congested. There are also fewer areas to cool down. Take advantage of the 8am opening and use the FastPass rides to minimise queuing.

Some of the cast at Disney's Animal Kingdom

© Disney

DISNEY'S ANIMAL KINGDOM

THE OASIS
1 The Oasis Tropical Garden

DISCOVERY ISLAND
2 The Tree Of Life
3 Discovery Island Trails
4 It's Tough To Be A Bug!

CAMP MINNIE-MICKEY
5 Pocahontas And Her Forest
  Friends
6 Character Greeting Trails
7 Festival Of The Lion King

DINOLAND USA
8 Dinosaur
9 The Boneyard
10 Tricera Top Spin
11 Chester & Hester's Dinorama
12 Tarzan Rocks!
13 Primeval Whirl

AFRICA
14 Harambe
15 Kilimanjaro Safaris
16 Pangani Forest Exploration Trail
17 Rafiki's Planet Watch

ASIA
18 Flights Of Wonder
19 Maharajah Jungle Trek
20 Kali River Rapids
21 Rainforest Cafe

MAHARAJAH JUNGLE TREK

KALI RIVER RAPIDS

Take the Wildlife Express from Harambe in Africa to explore Rafiki's Planet Watch

ASIA

AFRICA

DINOLAND U.S.A.

DISCOVERY ISLAND

THE OASIS

CAMP MINNIE – MICKEY

ENTRANCE PLAZA

5

Disney's Animal Kingdom Theme Park at a glance

Location	Directly off Osceola Parkway, also via World Drive and Buena Vista Drive
Size	500 acres divided into 6 'lands'
Hours	8am to 6, 7 or 8pm
Admission	Under 3, free; 3–9, $38 (one-day ticket), $152 (4-Day Park Hopper), $197 (5-Day Park Hopper Plus); adult (10+) $48, $192, $247.
Parking	$6
Lockers	Yes; either side of Entrance Plaza; $5 ($2 refundable)
Pushchairs	$7 and $13 ($1 refundable) at Garden Gate Gifts, through entrance on right
Wheelchairs	$7 ($1 refund) and $40 ($10 refund), same location
Top Attractions	Dinosaur, Kilimanjaro Safaris, It's Tough to Be a Bug, Kali River Rapids, Festival of the Lion King
Don't Miss	Pangani Forest Exploration Trail, Maharajah Jungle Trek, Conservation Station, dining at Rainforest Café
Hidden Costs	**Meals** Burger, chips and coke $7.90
	Kids' meal $3.25
	T-shirts $19–$34
	Souvenirs $2.25–$700
	Sundries Caricature drawings $12–$25

Getting there

If you are staying in the Kissimee area, *Disney's Animal Kingdom* Theme Park is the easiest to find. Just get on the (toll) Osceola Parkway and follow it all the way to the toll booths, where parking costs $6. Alternatively, coming down I4, take the new Exit 26C which puts

> BRIT TIP: The early start is especially advised for Kilimanjaro Safaris. You will see far more in the first few hours of the day than during the afternoon.

you on Osceola Parkway. From western Highway 192, come in on Sherberth Road (turn right at the first traffic lights).

If you arrive early (which is advisable), you can walk up to the Entrance Plaza. Otherwise, the usual tram system will take you in, so make a note of the area in which you park (e.g. Unicorn, row 67). The Plaza is overlooked by the mountainous **Rainforest Café**, with its 65ft waterfall, which is a must for an early lunch or dinner (rarely busy). The park's scheduled opening time is 8am to allow the animals the earliest opportunity to roam their habitats (they return to secure pens at night). With Orlando so hot through the summer months, this early start also gives visitors the best chance to see the animals before they seek shade.

For the early birds, here is your best plan of campaign. Once through the gates, animal lovers should head first for Kilimanjaro Safaris, through the Oasis, Discovery Island and into Africa. After the Safari, go straight to Pangani Forest Exploration Trail and you will have experienced two of the park's best animal encounters. Alternatively, thrill-seekers should turn right in Discovery Island for DinoLand USA, where the DINOSAUR ride (formerly Countdown to Extinction) is the big attraction. With that one safely under your belt before the serious crowds arrive, head back through the Island to Asia and Kali River Rapids raft ride, followed by the scenic Maharajah Jungle Trek. The best combination for the first arrivals is to get a FastPass for Dinosaur then head straight for the Safaris, and, once you have done that (and depending on your FP time), either do your Dinosaur ride (followed by a Kali River Rapids FP) or go straight to the Rapids. Check your show schedule for the Legend of the Lion King and try to catch one of the first two performances as the later ones draw sizeable queues. The 'wait time' board at the entrance to Discovery Island is also helpful.

Right, those are your main tactics, here is the full rundown.

The Oasis

This is a gentle, walk-through introduction to the park, a rocky, tree-covered area featuring several animal habitats, studded with streams, waterfalls and lush plant life. Here you will meet miniature deer, macaws, parrots, iguanas, sloths and tree kangaroos in a wonderfully understated environment that leads you across a stone bridge and to the main open park area. AAA.

Discovery Island

This hugely colourful 'village' is the hub of *Disney's Animal Kingdom* Theme Park, from which the other four lands radiate. Its theme is a tropical artists' colony, with animal-inspired artwork everywhere, four main shops and two eateries.

The Tree of Life: this 145ft-high arboreal edifice is the park centrepiece, an awesome creation that seems to give off a different perspective from wherever you view it. The 'trunk' and 'roots' are covered in 325 animal carvings representing the Circle of Life, from the dolphin to the lion. Trails lead round the Tree, interspersed with more natural animal habitats that showcase flamingos, otters, ring-tailed lemurs, macaws, axis deer, cranes, storks, ducks and tortoises. For stats lovers, the Tree canopy spreads 160ft wide, the trunk is 50ft wide and the roots spread out 170ft in diameter. There are 103,000 leaves (all attached by hand) on more than 8,000 branches! AAAA.

It's Tough to Be a Bug!: winding down among the Tree's roots brings you 'underground' to a 430-seat theatre and another example of Disney's artistry in 3-D films and special effects. This hysterically funny 8-minute show, a homage to 80 per cent of the animal world, features grasshoppers, beetles, spiders, stink bugs and termites (beware the 'acid' spray!) as well as a number of tricks I couldn't possibly

BRIT TIP: The dark, special effects and creepy-crawlies often scare young ones in this show.

© Disney

The Tree of Life

reveal. Sit towards the back in the middle of a row (allow a good number of people in first as you fill up the rows from the far side) to get the best of the 3-D effects. Queues build up from midday onwards, but they do move quite steadily. Don't miss the 'forthcoming attractions' posters in the foyer for some excruciating bug puns on well-known films. AAAAA (FP).

Shopping is at its best here, with a huge range of merchandise, souvenirs and gifts (notably in **Wonders of the Wild** and **Island Mercantile**), while the two counter-service restaurants, **Pizzafari** and **Flame Tree Barbecue**, are both fairly decent options. Indeed, provided it is not too hot, the Barbecue offers a relaxing and picturesque experience, set among pretty gardens, pools and fountains on the edge of Discovery River.

Camp Minnie-Mickey

This woodland retreat features gently winding paths and more of

Disney's clever scenery, like the benches, lighting and the gurgling stream, with Donald Duck and his nephews hiking down the side, that develops into a series of kid-friendly squirt fountains.

Character Greeting Trails: here, four trails lead to a series of jungle encounters with Disney characters like Mickey and Minnie (naturally), Winnie the Pooh and Tigger, Chip 'n Dale, Baloo and King Louie, Timon and Rafiki. AAAAA (for kids).

Pocahontas and Her Forest Friends: based on characters from the Disney film *Pocahontas*, this 15-minute show sees various animals – raccoons, rabbits, cranes, a skunk, armadillo and porcupine – interacting with the central actress and Mother Willow in the question of 'Who can save the forest?'. It doesn't seem to do much for small children, there is not much shade in summer and it is standing room only once the 350 seats have been filled. AAA.

© Disney

The Festival of the Lion King

Festival of the Lion King: not to be missed, this high-powered 40-minute production brings the hit film to life in spectacular fashion with giant, moving stages, huge animated figures, singers, dancers, acrobats and stilt-walkers. All the well-known songs are given an airing in a coruscation of colour and sound, and it serves to underline the quality Disney bring to their live shows. Its quality is matched only by its popularity – people begin queuing 30 minutes in advance for the 1,000-seater theatre, so try to take in one of the earlier shows of the day. AAAAA.

DinoLand USA

Rather at odds with the natural theming of the rest of the park, DinoLand USA is a full-scale palaeontology exercise, with this mock 'town' taken over by a university fossil dig. Energetically tongue-in-cheek (the 'students' who work in the area have the motto 'Been there, dug that', while you enter under a mock brachiosaurus skeleton, the Oldengate Bridge – groan!), it still features some glimpses into dinosaur research and artefacts.

DINOSAUR: this was re-named after Disney's big animated film and its original fast, jerky ride has been toned down a little for a more family-friendly ride (although the dinosaur menace is still too scary for many children). It is a wonderfully realistic journey back to the end of the Cretaceous Period and the giant meteor that put paid to dinosaur life. You enter the high-tech Dino Institute, 'a discovery center and research lab dedicated to uncovering the mysteries of the past', for a multimedia show of dino history that leads to a briefing room for your

> BRIT TIP: Ride at the front left of your Time Rover car for maximum effect of the twists and turns and the dinosaur menace.

'mission' 65 million years in the past to view Cretaceous life. However, one of the Institute's scientists 'hijacks' your journey for his own

© Disney

The Boneyard Adventure Playground

project, to capture a dinosaur before the fateful meteor's arrival, and you go careering back to a prehistoric jungle in your 12-passenger Time Rover. The threat of a carnivorous carnotaurus and the impending doom of the meteor add up to a breathtaking whiz through a stunning environment. You will need to ride at least twice to appreciate all the clever detail, but queues build up quickly, so go either first thing or late in the day. Restrictions: 3ft 4in. TTTT plus AAAAA (FP).

The Boneyard: a hugely imaginative adventure playground, it offers kids the chance to slip, slide and climb through the 'fossilised' remains of triceratops and brontosaurs, explore caves, dig for bones and splash through a mini-waterfall. The amusing signage will go over the heads of most kids, but it is ideal for parents to let their young 'uns loose for up to an hour (although not just after the neighbouring Tarzan show has finished). TTTT (kids only).

Tarzan™ Rocks!: and he really does. This amazing show is basically a 30-minute rock concert show-casing the songs from the animated film, with special effects provided by dancers, acrobats and roller-bladers, all in wonderful costumes and superbly choreographed. Tarzan and Jane make only a brief appearance, and then mainly as acrobats (ladies – no staring at that loincloth!), while

5

its loud, high-energy style is not everyone's cup of tea (especially for sensitive young ears), but it is visually stunning and the quality of the performers – singers, musicians and acrobats – leaves you gasping. AAAA.

Chester & Hester's Dino-Rama!: due to open in time for the 100 Years of Magic celebration is this new mini-land of rides, fairground games and stalls. It's main icon is a towering Concretosaurus (!), and it is designed to have a quirky, tongue-in-cheek style reminiscent of 1950s American roadside attractions. The standout features are: **TriceraTop Spin**, another version of the Dumbo/Aladdin rides in the *Magic Kingdom* Park, a flying, twirling, spinning top that bounces you around, up and down (but watch for the surprise dino appearance at the top!). AA (or TTTT for under 5s). **Primeval Whirl:** coaster fans should get a laugh out of this wacky offering that sends its riders through a maze of curves, hills and (quite sharp) drops that make it seem much faster than it actually is. The extra fun is provided by the cars being free-spinning, which means an extra, unpredictable element to each ride, which also plunges through the jaws of the inevitable hungry dino at one point! TTTT (expected).

Dining options include the **Restaurantosaurus**, counter-service

BRIT TIP: The Restaurantosaurus also features Donald's Prehistoric Breakfastosaurus 7.30–10.30am with Mickey, Donald Duck and other character favourites. It costs $14.95 for adults and $8.95 for 3–11s.

burgers and hot-dogs (presented by McDonald's, so you get McDonald's fries, Chicken McNuggets and Happy Meals but no Big Macs) and a snack bar, while shopping is centred on **Chester and Hester's Dinosaur Treasures**, the 'Fossiliferous Gift Store' with groan-inducing slogans like Merchandise of Extinction, Prehistoric Prices and Last Stop for 65 Million Years!

Africa

The largest land in *Disney's Animal Kingdom* Theme Park, it recreates the forests, grasslands and rocky homelands of equatorial Africa's most fascinating residents in a richly landscaped setting that is part run-down port town setting and part endless savannah. The outside world seems thousands of miles away and there is hardly a glimpse of *Walt Disney World Resort in Florida* (there is one, but I'm not telling!).

Harambe, a reconstruction Kenyan port village, complete with white-coral walls and thatched roofs, is the starting point of your adventure. The Arab-influenced Swahili culture is depicted in the native tribal costumes and architecture. Here you will find two more shops, including the **Mombasa Marketplace Ziwani Traders**, where you can suit up safari-style, and the counter-service **Tusker House Restaurant** for rotisserie chicken, fresh fish, salads, vegetarian sandwiches and a special African dish (a slightly healthier offering than most, but a touch expensive, I find), as well as four snack and drink outlets.

Kilimanjaro Safaris: the queuing area alone earns high marks for authenticity, preparing you for the sights and sounds of the 110-acre savannah beyond. You board a 32-passenger truck, with your driver/guide relaying information

BRIT TIP: The best (i.e. most jolting) ride is at the back of the truck, while the Safari is best avoided from midday to late afternoon when many animals take a siesta.

about the flora and fauna on view and a bush pilot overhead relaying stats on the wildlife, including the dangers threatening them in the real world. Hundreds of animals are carefully spread out in various habitats, with no fences in sight – the ditches and barriers are all well concealed – as you splash through fords and cross rickety bridges, and you are likely to get a close-up of rhinos, elephants, giraffes, zebras, lions, baboons, antelope, ostriches and hippos.

Halfway round, your journey becomes a race to stop elephant poachers, though the outcome is fairly obvious. Once again, the authentic nature of all you see (okay, some of the tyre 'ruts' and termite mounds are concrete and the baobab trees are fake) is quite awesome with the spread of the vegetation and the landscaping, and the only drawback is the lack of photo stops along the way (and the ride can be pretty bumpy). The animals can also roam over a wide area and disappear from view. The ride is not recommended for expectant mothers or anyone with back or neck problems. AAAAA (FP).

Pangani Forest Exploration Trail: as you leave the Safari you turn into an overgrown nature trail that showcases gorillas, hippos, meerkats, rare tropical birds and naked mole rats(!). You wander the trail at your own pace and visit several research stations where you can learn more about the animals on display, including the swarming, ant-

like colony of naked mole rats (see, I wasn't making it up), the underwater view of the hippos (check out the size of a hippo skull and those teeth!) and the savannah overlook, where giraffe and antelope graze and the amusing meerkats frolic. The walk-through aviary gives you the chance to meet the carmine bee-eater, pygmy goose, African green pigeon, ibis and brimstone canary, among others, but the real centrepiece is the silverback gorilla habitat, in fact, two of them. The family group are often just inches away from the giant plate-glass window, while the bachelor group further along can prove more elusive. Again, the sheer natural aspect of the Trail is breathtaking and it provides a host of good photo opportunities. It is best to visit early in the day to see the animals at their most active. AAAAA.

Rafiki's Planet Watch: the little train journey here, with its peek into some of the backstage areas, is just the preamble to the park's interactive and educational exhibits. The three-part journey starts with **Habitat Habit**, where you can see cotton-top tamarins and learn how conservation begins in your own back garden. **Conservation Station** is next up, a series of exhibits, shows and hands-on information stations about the environment and its ecological dangers, aimed primarily at children. Look out for *Song of the Rain Forest*, the story of endangered species at the *Mermaid Tales Theater* and the *Eco-Heroes* trying to redress the balance (who can be quizzed on screen), then take a self-guided tour of the park's backstage areas such as the veterinary treatment centre, the hatchery and neo-natal care. You can easily spend an hour absorbing the environmental message here, along with that of Disney's Wildlife Conservation Fund. Plus, youngsters can also meet Rafiki and some of his animal chums at various times. The

© Disney

Kilimanjaro Safari

Affection Section, a petting zoo of lambs, goats, donkeys, sheep and guinea pigs, completes the Planet Watch line-up.

Asia

The final land of the park is elaborately themed as the gateway to the imaginary south-east Asian city of Anandapur, with its temples, ruined forts, landscape and wildlife.

Flights of Wonder: another wildlife show, this showcases the talents and traits of a host of birds, built into a production of mythical proportions as a treasure-seeking student encounters Phoenix, the birds' guardian, in a crumbling, fortified town. Vultures, eagles, toucans, macaws and many other feathered friends take a bow as Phoenix reveals the treasures of the avian world. Unfortunately, the Caravan Stage where all this takes place is not air-conditioned and is fiendishly hot in summer. AAA.

Kali River Rapids: part thrill-ride, part scenic journey is this bouncy, raft-ride journey that will get you pretty wet (not great for early morning in winter unless you bring a change of clothes). It starts

Kali River Rapids

© Disney

out in tropical forest territory before launching into a scene of logging devastation, warning of the dangers of clear-cut burning. Your raft then plunges down a waterfall (and one unlucky soul – usually the rider with their back to the drop – gets seriously damp) before you finish the journey more sedately, albeit with a few more watery encounters. Queues are quite long through the main part of the day, so make good use of the FastPass here, and you will probably want to ride at least twice to appreciate all the clever detail. Restrictions: 3ft 6in (although a few rafts have adult-and-child seats allowing smaller children to ride). TTT (plus AAAA) (FP).

Maharajah Jungle Trek: Asia's version of the Pangani Forest Trail, this is another picturesque walk-through journey past decaying temple ruins and various animal encounters. Playful gibbons, tapirs, Komodo dragons and a bat enclosure (including the world's largest variety, the flying fox-bat) lead up to the main viewing area, the five-acre Tiger Range, which includes a pool and fountains, a popular playground early in the day for these magnificent big cats. An antelope enclosure and walk-through aviary complete this breathtaking Trek in fine style. AAAAA.

Finally, returning to the front entrance gives you the chance to sample or just visit (and shop at) the **Rainforest Café**, the second in *Walt Disney World Resort in Florida*. If you haven't seen the one at *Downtown Disney* Marketplace, you should definitely call in to witness the amazing jungle interior with its audio-animatronic animals, waterfalls, thunderstorms and aquariums. A three-course meal will set you back about $25 (kids' meals at $5.99), but the setting alone is worth it and the food is above average.

100 Years of Magic

In addition to the new fun and rides of Chester & Hester's Dino-Rama!, the park also has its **interactive kiosks** to allow guests to *Discover The Stories Behind the Magic* of Walt and his creations, while the special **Disney pins** provide some more Magic Moments at various points. The other dramatic new development due to debut on 1 October 2001, is the park's first big parade, a tour de force called **Mickey's Jammin' Jungle** Parade. Here, the Imagineers have created a series of fanciful, individually-designed 'Expedition Rovers' that give various Disney characters the chance to celebrate all the animals who live here. The Parade will be enhanced by stilt-walkers, puppets, mobile sculptures and different 'party animals,' plus live percussionists atop some of the sculptures, as it snakes a narrow path from Harambe Village, around Discovery Island and back to Harambe. It promises a real close-up encounter with the likes of Rafiki, Mickey, Minnie, Donald and Goofy, with the whole parade set to a special world-beat musical backing. It sounds truly delightful and another spectacular party offering, while there will also be up to 25 park guests chosen to appear in the parade each day, travelling on the back of amusingly-designed rickshaws which follow each of the character jeeps.

Finally, for a behind-the-scenes look at the park, the **Backstage Safari** is a wonderful 3-hour journey into the handling and care of all the animals ($65, not for under 16s. Call 407 393 8687 to book).

5

DISNEY'S ANIMAL KINGDOM PARK with children

Here is our general guide to the rides which appeal to the different children's ages in this park:

Under 5s
Character Greetings Trails, Festival of the Lion King, Discovery Island Trails, Kilimanjaro Safaris, Pangani Forest Exploration Trail, Affection Section, Maharajah Jungle Trek, TriceraTop Spin, The Boneyard.

5–8s
All the above, plus Pocahontas and Her Forest Friends, Habitat Habit, Conservation Station, Kali River Rapids, Flights of Wonder, and It's Tough To Be A Bug and DINOSAUR with parental discretion.

9–12s
All the above, plus It's Tough To Be A Bug, DINOSAUR, Primeval Whirl, Tarzan Rocks!

Over 12s
Festival of the Lion King, It's Tough To Be A Bug, Kilimanjaro Safaris, Pangani Forest Exploration Trail, Kali River Rapids, Maharajah Jungle Trek, Flights of Wonder, DINOSAUR, Tarzan Rocks!, Primeval Whirl.

Walt Disney World Resort in Florida at Christmas

If you can visit prior to the seriously busy days from just before Christmas Day to New Year's Day, you get the benefit of all the added decorations and atmosphere and none of the overwhelming crowds. Each of the parks takes on a festive character, with the addition of artistic artificial snow, Christmas lights and a huge, magnificently decorated fir tree.

Disney-MGM Studios also features an eye-popping extravaganza of exterior house decorations on the Backlot Tour with over 2 million lights! Donated by the Osborne family, they open up as a walk-through attraction every evening.

The **Magic Kingdom** Park turns Main Street into its Christmas extravaganza, with the 60-foot tree dominating the scene. There is also the unmissable Mickey's Very Merry Xmas Parade, which replaces the main 3pm parade in December, a positive delight for its lively music and eye-catching costumes. Another seasonal extra is the lively *Twas the Night before Xmas* show at the Galaxy Palace Theater.

Epcot is the jewel in the Christmas crown, though, with two outstanding features. At 6pm, the daily Christmas tree lighting ceremony is quite breathtaking as the rest of the park lights go out and then the World Showcase bridge and the tree itself are illuminated in dramatic stages to some grand musical accompaniment. The nightly Candlelight Processional also draws a crowd, with a guest narrator telling the story of Christmas to the backdrop of a large choir and elaborate candle parade. It is tasteful, dramatic and eye-catching, but you should arrive early as people start queuing two hours in advance.

Five More of the Best
(or, Expanding Orlando's Universe)

It is time to leave wonderful **Walt Disney World and venture out into the rest of central Florida's great attractions. And, believe me, there is still a terrific amount in store.**

For a start, they don't come much more ambitious than Universal Orlando. The area that used to consist of just the one theme park, Universal Studios Florida, is fast developing into a fully fledged resort of similar scope to Disney's. A second dynamic theme park, Universal's Islands of Adventure, opened in 1999, hot on the heels of the 30-acre CityWalk entertainment district. The first resort hotel, the Portofino Bay, also made its debut in 1999, followed by the Hard Rock Hotel in 2000, and the Royal Pacific Hotel is due in 2002.

There is also a waterway network connecting the hotels to the CityWalk hub of Universal Orlando, while their multi-storey car parks, handling more than 20,000 vehicles, have done away with the need for any other transport system, and it is quite convenient to move from park to park.

The marketing tie-up with SeaWorld and Busch Gardens, plus their buy-up of the Wet 'n Wild water park, has also proved a success, with the 14-day Orlando FlexTickets making for excellent value. The opening of Islands of Adventure has added a 2- and 3-Day Ticket (which includes a CityWalk Party Pass) allowing movement between the two parks. They have also introduced their **Universal Express** system for the most popular rides. Similar to Disney's FastPass, it allows all park guests to 'reserve' one ride at a time and then another once you have done that attraction, and so on. You just present your park entry ticket at the Distribution Center next to the Universal Express ride or show of your choice, and then return at the allotted time for what should be no more than a 15-minute wait (instead of an hour or more at peak periods). *Universal resort hotel guests also benefit from Express ride priority all day by producing their room key.*

Additionally, most of the rides have **Single Rider** queues which can save time if you are the only one in your group who wants to do, say, Dr Doom's Fearfall, or if you don't mind being split up. Once again, any height restriction is noted and Universal Express attractions are indicated UE.

BRIT TIP: Reader Tom Burton advises, 'If you buy an Orlando Flexticket giving you 14 consecutive days at Universal, etc., try going to their parks a couple of times in the evenings only. There are virtually no queues this late in the day and I got on the Hulk coaster five times in an hour!'

Universal Studios Florida

Universal opened its Florida park in June 1990 (it has had its original Los Angeles site open to the public since before World War II) and quickly became a serious competitor to Disney. For the visitor, it means a consistently high standard and good value in everything on offer (although the choice is beginning to be utterly bewildering!). Also, if you have already been to the LA Universal Studios, this one is better.

The obvious question to ask here is whether you need to go to Disney-MGM Studios as well as Universal, and the answer is an emphatic YES! Universal is a very different kettle of fish to Disney, with a more in-your-face style of entertainment that goes down well with older kids and younger adults. Younger children are also well catered for in Woody Woodpecker's KidZone. Universal can require more than a full day in high season. As with Disney's parks, the strategies

Universal Studios Florida at a glance

Location	Off Exits 30A and 29B from I4; Universal Boulevard and Kirkman Road		
Size	110 acres in seven themed areas		
Hours	9am–7pm off peak; 9am–10pm high season (Washington's birthday, Easter, summer holidays, Thanksgiving, Christmas)		
Admission	Under 3, free; 3–9, $39 (one-day ticket), $77 (2-Day Escape Pass), $92 (3-Day Escape Pass), $128 (4-Park Flex Ticket), $158 (5-Park Flex Ticket); adult (10+) $48, $90, $105, $160, $197.		
Parking	$7		
Lockers	Yes; immediately to left in Front Lot; $5 ($2 refundable)		
Pushchairs **Wheelchairs**	$8 and $14 (next to Locker hire) $7 and $35 (same location)		
Top Attractions	Men In Black, Jaws, Back to the Future, ET, Earthquake, Kongfrontation, Terminator 2 3-D		
Don't Miss	Curious George Playground (for kids), The Blues Brothers		
Hidden Costs	**Meals**	Burger, chips and coke $7.48 Three-course dinner $25 (Finnigan's)	
	Kids' meal	$4.95–$6.95 (Finnigan's and Lombard's Landing only)	
	T-shirts	$16–$28	
	Souvenirs	$1.50–$199	
	Sundries	Portrait studio photo $24.95 and $26.95	

1 Kongfrontation
2 Twister
3 Guest Services
4 Studio Audience Center
5 Production Central
6 Hitchcock's 3-D Theater
7 Nickelodeon Studio Tour
8 Terminator 2 3-D
9 The Funtastic World Of Hanna-Barbera
10 Lucy: A Tribute
11 The Bone Yard
12 Earthquake – The Big One
13 Jaws
14 Beetlejuice's Graveyard Revue
15 The Wild, Wild, Wild West Stunt Show
16 Men In Black: Alien Attack
17 Back To The Future … The Ride
18 Animal Planet Live!
19 Fievel's Playland
20 ET Adventure
21 The Gory, Gruesome & Grotesque
     Horror Make-Up Show
22 A Day In The Park With Barney
23 The Blues Brothers
24 Woody Woodpecker's Nuthouse
     Coaster
25 Curious George Playground

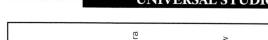

6

for a successful visit are the same. Arrive EARLY (up to 30 minutes before the official opening time), do the main rides first, avoid main meal times if you want to eat, and step out for a few hours in the afternoon (try shopping or dining at CityWalk) if it gets too crowded.

Location

Universal Studios Florida® is sub-divided into six main areas, set around a huge, man-made lagoon, but there are no great distinguishing features between many of them so keep your map handy to steer yourself around. The main entrance is found just off the new exit to I4 or by the Universal Boulevard link from International Drive by Wet 'n Wild. Parking costs $7 in their massive multi-storey car park and there is quite a walk (with some moving walkways) to the front gates.

Once through with the madding crowd, your best bet is to turn right on to Rodeo Drive, along Hollywood Boulevard and Sunset Boulevard and into World Expo for Back to the Future ... The Ride and Men In Black. From there, head straight across the bridge to Jaws, then go back along the Embarcadero for Earthquake and into New York for Twister and Kongfrontation. This will get most of the main rides under your belt early on before the crowds really build up, and you can then take it a bit easier by putting your feet up for a while at one of the several shows or taking advantage of the Universal Express system. Or, try to be among the early birds flocking to the blockbuster Terminator show at the entrance to Hollywood Boulevard to avoid the queues that build up quickly here, then use Universal Express for the likes of Back to the Future and Men In Black.

Here's a full blow-by-blow guide to the Studios. For the rundown on CityWalk, see Chapter 9.

Production Central

Coming straight through the gates brings you immediately into the administrative centre, with a couple of large gift stores (have a look at these in mid-afternoon) plus The Fudge Shoppe. Call at Guest Services here for written guides for disabled visitors, TDD and assisted listening devices, and to make restaurant bookings. If you are here early, you can sign up to be in the audience for one of Universal's TV shows at the **Studio Audience Center**. First aid is available here and on Canal Street between New York and San Francisco, while there are facilities for nursing mothers at Family Services by the bank through the gates on the right. Coming to the top of Plaza of the Stars brings you finally to the business end of the park.

Hitchcock's 3-D Theater: this tribute to the film-making genius of the late Alfred Hitchcock is a touch long for most children at 40 minutes, although it has three separate elements to keep you amused. The effects from his horror film *The Birds* come to the rescue of the first section, which is basically a series of clips from Hitchcock's 53 films for Universal Studios. Part two explores some of the effects and filming of his most famous film *Psycho* (including the shower scene). Part three goes 'inside the movies' as special effects from *The 39 Steps* are explained with film techniques. Queues build up quickly here after opening time, so save it for late in the day. It advises parental discretion for children under 13, but few seem put off by the horror elements, which are fairly tame by modern standards. TTT (UE)

Nickelodeon Studios: a lot of this American kids' TV series will be lost on us (although it's on satellite TV in Britain) as visitors are taken behind the scenes into the production set. All kids will be able to identify, however, with the chance to get gunged in green slime by the Gakmeister! And they'll love the restrooms which feature green slime 'soap' and sirens when you flush the loo. Long queues build up quickly, though. AAAA (for children only) (UE).

The Funtastic World of Hanna-Barbera: this is one of Universal's simulator rides that is always a big hit with kids. It involves a cartoon chase of the funniest order, with your seats becoming jet-propelled in the bid to save an all-star cartoon cast. Big queues, so go either first thing or late. Expectant mothers, those with heart, back or neck problems and children under 3ft 4in must use the stationary seats. TTTT (UE).

> BRIT TIP: The interactive do-it-yourself cartoon world as you exit the ride (in the Hanna-Barbera Store) is a great place for parents to unleash the kids for half an hour (or when it rains).

The Bone Yard: this is now a rather depleted area reserved for famous old props after they were discarded by the films in which they starred. AA. Watch out, also, for seasonal exhibits either here or in Hollywood offering a close-up look at props and scenery from recent Universal film releases. In 2001 it was *The Mummy Returns*.

The main eating outlet here is the magnificently themed **Monsters Café**, specialising in salads, pasta, pizza and chicken. The counter-service area is done up like Frankenstein's lab, with the dining areas sub-divided into Swamp, Space, Crypt and Mansion Dining, all to the accompaniment of old black and white horror film clips on the many video screens. There is also monster face painting for kids ($7–$16). Shopping includes the **Hanna-Barbera Store, Bates Motel Gift Shop** and the main **Universal Studios Store**.

New York

From Production Central you head on to New York and some great scene-setting in the architecture and detail of the buildings and streets. It's far too clean to be authentic, but the façades are first class and worth a closer look.

Twister: this experience, based on the hit film, brings audiences 'up close and personal' with the awesome destructive forces of a tornado. The five-storey terror will shatter everything in its path (okay, so it's pretty tame compared with the real thing), building to a shattering crescendo of destruction (watch out for the flying cow!). The noise is quite stunning, but it's a bit much for young children (parental discretion advised for under 13s). The pre-show area is almost a work of art but, unless you can get here early, save this for late in the day. TTT (UE)

Kongfrontation: Universal's engineers have really gone to town on this attraction, a full-scale encounter with the giant ape on a replica of the Roosevelt Island tram. The startlingly real special effects (King Kong even has banana breath!) and clever spiel of your tram driver all add up to a breathtaking experience that will have you convinced you have met King Kong and lived to tell the tale. It's only a 5-minute ride and queues regularly top an hour, so going early (or using Universal Express) is the best plan here. Restrictions: 4ft (but smaller children can ride with an adult). TTTT (UE).

The Blues Brothers: fans of the film will not want to miss this live show as Jake and Elwood Blues (well, pretty good doubles, anyway) put on a stormin' performance on New York's Delancey Street four or five times a day. They cruise up in their Bluesmobile and go through a selection of the film's hits before heading off into the sunset, stopping only to sign a few autographs. Terrific entertainment. AAAA.

For dining, you have the choice of two contrasting restaurants. **Finnegan's Bar and Grill** offers the likes of shepherd's pie, fish and chips, corned beef and cabbage along with more traditional New York fare like prime rib, burgers, fries and a good range of beers, as well as live Irish-tinged entertainment and Happy Hour from 3–5pm (half-price beer and wine). **Louie's Italian Restaurant** has counter-service pizza and pasta, Italian ice cream and tiramisu. For shops you have Safari Outfitters Ltd (and the chance to have your picture taken in the grip of King Kong!), The Aftermath for Twister

The five-storey tornado at Twister

Konfrontation

souvenirs, and Second Hand Rose for Coca-Cola merchandise and sweets. New York also boasts a noisy – and therefore kid-friendly – amusement arcade.

San Francisco/Amity

Crossing Canal Street brings you all the way across America to **San Francisco/Amity** and two of the biggest queues in the park.

Earthquake – The Big One: this three-part adventure has them lining up from first thing in the morning until almost last thing at night. Go behind the scenes first to two special stage sets where, with audience help, some of the special effects of the Charlton Heston film are explained. Then you enter the Bay Area Rapid Transit underground and arrive in the middle of a full-scale earthquake that will shake you to your boots. Tremble as the walls and ceilings collapse, trains collide, cars fall in on you and fire erupts all around, followed by a seeming tidal wave of water. It's not for the faint-hearted (or small children), while those who have bad backs or necks, or are pregnant, are advised not to ride. Restrictions: 4ft (but those under 4ft can ride accompanied by an adult, with discretion). TTTT (UE).

Jaws: the technological wizardry alone will leave you gasping on this attraction, where queues of more than an hour are commonplace. The man-made lagoon holds five million gallons of water; nearly 2,000 miles of wire run throughout the seven-acre site, which required 10,000 cubic yards of concrete and 7,500 tons of steel; and the 32-foot monster shark attacks with a thrust equal to a Boeing 727 jet engine! Yes, this is no ordinary ride, and its 6-minute duration will seem a lot longer as your hapless tour boat guide tries to steer you through an ever more spectacular series of stunts, explosions and watery menace from the Great White. Yes, of course it's only a model, but I defy you not to be impressed – and just a little terrified! TTTT (UE).

Beetlejuice's Graveyard Revue: *Disney-MGM Studios* has Beauty and the Beast and the Little Mermaid, Universal goes for Dracula, Frankenstein, the Wolfman, the Phantom of the Opera and Frankenstein's Bride in this 18-minute musical extravaganza. It eschews completely the twee prettiness of Disney's attractions yet still comes up with a fun family show, with versions of hits like *'Wild Thing'* and *'Great Balls Of Fire'* in a spectacular setting. AAAA (UE).

The Wild, Wild, Wild West Stunt Show: corny gags, fistfights, explosions, high-level falls and dramatic shootouts all add up to 15 minutes of rootin', tootin' Wild West adventure, Universal Studios style. A hilarious finale and some very loud bangs (not good for small children) are accompanied by large crowds, but the auditorium seats almost 2,000 so there is usually no serious queuing here (provided you arrive 15 minutes early). AAAA (UE).

San Francisco also has the best choice of eating establishments in the park, with **Lombard's Landing** the pick of the bunch (reservations accepted). Great seafood, pasta and sandwiches are accompanied by a good view over the main lagoon, and there's a separate pastry shop for desserts and coffee. **Richter's Burger Co.** offers a few interesting burger variations, while the **Midway Grill** serves smoked and Italian sausage hoagies. For a quick snack, **Chez Alcatraz** has shrimp cocktails, clam chowder and speciality hot sandwiches, while **Boardwalk Snacks** does corn dogs, chicken fingers, candy floss and frozen yoghurt.

For shopping, try **Quint's Nautical Treasures** for seaside gifts and **Shaiken's Souvenirs** for more up-market mementoes and apparel. The added attraction of this area is a boardwalk of fairground games (which will cost you an extra few dollars to take part), including a Guess Your Weight stall which usually attracts a good crowd for the fun patter of the person in charge.

Expo Center

Crossing the footbridge from Amity brings you into Expo Center and Universal's other five-star thrill attraction.

Back To The Future ... The Ride: simulators just do not come more realistic than this journey through space and time in Dr Emmit Brown's time-travelling De Lorean. The queues are immense, but a lot of the queuing time is taken up by some attention-grabbing pre-ride info on the TV screens above your head. Once you reach the front of the queue, there is still more information to digest and clever

Back to the Future

surroundings to convince you of the scientific nature of it all. Then it's into your time-travelling car and off in hot pursuit of baddie Biff, who has stolen another time-car. The huge, wraparound screen and violent movements of your vehicle bring the realism of the ride to a peak, and it all adds up to a huge experience, well worth the wait. Restrictions: 3ft 4in. TTTTT (UE).

Men In Black – Alien Attack: new in 2000 and huge fun (especially for kids) is this combination thrill/scenic ride which takes up where the hit film starring Will Smith left off. Visitors are secretly introduced to the MIB Institute in a wonderfully inventive mock-futuristic setting and enrolled as trainees for a battle around the streets of New York with a horde of escaped aliens. Your six-person car is equipped with laser zappers for an interactive shoot-out that is like a real-life arcade game as the aliens can also shoot back and send your car spinning out of control. The finale features a close encounter with a 30ft bug that is all mouth – will you survive? Only your collective shooting skill can save the day, and there are numerous ride variations according to your accuracy as each rider's score is totted up. Will Smith and Rip Torn are your on-screen hosts, and Will returns at the end to reveal if your score makes you Galaxy Defenders, Cosmically Average or Bug Bait! Fast, frantic and a bit confusing, this will have you coming back for more until you can score over 250,000 (Defender status). Restrictions: 3ft 6in. TTTT. (Beat my best score – 265,550)

For food here, there is the **Food Bazaar Pavilion**, a food court-style indoor diner offering burgers, sandwiches, meatball subs and salads (and in air-conditioned comfort).

Woody Woodpecker's KidZone

Animal Planet Live!: new in 2001, replacing the old Animal Actors Stage, is this highly amusing show version of the Animal Planet satellite TV channel. Several children are invited to take part as your hosts present a series of unlikely feats and stunts featuring a whole range of fairly tame wildlife, from a raccoon to a python, and on to domestic cats and dogs. Many have been rescued from various animal shelters and have gone on to feature in films before finding a home at Universal. It's a big theatre, too, and this is a good one to avoid the afternoon crowds. AAAA (UE).

> BRIT TIP: Along the lagoon in the World Expo/KidZone area is Central Park, a quiet area where you can escape the theme park whirl for a while.

Fievel's Playland: strictly for kids but also a big hit with parents for taking them off their hands for a good half-hour or so, this playground based on the enlarged world of the cartoon mouse offers youngsters the chance to bounce under a 1,000-gallon hat, crawl through a giant cowboy boot, climb a 30-foot spider's web and shoot the rapids (a 200ft water slide) in Fievel's sardine can. TTTT (young 'uns only!).

A Day in the Park with Barney: again, this is strictly for the younger set (ages 2–5). The purple dinosaur from the hugely popular kids' TV show is brought to Super-Dee-Duper life on stage in a 65,000-sq-ft arena that features a pre-show before the main event, which lasts about 15 minutes, plus an interactive post-show area. The show and its jokes are guaranteed to make mum and dad cringe, but the youngsters seem to love it and they are the best judges in this instance. NB: Check out the state-of-the-art restrooms! AAA (AAAAA under 5s) (UE).

ET Adventure: this is as glorious as scenic rides come, with a picturesque queuing area made up like the pine woods from the film and then a spectacular leap on the trademark flying bicycles to save ET's home planet. Steven Spielberg (Universal's creative consultant) has added some special effects and characters, and the whole experience is a huge hit with young to teenage kids and their parents. Queues here occasionally touch two hours at peak periods, so be aware you need to do this one either early or late (or, again, through Universal Express). There is a 4ft height restriction, but smaller children can ride with parents. AAAAA (UE).

Woody Woodpecker's Nuthouse Coaster: anchoring this excellent under 10s' adventure land is this child-sized but still quite racy roller-coaster. The brilliant red 800ft track reaches only 28ft high and 22mph, but it seems the real deal to youngsters. There is still a 3ft height ride restriction, however. TTTT (juniors only).

Curious George Goes to Town: this American children's book character means little to me, but kids of all ages will just love this amazing adventure playground with its huge range of activities – and plenty of opportunities to get wet (it is definitely advisable to bring swimsuits or a change of clothing for them here). It combines toddler play, water-based play stations and a hands-on interactive ball area, and adds up to a real boon to harassed parents. The town theme, on which Curious George has wreaked havoc, includes buildings to climb, pumps, hoses and sprays to get wet with, a

ball factory in which to shoot, dump and blast thousands of foam balls and – the tour de force – two 500-gallon buckets of water on the clock tower balconies which regularly dump their contents in spectacular fashion on the street below. TTTTT (under 12s).

For snacks, **Animal Crackers** offers hot-dogs, chicken fingers, smoked sausage hoagies and frozen yoghurt. Shop at the **Cartoon Store**, **Barney Store** or **ET's Toy Closet and Photo Spot**.

Hollywood

Finally, your circular tour of Universal brings you back towards the main entrance via **Hollywood** (where else?). Here, you'll find the **Gory, Gruesome and Grotesque Horror Make-Up Show** (not recommended for under 13s) which demonstrates some of the often amusing ways in which films have attempted to terrorise us. It's a 20-minute show, queues are rarely long and the secrets of the special effects are well worth learning. AAA (UE).

Terminator 2 3-D Battle Across Time: another first-of-its-kind attraction, this is hard to describe accurately. Part film, part show, part experience but all action, it cost a staggering $60million to produce and is guaranteed to leave its audience stunned and awed. The 'Wow!' factor works overtime as you go through a 10-minute pre-show to represent a trip into the workshops of the Cyberdyne Systems, from the Terminator films, and then into a 700-seater auditorium for a 'presentation' on their latest robot creations. Needless to say, nothing runs to plan and the audience is subjected to a mind-boggling array of (loud) special effects, including indoor pyrotechnics, real actors interacting

6

Men in Black Alien Attack

with the screen and the audience, and a climactic 3-D film finale that takes the Terminator story a step further. The original cast, including Arnold Schwarzenegger and director James Cameron, all collaborated on the new 12-minute film footage (which, at $24million, is the most expensive frame-for-frame film ever made) and the overall effect of this technological marvel is dazzling. Needless to say, you need to arrive early or expect queues well in excess of an hour all day (parental discretion for under 13s). TTTTT (UE).

The last attraction (or first, depending on which way you go round the park) is **Lucy: A Tribute**, which will mean little to all but devoted fans of the late Lucille Ball and her 60s TV comedy *The Lucy Show*. Classic shows, home movies, costumes and scripts are all paraded for close viewing, but youngsters will find it tedious. AA.

If you haven't eaten by now there is a choice of four contrasting but highly enjoyable eateries. **Mel's**

Woody Woodpecker's Nuthouse Coaster

Drive-In, a re-creation from the film *American Graffiti*, serves all manner of burgers, hot-dogs and milkshakes, while **Café La Bamba**, offers rotisserie chicken, ribs, salad and burgers, plus margaritas and beer (Happy Hour 3–5pm). There is also **Schwab's Pharmacy** for sandwiches, old-fashioned milkshakes, sundaes and ice cream

Terminator 2 3-D

and the **Beverly Hills Boulangerie** for baked breakfast treats, pastries, juices and coffee. Shop for hats in the **Brown Derby**, for Terminator gifts and clothing in **Cyber Image**, for movie memorabilia (especially Lucille Ball) at **Silver Screen Collectibles** and for some of the smartest but most expensive gear at **Studio Styles**.

Photo opportunities

In addition to all the set-piece action, watch out for photo and autograph opportunities with cartoon characters like Scooby Doo, Fred Flintstone, Woody Woodpecker and Yogi Bear, and filmstar lookalikes of Charlie Chaplin, WC Fields, Marilyn Monroe and Groucho Marx.

The Studios also feature some brilliant extra entertainment for **Mardi Gras** (a major parade, plus music, street entertainment and authentic New Orleans food each night at 6pm from mid-February to April 1) and **Halloween Horror Nights** (throughout much of

Excitement at the Terminator 2 experience

October) as well as **New Year's Eve** and the **4th of July**, when the park gets in full party mode. The Horror Nights, though, have become a real Universal trademark and add a wonderfully bloodthirsty touch (although there is an extra charge – about $46, or an extra $19–$25 if you up-grade your Universal Studios ticket on the day). The park is transformed with some highly imaginative recreations and set-pieces from various horror movies, with a parade and shows that include live (terrifyingly so, in some cases!) character interaction. This over-the-top extravaganza is definitely not for kids, but goes down a treat with adults with the right sense of humour and begins each evening at 7.30pm.

Sadly, as part of their on-going updating process, Universal have closed down their Dynamite Nights water stunt show which used to be the evening finale and there is no news of a replacement for the central lagoon area. The Hercules and Xena show (which replaced the original Murder She Wrote Mystery Theater) has also bitten the theatrical dust and we await developments with interest as the park has developed a couple of 'dead' spots as a result. As ever, for up-to-the-minute Universal hints, gossip and advice, check out www.usinfo.com.

UNIVERSAL STUDIOS with children

Under 5s
Nickelodeon Studios, Animal Planet Live, A Day In The Park With Barney, Curious George Goes To Town, Fievel's Playland, ET Adventure.

5–8s
Nickelodeon Studios, Animal Planet Live, Curious George Goes To Town, Fievel's Playland, ET Adventure, Woody Woodpecker's Nuthouse Coaster, Funtastic World of Hanna-Barbera, Wild, Wild, Wild West Stunt Show, Men In Black, plus Earthquake and Kongfrontation (with parental discretion).

9–12s
Funtastic World of Hanna-Barbera, Terminator 2: 3-D, Twister, Kongfrontation, Earthquake, Animal Plant Live, Curious George Goes to Town, Woody Woodpecker's Nuthouse Coaster, Wild, Wild, Wild West Stunt Show, ET Adventure, Beetlejuice's Graveyard Revue, Jaws, Men In Black, Back To The Future – The Ride.

Over 12s
Terminator 2: 3-D, Gory, Gruesome & Grotesque Horror Make-Up Show, Funtastic World of Hanna-Barbera, Alfred Hitchcock: Making Movies, Twister, Kongfrontation, Earthquake, Blues Brothers, ET Adventure, Beetlejuice's Graveyard Revue, Jaws, Wild, Wild, Wild West Stunt Show, Men In Black, Back To The Future – The Ride.

Islands of Adventure

In May 1999, Universal's creative consultant Steven Spielberg officially opened £1billion IoA, as it is known, with the words: 'These are not just theme park rides, these are entertainment achievements beyond anything I have ever seen anywhere else in the world.'

And that's only the beginning. Here is the most complete and thrilling theme park on offer. Complete, because the park is a genuinely rounded and consistent concept that has been carried through to the full extent of its designers' aims. And thrilling because it contains more T-rides (and the first TTTTT+ ratings) per square inch than almost all the other parks combined.

It has a full range of attractions from the real adrenalin overloads to pure family entertainment, the shopping and eating opportunities are above average, and it even sounds good (with some 40 pieces of original music, you can buy the CD of the theme park!).

Okay, so they are not really islands (the six themed 'lands' form a chain around the central lagoon), but that's the only illusion. And you do get a lot for your money here, unless you have extremely timid children or under 5s, in which case the *Magic Kingdom* is still your best bet. Seuss Landing has enough to keep them amused for several hours, and Camp Jurassic is a clever adventure playground for the 5–12 age range, but the rest of the park, with its seven five-star thrill rides and other heavyweight attractions, is primarily geared to kids of 8-plus, their parents, and especially teenagers. There are five elements that look truly alarming (two of which produce moments of supreme terror), but don't be put off – they all deliver immense fun. There is also great spectator value in many of the attractions!

If there is one ride that sums up IoA, it is the Amazing Adventures of Spider-Man, the world's first moving 3-D simulator ride. It is sure to leave you in awe of its technological wizardry and imagination, and it is the only ride I have ever seen where people actually applaud at the end!

Port of Entry

You arrive for IoA as you do for Universal Studios Florida in the big multi-storey car parks ($7) off Universal Boulevard and either walk or ride the moving walkways into CityWalk, where you continue through to the entrance plaza (head for the 130ft-high Pharos Lighthouse).

Once through the gates, the lockers, pushchair and wheelchair hire are all immediately to your left as the **Port of Entry** opens up before you. This elaborate 'village' consists of shops and eateries, so push straight on until you hit the main lagoon. Later in the day, return to Port of Entry to check out the fully-themed retail experience at places like the **IoA Trading Company** and **Ocean Trader Market**, enjoy a snack from **Spice Island Wings & Fries** or the **Croissant Moon Bakery** or chill out with a soft drink or ice cream from **Arctic Express**. Alternatively, sit down for lunch or dinner (great steak, pasta, burgers and salads) at **Confisco Grille** or grab a beverage at the **Backwater Bar** (Happy Hour 3–5pm) Above all, take a closer look at the wonderful architecture, which borrows from Middle East, Far East

Islands of Adventure at a glance

Location	Off Exits 30A and 29B from I4; Universal Boulevard and Kirkman Road
Size	110 acres in six 'islands'
Hours	9am–7pm off peak; 9am–10pm high season (Washington's Birthday, Easter, summer holidays, Thanksgiving, Christmas)
Admission	Under 3, free; 3–9, $39 (one-day ticket), $77 (2-Day Ticket), $92 (3-Day Ticket), $128 (7-Day, 4-Park Flex Ticket), $158 (10-Day, 5-Park Flex Ticket); adult (10+) $48, $90, $105, $160, $197.
Parking	$7
Lockers	Yes; immediately to left through main gates; $5 ($2 refundable)
Pushchairs Wheelchairs	$8 and $14 (next to Locker hire) $7 and $35 (same location)
Top Attractions	Amazing Adventures of Spider-Man, Dueling Dragons, Incredible Hulk Coaster, Jurassic Park River Adventure, Dudley Do-Right's Ripsaw Falls
Don't Miss	Eighth Voyage of Sindbad, Poseidon's Fury, Jurassic Park Discovery Centre, If I Ran the Zoo playground (for kids), Firework Finale (high season only)
Hidden Costs	**Meals** Burger, chips and coke $7.28 Three-course dinner $30 (Mythos Restaurant)
	Kids' meal $5.99
	T-shirts $18–$25
	Souvenirs $2.50–$310
	Sundries Dr Seuss character photos $12.95 and $17.95

6

and African themes and includes odd bits of bric-a-brac from all over the world dotted around the balconies.

When you come to the end of the Port thoroughfare, you are faced with three choices, and this is where you need a plan of campaign. There are five attractions where the queues build up quickly and remain that way. If you are here for the big thrill rides, turn left into Marvel Super-Hero Island and head straight to Spider-Man, then do Dr Doom's Fearfall and the Incredible Hulk Coaster, taking advantage of the Universal Express system.

Alternatively, dinosaur fans should jump in one of the Island Skipper boats for the trip across the lagoon to Jurassic Park, where you should be able to do the Triceratops Encounter and River Adventure before the majority arrive. Once you are nice and wet, you might as well go straight to Toon Lagoon and get Ripsaw Falls and the Bilge-Rat

PORT OF ENTRY
1 Island Skipper Tours
2 Confisco Grille

MARVEL SUPER-HERO ISLAND
3 Incredible Hulk Coaster
4 Café 4
5 Doctor Doom's Fearfall
6 The Amazing Adventures of Spider-Man
7 Storm Force Accelatron

TOON LAGOON
8 Comic Strip Café
9 Popeye & Bluto's Bilge-Rat Barges
10 Me Ship, The Olive
11 Dudley Do-Rights' Ripsaw Falls

JURASSIC PARK
12 Jurassic Park River Adventure
13 Thunder Falls Terrace
14 Camp Jurassic
15 Pteranodon Flyers
16 Triceratops Encounter
17 Jurassic Park Discovery Center

THE LOST CONTINENT
18 Dueling Dragons
19 The Enchanted Oak Tavern (and Alchemy Bar)
20 The Flying Unicorn
21 The Eighth Voyage of Sindbad
22 Poseidon's Fury
23 Mythos Restaurant

SEUSS LANDING
24 Picture This! Photo Gallery
25 Green Eggs and Ham Café
26 If I Ran The Zoo
27 Caro-Seuss-el
28 Circus McGurkus Café Stoo-pendous
29 One Fish Two Fish Red Fish Blue Fish
30 The Cat in the Hat

ISLANDS OF ADVENTURE

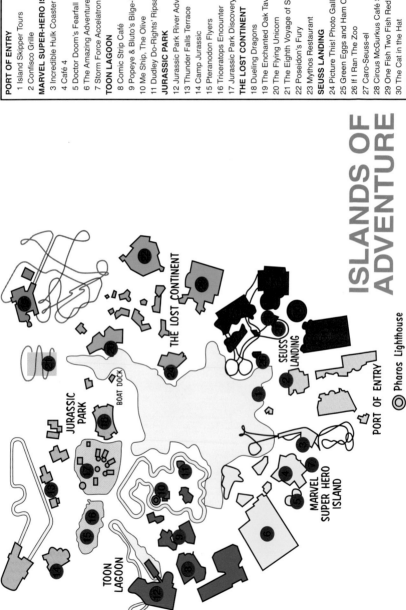

THE LOST CONTINENT

SEUSS LANDING

JURASSIC PARK

BOAT DOCK

PORT OF ENTRY

Pharos Lighthouse

MARVEL SUPER HERO ISLAND

TOON LAGOON

Barges under your belt. If you have younger children, turn right into the amazing multi-coloured world of Seuss Landing and enjoy the Cat In The Hat and other family-type rides prior to the crowd build-up.

Marvel Super-Hero Island

Taking the journey clockwise, you arrive first in the elaborate comic-book pages of the super-heroes. As with all the Islands, the experience is total immersion! The amazing façades of this world surround you with a totally credible alternative reality that is one of the park's triumphs – and that's before you have tried the rides.

The Incredible Hulk Coaster: roller-coasters don't come any more dramatic than this giant green edifice that soars out over the lagoon, blasting 0–40mph in 2 seconds and reaching a top speed of around 65mph. It looks awesome, it sounds stunning, and it rides like a demon as you enter the gamma-ray world of Dr David Banner, aka the Incredible Hulk. You zoom straight into a weightless inversion 100ft up, and it keeps getting better!

> **BRIT TIP:** Keep left where the queue splits up and you will be in line for the front car for an even more extreme experience.

Just watching is quite mind-boggling, and the after-effects are distinctly brain-scrambling. You will need to deposit ANY loose articles (sunglasses, cameras, coins, etc.) in the lockers provided at the front of the building as the ride is guaranteed to shake just about anything free. Crowds build up rapidly, but the queues move quite quickly.

Restrictions: 4ft 6in. TTTTT+ (UE).

The Amazing Adventures of Spider-Man: just queuing is a novel experience as your visit to the Daily Bugle, home of ace reporter Peter Parker (or Spider-Man to his enemies), unravels into a reporting secondment in one of the 'Scoop' vehicles. Prepare for an audio-visual extravaganza as the combination of 3-D and motion simulator takes you into a battle between Spidey and arch-villains like Dr Octopus with his anti-gravity gun, culminating in a 400ft sensory drop off a skyscraper as the contest literally hots up. There are numerous jaw-dropping special effects and you will probably need to ride at least twice to appreciate all there is to see. In fact, you'll see it and you still won't believe it. Do this ride early or expect queues of an hour or more. Restrictions: 3ft 4in. TTTTT+ (UE).

Dr Doom's Fearfall

Dr Doom's Fearfall: stand by for one of those two moments of supreme terror I mentioned earlier. This is where, O hapless visitor, you wander into the lair of the evil Dr Doom – arch-enemy of the Fantastic Four – and his sinister cohorts. His latest creation is the Fearfall, a device for sucking every ounce of fear out of its victims, and YOU are about to test it. Four riders at a time are strapped into chairs at the bottom of a 200ft tower, the dry ice rolls, and whoooosh! Up you go at breakneck speed, only to plummet back seemingly even faster, with an amazing split-second in between when you feel suspended in mid-air. Summon up the courage to do this and I promise a truly astonishing (if brief!) experience. Queues are also substantial during the main part of the day. Restrictions: 4ft 4in, and I reckon this is way too scary for under 10s. TTTTT+ (UE).

You exit Fearfall into the inevitable high-energy video arcade, or you may prefer to calm your nerves with a meal at the Italian buffeteria **Café 4** (pizza, spaghetti, sandwiches and salads) or a burger at the **Captain America Diner**. For shopping, each of the rides has its own character merchandise, while the **Comics Shop** and **Marvel Alterniverse** sell other souvenirs.

Storm Force: this new ride, aimed primarily at youngsters, puts you in the middle of a whirling, twirling battle between X-Men super-heroine Storm and arch-nemesis Magneto, with a range of special effects. It is basically an updated version of a fairground spinning-cup ride, but with some neat twists (there is a three-way rotation and the cars look like they will collide at any moment!). TTT (TTTTT under 12s) (UE).

You can also meet the **Marvel Super-Heroes** for character autographs several times a day as they patrol the island.

Toon Lagoon

The thrills continue here with a watery theme and more comic-book elements as the newspaper cartoon characters take a bow. Children will love the chance to play with the fountains, squirt pools and overflowing fire hydrants, plus a purpose-built playland **Me Ship, The Olive**, a three-storey boat full of interactive fun and games, including slides, bells and water cannons (with which to squirt passers-by on the Bilge-Rat Barges below) in best Popeye style. TTTT (youngsters only).

Popeye & Bluto's Bilge-Rat Barges: every park seems to have a variation on the white-water raft ride, but none is so outrageously themed and downright wet as this. It's fast, bouncy and unpredictable, with water coming at you from every direction, a couple of sizeable drops and a whirl through the Octoplus Grotto that adds to the fun. If you don't want to get wet, don't ride, because there is no escaping the deluge here. This is also one of the top five rides for queues, but it's worth the wait. Restrictions: 4ft. TTTTT (UE).

> BRIT TIP: A change of clothes is often advisable after riding the Barges, unless it's so hot you need to cool down in a hurry. Bring a waterproof bag for your valuables, too.

Dudley Do-Right's Ripsaw Falls: Universal's designers have again taken an existing ride concept and given it a new spin as this becomes the first flume ride to send its passengers through the water surface and out the other side at high speed. You join guileless mountie Dudley Do-Right in a bid

to save girlfriend Nell from the evil Snidely Whiplash. The action builds to an 'explosive' showdown at the top of a 60ft precipice that drops you, in almost sheer fashion, through the roof of a ramshackle dynamite shack and into the lagoon below. Just awesome – as are the queues from mid-morning to late afternoon. Wet? You bet!
Restrictions: 3ft 8in. TTTTT (UE)

After you have dried off, take a walk along **Comic Strip Lane** to meet up with characters like Beetle Bailey, Hagar the Horrible, Krazy Kat and Blondie (some of whom will mean little to a British audience). There is the usual array of character shopping outlets, like **Gasoline Alley** and **Toon Extra**, while you can grab a truly humongous sandwich at **Blondie's: Home of the Dagwood**, a trademark hamburger or hot-dog at **Wimpy's**, sample the **Comic Strip Café** food court (Mexican, Chinese, American and Italian) or tuck into something colder at **Cathy's Ice Cream**. Watch out for appearances of the **Toon Lagoon Beach Bash** for a meet-and-greet with the characters.

Jurassic Park

Leaving the comic-book lands behind, you travel back in time to the Cretaceous period and the utterly credible make-believe of the dinosaur film world. Again, the immersive experience is first class and the lavish scenery is enough to have you looking over your shoulder for stray dinos.

Jurassic Park River Adventure: the mood change from scenic splendour to hidden menace is startling as your journey into this magnificent waterborne realm brings you up close and personal with the most realistic dinosaurs created to date. Inevitably, your passage is diverted from the safe to the hazardous, and the danger increases as the 16-person raft climbs into the heights of the main building – with raptors loose everywhere. You are aware of something large lurking in the shadows – will you fall prey to the T-Rex, or will your boat take the 85ft plunge to safety (with a good soaking for all concerned)? Queues usually move quite briskly here.
Restrictions: 3ft 6in. TTTTT (UE).

Triceratops Encounter: this is your face-to-face meeting with the park's resident 4-ton, 24ft-long 'living' dinosaur, which reacts to both its handler and visitors. The spiel is amusing and educational and the 'Trike' pretty convincing, especially for children. It also draws a crowd and there is little shade (one of the few minus points), but the queues move steadily. AAAA. (UE).

Pteranodon Flyers: the slow-moving queues are a major turn-off, especially for a fairly average ride, which glides gently over much of Jurassic Park. It is designed mainly for kids, though, and the height range of 3ft-4ft 8in requires anyone over the upper limit (usually that is over 11s) to be accompanied by a child of the right height! TT (TTTT under 9s).

Camp Jurassic: more excellent kids' fare here with the mountainous jungle giving way to an 'active' ancient volcano for youngsters to explore, climb over and slide down. Squirt guns and 'Spitter' dinosaurs add to the fun. TTTT (children first, but parents may explore too!).

Discovery Center: the designers' imagination has gone into overdrive here with terrific results. Interactive opportunities include creating a dinosaur through DNA sequencing, mixing your own DNA with a dino via a computer touchscreen, seeing through the eyes of various large reptiles and even watching a baby raptor hatch, plus a host of other hands-on exhibits that are fun and educational. This is also a good visit

6

Jurassic Park River Adventure

in the hotter part of the day. AAAA.

Best of the shopping is in the Discovery Center itself, while you can chow down at the **Burger Digs** there, visit the **Pizza Predattoria** or the **Watering Hole**, or go for the rotisserie chicken at the rustic **ThunderFalls Terrace** (counter service), which boasts a great view of the River Adventure splash-down.

The Lost Continent

This is one of my favourite lands for its original theming, gentle contrast after Jurassic Park, superb attractions, great eating options and a few amusing 'extras'.

Dueling Dragons: there is no disguising the intense nature of this magnificent double coaster, with its 100ft drop, multiple loops, twists and three near-miss encounters. There is a lot more, too, as the queuing area is a real mind-boggler – 1,060 yards, most of it along a dark tortuous path through the ancient castle that is the domain of the dragons, Fire and Ice. You get their story while you stand in line, and Merlin arrives in time to cast a spell to ensure you survive. You choose which dragon to ride (the tracks differ slightly), and you can join an additional queue for the front seats. Unlike the Hulk, this is a suspended coaster, so your legs dangle free, and the initial drop is like going into free-fall (Supreme Terror moment Number Two!). Coaster aficionados reckon the best ride is in the back of

Dueling Dragons roller-coaster

The Flying Unicorn

the Ice (Blue) dragon, but it's all pretty amazing. Restrictions: 4ft 6in, and you will need to take advantage of the lockers provided to the left of the entrance in which to leave your loose articles. TTTTT+ (UE).

The Flying Unicorn: this junior-sized coaster is also aimed primarily at youngsters and features a wizard's workshop, hidden in an enchanted wood, that is the gateway to a magical journey inspired by the Unicorn. There are no big drops, but it delivers a surprisingly fast-paced whirl for its size. TTTTT (for 6–12s) (UE).

The Eighth Voyage of Sindbad: this stunt and special effects show is another marvel, as much for its elaborate staging as its performance. Mythical adventurer Sindbad and his side-kick Kabob (a name that's the cue for a truly awful pun) tackle the evil witch Miseria in a bid to rescue Princess Amoura, and the action springs up in surprising places. There are several loud bangs which could scare young children, but otherwise it is good, family fun. At peak times, arrive 15 minutes before showtime, but everyone usually gets in. TTT/AAAA (UE).

Poseidon's Fury: this is a walk-through show that puts its audience at the heart of the action as you journey beneath the sea to the lost temple of Poseidon, passing through an amazing water 'vortex' en route, with your 'archaeological expedition'

One Fish Two Fish

taking a wrong turn and awakening an ancient demon. Again, there is a terrific element of suspense, so I won't reveal any surprises, but the showdown between Poseidon and the evil demon is amazing as the arena seems to explode in water and fire around you. Queuing is a bit slow, but that's a bonus in summer as you are inside. TTT (UE).

Check out **Metal Smiths** for unusual trinkets, **Treasures of Poseidon** and **Shop of Wonders** for more up-market gifts and the **Psychic Readings** tent in Sindbad's Village for something new. The **Fire-Eater's Grill** (sausages, fries and drinks) and **Frozen Desert** (sundaes and sodas) provide the snacks, while there is the magnificent **Enchanted Oak Tavern** (in the dark, cool interior of a vast, sculpted oak tree, and with its Alchemy Bar) for counter-service meals (hickory-smoked chicken, ribs and salads) which has to be seen to be believed. The ultra-elaborate **Mythos Restaurant** provides the best dining experience in IoA, though. Not only is the food excellent (seafood, grills, pizza and pasta), but the setting, inside a dormant volcano with streams, fountains and clever lighting, is an attraction in its own right.

Finally, watch out for **The Mystic Fountain** in Sindbad's Village – it has the ability to get you very wet when you least expect it!

Seuss Landing

There is not a straight line to be seen in this vivid 3-D working of the books of Dr Seuss. The characters may not mean much to those unfamiliar with the children's stories, but everyone can relate to the fun here (although queues build up quickly for all rides). There is so much clever detail packed in, from squirt ponds to beach scenes, it is easy to miss something, so take your time.

Caro-Seuss-el: this intricate carousel ride on some of the Seuss characters – like cowfish, elephant-birds and dog-a-lopes – has rider-activated features sure to go down well with the young ones. AAA (AAAA under 5s) (UE).

One Fish Two Fish Red Fish Blue Fish: another fairground ride is given a twist as you pilot these Seussian fish up and down according to the rhyme that plays while you ride. Get it wrong and you get squirted! A big hit with the kids. TTT (TTTTT under 5s) (UE).

The Cat In The Hat: prepare for a ride with a difference as you board these crazy six-passenger 'couches' to meet the world's most adventurous Cat and his friends, Thing One and Thing Two. You literally go for a spin through this storybook world, and it may be a bit too much for very young children. The slow-moving queues are a bit of a drag, so try to get here early or leave it until much later in the day (or use the Express system). AAAA/TTT (UE).

If I Ran The Zoo: interactive playgrounds don't get much more fun for the pre-school brigade than with the 19 different Seuss character scenarios, most of which can get them quite wet. Hugely imaginative and great fun just to watch. TTTTT (young 'uns only).

The Circus McGurkus Seussian Sing-a-Long: especially for the youngsters inside the café Circus (see below) is this 20-minute musical performance as Ringmaster McGurkus introduces The Cat In The Hat and his friends, with interruptions from The Grinch. AA (AAAA under 5s).

If you have been captivated by the land, you can buy the book at **Dr Seuss' All the Books You Can Read** store, or visit the **Mulberry Street Store** for all the characters.

Snookers & Snookers Sweet Candy Cookers is a super sweet shop, while snacks and drinks can be had at **Hop on Pop Ice Cream Shop** and **Moose Juice Goose Juice**. The **Circus McGurkus Café Stoo-pendous** is a mind-boggling cafeteria for fried chicken, lasagne, pizza and spaghetti, complete with clowns and pipe organs (and the Sing-a-Long show – plus special birthday celebrations every afternoon at 2.45), while **Green Eggs and Ham Café** is a must for all Seuss fans to try the meal of the same name (and the eggs *are* green!).

To make sure they are extra family-friendly, there are private nursing facilities, an open area for feeding and resting (with high-chairs) and nappy-changing stations at the **Family Service Facility** at guest services (to the right inside the main gates), while ALL restrooms throughout the park are equipped with **nappy-changing** facilities. **First aid** is provided in Sindbad's Village in the Lost Continent, across from Oasis Coolers.

In high season, there is even a nightly **firework show** on the Lagoon that provides a fitting and spectacular finale to the day.

And that, my friends, is the full low-down on very possibly the best theme park in the world to date. Miss it at your peril.

6

ISLANDS OF ADVENTURE with children

Here is our guide to the rides which generally appeal to the different age groups:

Under 5s
Caro-Seuss-el, If I Ran The Zoo, The Cat In The Hat, One Fish, Two Fish, Red Fish, Blue Fish, Circus McGurkus Sing-a-Long, Eighth Voyage of Sindbad, Jurassic Park Discovery Center, Me Ship The Olive.

5–8s
All the above, plus Flying Unicorn, Triceratops Encounter, Pteranodon Flyers, Camp Jurassic, Amazing Adventures of Spider-Man, Storm Force Accelotron, and Jurassic Park River Adventure (with parental discretion).

9–12s
The Cat In The Hat, Flying Unicorn, Dueling Dragons, Eighth Voyage of Sindbad, Camp Jurassic, Pteranodon Flyers, Jurassic Park River Adventure, Triceratops Encounter, Jurassic Park Discovery Center, Dudley Do-Right's Ripsaw Falls, Popeye and Bluto's Bilge Rat Barges, Amazing Adventures of Spider-Man, Dr Doom's Fearfall, Storm Force Accelatron, Incredible Hulk Coaster.

Over 12s
Dueling Dragons, Eighth Voyage of Sindbad, Jurassic Park River Adventure, Jurassic Park Discovery Center, Dudley Do-Right's Ripsaw Falls, Popeye and Bluto's Bilge Rat Barges, Amazing Adventures of Spiderman, Dr Doom's Fearfall, Storm Force Accelatron, Incredible Hulk Coaster.

SeaWorld Adventure Park

SeaWorld has quickly become one of the most popular parks with British visitors for its more peaceful and naturalistic aspect, the change of pace it offers and the general lack of any substantial queues. It is a big hit with families in particular, but also possesses some pretty dramatic rides and attractions.

An extensive development programme by corporate owners Anheuser-Busch has also given SeaWorld the big-park treatment in recent years, with an impressive new 12-acre entrance plaza and rebranding as an Adventure Park, and it now demands a full day's attention. The opening, in summer 2000, of an exclusive sister park – Discovery Cove, an exotic tropical island with dolphin, stingray and snorkelling adventures – has added even more to this process.

Happily, the queues and crowds have yet to reach the monster proportions of elsewhere, so this is a park where you can still proceed at a relatively leisurely pace, see what you want to see without too much shoulder-jostling and yet feel you have been superbly entertained (even if meal-times do get crowded in the various restaurants around the park).

SeaWorld is also a good starting point if this is your first visit to Orlando as it will give you the hang of negotiating the vast areas, navigating by the various maps and learning to plan your visit around the different showtimes. There is also a strong educational and environmental message, plus three hour-long behind-the-scenes tours (book up as soon as you enter) to provide a greater insight into SeaWorld's marine conservation, rescue and research programme, as well as their entertainment resources. The **Polar Expedition** provides a close-up of the penguin and polar bear environments, **To the Rescue** showcases the park's animal rescue and rehabilitation programme, and **Sharks!** offers a

SeaWorld Adventure Park

1 Manatees: The Last Generation?
2 Journey To Atlantis
3 Penguin Encounter
4 Pacific Point Preserve
5 Sea Lion & Otter Stadium
6 Terrors Of The Deep
7 Nautilus Theater
8 Clydesdale Hamlet
9 Anheuser-Busch Hospitality Center
10 Shamu's Happy Harbor
11 Wild Arctic
12 Atlantis Bayside Stadium
13 Hawaiian Rhythms
14 SeaWorld Theater
15 Tropical Reef
16 Key West Dolphin Stadium
17 Shamu Stadium
18 Information
19 Key West at SeaWorld
20 Turtle Point
21 Stingray Lagoon
22 Tide Pool
23 Dolphin Nursery
24 Dolphin Cove
25 Kraken

SEA WORLD

6

backstage view of Terrors of the Deep. You have to pay an extra $7.95 ($6.95 for 3–9s) for these tours, but they are worth it and, if you take one of them early on, they will increase your appreciation of the rest of the park.

Two recent additions are the six-hour **Adventure Express Tour**, which offers guests their own guide to tour the park, with back-door access to the rides, reserved seating at shows and animal feeding opportunities (an extra $55 for adults, $50 for 3–9s; book up first thing at the Guided Tours counter or call 1-800 406 2244), and the

Trainer For A Day, an 8-hour programme open to just three people (at least 13 years old and in good physical condition) each day, which shows how SeaWorld trainers care for and train their animals (cost is $349, including T-shirt, waterproof disposable camera and lunch with trainers; for reservations, call 407 370 1382).

Location

SeaWorld is located off Central Florida parkway, between I4 (exit 27A going [north] east or 28 heading [south] west) and International

SeaWorld Adventure Park at a glance

Location	7007 SeaWorld Drive, off Central Florida Parkway (Junctions 27A and 28 off I4)		
Size	More than 200 acres, incorporating 25 attractions		
Hours	9am–7pm off peak; 9am–10pm high season (Easter, summer holidays, Thanksgiving, Christmas)		
Admission	Under 3, free; 3–9, $39 (one-day ticket), $128 (4-Park Orlando FlexTicket), $158 (5-Park Flex Ticket); adult (10+) $48, $160, $197		
Parking	$6		
Lockers	Yes, by main entrance; $1.50		
Pushchairs	$11 and $15 ($2 refundable; from Information Centre, to left of main entrance)		
Wheelchairs	$9 ($2 refundable) and $35 ($5 refundable) same location		
Top Attractions	Shamu Stadium, Terrors of the Deep, Journey to Atlantis, Kraken, Wild Arctic		
Don't Miss	Rock 'n Rockets Fireworks, Manatees: The Last Generation?, Behind-the-Scenes Tours, Cirque de la Mer		
Hidden Costs	**Meals**	Burger, chips and coke $7.68	
	Kids' meal	$3.49 and $6.29 (in Bimini Bay Café)	
		Three-course lunch (Bimini Bay) $19	
	T-shirts	$14.99–$26.95	
	Souvenirs	$0.99–$1,500	
	Sundries	Caricature Drawings $12.95–$22.95	

Drive, and the parking fee is $6. It is still a good idea to arrive a bit before the officially scheduled opening time so you're in good position to book one of the backstage tours at a time convenient to you or scamper off to one of the few attractions that does draw crowds, like Journey to Atlantis.

The park covers in excess of 200 acres, with nine shows (10 with the nightly **Aloha Polynesian Luau** Dinner Show which costs an extra $36, $26 for 8–12s and $16 for 3–7s, and for which you don't necessarily have to visit the rest of the park; nightly 6.30–8.45pm, tel 407 351 3600 to book), nine large-scale continuous viewing attractions and nine smaller ones, plus relaxing gardens, a kids' play area and a smart range of shops (a noticeable feature of Anheuser-Busch parks). Their hire pushchairs (strollers) are also the most amusing – shaped like baby dolphins so you push them along by the tail. Be warned, though, the size of the park will take you by surprise and requires a lot of to-ing and fro-ing to catch the various shows, which can be wearing. Keep a close grip on your map and entertainment schedule and try to establish your own programme that gives you regular time-outs to sit and enjoy some of the quieter spots. For something different, you can also sign up for the free 35-minute Anheuser-Busch Beer School at the Hospitality Center for a glimpse into beer-making (and tasting!).

Wild Arctic: this interactive ride-and-view experience provides a realistic environment that is both educational and thrilling. It consists of an exciting simulator jet helicopter journey into the Arctic wilderness arriving at a clever research base, Base Station Wild Arctic, where the 'passengers' are disgorged into a frozen wonderland to meet polar bears, Beluga whales and walruses. The imaginative detail

includes a replica sunken galleon and other nautical touches, as well as some scientific research. Not to be missed (but not just after a Shamu show when the hordes descend). Restrictions: 3ft 6in. TTTT plus AAAAA.

Shamu Stadium: SeaWorld has long since outgrown its tag as just the place to see killer whales, but the Shamu show is still one of its most amazing experiences. See the killer whales and their trainers pull off some spectacular stunts, as well as explaining all about these majestic creatures.

> BRIT TIP: Reader David Snelling from Cheshire, warns, 'Gentlemen, do not volunteer to participate in the Shamu display – it will be chauvinistically humiliating.'

There are two distinct shows, the more humorous Shamu Adventure during the day (25 minutes) and the louder Shamu Big Chill at night (20 minutes). Both are worth seeing, and are easily the park's most popular events, so do make an effort to arrive early (especially as there is an amusing pre-show). Also, the first 14 rows get VERY wet (watch out for your cameras) – when a killer whale leaps into the air in front of you, it displaces a LOT of water on landing! AAAAA.

Shamu: Close-up: this backstage exhibit can be found at the opposite side of Shamu Stadium, affording a much closer and more natural look at the killer whales while at their leisure. Attendants are on hand to answer all your questions. AAA.

Sea Lion & Otter Stadium: this is home to the new show, Clyde and Seamore Take Treasure Island, featuring the resident sea lions who, with their pals the otter and walrus

Shamu the killer whale

(plus a couple of humans to be the fall-guys!), put on a hilarious 25-minute performance of watery stunts and gags. Arrive early for some first-class audience mickey-taking from the resident pirate mimic. AAAA.

Key West Splash Fest: more breathtaking marine mammal stunts and tricks in a funky beach theme, with the accent again on informing and educating in a gentle manner on the current state of research into dolphins and false killer whales and the dangers they face. The show lasts almost 20 minutes and is rarely over-subscribed, but once again the first few rows face a soaking. AAAA.

Bayside Stadium: this arena showcases the half-hour Intensity Games Water Ski Show, with an

BRIT TIP: The weather may occasionally mean the outdoor entertainment is cancelled, but don't let it stop you enjoying yourself. Cheap, plastic ponchos will appear in the shops at the first sign of rain!

explosion of high-energy action in water stunts, featuring some breathtaking water-skiing, wake-boarders, jet skis and more. AAAA.

SeaWorld Theater: this air-conditioned venue is a little haven when it's hot during the main part of the day. Pets Ahoy! is the show here, a 25-minute giggle featuring the talents of a menagerie of dogs, cats, birds, rats, pot-bellied pigs and others, the majority of which were rescued from animal shelters. AAA.

Nautilus Theater: this is home to the spectacular Cirque de la Mer show, a unique 35-minute adventure of athleticism, acrobatics, modern dance, music and special effects. The South American cast exhibit a terrific élan as they illustrate the story of the Flight of the Condor. It's all air-conditioned, too. AAAAA.

Hawaiian Rhythms: an amusing song-and-dance pastiche of Polynesian culture on the Beach Stage, lasting 20 minutes and with a welcome beverage service. Beware if you are chosen to go on stage – it's an embarrassing experience! AAA.

Clydesdale Hamlet: these

The Key West Splash Fest

BRIT TIP: For all the
main shows, try to arrive
20 minutes early during
peak periods to grab one of
the better seats and avoid
the last-minute rush.

massive stables are home to the
Anheuser-Busch trademark
Clydesdale dray horses. They make
great photo opportunities when fully
harnessed, and there is a life-size
statue outside on which to sit the
kids to take their picture. The new
Hitching Barn shows how the horses
are prepared for the twice-daily
parade, including washing,
grooming and braiding. AA.

**Anheuser-Busch Hospitality
Center:** adjoining Clydesdale
Hamlet, this offers the chance to
sample the company's most famous
product, beer (in fact, the world's No
1 bottled beer, Budweiser, and its
cousins). Sadly, it's only three small
samples per over-21 visitor, but it
still makes a nice gesture, and you
can take your free drink and sit on
the outdoor terrace which makes for
a pleasant break from all the usual
theme park hustle and bustle. AAA.
It is also home to the **Beer School**,
while **The Deli** restaurant here is an
attractive proposition, serving fresh-
carved turkey and beef, German
sausage, sauerkraut, fresh-baked
breads and delicious desserts.

**Manatees: The Last
Generation?:** here is an exhibit that
will really tug at your heart-strings
as the tragic plight of this
endangered species of Florida's
waterways is illustrated. Watch these
lazy-looking creatures (half walrus,
half hippo?) lounge around their
man-made lagoon from above, then
walk down the ramp to the special
circular theatre where a 5-minute
film with amazing 3-D effects will
reveal the full dangers facing the

The touch pool at Stingray lagoon

harmless manatee. Then pass into
the underwater viewing section, with
hands-on TV screens offering more
information about them. It's a
magnificent exhibit and often
provokes a few tears at the animals'
uncertain future. It is also right
behind the Key West Dolphin Fest,
so DON'T go just after one of the
shows there. AAAAA.

Pacific Point Preserve: another
SeaWorld first, this carefully
recreated rocky coast habitat shows
the park's seals and sea lions at their

Journey to Atlantis

most natural. A hidden wave-making machine adds the perfect touch of reality, while park attendants are on hand intervals to provide informative talks. You can also buy small packs of smelt from two stalls to throw to the ever-hungry sea beasts. AAAA.

Shamu's Happy Harbor: three acres of brilliantly designed adventure playground await youngsters of all ages here, with all things climbable or crawlable. Activities include a four-storey net climb, two tented 'ball rooms' to wade through, and a giant 'trampoline' tent. It does get busy in mid-afternoon, but the kids seem to love it at any time. Next door is the clever **Shamu Splash Attack** (water-balloon catapults), the inevitable video arcade and some funfair games for a few extra dollars. TTTTT.

Terrors of the Deep: the world's largest collection of dangerous sea creatures can be found here, brought vividly and dramatically to life by the walk-through tubes that surround you with prowling sharks, barracudas and moray eels. It's an eerie experience (and perhaps too intense for small children), but brilliantly presented and, again, highly informative. Queues do build up here at peak times, though. AAAA or TTTT. Take your pick!

Tropical Reef: after the dramas and amusements elsewhere, this may seem a little tame, but stick with it. Literally thousands of colourful fish inhabit the centrepiece 160,000-gallon tropical reef, while smaller tanks show off other intriguing species. AAA.

Penguin Encounter: always a hit with all the family (and hence one of

the more crowded exhibits at peak periods) are the eternally comical penguins in this brilliantly presented (if decidedly chilly) showpiece. You have the choice of going close and using the moving walkway along the whole of the display or standing back and watching from a non-moving position, while both positions afford views of how the 17 different species are so breathtaking under water. Feeding time is the most popular time for visitors, so arrive early if you want a prime position, while there is also a special question-and-answer session at 2pm every day – the winner gets to pet a penguin. AAAA.

Key West at SeaWorld is a whole collection of exhibits grouped under the clever Key West theme. **Stingray Lagoon**, where you can feed and touch fully grown rays, includes a nursery for newborn rays, while the park's rescued and rehabilitated sea turtles are exhibited at **Turtle Point**, which helps to explain the dangers to these saltwater reptiles. The centrepiece exhibit, the 2.1-acre **Dolphin Cove**, is a more spectacular, naturalistic development and offers visitors the chance to get right up close and feed this friendly community of Atlantic bottlenose dolphins. There is an underwater viewing area to the 700,000-gallon lagoon, which also features waves, a sandy beach and a recreated coral reef.

The whole area is designed in the tropical, seaside flavour of America's southernmost city, Key West, with beach huts, lifeguard chairs, dune buggies, themed shops and other eclectic lookalike elements, but it also underlines the environmental message of conservation through a series of interactive graphics and video displays adjacent to the animal habitats, and children of all ages will find it a fun, educational experience. The shops are above average, too. AAAA.

BRIT TIP: Touching the rays and dolphins is an experience at SeaWorld you won't easily forget.

Journey to Atlantis: unique in Orlando, this terrific 'water-coaster' gave SeaWorld its first five-star thrill attraction in 1998. The combination of extra elements here ultimately makes it unique, with a series of illusionary special effects giving way to a high-speed water ride that becomes a runaway roller-coaster. An amusing TV show preamble about the 'discovery' of Atlantis opens the way to your eight-passenger Greek fishing boat, which sets off gently through the lost city. The evil spirit Allura takes over and riders plunge into a dash through Atlantis, dodging gushing fountains and water cannons, with hundreds of dazzling holographic and laser-generated illusions, before the heart-stopping 60ft drop, which is merely the entry to the roller-coaster finale back in the candle-filled catacombs. An amazing creation. Once again, be prepared to get seriously wet (like, soaked) in the course of the ride, which is great in the heat of the summer but not so clever first thing in the morning in winter. Restrictions: 3ft 6in. TTTTT. Riders exit into the **Sea Aquarium Gallery**, a combination gift shop and 25,000-gallon aquarium full of sharks, stingrays and tropical fish (don't forget to look up!).

Kraken: brand new in 2000 was this outrageous addition to the coaster family, the longest, fastest and highest in central Florida. Based on the mythical sea monster, Kraken is an innovative pedestal ride (you are effectively sitting in a chair without a floor – pretty exposed!) that plunges an initial 144ft, tops speeds of 65mph, dives underground three times, adds seven inversions (including a 119ft vertical loop, a 101ft diving loop, a zero-gravity roll and a cobra roll) and a flat spin before riders escape the beast's lair. The ride from the front row, especially down that opening drop at an angle that can best be described

as ludicrous, is positively blood-curdling, and the rear seats are pretty neat, too. Restrictions: 4ft 6in. TTTTT+.

SeaWorld Specials

In addition to the **Shamu Rocks America** show, night-time at SeaWorld is marked by an end-of-evening fireworks extravaganza in front of the Atlantis Bayside Stadium called **Rock 'n Rockets**. This 15-minute curtain-call features lasers, fountains and pyrotechnics and is well worth staying for. AAAAA.

There is also live entertainment daily around the Key West attractions, including the trademark **Sunset Celebration** street party.

Through the summer, when the park tends to stay open until at least 9pm, SeaWorld also hosts **Rockin' Summer Nights**, with outdoor DJs, live music, dancers and games, with teens getting their own music scene, Club Shamu, next to Kraken. The programme includes the Shamu's Big Chill show, leading up to the nightly pyrotechnic extravaganza.

As well as all the main set-pieces, there are several smaller ones which can be equally rewarding for their more personal touch. There are the **Flamingo, Pelican** and **Spoonbill Exhibits**, while **Tide Pool** is another hands-on experience with starfish and sea anemones, and, for an extra $3, you can ascend the **Sky Tower** for a lofty overview of the park (and International Drive). Then there are the flamingo pedal-boats, which rent for $6 per half-hour (for two people) in one corner of the lagoon. Look out, too, for the best photo opportunity of the day as a big, cuddly Shamu greets kids just inside the main entrance.

There are also nine different places to eat, with the **Dockside Smokehouse** (barbecued, mesquite-

6

The Kraken roller-coaster

grilled chicken, ribs and beef), **The Deli** (mentioned, above, in the Anheuser-Busch Hospitality Center), **Bimini Bay Café** (for a relaxing, full-service lunch or dinner) and **Mango Joe's Café** (delicious grilled fajitas, speciality salads and sandwiches) the best of the bunch. As in the other main parks, try to eat before midday or after 2.30pm for a crowd-free lunch, and before 5.30pm if you want a leisurely dinner.

Your wallet will also be in severe peril in any of the 24 shops and photo-opportunity kiosks. Make sure you visit at least **Shamu's Emporium** (for a full range of cuddly Shamu toys and souvenirs), **Manatee Cove** (more cuddlies), **Friends of the Wild** (dedicated to animal lovers everywhere) and **The Label Stable** for Anheuser-Busch gifts and merchandise (some of it extremely smart). Your purchases can be forwarded to Package Pick-up in Shamu's Emporium for you to collect on your way out, provided you leave at least an hour for this service to work.

Finally, non-drivers will want to make a note of the special daily bus service from SeaWorld (and other points on International Drive) direct to sister park Busch Gardens (see page 160). There is also a SeaWorld/Busch Value Ticket, providing one visit at each park and an additional day at either park for $94 (adults) and $78 (3–5s).

SEAWORLD with children

Here is a general idea of the appeal of SeaWorld's attractions to the different age-groups:

Under 5s
Shamu Adventure Show, Key West Splash Fest, Clyde & Seamore Take Pirate Island, Pets On Stage, Wild Arctic (without the ride), Manatees: Last Generation?, Penguin Encounter, Tropical Reef, Pacific Point Preserve, Clydesdale Hamlet.

5–8s
All the above, plus Wild Arctic (with the ride), Intensity Games Water Ski Show, Cirque de la Mer, Rock 'n Rockets, Terrors of the Deep, Shamu's Happy Harbor.

9–12s
All the above, plus Kraken and Hawaiian Rhythms.

Over 12s
Kraken, Journey to Atlantis, Wild Arctic, Terrors of the Deep, Shamu Adventure Show, Intensity Games Water Ski Show, Clyde & Seamore Take Pirate Island, Cirque de la Mer, Rock 'n Rockets.

Discovery Cove

Fancy a day in your own tropical paradise, with the chance to swim with dolphins, encounter sharks, snorkel in a coral reef and dive through a waterfall into a tropical aviary? Well, this is the place for you. The unique Discovery Cove is all that and more. The only drawback is the price. This mini theme park comes at a premium because it is restricted to just 1,000 guests a day, making for an exclusive experience, and the admission fee reflects that – a whopping $199, plus tax, per person, and no reduction for children (except to $99 for 3–5s; see full pricing below).

Snorkelling in the Coral Reef

So, just what do you get for your money? Well, as you would expect, it is a supremely personal park. You check in as you would for a hotel rather than a theme park (the entrance lobby is wonderfully impressive), and you have a guide to take you in and get you set for the day. All your basic requirements – towel, mask, snorkel, wet-jacket, lockers, beach umbrellas, lunch and soft drinks – are included in the

Discovery Cove

The author at Discovery Cove

price, and the level of service is excellent. A valuable seven-day pass for SeaWorld is also included. The lunch provided at the buffet-style **Laguna Grill** is pretty good, but you have to pay for any further snacks and any alcoholic drinks, while the gift shop and photographic prices reflect the entrance fee, i.e. expensive.

The whole of the 30-acre park is magnificently landscaped, with lovely thatched buildings, palm trees, lush vegetation, brilliant white-sand beaches, gurgling streams and even hammocks, and the overall effect is as if you have been transported to some Caribbean or South Seas oasis.

The usual tourist hurly-burly is left far behind. The five-star resort feel is enhanced by the high staff-to-guest ratio (the lifeguards can outnumber the guests at times, it seems). There should be no queues for anything (okay, the buffet-service restaurant may get a little busy at lunchtime) and the highlight dolphin encounter is unquestionably world class. The ultimate effect is of total relaxation, a holiday from your holiday, and a real feeling of escape from the everyday.

Guests with disabilities are also well catered for, with special wheelchairs which can move across the sand and into shallow water and an area of the Dolphin Lagoon designed to allow those who can't enter the water still to be able to touch the dolphins.

The essence of a day at Discovery Cove involves close encounters with all the animals – although not too close in the case of the sharks – with a strong underlying conservation message, as you get with SeaWorld. Here are the main attractions:

Coral Reef: a huge rocky pool, filled with several thousand tropical fish, offers the most amazing man-made snorkelling experience you'll find. The water teems with silverjacks, angelfish and yellowtail snapper and, even if the 'coral' is hand-painted concrete, it is a clever environment. Some of the larger stingrays inhabit the bottom of the reef and it is fascinating to watch them moving effortlessly around. Swimmers also come within inches of sharks and barracuda – all safely behind a Plexiglass partition – which adds another novel element. If you stay reasonably still in the water, many of the fish will crowd around you to inspect their latest pool-mate! AAAAA/TTTT.

Ray Lagoon: another carefully sculpted pool provides the opportunity to paddle among several dozen southern and cownose rays, quite harmless, but with just a hint of menace to the fascination. AAAA.

Tropical River: this 800-metre circuit of gently flowing bath-warm water is a variation on the lazy river feature of many of the water parks, although with a far more naturalistic aspect and none of the inner-tubes. It is primarily designed for snorkellers and features rocky lagoons, caves, a beach section, a tropical forest segment, sunken ruins, and an underwater viewing window into the Coral Reef. The lack of fish makes it seem a bit bland after the Tropical Reef and Ray Lagoon, but again, it is as much about relaxing as about having fun. AAA.

Aviary: this is both an area in its own right and a 30-metre section of the Tropical River. You can walk in off the beach or swim in through one of the two impressive waterfalls which guard each end, a beautifully scenic touch and fun for snorkellers. Some 200 tropical birds fill the 10m-high enclosure and, if you stand still for a while, they are likely to use you for a perch. There are guides to introduce you to specific birds, which you can also hand-feed, and tell you about their habits, habitats and conservation issues. AAAAA.

Animal Encounters: a minor additional touch, but sure to be a hit with children in particular, is the chance to meet some of the Cove's lesser lights, like macaws, tree-sloths and anteaters on an individual basis at various points around the park. AAA.

Dolphin Swim: the headline attraction at Discovery Cove is the encounter with the park's Atlantic bottlenose dolphin community. A 15-minute orientation programme in one of the four thatched beach cabanas, with a film and instruction from two of the animal trainers, sets you up for this deeply thrilling experience. Groups of 12–20 guests go into the huge lagoon with careful supervision from the trainers and, starting off by standing in the waist-deep (and slightly chilly) water as one of the dolphins comes to you, you gradually become more adventurous until you are swimming next to them. Timid swimmers are catered for and there are life-jackets for those who feel they need them, but the lagoon is up to 12ft deep so there is a feeling of really being in the dolphins' environment. You will learn how the trainers use hand-signals and positive reinforcement to communicate with them, and get the chance to stroke, feed and even kiss (!) your dolphin. The encounter comes to a dramatic conclusion as you are towed back to shore by one of these awesome animals, which can be anywhere from 300-600lb (although the activities can vary according to the dolphins' own attention span). You spend about half an hour in all in the water and it is genuinely unforgettable. TTTTT+.

Truly, this is an attraction with huge style and appeal – not to mention the stuff of which cherished memories are made – but it will take a big bite out of your holiday budget. The entrance fee plus tax adds up to $210.94 per person, and the only reduction is to $104.34 for those not wishing to do the Dolphin Swim and for 3–5s (under 6s are not allowed into the dolphin lagoon; under 3s are free). That means a family of four, with children of 6 or older, would pay $843.76 for the day and, even with the 7-day SeaWorld pass included, it is a massive outlay. The charge for 3–5-year-olds is also pretty steep, in my opinion.

The park is located on Central Florida Parkway, almost opposite the SeaWorld entrance, and is open year-round from 8.30am–5.30pm. Parking is free. The weather can get distinctly cool in the winter months, but the water is always heated (apart from the dolphin lagoon, which remains at a sea-water 72°F) and full wet-suits are also available to keep out the chill.

In the winter of 2000/2001, when the temperature in Florida hit freak lows (almost freezing at night), Discovery Cove came to its guests' aid by installing temporary heaters around the park and providing complimentary coffee and hot chocolate! Their attention to detail is really that good, and the guest satisfaction ratings remained extremely high. However, if any element falls below your expectations, it is worth bringing it to the attention of the park manager at the time as they are always keen to rectify any apparent oversights.

For more details, look up www.discoverycove.com. You can book on-line or call 407 370 1280.

Busch Gardens

Question: when is a zoo not a zoo? Answer: when it is also a theme park like 335-acre Busch Gardens in nearby Tampa.

Busch Gardens, the second big Anheuser-Busch park in the area, started life as a mini-menagerie for the wildlife collection of the brewery-owning Busch family. In 1959, they opened a small, tropical-themed hospitality centre next to the brewery and things have mushroomed ever since. Now, it is a major, multi-faceted family attraction, the biggest on Florida's west coast and just an hour or so from Orlando.

It is rated among the top four zoos in America, with more than 2,700 animals representing more than 320 species of mammals, birds, reptiles, amphibians and spiders. But that's just the start. It boasts a safari-like section of Africa spread over 65 acres of grassy veldt, with special tours to hand-feed some of the animals. Interspersed among the animals are more than 20 bona fide theme park rides, including the mind-numbing roller-coasters Kumba, Montu and Gwazi, which guarantee a new experience for coaster addicts, and yet another in the series of simulator rides, the amusing and novel Akbar's Adventure Tours. There are animal shows, comedians, musicians, strolling players and a family show extravaganza in the impressive Moroccan Palace Theater, World Rhythms on Ice.

The overall theme is Africa, hence the park is subdivided into areas like Nairobi and the Congo, and the dining and shopping opportunities are the equal of most of the other theme parks. It doesn't quite have the pizazz of an *Epcot* or Universal, and the staff are a bit more laid back.

In a way, it is like the big brother of the Chessington World of Adventures in Surrey, although admittedly on a much grander scale (and in a better climate). But it has guaranteed, five-star family appeal, especially with its selection of rides just for kids, and it is a big hit with the British market in particular.

Location

Busch Gardens is the hardest place to locate on the sketchy local maps and the signposting is not as sharp as it could be, but, from Orlando, the directions are pretty simple. Head (south) west on I4 for almost an hour (it is 55 miles from I4's junction with Highway 192) until you hit the intersecting motorway I75. Take I75 north for 3½ miles until you see the exit for Fowler Avenue (Highway 582). Continue west on Fowler for another 3½ miles, then just past the University of South Florida on your right, turn LEFT into McKinley Drive. A mile down McKinley Drive, Busch Gardens' car park entrance will be on your left, where it is $6 to park.

Those without a car can use the brilliant daily **Busch Gardens Shuttle Express** bus service, with five round-trips a day (and connections from 40 other locations in central Florida) from Orlando at $5 a time (free if you have a 5-Park FlexTicket). You board the Shuttle at SeaWorld, the Mercado Center, Lake Buena Vista Factory Stores, Universal Orlando or Old Town in Kissimmee and pick-up times range from 8–10.15am for the one-hour journey, returning at 5, 6 and 8pm. You book at the Guest Services window at SeaWorld or call 1-800 511 2450.

You may think you have left the

1 CONGO
2 Congo River Rapids
3 Kumba
4 The Python
5 TIMBUKTU
6 Dolphin Theater
7 The Scorpion
8 Festhaus
9 STANLEYVILLE
10 Tanganyika Tidal Wave
11 Stanley Falls
12 Stanleyville Theater
13 LAND OF THE DRAGONS
14 BIRD GARDENS
15 Koala Display
16 Hospitality House/Beer School
17 Lory Landing
18 MOROCCO
19 Moroccan Palace Theater
20 MYOMBE RESERVE
21 CROWN COLONY
22 Skyride Station
23 Crown Colony Restaurant & Hospitality
    Center
24 Clydesdale Hamlet
25 EGYPT
26 Akbar's Adventure Tours
27 Tut's Tomb
28 Montu
29 SERENGETI PLAIN
30 Edge of Africa
31 GWAZI
32 Rhino Rally
33 Train Stations
34 Marrakesh Theater

BUSCH
GARDENS

Busch Gardens at a glance

Location	Busch Boulevard, Tampa; 75–90 minutes drive from Orlando
Size	335 acres in 11 themed areas
Hours	9.30 or 10am–6pm off peak; 9am–9pm high season (Easter, summer holidays, Thanksgiving, Christmas)
Admission	Under 3, free; 3–9, $39 (one-day ticket), $78 (3-day Value Ticket with SeaWorld), $158 (5-Park Flex Ticket, inc. Universal Studios, SeaWorld and Wet 'n Wild); adults (10+) $48, $94, $197
Parking	$6
Lockers	Yes; in Morocco, Congo, Egypt and Stanleyville; $1
Pushchairs Wheelchairs	$9 and $15 ($2 refundable; in Morocco) $9 ($2 refundable) and $35 ($5 refundable; same location)
Top Attractions	Rhino Rally, Kumba, Congo River Rapids, Edge of Africa, Elephant Wash, Mystic Sheikhs Band
Don't Miss	*World Rhythms on Ice*, Myombe Reserve, Edge of Africa, Elephant Wash, Mystic Sheikhs band
Hidden Costs	**Meals** — Burger, chips and coke $7.38 / 3-course meal $21 (Crown Colony House)
	Kids' meal — $3.99 ($4.50–$4.75 Crown Colony House)
	T-shirts — $15.99–$24.99
	Souvenirs — $0.79–$595
	Sundries — Clydesdale family photo $19.95

crowds behind in Orlando, but, unfortunately, in high season you'd be wrong. It is still advisable to be here in time for opening, if only to be first in line to ride the amazing new Rhino Rally or the dazzling roller-coasters Gwazi, Kumba and Montu, which all draw queues of up to an hour. The Congo River Rapids, Stanley Falls log flume ride and Tanganyika Tidal Wave (all opportunities to get wet!) are also prime rides, as is Akbar's Adventure Tours and the other two roller-coasters, Python and Scorpion. The queues take longer to build up here, so for the first few hours you can

enjoy a relatively crowd-free experience, even in high season.

Busch Gardens is divided into 11 main sections, with the major rides all a bit of a hike from the main entrance. Rhino Rally, which opened in summer 2001, looked sure to attract the majority of early birds, so I would definitely head here first (especially as the animals are more visible early in the day). Bear right through Morocco, turn left into Nairobi, pass the train station and the Rally entrance is opposite the elephant habitat. Gwazi, the fabulous wooden double-coaster, is another to draw a crowd relatively quickly, so, if you are tempted by this first, bear left through Morocco past the Zagora Café and you will soon arrive in its own purpose-built area. Then go through Stanleyville to Congo for Kumba, and retrace your steps to do Congo River Rapids, the Python and the other two water rides. Alternatively, turn right through the main entrance and visit Egypt for Montu and Akbar's. Here is the full 335-acre layout.

Morocco

Coming through the main gates brings you first into **Morocco**, home of all the main guest services and a lot of the best shops. *Epcot's* Moroccan pavilion sets the scene rather better, but the architecture is still impressive and this version won't overtax your wallet quite as much as Disney does! For a quick meal try the **Zagora Café**, especially at breakfast when the marching, dancing, eight-piece brass band **Mystic Sheikhs** swing into action to entertain the early crowds. Alternatively, the wonderfully enticing **Sultan's Sweets** serves coffee and pastries. Watch out, too, for the strolling **Men of Note**, a scintillating four-piece a cappella group, and the costumed characters like TJ the Tiger and Hilda Hippo. The **Sultan's Tent** provides a first animal encounter in the form of a resident snake charmer, while turning the corner brings you to the alligator pen. Morocco is also home to two of the park's biggest shows. The **Marrakesh Theater** offers the new 25-minute *Moroccan Roll* song and dance show, with live musicians, top-notch singers and energetic dancers all in an amusing pastiche of pop and rock with a desert theme (hence songs like *Midnight At The Oasis* and *Rock The Casbah*). AAA. The **Moroccan Palace Theater** houses the award-winning and unmissable *World Rhythms on Ice*

show. Even if the thought of an ice show doesn't immediately appeal to you, think again, because this is a surprising and highly entertaining 30-minute spectacular celebrating different cultures around the world. The costumes (some 95 of them) are terrific, the music is vibrant and enhanced by video screens to either side of the stage, and there are a several breathtaking special effects which sum up a brilliant concept here. It is also air-conditioned, a welcome relief in summer. AAAAA.

Crown Colony

This area sits in the park's bottom right corner and has five distinct components. Here, you can take the **Skyride** cablecar (AAA) on a one-way trip to The Congo (and providing a great look at Rhino Rally). The **Clydesdale Hamlet** is also here, but if you've seen the massive dray horses and their stables at SeaWorld, the set-up is pretty similar (AA). The **Showjumping Hall of Fame** can also be found here, for equine devotees.

Akbar's Adventure Tours (actually part of Egypt's attractions but located in Crown Colony because it replaced the Questor ride in 1998): another in the array of simulator rides, this relies as much on fun as thrills. The TV pre-show leads its audience into the world of down-at-heel Akbar (brilliantly played by comedian Martin Short) and his home-made (and untried) excursion machine. It explores, in unconventional fashion, the secrets and treasures of ancient Egypt, but don't expect a smooth ride – a mysterious force takes control in the forbidden tomb and the trip takes a high-speed turn for the unexpected! It is not recommended for anyone with back or neck problems or expectant mothers, while the height restriction is 3ft 6in. TTTT. The **Crown Colony Restaurant,**

Rhino Rally

Provisions and Terrace: this large Victorian-styled building overlooks the Serengeti Plain and affords counter-service salads, sandwiches and pizzas (downstairs) or a full-service restaurant upstairs with magnificent views of the animals roaming the Plain. For a memorable lunch, book here early in the day or, better still, come back for dinner in the early evening and see the animals come down to the water hole.

Serengeti

The **Serengeti Plain** itself is a 49-acre spread of African savannah that is home to buffalo, antelope, zebra, giraffe, wildebeest, ostriches, hippos, rhinos and many exotic birds, and can be viewed for much of the journey on the **Serengeti Express Railway**, a full-size, open-car steam train that chugs slowly from its main station in Nairobi to Egypt and all the way round to Congo, Stanleyville and back (AAA). It is a good ride during the main part of the day when queues build up at the thrill rides.

Rhino Rally: new in summer 2001 was this wonderfully dramatic and scenic ride which starts out as an off-road jeep safari and changes into an innovative raft adventure as your 17-passenger vehicle gets caught up in a flash flood. The blockbuster 8-minute whirl through the wilds of Africa includes encounters with elephants, rhinos, crocodiles, antelope and more, as the off-road part of the ride is just about as 'real' as they can make it. Your driver adds to the fun with some amusing spiel about the Rally and your purpose-built (by Land Rover) vehicle, but it soon becomes clear your 'navigator' (the front seat passenger) has led you up the garden path into a blind gully. An unused pontoon bridge is your only way out, but fate (or rather, the ride designer!) has a unique twist in store, which opens the way to part two of the ride and the thrilling raging river section that is unlike any attraction to date. Check this out (but get here early to beat the queues). TTTT/AAAAA. Height restriction is just 3ft.

Edge of Africa

This 15-acre safari experience guarantees a close-up encounter almost as good as the real thing. The walk-through attraction puts you in an authentic setting of natural wilds and native villages (right down to the imported plants and even the smells), from which you can view giraffes, lions, baboons, meerkats, crocodiles, hyenas, vultures and even get an underwater view of a specially designed hippopotamus habitat. Look out for the abandoned jeep – you can sit in the front cab while lions lounge in the back! Wandering

Hippos at the Edge of Africa

BRIT TIP: Edge of Africa offers some wonderful photo opportunities, but, in the hot months, come here early in the day as many animals seek refuge from the heat later in the day.

'safari guides' and naturalists offer informal talks, and the attention to detail is wonderful. AAAAA. You can also sign up here for the Serengeti Safari by truck (see below).

Nairobi

Nairobi is home to the awesome **Myombe Reserve**, one of the largest and most realistic habitats for the threatened highland gorillas and chimpanzees of central Africa. This 3-acre walk-through has a superb tropical setting where the temperature is kept artificially high and convincing with the aid of lush forest landscaping and hidden water mist sprays. Take your time, especially as there are good, seated vantage points, and be patient to catch these magnificent creatures going about their daily routine. It is also highly informative, with attendants usually on hand to answer any questions. AAAAA.

At **JR's Gorilla Hut** you can buy your own cuddly baby gorilla (a cuddly toy, of course!) while you can get a snack or soft drink at the **Myombe Outpost**. This is also the place to see the Gardens' Asian elephants (check the advertised times for the **Elephant Wash**, which is always worth watching) and the **Animal Nursery**, which houses all manner of rehabilitating and hand-reared creatures that can be seen close up. Continuing round the Nursery brings you to the **Reptile House and Tortoise Habitat**. The **Curiosity Caverns**, just to the left

of the Nursery, are easy to miss but don't if you want to catch a glimpse of various nocturnal and rarely seen creatures in a clever, cave-like setting.

Timbuktu

Passing through Nairobi brings you to the more ride-dominated area of the park, starting with **Timbuktu**. Here in a North African desert setting you will find many of the elements of a traditional fun fair, with a couple of brain-scrambling rides and two good shows.

Scorpion: a 50mph roller-coaster, this features a 62ft drop and a 360-degree loop that is guaranteed to dial D for dizzy for a while afterwards. The ride lasts just 120 seconds, but it seems longer! The queues build up here from late morning to mid-afternoon, and you have to be at least 3ft 6in tall to ride. TTTT. **The Phoenix** is a positively evil invention, sitting its passengers in a gigantic, boat-shaped swing that eventually performs a full 360-degree rotation in dramatic, slow-motion style. Don't eat just before this one! TTTT. **Sandstorm** is a fairly routine whirligig contraption that spins and levitates at fairly high speed (hold on to your stomach). TTT. The **Crazy Camel** is an odd sort of ride resembling a giant sombrero that spins and tilts its riders into a state of dizziness. TT. Then there are a series of scaled-down **Kiddie Rides** that always seem popular with the under 10s (and give mum and dad a break as well). The **Carousel Caravan** offers the chance to ride a genuine Mary Poppins-type carousel, while there is also the inevitable **Electronic Arcade** and a **Games Area** of side shows and stalls that require a few extra dollars to play. **Das Festhaus** is a combined German Bierfest and entertainment hall, offering a

6

mixture of German and Italian food. It's a jolly, rather raucous establishment, with the 25-minute *International Celebration* show featuring singers, dancers and musicians four or five times a day (AAA). The final element is the **Dolphin Theater**, complete with its aluminium sculpture outside that is a homage to the value of recycling. The 25-minute Dolphins of the Deep show borrows heavily from SeaWorld's education-orientated dolphin offering, but still comes up with some terrific leaps, stunts and tricks. AAAA.

Congo

You're into serious ride territory here, with the unmistakable giant turquoise structure of **Kumba** looming over the area. First of all, it's one of the largest and fastest roller-coaster in the south-east United States and, at 60mph, it features three unique elements: a diving loop which plunges the riders a full 110ft; a camelback, with a full 360-degree spiral that induces a feeling of weightlessness for three seconds; and a 108ft vertical loop. For good measure, it dives underground at one point! It looks terrifying close up, but it is absolutely exhilarating, even for non-coaster fans. The height restriction here is 4ft 6in. TTTTT.

The **Congo River Rapids** look pretty tame after that, but don't be fooled. These giant rubber tyres will bounce you down some of the most convincing rapids outside of the Rockies, and you will end up with a fair soaking for good measure. TTTT. The **Ubanga-Banga Bumper Cars** are just that, typical fairground dodgems (TT), and you won't miss anything by passing them by for the more daring **Python**, the fourth of Busch Gardens' roller-coasters, with this one featuring a

double spiral corkscrew at 50mph from a drop of some 70ft. Height restriction here is 4ft, and the whole ride lasts just 70 seconds, but it's a blast. TTTT. There are also some more **Kiddie Rides** for the smaller visitors. The **Vivi Storehouse Restaurant** offers chicken fajitas, club sandwiches, salads and desserts, and there are two gift shops, including the **Tiger's Den**.

Stanleyville

You pass over Claw Island, home of the park's spectacular rare white Bengal tigers, to get to **Stanleyville**, which all rather merges into one area from the Congo. Here there are more watery rides, with the popular **Stanley Falls Log Flume** ride (almost identical to the ones at Chessington, Legoland, Thorpe Park and Alton Towers), which guarantees a good soaking at the final drop (TTT) and the distinctly cleverer **Tanganyika Tidal Wave**, which takes you on a scenic ride along 'uncharted' African waters before tipping you down a two-stage drop which really does land with tidal-wave force. TTTT.

> BRIT TIP: Don't stand on the bridge into the neighbouring Orchid Canyon unless you want to catch the full weight of the Tidal Wave!

Stanleyville Theater is a good place to relax and put your feet up for a while as you are entertained by the unusual *Jungle Fantasy* show, a mix of circus and acrobatics (direct from St Petersburg, Russia) which provide 30 minutes of offbeat entertainment (AAA). For a hearty, if somewhat messy, meal, visit the **Stanleyville Smokehouse** – their wood-smoked ribs platter is a delight. As you leave Stanleyville behind, say hello to the muntjac deer and orang-utans (who are rarely active during the day) in the large pens either side of the Train Station.

Land of the Dragons

Parents will want to know about this large, wonderfully clever area of activities, entertainment, rides and attractions purely for the young 'uns. It features a three-storey treehouse complete with towers and maze-like stairways, a rope climb, ball crawl and outdoor **Dragon's Tale Theater**, which features the 15-minute show with *Captain Kangaroo's Roo Crew* – fun, friendship and ping-pong balls! It is all good, knockabout, well-supervised stuff, and some of the kiddie rides are superbly inventive, as well as offering plenty of opportunity to get wet. TTTTT (youngsters only – but mums and dads can watch!).

Bird Gardens

Your anti-clockwise route now brings you to the most peaceful area, the **Bird Gardens**. Here it is possible to unwind from the usual theme park hurly-burly. The exhibits and shows are all family-orientated, too, with the 30-minute *For The Birds* presented in the **Bird Show Theater** (part of the original park attraction in 1959; AAA) and the **Hospitality Patio**, where the resident band plays a mix of musical favourites, past and present. **Lory Landing** is a desert island-themed walk-through bird encounter featuring lorikeets, hornbills, parrots and more, with the chance to become a human perch and feed the friendly lorikeets (and have your ear nibbled!). A cup of nectar costs $1, but is a great investment for a memorable photo. Take a slow walk round to appreciate the lush, tropical foliage, and special displays such as the walk-through **Aviary, Flamingo Island, Eagle Canyon** and the emus. The highlight of the Bird Gardens, confusingly enough, is the **Koala Display**, in the bottom corner, where these natives of Australia happily sit and seemingly do nothing all day while drawing large crowds for doing so. A moving walkway takes you through this gentle exhibit, which also showcases kangaroos and ring-tailed lemurs.

A free taste of Anheuser-Busch products is on offer in **Hospitality House**, and you can also enroll for **Beer School**, a 40-minute session into the process of beer-making. It offers a fascinating glimpse into the brewery world, and is excellently explained, with the bonus of some tasting! You also get a Brewery Master certificate. AAA (21s and over only).

Gwazi: now included as part of the Bird Gardens, although it started life as an area in its own right, Busch's most recent roller-coaster is a massive 'duelling' wooden creation in the classic mould (i.e. no inversions). The two sets of cars, the Gwazi Lion and Gwazi Tiger, each top 50mph and generate a G-force of up to 3.5 as they career around nearly 7,000ft of track with six fly-by encounters. You get to choose your ride in the intricately themed 8-acre village plaza and then you are off up the 90ft lift for a breathtaking 2½ minutes. The shake, rattle 'n' roll effect of a classic coaster is cleverly re-created and the Lion and Tiger rides are slightly different so you need to do both. Even if you don't like coasters, try this one. Restrictions: 4ft. TTTTT. Next door is the River Rumble game for kids, a series of catapults that fire water-filled balloons guaranteed to get everyone wet. TTTT (for under 12s). This actually costs an extra $3 for a bucket of 9 balloons (or $5 for two buckets).

6

The breathtaking Montu roller-coaster

Egypt

The final area of Busch Gardens is tucked away through the Crown Colony, so it is best visited either first thing or late in the day. **Egypt** is 8 acres of carefully recreated pharaoh country, dominated by the trademark roller-coaster **Montu**, named after an ancient Egyptian warrior-god. It is a truly breathtaking creation, one of the world's tallest and longest inverted

Congo River Rapids

coasters, covering nearly 4,000ft of track at speeds topping 60mph and peaking with a G-force of 3.85! Like Kumba, it looks terrifying, but in reality it is an absolute five-star thrill as it leaves your legs dangling and swoops and plunges (underground at two points) for almost 3 minutes of brain-scrambling fun. Restrictions: 4ft 6in. TTTTT.

You can travel back in time on a tour of **Tut's Tomb**, as it was discovered by archaeologist Howard Carter, with clever lighting, audio and even aroma effects. AAA. There is also a neat **Sand Pit** that invites youngsters to undertake their own excavations (with some little 'treasures' to be found!), while the shopping here takes on a high-quality air with its hand-blown glass items, elaborate sculptures and authentic cartouche paintings.

You should finally return to Morocco for a spot of shopping in the area's tempting bazaars. Middle

Lory Landing

Eastern brass, pottery and carpets will all tempt you into opening your wallet yet again, while there is a full range of Anheuser-Busch products and gift ideas if you haven't already fallen prey to the array of gift shops and cuddly-toy emporiums around the park.

And ...

In addition to all the aforementioned activities, you can enhance your visit by taking the **Serengeti Safari** tour, an excursion aboard flat-bed trucks to meet the Plain's giraffes, zebras, ostriches and rhinos close up and

learn more about the park's environmental efforts. You book up at the entrance to Edge of Africa for an extra $20, and places soon fill up (children must be at least 5 to take part).

For a full family day out, you can combine Busch Gardens with next-door water park **Adventure Island** (on McKinley Drive) which is particularly welcome when it hots up (provided you plaster on the sun tan cream). The 25 acres of watery fun, in a Key West theme, offer a full range of slides and rides, like the Wahoo Run adventure ride, the 76ft free-fall plunge of the Tampa Typhoon and the spiralling Calypso Coaster, kids' playground, cafés, gift shops, arcades and volleyball, plus the wonderful Splash Attack adventure, a water activity maze culminating in a 1,000-gallon bucket dump on the unwary! Adventure Island is open from mid-February to late October (weekends only Feb–Mar and Sept–Oct) 10am–5pm (later in high season) and a combined ticket with Busch Gardens costs $60 for adults and $50 for 3-9s.

Well, that's the full low-down on all the main theme parks now, but there are still a host of other attractions to consider. Let's move on ...

The Serengeti Safari

7

The Other Attractions
(or, One Giant Leap for Tourist Kind)

If you think you have seen everything Orlando has to offer by simply sticking to the theme parks, in the words of the song, 'You ain't seen nothin' yet'. It would be relatively easy to add the Kennedy Space Center to Chapter 6 because, although it's not strictly a theme park, it is adding new attractions all the time and is fast becoming a full day's excursion from Orlando to the east or 'space' coast.

Then there are Cypress Gardens and Silver Springs to give you a taste of the more natural things Florida has to offer, the Kissimmee attraction Splendid China for a completely different park experience, the mind-boggling Gatorland, with its alligators, crocs and gator shows (and great value, too), and the one-off family centres like Guinness World Records Experience, WonderWorks, the Orlando Science Center and Ripley's Believe It Or Not.

For more individual attractions, you have the unique aviation experience of Fantasy of Flight, and the Warbirds Air Museum, the hair-raising haunted house walk-through of Skull Kingdom plus the area's magnificent array of water fun parks.

Chapter 8 then introduces a range of alternatives that help you Get Off the Beaten Track and discover some of the real Sunshine State, while Chapter 9 unveils all the options for an evening out in Orlando by Night. The choice is yours, but it is an immense selection. Let's start here with One Giant Leap for Mankind.

Kennedy Space Center

The recent change to a fully ticketed entrance fee is a reflection of the massive amount of new development that has taken place at the home of NASA's space programme. More than $120 million has been spent on revamping the Kennedy Space Center's Visitor Complex in the last couple of years and, while it was always a great visit in the past, now it is simply unmissable, in my opinion, for its hugely imaginative depiction of the past, present and future of space exploration.

There are five continuous-running shows or exhibitions, four static showcases, a kids' play area (and a new show designed specifically for them), an art gallery, the all-new Astronaut Encounter, two splendid IMAX films and a full bus tour of the Space Center, which adds up to great value for the entrance fee.

You enter through the futuristic new ticket plaza and can spend several hours wandering around the exhibits and presentations of the 70-acre complex.

Robot Scouts is a walk-through display-cum-show in the company of Starquester 2000, your robot host who will explain the history of NASA's unmanned space probes in surprising and often amusing style. Next door, the **Quest for Life** film – narrated by *Deep Space Nine* star Avery Brooks – provides another illuminating view in the Universe Theater. Head on out and see some of the hardware of space flight in the **Rocket Garden**, and don't forget to stop by the **Astronaut Memorial**, a stark, sombre but very moving tribute to the men and women who have died in advancing the space programme.

Shuttle Plaza gives you the chance to inspect a full-size replica space shuttle, while the **Launch Status Center** displays actual flight hardware, plus live mission briefings. Free walking tours are available several times a day.

Early Space Exploration is a clever and coherent walk-through trip into the recent past of the space programme, including the *Hall of Discovery*, the *Mercury Mission Control Room* – the original consoles from America's first manned space flights – and the *Hall of History*. The futuristic **Exploration in the New Millennium** exhibit provides more appeal for youngsters, with a fun educational element from the spaceship-like *Exploring Gallery*, the *Mars Rock* exhibit and a series of interactive panels. New in 2001 was the kid-friendly **Mad Mission To Mars 2025** show, a mix of educational messages and pure fun theatricals, with lots of special effects, audience participation and even its own hip-hop song, *The Newton Rap*. Children from eight up should have a laugh or two here.

Perhaps the most innovative feature, though, is the **Astronaut Encounter**, with personal briefings, Q&A sessions, video footage and anecdotes from various veterans of the Mercury, Gemini and Apollo programmes, plus several Space Shuttle astronauts. It is an amazingly insightful, inspirational and engrossing feature, and takes place up to three times a day at the Center Plaza. Kids have their own playground, too, inside the **Children's Play Dome**, complete with a one-fifth scale space shuttle.

Owners Delaware North Parks Services have lavished a fortune on upgrading the Center and, for my money, it's an essential experience for all but pre-school children. In many ways, it knocks the artificiality of Disney and Co. into a cocked hat.

The air-conditioned **coach tour**, fully narrated throughout, makes three important stops in addition to driving around much of the working areas of the Space Center, including the truly massive Vehicle Assembly Building. The first stop is the new $7m **LC39 Observation Gantry**, just one mile from shuttle launch pad 39A, a combination four-storey observation deck and exhibition centre. The exhibits consist of a 10-minute film on the preparation of a shuttle for launch, models and videos of a launch countdown and touch-screen information on the shuttle programme. Next is the awesome **Apollo/Saturn V Center**, one of the area's truly great exhibits, where you can easily spend 90 minutes. It highlights the Apollo programme and first moon landing with two deeply impressive theatrical presentations on the risks and triumphs, with an actual 363ft Saturn V rocket and a hands-on gallery that brings the past, present and future of space exploration into sharp focus. It is also quite a humbling experience. Third stop is the **International Space Station Center**, another interactive attraction featuring the construction of this current project, with incredibly detailed mock-ups of the modules and a fascinating viewing gallery showing the workings of the Center. You should allow 3–4 hours to do the tour justice.

Additional tours are available at an extra $20 per person (adult or child). **Cape Canaveral: Then and Now** is a 2-hour-plus in-depth journey into the early days of space exploration around the older part of the facility. Highlights include the Air Force Space Museum, Mercury launch sites and Memorial, original astronaut training facility and several

KEY TO ORLANDO – MINOR ATTRACTIONS

A	Winter Park	S	Grand Cypress Equestrian Center
B	Aquatic Wonders Tours	T	Horse World Riding Stables
C	Boggy Creek Airboat Rides	U	Pirates Dinner Show
D	Port Canaveral	V	TD Waterhouse Center
E	Leu Gardens	W	Citrus Bowl Stadium
F	Warbird Air Museum	X	Osceola County Stadium
G	Green Meadows Petting Farm	Y	Central Florida Zoo
H	Sanford-Rivership Romance	Z	Sak Comedy Lab
I	WonderWorks	A1	Sleuth's Mystery Dinner Shows
J	Trolley and Train Museum	B1	Arabian Nights
K	Disney's Wilderness Preserve	C1	Forever Florida
L	Marriott's Orlando World Center	D1	Orlando Science Center
M	West Orange Trail Bikes	E1	Orange County History Center
N	Kissimmee Rodeo	F1	Lake Eola
O	Richard Petty Driving Experience	G1	Medieval Times
P	Black Hammock Fish Camp	H1	Guinness world Records Experience
Q	Dave's Ski School		Titanic, Ship of Dreams
R	Katie's Wekiva River Landing	J1	Skull Kingdom

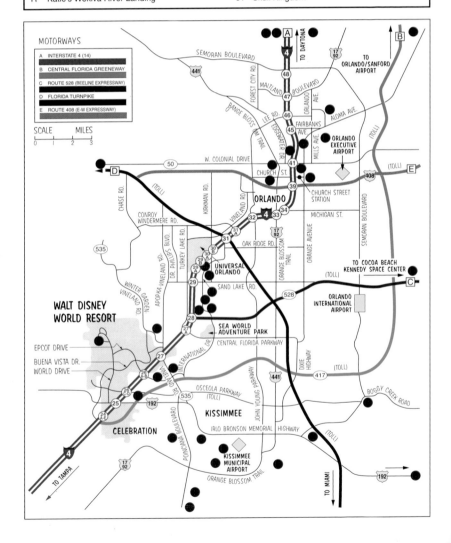

active launch pads, all of which are otherwise off-limits. The 90-minute **NASA Up Close** takes visitors along the astronaut's launch day routine, with a look at both launch pads, the Vehicle Assembly Building and the gigantic crawler transports.

Equally impressive are the IMAX cinemas – 55ft screens which give the impression of sitting on top of the action. The 37-minute film **The Dream Is Alive** puts you inside a space shuttle mission, and the 3-D **L5: First City in Space** is a breathtaking slice of science fiction based on science fact. Both films are included in the admission price.

The Visitor Complex boasts an excellent **Space Shop**, four restaurants, including the full-service **Mila's**, and three snack counters. Even the Apollo/Saturn V Center has its own café where you can sit and marvel at it all.

To get to the Kennedy Space Center, take the Beeline Expressway out of Orlando (Highway 528, and it's a toll road, remember) for about 45 minutes, then bear left on the SR 407 (Don't follow the signs to Cape Canaveral or Cocoa Beach at this point) and turn right at the T-junction on to SR 405. The Space Center's Visitor Center is located 6 miles along SR 405 on the right-hand side. Opening hours are 9am to dusk every day except Christmas Day, and the Center gets busiest around lunchtime. The complex is open daily (but not on Shuttle launch days – call 321 449 4444 to check if you may be affected) from 9am and the first tours and IMAX presentations start at 9.30am, while the final tour of the day is 2 hours before dark. Adult admission is $25 and $15 for children 3–11. Parking is free. For more details, log on to www.kennedyspacecenter.com. Total attraction rating: AAAAA.

The greatest thrill of all, however, is an actual **shuttle launch**, of which there are six or seven a year. You can call 321 449 4444 for dates and information, while Launch Transportation Tickets to a viewing area just 6 miles from the launch pad are available to buy online or by calling the number above. Adult tickets cost around $40, while children (3–11) cost around $29. However, in the event of a launch cancellation, there are NO refunds, and the traffic in the area is usually humongous, taking anything up to 3 hours to get from Orlando to the KSC. Alternatively, prime viewing sites are available outside the Space Center along Highway 1 in Titusville and Highway A1A through Cape Canaveral and Cocoa Beach. To be on hand for a shuttle launch is an awe-inspiring experience.

Astronaut Hall of Fame

7

While the Kennedy Space Center tells you primarily about the machinery of putting men in space, the neighbouring Astronaut Hall of Fame (on SR 405, just before the main entrance to the Space Center)

Kennedy Space Center

gives you the full low-down on the people involved. This museum to the space programmes houses some fascinating memorabilia, interactive exhibits and engaging explanations of the people behind the spacesuits. Prepare to be amazed at how incredibly small the cockpits of the early manned spaceflights were and amused by personal touches like Buzz Aldrin's High School report!

A chronologically coherent approach divides the Hall of Fame into six main sections. The **Entry Experience** introduces the visions of space flight, with an 8-minute video of the astronauts as modern explorers, and leads into **Race to the Moon**, the stories of the Mercury, Gemini and Apollo missions and their people. The **New Frontier** opens the way for Skylab and Shuttle missions, adjacent to the **Astronaut Hall of Fame**, the museum's heart and soul. **Space Explorers Today and Tomorrow** includes the audio-visual experience aboard the replica Shuttle to Tomorrow and a glimpse of the Space Camp for kids, before introducing the hands-on **Astronaut Adventure** with its working models, G-force and flight simulators (a cabin that does six 360-degree rolls!), space-walk 'chairs', moon exploration, interactive computers and Mars Mission experience. Active minds will be more than rewarded. The **First on the Moon** exhibit also focuses on the selection of the Apollo 11 crew.

Admission is $13.95 for adults and $9.95 for kids (6–12; 5 and under

BRIT TIP: Every Friday is Space Camp graduation day, so avoid the Hall of Fame then unless you want to be surrounded by dozens of highly enthusiastic 'space cadets' and their parents.

free), with opening hours 9am–5pm (7pm in holiday periods), 7 days a week. If you enjoyed the Kennedy Space Center, try to spend a couple of hours here. Total attraction rating: AAAA.

There is also the usual gift shop, with refreshments provided by the **Cosmic Café**. The residential **Space Camp** may be of interest to you if you have children of 9–12 who would like to train to be junior astronauts for 5 days. It's not a cheap programme – $699/child – but it is a magnificent educational recreation for kids, and the Camp is happy to take visitors from the UK. You have to book up about 2 months in advance, but then just bring your youngsters along on Sunday afternoon and they are taken off your hands until Friday morning. They are arranged into groups and go through activities like flight and space-walk simulators, simulated space missions, studying rocket propulsion, space technology and other scientific experiments. If your youngster is mad keen on being an astronaut, sign him or her up for Space Camp! For details, phone 407 267 3184 or, look up their website at www.AstronautHallofFame.com.

Cypress Gardens

Turning from the futuristic to the more natural, Cypress Gardens offers more than 200 acres of immaculate botanical gardens, spectacular flower festivals, world-famous water-ski shows and plenty of good ol' southern hospitality. It was, in fact, the first 'theme park' in Florida, pre-dating *Walt Disney World* by 35 years, and it has gradually expanded to remain a pleasant alternative to the usual park experience. A new mini water park also now provides a real child-friendly aspect for the first time.

It is about a 45-minute drive from

Kissimmee, down I4, turning off at Exit 23. Go south on Highway 27 for 20 miles and then right on to SR 540. Cypress Gardens is 6 miles along SR 540, on the left.

After the major tourist hustle of Orlando, the Gardens are an island of peace and tranquillity. Plan on spending the best part of a day here, too, as there is plenty to keep everyone amused. Start with a boat tour round the canals of the **Botanical Gardens** (NB: this attraction had to close in summer 2001 because the drought situation meant water levels were too low to operate boats), then stroll round the gardens themselves, taking note of the immense **Banyan Tree** (unlike the *Magic Kingdom* Park's Swiss Family Treehouse, this one is real!), the photogenic **Southern Belles** in their colourful period outfits and the beautiful **Gazebo**, which hosts more than 300 weddings a year.

Retracing your steps brings you to the spectacular **Water Ski Show**, which features world-class skiers and world-famous routines (odd fact: Cypress Gardens' ski show is the world's longest-running single attraction, operating every day since 1942). There is also a water-ski adventure programme for $25 per person and a deluxe package with VIP backstage tour, T-shirt and souvenir photo for $50 (visit the Information Desk on your way in to book a place).

Continue on and have your picture taken in front of the **Mediterranean Waterfall**, then marvel at the delights of the centrepiece garden attraction: the **Spring Flower Festival** runs from March to May, the **Victorian Garden Party** (featuring clever topiary 'statues') all year long, the **Mum Festival** (featuring more than 2.5 million chrysanthemum blooms) in November and the **Poinsettia Festival/Festival of Trees** from the end of November to early January.

Next up are the **Plantation Gardens**, which offer the practical side of gardening with tips on 'how to grow' herbs, vegetables, roses and other flowers. Also here is the **Wings of Wonder** exhibit, a huge butterfly house where more than 1,000 butterflies hatch from glass cabinets and flutter around in tropical splendour. Stop off for a *Gone with the Wind* experience at the beautifully restored **Magnolia Mansion**. The **Island in the Sky** will then lift you up 15 storeys on its circular revolving platform for a grandstand view of the park. Model railway fans are also well catered for at the indoor, 20-train **Cypress Junction**, with replicas of various US landmarks on 1,100ft of track, while next door is **Carousel Cove**, a selection of games, rides and other activities to keep the youngsters amused for a while. New in 2001, just through Carousel Cove, is the **Wacky Water Park** (open from 10.30am–5pm daily; closed in winter), which offers kids – from toddlers to teens – the chance to really expend some energy on a series of pools, slides, flumes and splash areas. The main pool is geared primarily for under 8s, with a zero-depth entry and greatest depth of only 18 inches. It features an array of squirting animals, small slides and splash zones (including a tropical 'volcano'!), while the Flumarama section has six slides and one tube ride, from the rather tame (by Blizzard Beach standards) Coral Reef to the whizzier Typhoon Twister. Changing rooms and lockers are also available here as the park adds a completely different dimension to its appeal.

Also new in 2001 was the huge **FloraDome**, a beautiful covered flower exhibit of thousands of blooms that changes several times a year, with the extra scenic elements of waterfalls, streams and a large-scale model railway.

7

The beautiful Gazebo

In addition to the water-ski extravaganza, there are two other notable shows offering contrasting live entertainment at various times. The **Palace Theater** houses the spectacular *Moscow on Ice* show (in great air-conditioned comfort), while **Nature's Arena** offers *Calling All Animals* – featuring macaws, a playful coatimundi, a gator and 15ft albino python – three times daily. A mini zoo showcases the likes of wallabies, fallow deer and cotton-top tamarins in **Nature's Way** and **Nature's Boardwalk** (including the inevitable Gator Gulch), while the **Birdwalk Aviary** is a walk-through encounter with lorikeets and Australian parrots that eat out of your hand. The pretty **Southern Breeze** paddle wheel riverboat provides historical excursions on Lake Eloise during the day for a small extra fee and themed dinner cruises in the evening and for Sunday brunch (separate ticket required – call 863 324 2111 to book, or call at the ticket booth during your visit).

There are 14 shops and gift stores

to tempt you into buying yet more souvenirs, from the children-friendly **Butterfly Shop**, to **Sweet Creations** (home-made fudge and real citrus juice, marmalades and jellies). The **Village Fare** food court offers a good choice of eating, from freshly carved roast beef to pizza and salads, while the **Cypress BBQ** serves up barbecue-smoked chicken and ribs, and the **Crossroads Restaurant** is full-service dining in air-conditioned comfort. Again, there's no shortage of choice, quality is consistently high and value for money is good.

Cypress Gardens is open 9.30am–5pm, with extended hours during the festivals, including until

The Spring Flower Festival

8pm for the spectacular **Spring Lights** (Feb 1–April 30) and 9pm for the **Garden of Lights Holiday Festival** (Nov 21–Jan 6), neither of which should be missed if you have the chance. The former features more than four million twinkling lights, a 110ft Tree of Light and fireworks every Saturday evening, while the latter is themed to a Christmas story, with festive set-pieces and a positive explosion of glistening lights, and a 116ft Christmas tree which alone boasts some 25,000 lights.

Admission is $32.95 for adults and $16.95 for 6–12s (under 6s free). Check out www.cypressgardens.com for the latest info. Parking is $5. Total attraction rating: AAAA.

Ski show at Cypress Gardens

Silver Springs

Continuing the theme of more natural attractions, we have Silver Springs, just under 2 hours' drive to the north of Orlando. This peaceful 350-acre nature park (don't worry, you won't have to walk round all of it) surrounds the headwaters of the crystal-clear Silver River. Glass-bottomed boats take you for a close-up view of the artesian springs (the largest in the world) that bubble up here, along with plenty of wildlife. Expect close encounters with alligators, turtles, raccoons and plenty of waterfowl, while the park also contains a collection of more exotic animals, like bears, panthers, giraffes, camels and zebras that can be viewed from either land or water. Four animal shows, an alligator and crocodile encounter, the world's largest bear exhibit, a petting zoo, a kids' adventure playground and a white alligator exhibit complete the attractions. To ruin a few more illusions of the film industry, this was the setting for the 1930s and 40s Tarzan films starring Johnny Weissmuller. And, once you have absorbed the timeless tropical nature of the landscape, you will understand why they decided to save on the cost of shipping the film crew to Africa.

> **BRIT TIP:** Silver Springs and Wild Waters are both busy at weekends. Otherwise, you shouldn't encounter many queues here.

Silver Springs is located on SR 40 just through the town of Ocala, 72 miles to the north of Orlando. Take the Florida Turnpike north (it's a toll road, remember) until it turns into I75 and, 28 miles further north, you turn off and head east on SR 40. Another 10 miles brings you to Silver Springs, just past the Wild Waters water park on your right (NB: The park will be closed Monday-Wednesday from early September to February 1).

Silver Springs' main attraction (dating back to 1878) is its **Glass-bottomed Boats**, 20-minute rides which go down well with all the family and give a first-class view of the seven different springs and a host of water life. Similarly, the **Lost River Voyage** is another 20-minute boat trip down one of the unspoilt stretches of the Silver River including a visit to the park's animal hospital where the local park ranger introduces you to all his current charges. The third boat trip on offer, the **Jungle Cruise**, is effectively a water safari, where animals from six continents, including giraffes, ostriches and antelope, are arranged in natural settings along the riverbanks.

As an alternative to messing about on the river, the **Jeep Safari** is a 15-minute ride in the back of an open trailer through a natural forest habitat, home to more animals from other corners of the world, such as tapirs, marmosets, antelope and vultures (plus a drive-through alligator pond!). Then there are the three **Ross Allen Island Animal Shows**, each one lasting 15 minutes and featuring an entertaining – and occasionally hair-raising – look at the worlds of reptiles, birds (including comical parrots, macaws and cockatoos) and creepy crawlies. The hair-raising occurs only if you are the unlucky victim chosen to

Silver Springs glass-bottomed boat

display a large tarantula, giant cockroach or scorpion. As you exit the animal shows take time to wander **Big Gator Lagoon** and the **Crocodile Encounter** in a one-acre cypress swamp habitat, viewed from a raised boardwalk. See the largest American crocodile in captivity, the 16ft, 2,000lb Sobek, as well as a collection of alligators, turtles and Galapagos tortoises. The **Florida Natives** attraction features a collection of snakes, turtles, spiders, otters and other denizens of the state. The **Botanical Gardens** then provide a peaceful haven to sit and watch the world go by for a while.

Other large-scale exhibits are the **World of Bears**, an educational presentation including conservation information in a 2-acre spread devoted to bears of all kinds (the largest of its type in the world), from grizzly to spectacled and black bears, and the **Panther Prowl**, with a unique look at the endangered Florida panther and Western cougar. Both of these have educational presentations on their welfare several times daily. **Birds of Prey** is a 30-minute show in the Silver River Showcase arena highlighting the strengths, beauty and conservation issues of the park's collection of hawks, eagles, owls, falcons and vultures in a dramatic free-flight demonstration.

Children are not forgotten, either. The **Kids Ahoy!** playland, with its centrepiece riverboat featuring slides, rides, an air bounce, ball crawl, 3-D net maze, carousel, bumper boats and games, and **Doolittle's Petting Zoo**, with its deer and goats, are both big draws for the young ones.

The usual collection of shops and eateries are fairly ordinary here, in contrast to the slick appeal of Orlando's parks, although the **Deli** offers some pleasant sandwich alternatives for lunch and the **Springside Restaurant** is above average. In all, you would probably want to spend a good half day here, with the possibility of a few hours in the neighbouring 9-acre water park of **Wild Waters**, which offers slides like the Twin Twister, a pair of 60ft-high flumes, the free-fall Thunderbolt, the twin-tunnelled Tornado, the 220ft-long Silver Bullet and the helter-skelter Osceola's Revenge, as well as a 400ft tube ride on the turbo-charged Hurricane, a huge wave pool, and various kid-sized fun in Cool Kids Cove and Caribbean Sprayground.

Parking is $5 and admission fees are $31.95 for adults, $28.95 for seniors (55+) and $22.95 for children under 48 inches tall (under 3s free). A joint ticket (Silver Springs and Wild Waters) is $33.95 and $24.95. Open 10am–5pm seven days a week Mar–Sep, Thursday–Sunday only Sep–Feb (Wild Waters open 10am– 5 or 7pm Mar–Sep only). Look up www.silversprings.com for more info or call 352 236 2121. Attraction rating: AAAA.

Splendid China

New in 1994 and still expanding and modifying its various displays and exhibits, Splendid China is unique to central Florida and a completely different type of attraction (although it was having to rectify two years of mis-management in 2001 that had left the park looking rather run down). You won't find rides and other flights of fancy, but you will be taken on a fascinating journey through one of the biggest and most mysterious and breathtaking countries in the world.

This elaborate 76-acre park offers a range of intricate, miniaturised features like the Great Wall of China, the Forbidden City and the Stone Forest, some fascinating full-size exhibits, thrilling acrobats and martial arts experts, and, naturally enough, some great food. There is a play area for young children, but realistically, the park will not hold their attention for long, and, in summer there is little escape from the relentless heat. But where it scores impressively is in its amazing eye for detail, its air of authenticity (genuine Chinese craftsmen were brought in to hand-build every miniature) and its peaceful atmosphere – quite an achievement in the tourist bustle of Orlando!

Splendid China is located at the western end of the main tourist drag of Highway 192, three miles west of its junction with I4, just off the main road opposite the big Key W Kool Restaurant, on Splendid China Boulevard. The minimum time requirement is 3–4 hours, and you can easily spend half a day taking in all the different shows and attractions. Here's how its 10,000-mile journey through 5,000 years of history works. The four elements are essentially:

The exhibits: more than 60 painstakingly recreated scale models of China's greatest buildings, statues and landmarks. The **Great Wall** is one of the most striking, at half a mile long and up to 5½ft high. It is constructed of more than six million tiny bricks, all faithfully put into place by hand. Other highlights include Beijing's **Imperial Palace and Forbidden City**, the 26-storey **Grand Buddha of Leshan** (reduced to a 'mere' 36ft tall), and the **Mausoleum of Genghis Khan**. The stairs by the side of the **Mausoleum of Dr Sun Yat Sen** afford a wonderful high-rise overview of the park, while the famous **Terracotta Warriors** exhibit offers a chance to get in the air-conditioned cool for a minute or two. Splendid China is three-quarters the size of the *Magic Kingdom*, so it demands a fair amount of leg work to appreciate fully all the exhibits (which the new

management was actively involved in refurbishing after many had been allowed to slip into a rather unkempt state).

The shows: There are four centres for the performing arts which showcase the talents of some top musicians, artists, acrobats and martial arts exponents. Inside the park, the **Temple of Light Theater** is the main centre, staging internationally acclaimed acrobatic exhibitions of around 30 minutes a time. On the opposite side of the park is the **Pagoda Gardens Show Area**, which features gold medal-winning Martial Artists from China's Shandong Province. In the heart of the park is the **Imperial Bells Theater**, with Chinese traditional music and instruments, including ancient bells and drums. The highlight, though, is the **Golden Peacock Theater** next to the park entrance. During the day, dance and folk costume shows are presented, and, in the evening, it features the 90-minute spectacular (not on Mondays) *Mysterious Kingdom of the Orient*, which showcases the talents of some 50 dancers, acrobats and martial artists in magnificent costumes. You will need to get your entry ticket validated if you leave the park early and want to return for this show, or you can pay the $14.95 (children 5–12 $9.95) for the show on its own, which includes a free buffet-style meal.

The restaurants: the park sets great store by its food, whether it be in its sumptuous five-star restaurant or its cafeteria-style buffet. The jewel in the crown is the elegant **Suzhou Pearl Restaurant** for full-service, gourmet cuisine, while more budget-priced is the **Seven Flavors**, a cafeteria-style diner offering American food as well as Chinese dishes.

The shops: unlike the other theme parks, Splendid China's shopping opportunities are all located in the Chinatown front area of the park which is open to the general public without park admission. The ten gift shops are also one up on their counterparts by stocking a more up-market and distinctive range of goods, from Bonsai trees to furniture, jewellery to T-shirts, silk and satin clothing to children's toys, and antique curios to contemporary artefacts. In many instances you can watch the local craftsmen and women at work producing the various wares.

The mixture of Chinese and Floridian staff adds to the friendly atmosphere the park generates, but ultimately it is a difficult concept to describe so the best advice is to see it for yourself. Adult admission is $26.99 and children (5–12) are $16.99 (under 5s free). You can also take a guided walking tour for an extra $5.35 per person or do a guided tour by electric buggy (which takes five people) for $48.15. Opening hours are 9.30am–6pm 7 days a week and parking is free. Attraction rating: AAAA.

Splendid China

The spectacular Mysterious Kingdom of the Orient show at Splendid China

Gatorland

For another taste of the 'real' Florida, this is as authentic as it gets when it comes to the wildlife, and consequently it is popular with children of all ages. When the wildlife consists of several thousand menacing alligators and crocodiles in various natural habitats and four fascinating shows, you know you're in for a different experience. 'The Alligator Capital of the World' was founded in 1949 and is still a family-owned attraction, hence it possesses a home-spun charm which few of its big-money competitors can match.

Start by taking the new **Gatorland Express** railway around the park to get an idea of its 110-acre expanse. Wander through the natural Florida countryside beauty of the 2,000ft **Swamp Walk**, as well as the **Alligator Breeding Marsh Walkway**, with its three-storey observation tower, and get a close-up view of these great reptiles who seem to hang around the walkway in the hope someone might 'drop in' for lunch. Breeding pens, baby alligator nurseries and rearing ponds are also situated throughout the park to provide an idea of the growth cycle of the Florida gator and enhance the overall feeling that it is the visitor who is behind bars and not the animals. Many of the small-scale attractions have been designed with kids in mind and there is plenty

BRIT TIP: If you have an evening flight home, Gatorland is a handy place to visit on your final day. Conveniently located, it is the ideal place to soak up half a day or so.

to keep even the youngest amused, notably at **Lilly's Pad**, an imaginative water playground guaranteed to get them good and wet (swimming costumes definitely advisable). **Allie's Barnyard** is the petting zoo, while you can feed some friendly lorikeets at the **Very Merry Aviary**. Other animals on view include bats, iguanas, turtles, turkey vultures, tortoises, snakes, flamingos, emus, a Florida bear and deer.

However, the gators and crocs are the main attraction and it is the three shows which are the real draw (although you will never find yourself on the end of a queue here). The 800-seat **Wrestling Stadium** sets the scene for some real Cracker-style feats (a Cracker is the local term for a Florida cowboy) as Gatorland's resident 'wranglers' catch themselves a 7–8ft gator and proceed to point out the animal's various survival features, with the aid of some stunts that will have you questioning your cowboy's sanity. The **Gator Jumparoo** is another eye-opening spectacle as some of the park's biggest creatures use their tails to 'jump' out of the water and be hand-fed tasty morsels such as whole chickens! **Jungle Crocs of the World** features some of the deadliest animals of Egypt, Australia and Cuba, with authentic lairs and brilliant presentation, while the show element has its scare-raising moments as the (admittedly highly knowledgeable) guides enter the pens to tell you all about the inhabitants. The revamped **Upclose**

Encounters–Snake Show is another entertaining and highly amusing showcase of various creatures, from the obvious snakes to less obvious scorpions and cockroaches. Brave children can provide some great photo opportunities here!

Obviously, face-to-face encounters with the park's living dinosaurs is not everyone's cup of tea, but it's an experience you're unlikely to repeat anywhere else. In addition, you can dine on smoked alligator ribs and deep-fried gator nuggets (as well as burgers and hot dogs) at **Pearl's Smokehouse**, with excellent kids' meals at $3.99. The park is also home to hundreds of nesting herons and egrets, providing a fascinating close-up of the nests from March–August.

Gatorland also scores in its great value for money, with adult tickets at $16.93, children 3–12 $7.48, and it makes a great combination with an early-morning ride with nearby **Boggy Creek Airboats**. Gatorland is located on the South Orange Blossom Trail, 2 miles south of its junction with the Central Florida Greeneway and three miles north of Highway 192. Hours 9am–dusk and parking is free. Visit their website at www.gatorland.com for more info. Attraction rating: AAAA.

A Gatorland denizen

Fantasy of Flight

Another recent addition to central Florida is this aviation museum attraction which is an absolute must even for anyone not usually interested in the history of flight or the glamour of the Golden Age of flying. Just 25 minutes down I4 towards Tampa (take Junction 21, Polk City, go north on SR 559 for half a mile, then turn left into the main entrance), Fantasy of Flight is a five-part adventure featuring the world's largest private collection of vintage aircraft. You start by entering the **History of Flight**, a series of expertly recreated 'immersion experiences' into memorable moments in aviation history, like a dogfight over the trenches in World War I and a bomber mission with a real Flying Fortress in WWII. Audio-visual effects and film clips enhance the experience and give everything a feeling of authenticity that is quite awesome. You exit into the **Vintage Aircraft** displays in two huge hangers, with the exhibits ranging from a replica Wright Flyer, to a Ford Tri-Motor, a Mk-XVI Spitfire and the world's only fully working Short Sunderland flying boat. Recent acquisitions include a P51 Mustang and a B-25. From the museum's collection of 40 or so vintage planes, one is selected each day as the **Aircraft of the Day**, with a pilot holding a question-and-answer session about that plane before performing an aerial demonstration over Fantasy of Flight. The new **Guided Tours** are held several times a day, taking visitors into the backlot and restoration areas where they learn what it takes to restore one of these machines to airworthy status. Finally, **Fightertown** features eight incredibly realistic fighter simulators that take you through a WWII aerial battle. You get a pre-flight 'briefing' on how to handle your simulator (a Vought Corsair), and then climb in to the totally enclosed cockpit to do battle with the Japanese Air Force over the Pacific. It's difficult, absorbing, fun and totally addictive.

The whole experience is crafted in 1930s Art Deco style, including a full-service diner (the excellent **Compass Rose**) and original gift shop. There is strong British appeal with the war depictions and the exhibits, and admission is $24.95 for adults, $22.95 for seniors (60+) and $13.95 for kids (5–12, under 5s free). It is open 9am–5pm and parking is free.

Fantasy of Flight is the brainchild of American entrepreneur and aviation whiz Kermit Weeks and I have yet to encounter an attraction put together with more genuine love and care. In fact, it is as much a work of art as a tourist attraction, and the masses have yet to discover it, too. For more information call 863 984 3500 or look up their website at www.fantasyofflight.com. Attraction rating: AAAA.

International Drive Area

The long tourist corridor of I-Drive continues to be a fast-developing source of hotels, restaurants, shopping and, more importantly, fun. It now has its own development council, advertising 'Orlando's Most Dynamic Destination,' to emphasise it as an attraction in its own right. The I-Ride trolley service brings it all together in transport terms and www.InternationalDriveOrlando.com highlights all the possibilities. There is also an Official Visitors Guide with an I-Ride map and some valuable money-off coupons (which they will mail to the UK), and a freephone number – 1 866 2437 483 – to steer people in the right direction. Here's a look at the main attractions (See also Orlando By Night and Shopping to complete the picture):

Ripley's Believe It Or Not

You can't miss this particular attraction, next to The Mercado shopping village on International Drive, as its extraordinary tilted appearance makes it seem as though it was designed by an architect with an aversion to the horizontal. However, once inside you soon get back on the level and, for an hour or two, you can wander through this museum dedicated to the weird and wonderful.

BRIT TIP: Ripley's, *Titanic* and Guinness World Records (see below) are all handy retreats to keep in mind for the occasional rainy day.

Robert L Ripley was an eccentric and energetic explorer and collector who, for 40 years, travelled the world in his bid to assemble a collection of the greatest oddities known to man. The Orlando branch of this worldwide museum chain features 8,900sq ft of displays that include authentic artefacts, video presentations, illusions, interactive exhibits and music. The elaborate re-creation of an Egyptian tomb showcases a mummy and three rare mummified animals, while the Primitive Gallery contains artefacts from tribal societies around the world (some quite gruesome). Human and Animal Oddities, Big and Little galleries, Illusions and Dinosaurs all boast some recent up-dates and extra interactive elements. The collection of miniatures includes the world's smallest violin and a single grain of rice hand-painted with a tropical sunset. Larger-scale exhibits include a portion of the Berlin Wall, a two-thirds scale 1907 Rolls Royce built entirely out of matchsticks and a version of the Mona Lisa textured completely from toast!

Admission is $14.95 for adults and $9.95 for 4–12s and it is open 9am–1am daily (last ticket sold at midnight). Attraction rating: AAA.

Guinness World Records Experience

Right in front of The Mercado is one of the most refreshing and enjoyable smaller attractions. New in 2000, it is an interactive showcase for all the myriad of fun and bizarre facts which the famous book highlights, all presented in a unique way. You start in the Guinness World Theater for a look at how the book came to be and then pass through the 'Shrinkenator' which 'miniaturises' you so you can enter the book's database via the Computer Gateway (where you stop to play Guinness trivia on the 'Monster monitors'). The Micro-Tech Playground is next, with a variety of Records experiences (including the chance to set your own World Record!) and games (some of them quite energetic, and with a climb-and-slide area for kids), before you pass to the Molecular Expander/Transporter & Space Shuttle, which has more surprises in store (some rather gross, some quite breathtaking). The clever Space Shuttle segment brings you to Guinness Town and a multimedia streetscape of World Records brought to life in a host of amusing ways. Finally, you enter the Simulator Theater for a ride with a difference and exit into the inevitable gift shop. All in all, it is a novel way to spend a couple of hours and a great way to amuse the kids while mum and dad enjoy shopping or, perhaps, a drink in The Mercado itself. The Experience is open daily 10am–11pm and costs $12.95 for adults and $7.95 for 5–12s. Attraction rating: AAAA.

Immerse yourself in Fantasy of Flight

Titanic

A new attraction in 1999 inside The Mercado was *Titanic* – **Ship of Dreams**, the first permanent exhibit to the great maritime disaster of 1912. With a mixture of genuine artifacts, full-scale re-creations of the ship's interior, several clever scene-setting presentations (including a visit to the Harland and Wolff shipyard in Belfast during building of the 'unsinkable' liner), film memorabilia from *Titanic* and *A Night to Remember,* plus live interpretations by storytellers in period costume, you will see, hear and feel just about everything there is to know about the Titanic and her tragic fate. The excellent actor participation, which is carried right through the exhibit, makes for an enthralling and quite moving depiction of the tragedy. The full experience takes at least an hour, with the inevitable gift store at the end, and, while the basic premise is a touch macabre, there is no disguising the on-going fascination with the ship. Even the ticket hall is suitably atmospheric, and entry is $16.95 for adults and $11.95 for 6–12s (5 and under free). It is open 10am–9pm daily (last guided tour at 8.30pm). Attraction rating: AAAA.

Skull Kingdom

The walk-through haunted house idea takes on a new dimension here. Not content with a house, here is a full-blown castle on International

> BRIT TIP: Friday and Saturday evenings are peak periods for Skull Kingdom, with queues of up to 30 minutes.

Drive (opposite Wet 'n Wild) dedicated to frights, horrors and grisly goings-on at every turn. The setting and lavishness of the Kingdom of the Skull Lord marks it out as way above average, and the combination of elaborate light and sound effects, robotics and the scream-inducingly brilliant live actors (who are kept suitably creepy by two full-time make-up artists) makes for a hair-raising experience. The shock tactics are state of the art, with the best elements of horror films and haunted houses well

The grand staircase at *Titanic*

Skull Kingdom

maintained over the two-storey spread of mazes, caverns and other demonic challenges (watch out for the monster spit!).

There is also the inevitable Haunted Gift Shop and Ghoulish Arcade Games at the end of your 20–30-minute (depending on how much you 'enjoy' the experience!) Skull Kingdom immersion. It is open 6pm–11.30pm (Sun–Wed), noon–midnight (Thur–Sat), with extended hours in peak season, with admission $12.95. Go with a few friends, or have a drink or three first! Attraction rating: TTTTT (not recommended for under 12s).

Fun Spot

Here is another choice for full-scale, family-sized fun, just off I-Drive on Del Verde Way (look for the 102ft-

BRIT TIP: WonderWorks and Fun Spot are both open until midnight in high season, long after most of the theme parks are shut, meaning you can have a day at the park and then let the kids loose here for a while to really tire them out!

high Big Wheel past the junction with Kirkman Road). With four different and highly challenging go-kart tracks, bumper cars and boats, four quite daring fairground-type rides (check out the Spyder and Paratrooper), an impressive two-storey video arcade (one of the largest in Florida) and food court, plus six Kid Spot rides for the little ones, the 4.7-acre park promises several hours of fun. Parking and admission are free, but you must buy tickets for the rides, which are $3 each (or $22 for eight). Go-karts require two tickets, while the other rides are a ticket apiece. However, if you are planning on a visit of an hour or longer, their 'armband' tickets work out at better value. The 3-hour Unlimited Armband ($30) gives you three hours of go-kart riding plus all-day access to the other rides; the Rides Armband ($15) affords all-day access to just the 13 non-kart rides. Then there is the Freeplay Arcade (37 individual classic arcade games) for a $6 all-day ticket, and the spread of more than 100 token-driven games (some of them state-of-the-art). It opens 10am–midnight (high season), or 2pm–11pm (Mon–Fri), 10am–midnight (Sat) and noon–11pm (Sun) in low season. Call 407 363 3867 or log on to their website www.fun-spot.com for details. Attraction rating: TTTT.

WonderWorks

International Drive's most unmistakable landmark is the 'interactive entertainment centre' of **WonderWorks**, a three-storey chamber of real family fun with a host of novel elements. Unmistakable? You bet – how many buildings do you know that are upside down? That's right, all of the 82ft-tall edifice is constructed from the roof up! The basic premise (working on the theory that every attraction has to have a story behind it) is WonderWorks is a secret research facility into unexplained phenomena that got uprooted by a tornado experiment and dumped in topsy-turvy fashion in the heart of this busy tourist district (yeah, right!). Well you've got to give them full marks for imagination, and the interior attractions are almost as entertaining as the exterior façade.

You enter through an 'inversion tunnel' that orientates you the same way round as the building (look out of the window if you don't believe me) and there are then chambers of entertaining and mildly educational hands-on experiences that demand several hours to explore fully. Without ever using the words 'science' or 'museum', WonderWorks steers you through five 'labs' of interactive activities, including the **Bermuda Triangle Corridor**, the **Mystery Lab** (experience earthquakes and hurricanes and see famous disasters on a bank of computer monitors), **Physical Challenge Lab** (virtual basketball, table tennis, hang-gliding and even horse racing; a baseball test, health and lifestyle quizzes and the wonderfully creepy Shocker Chair, a high-voltage simulation that gives you the feeling of 2,000 jolts rather than volts – it's weird!), **Illusions Lab** (with the Bridge of Fire static electricity generator, a computer ageing process and 'elastic surgery', hall of mirrors and bubble table), plus the **WonderWorks Emporium** gift shop, souvenirs and **Mazzarella's Pizzeria**. A Lazer Tag game centre on the top floor adds even more appeal for youngsters. On no account miss the two virtual roller-coasters, a pair of amazing enclosed 'pods' which let you design and then ride your own coaster. Truly, a topsy-turvy experience! If you have already been to DisneyQuest, this may seem tame, while it isn't as educational as the Orlando Science Center. But under 12s seem to get a good kick out of it and it also offers a clever dinner-show option, **Night of Wonder** (see Chapter 9, Orlando By Night), with a good value combination ticket. WonderWorks costs $15.95 for adults, $11.95 for seniors (55+) and children 4–11; $5.95 for the Lazer Tag; $15.95 and $13.95 for Night of Wonder; $29.95 and $24.95 for the WonderWorks/dinner-show combo; $19.95 and $14.95 for WonderWorks/ Lazer Tag; and $31.95 and $26.95 for all three elements. Check out their website at www.wonderworksonline.com for more info. Open 9am–midnight daily. Attraction rating: AAA/TTT.

Trolley and Train Museum

The large-scale steam engine around the outside of the building (just south of the huge Race Rock restaurant) marks this out as a must for all train and model railway enthusiasts. New in 2001 and still developing, the Trolley and Train Museum features a 4,000sq ft G-gauge lay-out inside, beautifully crafted and with three main, highly-elaborate sections – the Pennsylvania backwoods, the Town, and the Industrial Area. The mountains, bridges, town streets and buildings, coal mines, lakes, rivers and waterfalls have all been painstakingly hand-built from scratch, and some 14 trains are constantly on the go, with the longest track completing a mazy, 960ft circuit of the whole premises. There is also a scavenger hunt for children to keep them amused while they wander round and birthday parties can also be held here (call 407 363 9002 for details). The gift shop stocks a huge range of model train, track and accessories and has a Thomas the Tank Engine play area for the young 'uns. And then there are the purpose-built outdoor locomotive Lady Liberty (with two open-sided – and wheelchair accessible – passenger cars) and the hand-crafted Victorian-style trolley on the 2ft narrow-gauge line, which are likely to be magnets for children of the right age. The quarter-mile route around the Museum lasts just 5 minutes, but a ticket here is valid all day, which means youngsters can ride as often as they like! The Museum itself costs $6.95 for adults, $5.95 seniors and $4.95 children, while the combination pass (Museum and outdoor rides) is $8.95, $7.95 and $6.95. For the train/trolley rides alone, the fee is $3 for adults and seniors and $2 for children. Hours are 10am–9pm (10am–8pm Sun). www.trolleyandtrainmusum.com is their website for more info. Attraction rating: AAA.

Downtown Orlando

The last couple of years have seen a significant move towards regenerating the city centre – the 'Downtown' area – with new offices, apartments, shops and restaurants. This has also brought several significant developments in tourist attractions, too.

And, because this is Orlando, there is no such thing as a simple museum or science centre. Everything must be all-singing, all-

dancing just to compete. Hence, the **Orlando Science Center** is more than a mere museum and far more fun than the average science centre. Here, you get a series of hands-on experiences and habitats that entertain as well as inform, and school-age children in particular will get a lot from it.

The Science Center has eight main components, plus an inviting café, a night sky observatory and an IMAX cinema. **Natureworks** creates a number of typical Florida habitats (with several shows and a series of hands-on field stations), **Science City** introduces fun ways to understand and use physical science and maths (including some mind-bending puzzles) and the **Cosmic Tourist** offers a trip round our solar system with an amusing travel theme. The **Darden Adventure Theater** takes up more 'science is fun' topics with the Einstein Players. **Bodyzone** offers some fascinating insights into the human body, with a new interactive element called Measure Me which explores your size, strength, flexibility, agility and sensory abilities. Next door, **TechWorks** is a four-part adventure into light, imaginary landscapes, showbiz science and a micro-world of microscopic investigation. For those a bit too young for the educational element, **Kids' Town** has plenty of junior-sized fun and games for under 8s. You'll be amazed at how much you learn in the course of having fun. New in summer 2001 was **DinoDigs: Mysteries Unearthed**, a gift from the Walt Disney Company of their former

BRIT TIP: The CineDome film and laser show can operate until midnight on Friday and Saturday for a show independent of the Science Center.

The upside-down world of WonderWorks

Dinosaur Jubilee exhibit in the DinoLand area of *Disney's Animal Kingdom*. It has been recreated in the OSC as a palaeontological excavation site, complete with eight full dinosaur skeleton replicas and a number of genuine fossils.

In addition, the Center has two separate programmes based in the Dr Phillips **CineDome**, a 310-seat cinema that practically surrounds its audience with large-format films, digital planetarium shows (a virtual tour of the universe, anyone?) and 3-D laser shows. The CineDome also boasts a 28,000-watt digital sound system that helps make the experience unforgettable. The Science Center is located on East Princeton Street in downtown Orlando, just off exit 43 of I4 (as you go east on Princeton, the Center will be on your left but the multi-storey car park is on the *right*), and is open 9am–5pm Tue–Thur, 9am–9pm Fri and Sat and noon–5pm Sunday (closed Mondays, except school holidays), and costs $9.50 for adults, $8.50 for seniors (55+) and $6.75 for 3–11s; it is $12.50, $11.50 and $9.25 with one CineDome show (film or planetarium) and $14.50, $13.50 and $11.25 with two shows; the CineDome film only is $6.00, $5.50 and $4.50 for one film. Parking is $3.50. It is closed on Thanksgiving Day in November, Christmas Eve and Christmas Day. Attraction rating: AAAA.

The new **Orange County History Center** offers an imaginative and entertaining journey into central Florida history, from the wildlife and Native Americans to today's tourist issues and the space programme. Again, the accent is on the interactive, with hands-on exhibits and audio-visual presentations, and it is very much a journey through time, starting outside in renovated Heritage Square, complete with its cypress trees and fountains. The History Center itself is in the former 1927 Orange County Courthouse, with the foyer converted into a Dome featuring more than 150 icons unique to central Florida (see how many you can identify before and after your tour). The four-storey adventure starts at the top with the *Orientation Theater* for a 14-minute multimedia presentation as you sit in rocking chairs on the 'front porch.' Then you visit the *Natural Environment* and *First Peoples* exhibits (12,000 years ago), before First Contact brings in the European element. Jump into the 1800s and you visit a *Seminole* settlement, an early Pioneer Cracker home (the first true 'cowboys'), hear tales of the early *Cattle* ranching days and learn about the *Citrus* industry. The early 20th century brings the story of *Transportation, Tin Can Tourists, Aviation* and the great land boom *(Selling Central Florida)*. Then witness how the region dramatically altered with the development of the *Space programme* and the arrival of a certain Walt Disney in *The Day We Changed*. From there, you move on to the beautifully restored *Courtroom B* for some more real-life Orlando history. Finally, come up to date with the Central Florida story in the *Community* exhibit, a spotlight on famous places, people and activities in the area, and a chance to view the Dome from the top, testing all your new-found knowledge of the icons.

> BRIT TIP: Combine a visit here with lunch at the wonderfully eclectic Globe restaurant on the corner of the Square.

You will also find various periodical travelling exhibits here, as well as the Historium gift shop. Admission is $7 for adults, $3.50 for 3–12s and $6.50 for seniors (60+), and it is open 9am–5pm (Mon–Sat) and 11am–5pm (Sun). The History Center can be found off Central Boulevard and Magnolia Avenue downtown (Exit 38 off I4, left on to Magnolia, right on to Central Blvd). Best place to park is the Orlando Public Library multi-storey car park on Central Boulevard (History Center admission includes two hours free parking there if you show your car park ticket). For more information, call 407 836 8500 or visit their website at www.thehistorycenter.org. Attraction rating: AAA½.

Other Downtown developments include the free **Lymmo** bus service which connects the central stretch along Magnolia Avenue, from South Street to the TD Waterhouse Center (formerly the Orlando Arena for sports and concerts) on Amelia Street, the **Downtown Arts District** and **Arts Market**, plus new shops and restaurants around **Lake Eola**. See www.downtownorlando.com for the latest info (see also Chapter 8, Off The Beaten Track, and Chapter 9, Orlando By Night).

The Holy Land Experience

Not so much a conventional attraction but right in the heart of the tourist mainstream is this new 'living Biblical museum' which sets out to recreate in great detail the city of Jerusalem and its religious

significance from 1450BC to AD66. The staff are all in period costume, the architecture and landscaping are impressive and the background music throughout both the indoor and outdoor areas is all original and suitably atmospheric as the Experience aims to provide an explanation and celebration of the Christian faith. From the **Jerusalem Street Market** entrance to the **Qumran Dead Sea Caves**, **Calvary's Garden Tomb** and on to the highly impressive **Temple of the Great King** (destroyed by the Romans in AD70), everything is portrayed in quite literal Biblical terms. The **Theater of Life** shows a dramatic, 25-minute film of a series of Bible landmarks, from Adam and Eve to the Crucifixion, while the **Wilderness Tabernacle** is a 25-minute theatrical portrayal of Old Testament worship, featuring the Holy Ark but also with lasers and pyrotechnics. A huge replica **Jerusalem Model** – which took more than a year to build – is explained in great detail several times a day in the form of a guided tour. Live performances include the *Garden Tomb Music & Drama* celebrating the Resurrection and an original musical drama *'Today's The Day'*, which plays out in the Plaza of Nations. There is even a Middle Eastern-style café where one of the menu items is a Goliath Burger (I'm not kidding). It is a thoroughly

Bears exhibition at Science Center

unusual 'attraction' (although they don't call it that), and sits rather awkwardly among the surrounding tourist offerings, but it may well pique the religious interest of some and should provide at least half a day's 'edutainment.' The Holy Land Experience can be found immediately off Exit 31A of I4, on the junction of Conroy and Vineland Roads (just north of Universal Orlando). It is open 9am–6pm (Mon–Thur), 9am–9pm (Sat) and noon–6pm (Sun), and costs $17 for adults and $12 for children 4–12. Parking is free. Call 407 367 2065 for more information or visit www.theholylandexperience.com.

The Water Parks

If anyone has been down the slides and flumes at the local leisure centre, they will have an inkling of what Orlando's five big water parks are all about. Predictably, *Walt Disney World Resort in Florida* weighs in with three of the most elaborate ones, but the Universal-owned Wet 'n Wild and Water Mania are equally adept at providing hours of watery fun in an amazing variety of styles that owe a lot to the imagination of the theme park creators.

BRIT TIP: While these parks are a great way of cooling down, it is easy to pick up a five-star case of sunburn. So don't forget high-factor, *waterproof* suntan lotion.

All five parks require at least half a day of splashing, sliding and riding to get full value from their rather high admission charges, but if you prefer to get your kicks in watery rather than land-borne fashion, these are definitely for you and you will want to try at least a couple.

Lockers are provided for valuables and you can hire towels.

Disney's Typhoon Lagoon Water Park

Until *Disney's Blizzard Beach* Water Park opened in 1995, *Disney's Typhoon Lagoon* was the biggest and finest example of Florida's water parks. In high season, it is also the busiest, so be prepared to run into more queues. The park's 56 acres are spread out around the 2½-acre lagoon fringed with palm trees and white-sand beaches. If it wasn't for the high-season crowds, you could easily convince yourself you had been washed up on some tropical island paradise. *Disney's Typhoon Lagoon* also goes in for some of the most extravagant landscaping and introduces some unique and clever details. The walk up Mount Mayday, for instance, provides a terrific overview of the park as well as adding scenic touches like rope bridges and tropical flowers. Sun loungers, chairs, picnic tables and even a few hammocks are provided to add to the comfort and convenience of restful areas like Getaway Glen (although you need to arrive early to bag a decent spot with some shade).

The park is overlooked by the 90ft Mount Mayday, atop which is perched the luckless Miss Tilly, a shrimp boat that legend has it landed here during the typhoon that gave the park its name. Watch for the water fountains that shoot from Miss

BRIT TIP: As the busiest of the water parks, *Disney's Typhoon Lagoon* can hit capacity quite early in the day in the summer. Call 407 824 4321 in advance to check on the crowds.

Tilly's funnel at regular intervals, accompanied by the ship's hooter, which signal the outbreak of another round of 6ft-high waves in the **Surf Pool** (where you can hire inner-tubes to bob around on or just try body-surfing). Circling the lagoon is **Castaway Creek**, a 3ft-deep lazy flowing river that offers the chance to float happily along on the rubber tyres that are provided for just this purpose (although around midday you may find yourself among hundreds who all have the same idea).

The series of slides and rides are all clustered around Mt Mayday and vary from the breathtaking three slides of **Humunga Kowabunga**, which drop you 214ft at up to 30mph down some of the steepest inclines in waterdom (make sure your swimming costume is SECURELY fastened!), to children's area **Ketchakiddee Creek**, which offers a selection of slides and fun pools for all youngsters under 4ft tall. In between, you have the three **Storm Slides**, more body slides which twist and turn through caves, tunnels and waterfalls, **Mayday Falls**, a 460ft inner-tube ride down a series of banked drops, **Keelhaul Falls**, an alternative tube ride that takes slightly longer, and **Gang Plank Falls**, a group or family ride whose tubes take up to four people down the 300ft of mock rapids. The hugely imaginative (but slightly chilly) **Shark Reef** offers the chance to snorkel around this upturned wreck and coral reef among 4,000 tropical fish and a number of real, but quite harmless, nurse sharks. Like all the areas, this one is carefully supervised, and those who aren't quite brave enough to dive in amongst the marine wildlife can still get a close-up through the underwater port holes of the sunken ship (the Reef is closed to swimmers during the coldest of the winter months). There are height and health restrictions on Humunga

Kowabunga (it's not suitable for anyone with a bad back or neck, or for pregnant women), while the queues for this slide, plus the Storm Slides and Shark Reef, can touch an arduous hour at times, which can take a lot of the fun out of it (an hour's wait for a 20-second slide? Not for me, thanks). Getting out of the sun can also be slightly problematic as the provision of shaded areas is not overwhelming, but a quick plunge into Castaway Creek usually solves any overheating problems.

For snacks and meals, **Lowtide Lou's** and **Let's Go Slurpin'** both offer snacks and drinks while **Typhoon Tilly's** and **Leaning Palms** serve a mixture of burgers, sandwiches, salads and ice cream. It is essential to avoid main meal-times here if you want to eat in relative comfort. You can, however, bring your own picnic along (unlike the main theme parks) as there are several scenic areas for this purpose (but no alcohol or glass containers are allowed). You CAN'T bring your own snorkels, inner-tubes or rafts, but snorkels are provided at Shark Reef and you need to hire inner-tubes (if required) only for the Lagoon. If you have forgotten a vital item like a sun-hat or bucket and spade for the kids, or even your swimsuit, they are all available (along with the usual range of gifts and souvenirs) at **Singapore Sal's**.

To avoid the worst of the summer crowds (when the park's 7,200 capacity is frequently reached), Monday morning is about the best time to visit (steer clear of the weekends at all costs), while, on other weekdays, arrive either 30 minutes before opening time or in mid-afternoon, when some people decide to call it a day to dodge the daily rainstorm. Early evening is extremely pleasant as the park lights up.

Opening hours are 9am to dusk every day, with admission $29.95 for

7

© Disney

Disney's Typhoon Lagoon Water Park

adults and $24 for kids 3–9 (under 3s free), and there is NO parking fee. It is free as one of the options with the Park Hopper Plus Passes. Attraction rating: TTTT/AAAAA.

Disney's River Country Water Park

At just a quarter of the size of *Disney's Typhoon Lagoon*, you might think this is a good, out-of-the-way spot most people overlook. But you'd be wrong. It may be smaller, but the same number of folk seem to cram in here. As it is not unknown for the gates to close by late morning because capacity has been reached, it is a good idea to arrive early or after 4pm (when admission is also reduced).

BRIT TIP: *Disney's River Country Water Park* is not the best of their trio in winter. Despite the heated pool, Bay Lake can be pretty cold and the park often closes for refurbishment. Call 407 824 4321 to check opening times.

However, just because it is the country cousin doesn't mean *Disney's River Country* is any less well organised or lacking in charm (although I believe it is looking a little ragged at the edges these days, especially the changing facilities). The overall theme is of an old-fashioned swimming hole, which gives it a rustic, backwoods America flavour straight out of *Huckleberry Finn*.

The heart of the park is **Bay Cove**, a roped-off section of Bay Lake which offers the chance to climb on ropes, tyre swings, a barrel bridge and boom swing, and ride the cable, all finishing with an emphatic splash into the lake. **Whoop-N-Holler Hollow** contains the two main thrill opportunities, a pair of similar body-slide flumes that end with a drop into Bay Cove. **White Water Rapids** is a more sedate trip via inner-tube down a series of chutes and pools that gives you a chance to admire the scenery, while young children are also very well catered for with their own area, **Kiddie Cove**, with several small slides, pools and a separate stretch of beach, and **Indian Springs**, a neat fountain-cum-squirt pool. **Upstream Plunge** is a large, free-form pool, and the **Slippery Slide Falls** drop you 7ft into it! Each of the main activities will occupy you for about half the time of those in *Disney's Typhoon Lagoon*, but there is a more relaxing feel to *Disney's River Country* that encourages you to stick around. You can also take a boat ride or walk the **Nature Trail**, a 1,000yd boardwalk through a pretty, well-shaded cypress grove. The animals, pony rides and petting zoo of the neighbouring Fort Wilderness are another handy diversion for young 'uns.

Pop's Place serves the usual array of fast food (and a Kid's Picnic Basket at $3.99) while the **Waterin' Hole** offers snacks and drinks.

There is no gift shop, however, and 3–4 hours may be all you need here.

To find *Disney's River Country Water Park*, aim for *Disney's Fort Wilderness Resort & Campground* and you will find the (free) parking area at Gateway Depot. From there, you must leave your car and use the bus service to *Disney's Fort Wilderness Campground*, where you walk the last 100 yards and bear left just before the boat jetty. Admission is $15.95 for adults and $12.50 for 3–9s, while it is free with a Park Hopper Plus Pass, and is open 10am to dusk. Attraction rating: TTT/AAA.

Disney's Blizzard Beach Water Park

Ever imagined a skiing resort in the middle of Florida? You haven't? Well, Disney have, and this is the wonderful result. *Disney's Blizzard Beach* Water Park puts the rest in the shade for size as well as extravagant settings, with the whole park arranged as if it were in the Rocky Mountains rather than the sub-tropics. That means snow-effect scenery, Christmas trees and water slides cunningly converted to look like skiing pistes and toboggan runs. It delivers a real feast for water lovers and Disney admirers in general, and the basic premise of snow-surfin' USA is an unarguable five-star knockout. Feature items are **Mount Gushmore**, a 90ft mountain down which all the main slides run (including the world's tallest free-fall speed slide, the terrifying 120ft-long **Summit Plummet**, which rockets you down a simulated ski jump at up to 60mph!), **Tike's Peak**, a kiddie-sized version of the park with scaled-down slides and a mock snow-beach and **Ski-Patrol Training Camp**, a series of slides and challenges for pre-teens. **Melt-Away Bay** is a one-acre pool fed by 'melting snow' waterfalls (actually blissfully warm),

BRIT TIP: Ladies, please remember, down some of the whizziest slides it is advisable to wear a one-piece swimsuit rather than a bikini. Your modesty could be at stake here!

and **Cross Country Creek** is a lazy-flowing half-mile river around the whole park which also carries floating guests through a bone-chilling 'ice cave' (watch out for the mini-waterfalls of ice-cold water!). A ski chair-lift operates to the top of Mt Gushmore, providing a magnificent view of the whole park and surrounding areas. Don't miss the outstanding rides – **Teamboat Springs**, a wild, family inner-tube adventure, **Runoff Rapids**, a one, two or three-person tube plunge, and the **Snow Stormers**, a daring head-first 'toboggan' run. **Toboggan Racers** give you the chance to speed down the 'slopes' against seven other head-first daredevils. All four go to new heights of water park imagination and provide good-sized thrills without overdoing the scare factor

Disney's Blizzard Beach Water Park

© Disney

(yes, I know, I'm a total coward).

The **Double Dipper** is two side-by-side slides which send you down 215ft-long tubes in a race that is timed on a big clock which you can see at the bottom, and which gives you a real jolt halfway down! For those not quite up to Summit Plummet lunacy, the wonderfully named **Slush Gusher** is a slightly less terrifying speed slide. There is also a 'village' area including the **Beach Haus** shop and **Lottawatta Lodge** fast-food restaurant, offering diners a grandstand view of Mt Gushmore and Melt-Away Bay beach. Snacks are also available at **Avalunch** (ouch!), the **Warming Hut** and **Polar Pub & Frostbite Freddie's**. Predictably, the crowds are suitably massive, so avoid the

BRIT TIP: For all the water parks, it can be advisable to bring a pair of deck shoes or sandals that can be worn in water.

weekends and from mid-morning onwards on Wednesdays to Fridays.

Disney's Blizzard Beach Water Park is located just north of *Disney's All-Star Resorts* off Buena Vista Drive, and charges are $29.95 per adult and $24 per child (3–9); again it is one of the free optional extras with Hopper Plus Passes, with opening times from 9am to early evening. Attraction rating: TTTTT/AAAAA.

Adjacent to Blizzard Beach is the wonderful **Winter Summerland** mini-golf challenge, with two elaborately themed courses, that makes for a great diversion with children.

Wet 'n Wild

If *Walt Disney World Resort in Florida* scores highest marks for its scenic

content, Wet 'n Wild, the world's first water park back in 1977, goes full-tilt for thrills and spills of the highest quality. This place will really test the material of your swimsuit to the limit!

Wet 'n Wild is repeatedly one of the best-attended water parks in the country, and its location in the heart of International Drive makes it a major tourist draw. It was also given a $1.5million facelift in 2000 to give it a fresh, new look. Consequently, you will once again encounter some serious crowds here, although the 12 slides and rides, **Lazy River** attraction, an elaborate kids' park (with mini versions of many of the slides), **Surf Lagoon** and restaurant and picnic areas all manage to absorb a lot of punters before the queues start to develop. Waits of more than half an hour at peak times are rare. Its popularity with locals means it is busiest at weekends, with July the month that attracts most crowds.

You are almost spoilt for choice of main rides, from the highly popular group inner-tube rides of the **Surge** and **Bubba Tub**, through the more demanding rides of **Raging Rapids** to the high-thrill factor of the two-person **Black Hole** (like the *Magic Kingdom*'s Space Mountain, but in water!), **Blue Niagara** (also enclosed, but this one's a body slide) and **Mach 5**, to the ultimate terror of **Der Stuka** and the **Bomb Bay**. These latter are definitely not for the faint-hearted. Basically they are two 76ft-high body slides with a drop as near vertical as makes no difference. Der Stuka is the straightforward slide version, while the Bomb Bay adds the extra terror of being allowed to free-fall on to the top of the slide. And they call it fun?! Suffice it to say, your author has not put himself at risk on these particular contraptions, and has absolutely no intention of doing so! For some reason, only 15–25 per cent of the park's visitors pluck up the courage to try it. Can't think why. There are height restrictions (minimum 4ft required) on the Bomb Bay and Der Stuka and Blue Niagara, while older kids get their own chance for thrills on the huge, inflatable **Bubble Up**, which bounces them into 3ft of water.

There's also the thrilling toboggan-like **Fuji Flyer**, which takes four passengers in 8ft-long, in-line tubes which whoosh down more than 450ft of banked curves and speed-enhancing straights, and the bungee-like **Hydra Fighter**, a two-person swing equipped with a fire-type hose that sends the contraption into mad gyrations as you increase the water pressure! New in 2001 was **The Storm**, a pair of identical circular slides which are billed as 'body coasters!' The enclosed tubes – complete with storm sound and light effects – send the rider plunging into a circular bowl,

> BRIT TIP: The Children's Playground at Wet 'n Wild was built especially for those under 4ft – right down to the only junior wave pool in the world.

around which they spin at high speed before landing in the splash pool below. Huge fun.

The neighbouring lake is also part of the fun (although not in winter when its temperature drops below that of merely chilly), adding the opportunities to try the cable-operated **Knee Ski** and (for a nominal fee) ride the **Wild One** (large inner-tubes tied behind a speedboat). Alternatively, take a breather in the slow-flowing **Lazy River** or abandon the water altogether for one of several shaded picnic areas. Staying cool out of the water is rather harder, however,

especially at peak times when the best spots are quickly snapped up.

For the energetic, there is also beach volleyball and the chance to ride the **Robo Surfer** at selected times, a watery version of the mechanical bucking bronco. Lockers, showers, tube and towel rentals are all available, but, if you bring your own floating equipment, it must be checked by one of the lifeguards.

For food, **Bubba's Bar-B-Q** serves chicken, ribs, fries and drinks, the **Surf Grill** features burgers, hot-dogs, chicken and sandwiches and there are another seven snack bars offering similar fast-food fare, including a pizza bar and a kiddies' counter (for the likes of peanut butter sandwiches, hot-dogs and chips). Picnics can also be brought in, provided you don't include alcohol or glass containers.

Wet 'n Wild is located half a mile north of International Drive's junction with Sand Lake Road at the intersection with Universal Boulevard and is open year-round from 9am in peak periods (10am at other times) until variously 5, 6, 7, 8 or 10pm. The extended hours from late June to late August offer particularly good value as admission is $10 off after 5pm and you still have 5 hours of fun ahead of you. Admission is $29.95 for adults, $23.95 for 3–9s and free for under 3s, while Wet 'n Wild is included in the 14-day Orlando FlexTicket. Tube rentals are $4 ($2 deposit), towels $2 and lockers $5 ($2 deposit), or $9 for all three ($4

> BRIT TIP: Kids are again extremely well catered for, and Water Mania can even host birthday parties in Mr Kool's Party Land. Call 407 396 2626 for details.

Wet 'n Wild – the Fuji Flyer

deposit). Parking is $5. Check out www.wetnwild.com. Attraction rating: TTTTT/AAA.

The Hydra Fighter at Wet 'n Wild

Water Mania

If Wet 'n Wild attracts the serious water-thrill seekers, Kissimmee's version, Water Mania, is more family-orientated and laid back, with the crowds highest at weekends when the locals flock in and lowest early in the week. That's not to say Water Mania doesn't have its share of scary slides (or Wet 'n Wild doesn't cater for families), it's just their emphasis is slightly different and those looking to avoid the crowds often end up here. Where this 36-acre park scores a minor victory over its rivals is in the provision of 3 acres of wooded picnic area that makes a welcome change from the concrete expanses and feverish splashing activities. You are again welcome to bring your own picnic (although no glass items).

Eight different slides, including a patented non-stop surfing challenge called **Wipe-Out**, the usual **Cruisin' Creek**, a 720,000-gallon **Wave Pool** (waves every 15 minutes, up to 4ft high) and three separate kids' areas provide the main attractions, and there is again enough here to keep you occupied for at least half a day. Top of the list for those daring enough to throw

Water Mania

themselves down things like Der Stuka is the **Screamer**, an aptly named 72ft free-fall speed slide, and the **Abyss**, 380ft of enclosed-tube darkness. The **Anaconda** and **Banana Peel** both feature family-sized inner-tubes down long, twisting, turning slides, while the **Double Berzerker** offers two different ways to be whooshed along and spat out into a foaming pool.

However, the outstanding feature, for both trying and watching, is the **Wipe-Out**, one of only two such attractions in the world. The challenge is to grab a body surfboard and try to ride the continuous wave, risking going over the edge into another pool if you stray too wide, or being sent flying backwards if you lose your balance. A real blast!

Then, when it comes to pint-sized fun for the children, Water Mania is one of the best. The **Rain Forest** is designed for the 2–10s, with a 5,000-sq-ft pool ranging from 3in to 2ft deep and featuring a range of mini-slides, fountains and water guns, all arranged around a wonderful large-scale pirate ship, with more chances to climb, jump and generally swashbuckle. Other innovative recent additions are the **Rain Train**, a near life-size locomotive that sprays water out of its stack in the centre of a shallow pool, with other interactive play features and more slides; and **Tot's Town** for the toddlers (and their parents who want to relax a little from supervising their youngsters), which is a partly

fenced playground with sand beach and paddling area, with added shade and refreshment hut. Then there is the inevitable Electric Arcade of video games for the older children.

In addition to the cooling picnic areas, there are also several snack bars, a mini-golf course, volleyball and basketball courts and a large shop. Much of the park was refurbished in 1999, making it extremely good value for money.

Water Mania is located on Highway 192, just a mile east of the I4 intersection and is open 10am–5pm early March–end September, and Wed–Sat only in October (hours subject to change). Call 407 396 2626 for more details or check out www.watermania-florida.com. Admission is $16.95 for adults and children and parking is $5. Attraction rating: TTTT/AAA.

Okay, that sums up the main large-scale attractions, but many people are now looking for the 'something different' factor, so let's explore some alternatives to the mass-market experience …

7

Cruisin' Creek at Water Mania

8 Off the Beaten Track
(or, When you're All Theme Parked Out)

After several days in the midst of the hectic tourist whirl of mainstream Orlando, you may find yourself in need of a rest from the non-stop theme park activities. Or, you may be a repeat visitor looking for a different Central Florida experience. If either is the case, this chapter is for you.

Hopefully, you will already have noted the relatively tranquil offerings of Cypress Gardens and Silver Springs, but, to get away from it all more completely and to enhance your view of the area further, the following are guaranteed to take you well off the beaten tourist track. The chapter should really be subtitled 'A Taste of the Real Florida', as it introduces the areas of Winter Park, Seminole County, nature boat rides and eco-tours, and journeys by airboat, balloon, ship, train and plane.

Winter Park

Foremost among the 'secret' hideaways is this elegant northern suburb of Orlando, little more than 20 minutes' drive from the hurly-burly of areas like International Drive and yet a million miles from the relentless commercialism. It offers several renowned museums and art galleries, some fabulous shopping, numerous restaurants, several pleasant walking tours, a delightful 50-minute boat ride around several of the area's lakes and, above all, a chance to slow down.

The central area is **Park Avenue**, a classy street of fine shops, boutiques, two museums and a wonderfully shaded park. At one end of the avenue is Rollins College, a small but highly respected arts education centre which also houses the **Cornell Fine Arts Museum** (the oldest collection of paintings, sculpture and decorative arts in Florida, open 10am–5pm Tue–Fri, 1pm–5pm Sat–Sun, closed Mondays and main holidays, admission free) and the **Annie Russell Theater**. The museum features regular exhibitions and lectures, as well as having its own collection. The **Morse Museum of American Art** is a must for admirers of American art pottery, American and European glass, furniture and other decorative arts of the late nineteenth and early 20th centuries, including one of the world's foremost collections of works by Louis Comfort Tiffany. The dazzling Chapel restoration from the 1893 Chicago World Expo is now on display in its original form for the first time since the late 19th century and is worth the entrance fee alone. The museum is open 9.30am–4pm Tues–Sat, and 1–4pm Sun, admission $3 for adults, children under 12 free. See their website at www.morsemuseum.org. The **Albin Polasek Museum and Sculpture Gardens** are also worth a look for culture buffs and the serene, tranquil setting devoted to this Czech/American artist. Open 10am–4pm Wed–Sun, there is no admission charge and it is also a superb setting for weddings. The **Scenic Boat Tour** is located at the east end of

Morse Avenue, and offers a charming, narrated tour of the 'Venice of America', travelling 12 miles (weather permitting – the drought of early 2001 had severely restricted the route) around the lakes and canals for a fascinating glimpse of some of the most beautiful houses, boat houses and lakeside gardens (properties in the area start at $800,000 and top $4 million in several instances!). Tours run each day 10am–4pm and cost $7 for adults and $3 for children 2–11, and it is one of the most relaxing hours you will spend in Orlando. Take a look at their website at www.scenicboattours.com.

An alternative tour is with **Home Town Bicycle Tours** for a gentle but unique overview of this picturesque neighbourhood, including several parks and Rollins College, with full guide narration ($50/hour for groups up to 10; i.e. $5/person/hour, plus $20 bike hire; call 407 332 8703 or e-mail HomeTownBicycleTours@HotMail.com). You can also take the **Park Avenue Walking Tour**, with useful free maps provided by the Chamber of Commerce on New York Avenue.

The shops of Park Avenue are also a cut or two above anything you will encounter elsewhere, and, while you may find the prices equally distinctive, just browsing is an enjoyable experience with the charm of the area highlighted by the friendliness of everyone hereabouts. For shops that are both unique and fun, look out for **Panache** (jewellery), **Park Avenue Gallery** (art), **Kendyl's Kloset** (children's clothes and toys) and **The Doggie Door** (for pets). Regular pavement craft fairs and art festivals (especially the Spring Art Festival in March/April, which is a big part of the social scene) add splashes of colour to an already inviting scenario. In addition to the **Park**

Plaza Gardens, which specialises in continental cuisine (see Chapter 10, Eating Out), you can sample French, Italian and Thai cuisines, among many to choose from. Street parking here generally allows two hours free, but the new Sun Trust Building on the corner of Comstock and Park Avenue is a better bet. The **Central Park** area alongside Park Avenue, notable for its fountains and flowers, is due to be expanded in the near future, which should enhance things still further.

An additional high point of a visit to Winter Park is the **Kraft Azalea Gardens** on Alabama Drive (off Palmer Avenue at the north end of Park Avenue), 11 acres of shaded lakeside walkways, gardens and hundreds of magnificent azaleas. The main focal point, the mock Grecian temple, is a particularly beautiful setting for the many weddings that are held here. **Mead Botanical Garden**s, on Garden Drive (just off Highway 17/92) offers more beautiful trails through a sub-tropical forest with native birds and plants from around the world. There is no admission charge for either.

Midway between Winter Park and downtown Orlando is another botanical gem, **Leu Gardens**, a 50-acre retreat featuring formal gardens, peaceful walks and a boardwalk overlooking Lake Rowena. Leu Gardens are open daily from 9am–5pm (9am–8pm in summer) and cost $4 for adults and $1 for under 13s. They are on the corner of Forest and Nebraska Avenues, via Mills Avenue and Princeton St from Exit 43 of Interstate 4.

Winter Park is located off exit 45 of Interstate 4, Fairbanks Avenue. Turn right on to Fairbanks and head east for two miles until it intersects with Park Avenue and turn left.

8

Aquatic Wonders boat tours

To go further into the real world of Florida nature and its wildlife, **Aquatic Wonders** operates a delightful break from the theme park business on Lake Tohopekaliga in Kissimmee (the bigger of the two lakes; NOT East Lake Toho). Operated by Captain Ray Robida and limited to a maximum of six people per trip, the choice of seven cruises offers a series of gentle adventures that are entertaining and educational as well as relaxing. Every cruise on the 30ft covered pontoon boat is different depending on local conditions and Captain Ray's truly individual style, which is wonderfully laid back yet informative. His knowledge of the waterways and wildlife is outstanding and children with enquiring minds will get a lot out of it.

The 3-hour **Aquatic Wonders** cruise studies the complex of local lakes and rivers, water ecology and the fish, insects and other animals of the area ($35 for adults and children). The **Eagle Watch Tour** is an ornithologist's delight as it goes out for 2 hours to look at the nesting bald eagles on the lake, rare ospreys and many other species of birds ($18.95 for adults, $12.95 for 3–12s). The rather romantic **Sunset Sounds** is another 2-hour trip aboard the 'Eagle Ray' to enjoy the sights and sounds of dusk over the lake as the

birds come home to roost ($18.95 and $12.95). **Starlight Wonders** is a 2-hour tour for a spot of star-gazing, gentle music and Native American stories surrounding the origins of the constellations ($24.95 and $14.95). **Rivers in Time** is a 2-hour journey back in time to the days of the river boat and the Seminole Indian War, a fascinating live history

> **BRIT TIP:** Amazingly, the waterways feeding Lake Toho stretch all the way to Miami in the south. Captain Ray is a mine of fascinating geographical and historical information.

lesson with all the sights and sounds of the lake for good measure ($18.95 and $12.95). The **Gator Watch Tour** is a 2-hour night-time journey to view some of the locals hunting, nesting and just hanging out (and there are plenty of them out there!) as well as sounds of the lake at night ($24.95 and $14.95). **Family Fishing Adventures** offers 4–5 hours of fishing fun with all bait and tackle (but not fishing licence) provided, especially for beginners ($150 for 1 or 2 persons, $175 for 3 or 4, $200 for 5 or 6). There are also games and videos for the kids in case their attention wanders! All tours have non-alcoholic drinks and snacks provided (but you can also take your own), and Captain Ray is fully licensed by the US Coast Guard, so you are guaranteed a high level of safety as well as entertainment. The Eagle Ray departs daily from Big Toho Marina at the west end of Lakeshore Boulevard off Ruby Avenue in downtown Kissimmee (via Main Street and Broadway, turn left into Ruby and right at the end, Lakeshore Blvd). Call 407 846 2814 for more details and to make

Airboat ride

reservations for these tours, which are proving increasingly popular (or visit www.florida-nature.com).

Airboat rides

Florida also offers the thrill of airboat rides on many of its lakes, rivers and marshes. An airboat is a totally different experience to any boat ride you will have taken as it is more like flying at ground level. It is as much a thrill as a scenic adventure, but it also has the advantage of exploring areas otherwise inaccessible to boats. Airboats simply skim over and through the marshes, to give you an alternative, close-up and very personal view. Travelling at up to 50mph means it can be loud (hence you will be provided with headphones) and sunglasses are also a good idea to keep stray flies out of your eyes. It is NOT the trip for you if you are spooked by crickets, dragonflies and similar insects that

> BRIT TIP: Watch out for discount coupons in tourist literature offering up to $3 off airboat rides.

occasionally land inside the boat!

There are several operations offering airboat rides in the area, from you-drive boats that do barely 5mph to much bigger rides, but for safety and quality my tip goes to **Boggy Creek Airboat Rides**. Their airboats can be found on Lake Toho at Southport Park (all the way down Poinciana Boulevard, off Highway 192 between Markers 10 and 11, and across into Southport Road – about a 30-minute drive) or on East Lake Toho (their main site). For the latter, you either take Exit 17 off the Central Florida Greeneway (417) and go south on Boggy Creek Road,

then right into East Lake Fish Camp; better still, take Osceola Parkway all the way east until it hits Boggy Creek Road. Go left and then turn right at the Boggy Creek T-junction, then right into East Lake Fish Camp after 2 miles.

> BRIT TIP: Best time to ride is first thing on a weekday morning when the local wildlife is not hiding from the weekend boaters.

The **Fish Camp** is itself a little gem, offering a variety of boating and angling opportunities (call 407 348 2040 for details) as well as the wonderfully authentic rural Florida charm of the **restaurant and gift shop** (open 8am–9pm every day). If you are heading for a morning airboat ride, consider arriving early for one of their magnificent (huge!) all-day breakfasts, while the more adventurous will want to try the local delicacies – catfish, frogs' legs and gator tail. For another great slice of local eating, try their Friday and Saturday night buffets. They are fabulous value at $8.95 and $11.95 each on an all-you-can-eat basis.

Boggy Creek's **half-hour ride** features three of the most modern 18-passenger airboats in Florida, skimming over the local wetlands for a close-up view of the majestic cypress trees and wildlife that can include eagles, ospreys, snakes and turtles as well as gators.

> BRIT TIP: Want to sample the Florida Everglades but don't fancy the 3-hour trip south? Boggy Creek Airboats are the perfect substitute, and at a fraction of the cost.

8

You do not need to book in advance, just turn up and go (9am–5.30pm, 7 days a week), and rides cost $16.95 for adults and $10 for children 3–12 (don't forget the sunscreen as you can really burn out on the water). They also do a 1-hour **Night Tour** ($25, March–October only) for a completely different, and quite exhilarating, experience (gator eyes glow red in the dark!), but you do need to book at least three days in advance on 407 344 9550. Finally, they offer 45-minute **private tours** in their six-passenger boat ($45/person) which provide an even more personal view of this amazing area. Check out www.bcairboats.com for more info.

Boggy Creek Parasail

A new operation in 2001 and complementary to the airboat rides is this chance to float up and over East Lake Toho for one of the most breathtaking views of the area. You float up, with the greatest of ease, from the back of their 16-passenger boat going up to 400, 600 or 800ft (depending on the price you pay), descending again after about 15 relaxing minutes to land gently standing up – and completely dry (if you wish – see below). The sit-down harness they use requires no skill or effort on your part and makes it accessible to young and old alike, the able bodied and the physically challenged. The system is also deft enough to allow the operators to dip you in the water – upon request! Single flyers cost $45 (up to 400ft), $55 (600ft) and $65 (800ft), while double flyers are $75, $85 and $95. Observers may also ride free if there is space in the boat. Reservations are not usually required but it is often wise to check on 407 348 2700, and Boggy Creek parasail operate 7 days a week from 10am–5.30pm.

Balloon trips

Florida is one of the most popular areas for ballooning and, if you are up early enough in the morning, you will quite often see three or four floating over the countryside. The experience is a majestic one. If Orlando represents the holiday of a lifetime, then a balloon flight is the ride of a lifetime. Believe me, Disney has nothing to touch this one! The utterly smooth way in which you lift off into the early morning sky is breathtaking in itself, but the peace and quiet of the ride, not to mention the stunning views from 2,000ft above ground, are quite awesome. It is not a cheap experience, but it is equally appealing to all but the youngest children or those who suffer vertigo or a fear of heights. It is a highly personalised ride, as 6 people can make for a full trip. Some baskets take up to 9, but you need to be on good terms!

BRIT TIP: Dresses are not advisable for balloon trips and sensible shoes are essential.

Orange Blossom Balloons are the premier company in central Florida, with more than 16 years' experience and a wonderfully laid-back style that stems from their British-owned operation. You meet at the Days Inn Hotel Maingate West on Highway 192, half a mile past Splendid China, at 6am (the best winds for flying are always first thing in the morning) and then transfer to the take-off site, where you help the crew set up and inflate one of their three balloons. Owner-operator Richard Ornstein and his team are a real hoot, and you are soon up, up and away in awe-inspiring style, floating serenely up to 2,000ft or sinking down to skim the surface of one of the many lakes (disturbing the occasional gator or deer). After about an hour you come back to earth for a traditional champagne landing ceremony and return to Days Inn for a full breakfast and your special balloonist's certificate. The full experience lasts 3–4 hours and the cost is $175 per adult (inclusive of tax) and $95 for 10–15s (under 10s go free with their parents). Hotel pick-up is also available at $10 per person round-trip or you can pay $20 to be part of the chase crew and enjoy the champagne landing and breakfast. Call 407 239 7677 for reservations (they do get well-booked, even though they fly 7 days a week, weather permitting) or go to www.obballoons.com.

> BRIT TIP: I consistently receive some of the most impressive feedback from readers who try Aquatic Wonders, Boggy Creek Airboats and Orange Blossom Balloons.

Everglades and the Bahamas

Day trips are increasingly common from Orlando to the Everglades, Miami, the Florida Keys and the Bahamas and, if you are prepared to put up with a long day out (up to 16 hours) you can see a lot of the state this way. However, they are not well-suited to children, with long periods on a coach, while the half-hour airboat ride once you get to the Everglades can seem brief.

There are two companies worth recommending here, **Real Florida Excursions** and **International Divers**, who both offer quite a variety of tours, from an Orlando Shop Til You Drop excursion to a Miami-Bahamas 2-day getaway. For the latter, you travel down to Miami (3½ hours) by coach, get to shop at the smart Bayside Marketplace or take the popular 1½-hour Miami waterways cruise, before the 22-minute flight to the Bahamas for an overnight stay. The following day can be spent on the beautiful beaches or at your hotel in Freeport, the Bahamia Resort & Casino, before you cruise back to Fort Lauderdale in some style (great food in particular) and catch the coach back to Orlando. This excellent package costs just $149 for adults and $99 for children 2–12 (plus another $73 for local taxes). An overnight trip to **Miami** and the sizzling **South Beach** district, with its hot night-life, is another attractive proposition. You get deluxe transport, a guided tour, good quality accommodation and the best part of a day on the beach for $99 and $59 (3–12s). Alternatively, you could try their **Naples-Everglades Adventure**, with a 30-minute airboat ride through the Everglades, lunch in the beautiful city of Naples and a late afternoon cruise along the coastal waterways. This is $99 (adults) and $59 (3–12s), with an optional swamp buggy ride in the Everglades at $14 per adult (under 6s free). Call Real Florida Excursions on 407 345 4996, ext. 3012 (or look them up at www.werusa.com). **International Divers** offer several other contrasting and memorable tours, chief among which is their **Florida Adventure Tour**, a personal, all-day experience in the real Florida. It includes a breakfast buffet stop, a 2-hour boat trip and snorkel on the picturesque Crystal River (where you often encounter the harmless manatees!), a relaxing lunch at King's Bay, 45-minute airboat tour on the Withlacochee River and a jeep safari through a wildlife refuge that includes tigers, lions, kangaroos

8

Orange Blossom Balloons

and raccoons. Alternatively, their 2-day **Getaway to the Florida Keys** is an excellent proposition, visiting the Everglades en route, seeing an alligator wrestling and snake-handling show and taking an airboat ride before arriving at Key Largo for a beach barbecue. Part two of the adventure, after an overnight stay and breakfast at your beach resort, is the **dolphin encounter**, a two-hour programme of instruction, observation and interaction with the Key's tame resident dolphins (including one-on-one swims, dorsal tows and foot pushes!). With the dolphin encounter, the tour is $289 for adults and $279 for 7–9s, while without it is $189 and $179 (children must be at least 7 to participate in the dolphin swim). Call International Divers for details on 407 352 4646 (or visit them online at www.swimdolphins.com).

Flying Tigers Warbird Restoration Museum

Vintage aeroplane and nostalgia buffs will want to make a note of this offbeat museum adjacent to Kissimmee Airport, which builds and restores World War Two fighters and bombers. Kids who enjoyed building Airfix kits will especially enjoy the 1-hour tour of

the facilities, which basically represent a couple of large hangars with aircraft in various stages of restoration and repair. It is one of the most amazing programmes of its kind you will find, with the exhibits ranging from a fully restored B-25 Mitchell bomber and a P-51 Mustang to scraps of fuselages and engines that will gradually be incorporated into the latest rebuilding project. It's a place where you see, smell and touch the history of the old 1940s newsreels. The guides have a detailed working knowledge of everything they show you. You could be forgiven for thinking you have walked into a scrapyard, but the main hangars reveal the full scale of the operation, with the wholesale restoration of a B-17 Flying Fortress being their pride and joy. In fact, owner Tom Reilly insists: 'All those clean, tidy sterile museums you have seen in the past, well, this isn't one of them. We have oil on the floor we refer to as bomber blood and, if you are lucky, you might get some on you to take home as a souvenir.' In progress in 2001 was a unique project to restore a Focke-Wulf FW190 fighter-bomber back to flying condition. The site detail includes a charming gift shop that houses some more museum pieces, uniforms and memorabilia from World War Two. It is open 7 days a week 9am–5.30pm, and there's always some reconstruction work under way.

Fightertown at the Warbird Museum

Charges are $8 for adults, $7 for 60+ and $6 for under 12s (under 5s free). This 'living museum' can be found off Highway 192, half a mile down Hoagland Boulevard on the left.

Anyone captivated by the sights, sounds and stories of this magnificent exhibit (also known as Bombertown) can also join in. Warbird Restoration School is an intensive 5-day course covering the whole rebuild process, from sheet-metal fabrication to welding and fuel systems. It culminates with a flight in a restored B-25J Mitchell bomber, but is definitely for enthusiasts only – it costs $995. Call 407 933 1942 for details or see their website www.warbirdmuseum.com.

Warbird Adventures

Once you have seen the displays, you should consider neighbouring **Warbird Adventures**. This is the best ride in town, bar none, guaranteed. Not only do you get to fly in a 1945 T-6 Harvard fighter-trainer (one of three they operate), but also, after a while getting used to the front seat of this vintage two-seater … you get to fly it! And you don't just handle the controls, your instructor will get you doing loops, barrel rolls and all manner of aerobatics. This is simply the most memorable and exhilarating ride I have done anywhere in the world, enhanced by in-flight video and wingtip camera to record every moment. It is the only place where you can walk in off the street and, 20 minutes later, be flying a plane with *no previous flight experience*. My instructor was the excellent Thom Richard and, despite my initial reluctance and disbelief, he had me doing the full aerobatic business before long. Roller-coasters? They're for wimps! Mind you, this is not a cheap experience – a 15-minute flight costs $150, while a

30-minute trip is $250 and an hour $450. Aerobatics (on 30 or 60-minute flights only) cost $30, while the PAL video is $40 and the stills $15 (or all three 'extras' for $70), but this is truly a memory to last a lifetime, and the thought of it still thrills me to bits a good while after. Call 407 870 7366 for details or look up www.warbirdadventures.com.

Green Meadows Petting Farm

From one extreme to another, here is guaranteed fun for kids of 2 up to about 11, and their parents (and don't forget your cameras). It's the ultimate hands-on experience as, on your 2-hour guided tour, you (or rather, your children) can milk a cow, pet a pig, cuddle a chick or duckling, feed goats and sheep, meet a buffalo, chickens, peacocks and donkeys and learn what makes an animal farm tick. There are pony rides for the young ones and tractor-drawn hay rides for all, plus the Green Meadows Express steam train for a scenic ride through the farm and a play area of slides and swings. The shaded acres, free-roaming

The author takes the front seat with Warbird Adventures

8

animals and peaceful aspect all make for another pleasant change of pace, especially as Green Meadows is barely 10 minutes from the tourist hurly-burly of Highway 192 (south on Poinciana Boulevard). It is open 9.30am–5.30pm daily (last admission at 4pm) and costs $15 per person (under 2s free), and you should allow 3–4 hours for your visit. Drinks, snacks and gifts are available, but it is also the ideal place to bring a picnic. Call 407 846 0770 or visit www.greenmeadowsfarm.com.

Disney and cruising

Taking a cruise is fast becoming a regular option with your Orlando stay and, with the advent of *Disney Cruise Line* in 1998, you will now see a lot of publicity for these competitively priced 2-, 3-, 4- and 7-day sailings out of fast-developing Port Canaveral.

Although they are cruise newcomers, Disney have set their stall out with some of the most breathtaking hardware in the form of their first two ships, the 83,000-ton *Disney Magic* (1998) and *Disney Wonder* (1999), plus their own dedicated cruise terminal. Classic design plus the usual Disney imagineering have produced these two huge vessels incorporating special features for kids, teenagers AND couples without children. Both ships are a destination experience in their own right, each with four restaurants, a 1,040-seat theatre, cinema, night-club complex, sports club and a full health spa, while they visit the Bahamas, Caribbean and Disney's stunning private island. It is not a cheap option and the 3- and 4-day cruises can feel a little frenzied, but the new 7-day voyages – either to St Maarten and St Thomas or Key West, Grand Cayman and Cozumel in Mexico – offer a genuinely relaxing style that

is hard to beat anywhere in the world, and boast some novel touches with superb on-board entertainment, Disney character interaction and features like the adults-only champagne brunch, which is just to die for. Many tour operators offer Disney cruise packages but you can also book cruise-only at great rates with Dreams Unlimited Travel at www.dreamsunlimitedtravel.com.

The ships are identical in practical terms, and the week's cruise allows you to enjoy fully the wide range of facilities. The impact of the four-restaurant set-up (where you dine in a different one each night, including the amazing Animator's Palate which comes to life all around you), the fabulous entertainment 'district', the vast array of kids' facilities (including Buzz Lightyear's Cyberspace Command Post), the wonderfully picturesque beaches of Castaway Cay island and the sheer ocean-going quality knocks your socks off.

Other cruises out of Port Canaveral include the glitzy **Carnival Cruise Lines** (all-modern hardware, party atmosphere; tel 1-888 2276 4825) with 3- and 4-day Bahamas voyages, and **Royal Caribbean International** (another modern, glamorous vessel, tel 1-800 327 6700) with similar trips to Nassau and RCI's private island of CocoCay. For more advice, consult my book *Choosing A Cruise* and specialist UK travel agent The Cruise Line Ltd on 01273 835252.

For a smaller and more low-key approach, the **Rivership Romance**, daily out of downtown Sanford, is a great choice, especially for their lunch cruises on the wildlife-rich St John's River. Their old-fashioned steamer can take up to 200 in comfort and adds a fine meal, live entertainment and a river commentary, as well as providing a relaxing alternative to the usual tourist scenario. Choose from the

3-hour lunch cruise (Wed, Sat and Sun, 11am–2pm) at $35 a head, the 4-hour cruise (Mon, Tue, Thur and Fri, 11am–3pm) at $45 or an evening dinner-dance voyage (Fri and Sat, 7.30–11pm) at $50. For reservations and information call 407 321 5091 (or visit www.rivershipromance.com). Their dock can be found off exit 51 of I4, east into Sanford, then left on Palmetto Avenue.

Seminole County

Having arrived in the historic town of Sanford, the heart of Seminole County, it is worth pointing out the possible diversions of a day or two in this area that will get you well off the beaten track. The **Central Florida Zoological Park** is a private, non-profit-making organisation that puts a pleasant, natural accent on the zoo theme, set in 109 wooded acres of unspoilt Florida countryside and with boardwalks and trails around all the attractions. These include more than 100 species of animals, weekend feeding demonstrations, educational programmes, a picnic area, pony rides and a butterfly garden, plus the Zoofari Outpost gift shop. It's good value, too, at $7 for adults and $3 for kids 3–12, and the park (off exit 52 of I4) is open every day (except Thanksgiving Day and Christmas Day) 9am–5pm.

St John's River Cruise at Blue Spring State Park features a two-hour nature tour of this historic waterway, with interactive narration of the history, flora and fauna (which includes manatees in winter months). This immensely personable, family-run tour costs $14 for adults, $12 for seniors (60+) and $8 for children (3–12) and goes out several times a day from Orange City marina (take Highway 17/92 north from Sanford to French

Avenue and head west for one mile). Call 407 330 1612 to check times and book. **Bill's Airboat Adventures**, on the St John's River east of Sanford, offer 90-minute tours in the company of conservationist and river historian Captain Bill Daniel for $30 ($15 for under 14s). Call 407 977 3214 to book. **Possum Bay Fish Camp**, out on East SR 46, has a full range of airboat rides, fishing boat rentals, wave-runner rides, camping, picnics and country store (tel 407 349 0900), while **Skyline Watersports** offer speedboats, pontoon boats, fishing boats and wave-runners for rent (tel 407 321 0000). **Black Hammock Fish Camp and Restaurant** (off Exit 44 of the Central Florida Greeneway, take SR 434 east, turn left on Deleon St and left on to Black Hammock Road) is another peaceful backwater on Lake Jesup where you can try fishing or Gator Ventures airboating – and don't miss their great restaurant for local specialities (tel 407 365 1244). For a taste of all this – and more – the new **Seminole Safari** offers a full day excursion into the backwoods and backwaters for a real close-up with Florida nature. You will hike along the St John's River, visit the historic Cracker Ranch House (and learn about the Seminole Indian Wars), take an airboat ride and trek through the rich birdlife of the wetlands, stopping en route for lunch. Iced water is provided all day and stout footwear is advisable (as is bringing a towel). It costs $99 for adults and $79 for children 4–12 (under 4s free, but not really recommended). Call 407 349 2080 for more details or go to www.allseasonscommerce.com.

Of course, you can just head for one of the splendid **State Parks** in this area and take your own tour of the well-marked trails. Wekiva Springs State Park offers hiking, canoeing and swimming, plus picnic areas and shelters, while Little Big

Rivership Romance in Seminole County

Econ state forest is 5,048 acres of scenic woodlands and wetlands.

Sanford itself is a designated historic centre, full of brick-paved streets and antique shops. It is very much small-town America, having lost the growth battle with Orlando many years ago, but it makes a peaceful diversion with some lovely walks. It also offers the **Rose Cottage Tea Room**, one of the prettiest restaurants you will find in Florida, which serves a mouth-watering array of soups, sandwiches, salads and quiches, as well as fabulous fruit teas. This little treasure (open 11am–3pm Tue–Sat) can be found on Park Avenue, 13 blocks out of Sanford town centre, call 407 323 9448 for reservations (which are usually required). If you fancy a day or two staying in the area (highly recommended), check out one of the quaint B & B accommodations like The Higgins House (407 324 9238) or The Martin House (407 330 9013).

For more details on all of the above, go to www.visitseminole.com.

Caladesi Island

Eco-tourism

Genuine eco-tourism is still in its infancy, in general terms, in central Florida, but there are two major exceptions worth knowing about.

Forever Florida is, for my money, one of the most outstanding, non-theme park attractions of all. It is both a 4,700-acre wilderness preserve and a working ranch. As well as a close-up of Florida's flora and fauna and its conservation issues, you get a taste of the original cowboy life, Cracker style (Crackers were the 'real' cowboys, pre-dating their Western counterparts by 50 years), which is a fascinating slice of history. Eco-safaris, covered wagon tours, horse rides, bike trails, nature walks and, for the kids, pony rides and a free petting zoo, are the highlights, as well as the magnificent **Cypress Restaurant** and Visitor Center, which offers an essential 30-minute orientation programme into the Conservancy's creation. Forever Florida began as a dream of gifted young biologist and ecologist Allen Broussard and has been carried to fruition after his death from complications of Hodgkin's disease by his parents, Dr William and Margaret Broussard, who own the neighbouring Crescent J Ranch and continue to give their time and energy to building the wilderness as a non-profitmaking memorial to their son. The education element alone is awesome, and tours feature a strong conservation message in this tranquil, untouched corner of

Getting off the beaten track

Florida. The **Cracker Coach Tour** ($28 for adults, $18 for under 13s, daily at 9am, 12 noon and 3pm) – a kind of open-sided, large-wheeled buggy – is their stock-in-trade, a 2-hour-plus trundle around much of the woods, swamp and prairie that make up the ranch and Conservancy, in the company of an education coordinator who provides the low-down on the history and environmental issues of the ecosystems. You are likely to encounter alligators (at a safe distance), whitetail deer, armadillos and a host of bird-life – including bald eagles – and leave with a good understanding of the real Florida.

Guided horse rides vary from $35–$52 (1–3 hours; $24–$31 for children), and **covered wagon tours** of the Ranch are $28 and $18 (reservations required). **Trail bike** rentals are $8 an hour and **pony rides** $5 for the first ride, $3 for a second. There is even an overnight horse ride or ranch experience for the ultimate Cracker appeal, but it is distinctly expensive at $275 and $255. Regular tours run Fri–Sun at 9am, 12.30pm and 3.30pm but should be booked on 1-800 957 9794. A new **BioPark** is taking shape, which aims to showcase only native Floridian animals such as the panther and bear, and the original Cracker cattle (a distinctly ornery beast, by all accounts). For more details, visit www.foreverflorida.com. The Conservancy is a good 80-minute drive out of Orlando, some 40 miles east on Highway 192,

through St Cloud as far as Holopaw, then 7.6 miles south on US Highway 441, but it is well worth the journey. Rating: AAAAA.

Forever Florida

On an equally authentic scale is **Disney's Wilderness Preserve**, run by the Nature Conservancy in Poinciana, south of Kissimmee. This restoration of an 11,500-acre preserve is a work in progress and allows visitors in for various hiking trails, a 1-hour guided tour on Saturdays (at 9.30am) and 2-hour buggy tours on Sundays (1.30pm). Entry fee is $2 for adults and $1 for children, while the buggy tours are an additional $7 and $5. The Preserve is located at the end of Pleasant Hill Road (follow Hoagland Boulevard south off Highway 192). Call 407 935 0002 for more information. Rating: AAA.

The Kissimmee Convention and Visitors' Bureau also publishes an excellent eco-guide, if you drop by their Visitor Center on Highway 192.

Daytona Beach

Beach escapes

When it comes to beaches, and another key component of a Florida holiday, you are again spoiled for choice (see page 212). The sea, sand and surf of **Cocoa Beach** is only an hour's drive from Orlando east on the Beeline Expressway (528) then south on Highway A1A, and offers some good shopping (including the unmissable **Ron Jon's Surf Shop**, a massive neon emporium of all things water related) in addition to the two main public beaches. As it's the Atlantic, the sea can be pretty chilly from November to March, but Cocoa Beach is rapidly developing into a major coastal resort, so the facilities are excellent. Its more famous neighbour, just to the north, is **Daytona Beach**, which is still only an hour away if you take I4 all the way east. This is the prime site of the Atlantic coast scene, with an array of good beaches (some of which you can even drive on – for a $5 toll, speed limit 10mph), boating and fishing trips, sightseeing (including the **Ponce deLeon Inlet Lighthouse**) and surprisingly smart shopping (witness the redeveloped **Ocean Walk Village**). The beaches themselves are a lively affair around Spring Break (the big American pre-Easter college holiday) but fairly down to earth otherwise. Other highlights include the chance to cruise the intra-coastal waterway to

> BRIT TIP: Be warned, in summer months the locals all get the same urge to head for the beach at weekends, so unless you head out EARLY (i.e. before 9am) and come back late (i.e. after 8pm) you will encounter some serious traffic.

see the local dolphins at play – check out **A tiny Cruise Line** (call 904 226 2343) for this memorable outing – and the **Riverfront Marketplace**, the heart of downtown Daytona Beach, with a museum of local history, restaurants, nightclubs, coffee bars and a performing arts theatre, all in a quaint riverside setting. Your opportunities for dining out are particularly inviting along the Beaches, with Inlet Harbor and Lighthouse Landing among the best. The beaches themselves can be up to 500ft wide at low tide and all areas are open to the public year-round. **Lighthouse Point Park** is especially worthy of note, a 52-acre stretch of nature trails, fishing, observation deck, swimming and picnicking (open 8am–9pm, $3.50 per vehicle). For the latest information on all Daytona Beach has to offer, look up www.daytonabeach.com or call 020 7935 7756 in the UK. Of course, one of the biggest attractions is the Daytona USA racetrack (see Motor Sport at the end of the Chapter).

To the West you have the **Gulf Coast**, which is a good 90 minutes' drive down I4 and through Tampa on I275 south to **St Petersburg Beach** (105 miles) or **Clearwater Beach** (110 miles) or two hours-plus down I4 and then I75 to **Bradenton** (130 miles), **Sarasota** (140 miles) and **Venice** (160 miles), plus the beautiful islands of **Captiva Sanibel** (175 miles) . The beaches are less 'hip', that is, more relaxed and refined, and the sea a touch warmer and much calmer, so it is better for families with small children. You will find it easier to get away from the crowds here, too. **Naples** is further south still on Interstate 75 but is rated one of the most welcoming beach destinations in Florida.

Sport

In addition to virtually every form of entertainment known to man, central Florida is one of the world's biggest sporting playgrounds, with a huge range of opportunities either to watch or play your favourite sport.

Golf

Without doubt, the number one activity is golf, with almost 150 courses within an hour's drive of Orlando. The weather, of course, makes it such a popular pastime, but some spectacular courses add to the attraction, and there are numerous holiday packages geared towards keen golfers of all abilities. With an 18-hole round, including cart hire and taxes, from as little as $40 on some courses (and they average around $75), it is an attractive proposition and quite different for those used to British courses. If you go in for 36-hole days, it is possible to save up to $30 by replaying the same course, while it is cheaper to play Monday–Thursday than Friday–Sunday. Sculpted landscapes, manicured fairways and abundant use of spectacular water features and white-sand traps make for some memorable golfing. The winter months are the high season, hence the most expensive, but many courses are busy year-round. Be aware also many courses pair up golfers with little thought for ability, handicap, etc. So, if two of you turn up, the chances are you will play with two complete strangers ('a little frustrating when you get paired with

two middle-aged ladies from Switzerland who have only just taken up golf,' says reader John Cartlidge).

Virtually every course will offer a driving range to get you started, plus lockers, changing rooms and showers, while the use of golf carts is universal (and many include the amazing GPS positioning system which gives the yardage for every shot, plus the ability to order drinks or even lunch while you're on the course!). They all feature creature comforts like ice water stations and drinks carts that circulate the course (please don't forget to tip the trolley girls who drive them). A handful boast swimming pools while all can offer a decent bar and restaurant for that all-important 19th-hole session. Your best starting point is to visit one of the five **Edwin Watts** golf shops around Orlando to pick up a free copy of the *Golfer's Guide* or the *Guide To Golf* for a handy introduction to most of the courses available (and even pick up a new set of clubs at the Watts National Clearance Center just south of Wet 'n Wild on I-Drive; tel 407 352 2535 or visit their website at www.edwinwatts.com). Alternatively, Tee-Times USA (tel 1-888 465 3356) offer an excellent advice and reservation service.

For a unique and personable touch, you can't beat the all-in-one service of **Professional Golf Guides of Orlando**, led by PGA-qualified Phillip Jaffe, who take up to three at a time around one of 17 courses, providing tuition, the inside track of the course and some invaluable tips for developing your game. They supply transport, clubs (if necessary) and a playing lesson of the highest calibre. Phillip himself is a mine of golfing lore and knowledge, as well as being great company, and the keen golfer should call 407 894 0907 or visit www.progolfguides.com. Rates are from $350 for one, $500 for two and

BRIT TIP: An early-morning tee-off in the summer can provide some of the most peaceful and scenic golf you will find.

8

Florida's Beach

The huge spread of beaches and 'cities' from St Pete Beach to Clearwater (collectively known as Florida's Beach) represent the heart of the Florida beach experience, with a wonderful array of attractions in addition to the 35 miles of lovely white sands and average 361 days of sunshine a year. **St Petersburg** itself, just across the Howard Frankland Bridge from Tampa, is a bright, attractive and happening city, with a range of developments, both recent and historical, which make it a worthwhile visit. Take time here for the wonderful **Dali Museum** (open 9.30am–5.30pm Mon–Sat, 12 noon–5.30pm Sun; adults $10, under 11s free) and the new **Bay Walk** complex of shops, restaurants and 20-screen cinema. An additional assortment of surprising museums, pedestrian-friendly streets and The Pier all add up to a wealth of opportunity for the interested visitor. Out in the **Beaches**, from the 800-acre Fort De Soto Park in the south to stunning Caladesi Island in the north, there is a wonderful diversity of choice, too, with the likes of Treasure Island, Sand Key and St Pete Beach all receiving the Blue Wave Award for cleanliness and safety. **Fort De Soto Park** also offers free walking tours of its Spanish-American War era Fort and wilderness areas, in addition to boasting one of the quietest and prettiest beaches. **John's Pass Village & Boardwalk** is an unusual shopping district full of art galleries and restaurants, while **Dolphin Landings** in St Pete Beach is another big draw for its dolphin watch cruises, Shell Island day-trips and sunset sailings (the dolphin cruise is a real highlight for its guaranteed close-up animal encounters along the calm inland waterway; the 2-hour yacht voyage costs $25 for adults and $15 for children – call 727 367 4488 or visit www.dolphinlandings.com). Along at Indian Shores, the **Suncoast Seabird Sanctuary** is another must-see little hideaway, America's largest wild bird hospital, with more than 500 injured birds on display. **Clearwater Beach** boasts the Marine Aquarium and Pier 60, where they hold the daily sunset celebration, complete with craft stalls and live music. And, reaching **Caladesi Island** brings you to one of the most picturesque beach spots in the world and another Blue Wave award-winner. For those wishing to take it easy rather than get back in the hire car while they are here, the **Suncoast Beach Trolley** is the perfect transport link both along the beaches and into St Petersburg ($1/ride or $2.50 for an all-day pass). When it comes to accommodation, there is a suitably wide choice, too. A range of **Superior Small Lodgings** combine desirable beach-front locations with small-scale, personalised service (check out the Seahorse Cottages & Apartments on treasure Island Beach as the perfect example – with weekly rates from $385 for a one-bedroom cottage; call 727 367 2291 or look them up at www.beachdirectory.com/seahorse). Of course, there are also the more up-market hotels, and I can vouch for both the superbly-equipped **Tradewinds Beach Resorts** (a 1,100-room development of three resorts that combine their wide range of facilities; call 727 562 1221 or visit www.tradewindsresort.com) on St Pete Beach and the huge (and hugely impressive) **Sheraton Sand Key Resort** at Clearwater Beach, a 10-storey edifice with 10 acres of private beach and facilities ranging from floodlit tennis courts to a fitness centre, children's pool and playground (with supervised programmes in summer). Rates from $135-$480, call 727 595 1611 or check out www.beachsand.com. The area also boasts more than 2,000 restaurants and they – and much, much more – can be looked up on the essential website, www.floridasbeach.com.

$650 for three, to include all green fees and lunch (May 1–Oct 15; add $50 per player in high season), with an additional $50–$75 for a premium course like Disney or Grand Cypress. The lesson includes full on-course instruction, course management strategies, full game analysis and improvement suggestions, shot-making demonstrations and a wrap-up lesson afterwards. Group lessons are $100 (ratio 1:5) and range lessons are $75/hour, or $275 for a package of four.

The **Nick Faldo Golf Institute** on the lower portion of International Drive (tel 1-888 463 2536) is a great place to visit if you just want to hit a few golf balls.

Disney have been quick to attract the golf fanatic, with five championship-quality courses, including the 7,000yd Palm, rated one of Golf Digest's top 25. Fees vary from $100–$130 for *Walt Disney World Resort in Florida* guests and $110-$140 for visitors, with half-price reductions after 3pm. Call 407 939 4653 for tee-times.

Another luxury experience is afforded by the **Grand Cypress**, next door to *Walt Disney World Resort in Florida* on Vineland Road (tel 407 239 1904, rates from $130–$170 depending on season). It has three elegant nine-hole courses and a superb 18-hole links-style offering (all designed by the legendary Jack Nicklaus) which presents a truly magnificent challenge. **MetroWest Country Club**, on South Hiawassee Road to the north of Universal Studios (tel 407 299 1099; $79–$115) is a 7,051-yard masterpiece designed by Robert Trent Jones Snr and features elevated tees and greens, with rolling fairways and expansive bunkers. The superb **Keene's Pointe** in Windermere to the north of *Walt Disney World Resort in Florida* is Nicklaus's newest and most exciting

Golf at the Westin Innisbrook Resort

course, measuring 7,173yd if played off the pro Bear tees (there are always five tees for the various handicaps, ladies and seniors). Surrounded by lakes, it has a truly impeccable look, not to mention outstanding facilities, including a pool (tel 407 876 1461; $65–$115). The **Legacy Club at Alaqua Lakes** is a masterpiece of conservation and tranquility (it is part of the Audubon preservation and restoration scheme) as well as a tour de force of lush fairways and weird and wonderful greens (a signature feature of designer Tom Fazio). Winding through some spectacular forest in the suburb of Longwood in Seminole County, it is a serious challenge for serious golfers (tel 407 444 9995; $54–$64). Also in Seminole, **Magnolia Plantation** is another wonderful contrast, a heavily wooded and peaceful haven that feels miles from the theme park world and yet is less than half an hour away up I4. Woven among the Wekiva River basin, hence with a series of lakes and ponds, Phillip Jaffe rates it a 'must play' course here (tel 407 833 0818; $55–$85). **Falcon's Fire** in Kissimmee is another standout course, featuring the 'ProShot' digital caddy system and water coolers on all golf carts. Plenty of water elsewhere assures a testing 18 holes, but it is wonderfully picturesque (tel 407 239 5445; $75–$150). The **Orange Lake Country Club** is a huge vacation resort in Orlando (just four miles from Disney) with two 18-hole courses, a nine-hole course and a floodlit, par-3 nine holes. The new *Legends at Orange Lake* course (designed by Arnold Palmer) is their top-of-the-range offering (tel 407 239 1050; $70–$90). **Kissimmee Oaks** features some majestic moss-draped oaks and local wildlife as well as 18 holes of memorable golf that wind around some pretty lakes, all just 3½ miles south of Highway 192 in Kissimmee in the Oaks Community off John Young Parkway (tel 407 933 4055; $50–$80). Seminole County itself is another golf haven, with 18 public or semi-private courses, and offers golf-and-hotel packages from $65. Call 1-800 555 9589 for details or look up www.visitseminole.com.

Check when you book about each club's dress code, as there are a few differences from course to course.

Of course, this is only a small (if representative) sample and there are dozens of other choices. The Visit Florida organisation publishes an Official Golf Guide (tel 850 488 8374 or look up www.playfla.com), as does Daytona Beach (tel 1-800 881 7065, www.golfdaytonabeach.com.)

> BRIT TIP: Reader John Cartlidge, a keen Florida golfer, advises: 'Take your waterproofs with you. I was looking to buy some in Florida but could only find lightweight slipovers – no use in the UK.'

Mini-golf

Not exactly a sport, but definitely for tourist consumption are the many quite extravagant opportunities for mini-golf around Orlando. They are a big hit with kids and good fun for all the family (if you have the legs left for it after a day at the theme park!). Several attractions and parks offer mini-golf as an extra, but for the best, try out the self-contained centres, of which there are six main ones.

Predictably, Disney have come up with some terrific varieties of their own. **Disney's Fantasia Gardens Miniature Golf**, next to the Swan Hotel just off Buena Vista Drive, is a two-course challenge over 36 of the most varied holes of mini-golf you will find. Hippos dance, fountains leap and broomsticks march on the 18-hole crazy golf-themed **Fantasia Gardens** – its style is taken from the Disney animated classic Fantasia, and that means lots of cartoon fun along the way as the park's imagineers challenge you with a riot of visual gags as well as some diabolically difficult mini-golf. Watch out for *Toccata and Fugue in D Minor* where good shots are rewarded with musical tones, and *The Nutcracker Suite*, where obstacles include dancing mushrooms! **Fantasia Fairways** is a cunning putting course, complete with fairways, rough, water hazards and bunkers to test even the best golfers. The 18 holes range in length from 40 to 75ft, and it can take in excess of an hour to play a full round. Each course costs $9.25 (adult) and $7.50 (child), and they are open 10am–midnight every day. Their newest offering is the 36-hole **Winter-Summerland** course at the entrance to *Disney's Blizzard Beach* Water Park. Divided into two 18-hole courses, these mini works of art feature a 'Summer' setting of surf and beach tests (watch out for squirting fish), and a 'Winter' variety of snow and ice-crafted holes, all with a welter of visual puns as befitting the vacation resort of Santa's elves (yes, that's the theme, and kids will love it – there are even skid marks where Santa landed his sleigh!). An adult round is $9.25 (3–9s $7.50), a double round is 50 per cent off and it is open 10am–11pm.

Elsewhere, **Pirate's Cove** has a twin-course set-up at Lake Buena Vista (by the Crossroads shopping plaza) and International Drive (just south of the Mercado Center), with mountain caves, waterfalls and rope bridges to test your skill and please the eye. **River Adventure Golf** (on Highway 192, almost opposite Medieval Times) offers a Mississippi River adventure with rolling rapids, waterfalls and an authentic water wheel. **Bonanza Miniature Golf and Gifts** (next door to the Magic Mining Co. restaurant on west Highway 192) has another imaginative – and tricky – 36 holes set in a gold-mine theme. **Pirate's Island** (further along Highway 192 to the east) is another spectacular 36-hole spread, while arguably the most impressive of the lot is the **Congo River Golf and Exploration Co.**, which has courses on Highway 192, International Drive and Highway 436 in Altamonte Springs. They could almost be Disney-inspired, they are so artificially scenic. The Kissimmee location also has paddle boats to try, while International Drive has the option of go-karts, and all three have games and video arcades. Charges are $6–$8 per round, but look out for coupons which all have a couple of dollars off each one. They open 9am–10 or 11pm daily. **Million Dollar Mulligan** is also worthy of mention here, although it is neither mini-golf nor the real McCoy. Instead, Million Dollar Mulligan, just off Highway 192 on Florida

Plaza Boulevard (next to Old Town – look for the giant golf ball), is a nine-hole, floodlit pitch-and-putt course that looks spectacular at night with its lake and fountains lit up. It costs $11.75 for adults and $7.50 for children and seniors and is open from 10am–midnight (tel 407 396 8180).

Fishing

Fishing attracts a lot of specialist holiday-makers and is fast catching on as a highly enjoyable day out with us foreigners as well. The abundance of lakes and rivers makes for plentiful sport, with bass the prime catch. A 7-day licence costs $17 (available from all tackle shops, fishing camps, sports stores and Wal-Mart and K-Mart supermarkets), and there are dozens of boats for hire on the St John's River, Lake Toho in Kissimmee, Lake Kissimmee and both coasts for some serious sea fishing. Expect to pay $160–$195 for half a day and $200–$295 for a full day bass fishing. For the most complete angling service try **Cutting Loose Expeditions**, a highly experienced, personalised operator who can organise fresh or sea-water expeditions and arrange hotel pick-up if necessary. All your bait and licence requirements are included. The service is run by A Neville Cutting, one of America's leading fishing adventurers, and he maintains high standards with his guides and other staff. Rates start at $200 for a half day's bass fishing (two fishermen per boat with a licensed guide), but other trips, including offshore for marlin, can be arranged. Call 407 629 4700, visit www.ucutloose.com or write to Cutting Loose Expeditions, PO Box 447, Winter Park, Florida 32790-0447. Alternatively, **AJ's Freelance Bass Guide Services** specialise in trophy bass fishing on Lake Toho in Kissimmee with professional guides (all US Coastguard-licensed captains). Full-day trips (9 hours from first light) are $275 for one to two people, a half day (4½ hrs) is $200 and it is $75 or $50 extra per person, plus your licence and bait (sodas and ice provided, but you need to bring your own snacks). Hotel pick-ups ($30) can also be arranged, call 407 348 8764 or visit www.orlandobass.com.

Water sports

Florida is also mad keen on water sports of all persuasions. So, on any area of water bigger than your average pond, don't be surprised to find the locals water-skiing, jetskiing, knee-boarding, canoeing, paddling, wind-surfing, boating or otherwise indulging in watery pursuits. *Walt Disney World Resort in Florida* offers all manner of boats, from catamarans to canoes and pedaloes, and activities, from water-skiing to parasailing, on the main **Bay Lake**, as well as the smaller **Seven Seas Lagoon**, **Crescent Lake** and **Lake Buena Vista**. Parasailing (from *Disney's Contemporary Resort*) costs $75 solo

Waterskiing at Dave's

or $115 tandem, while boat rentals (from a range of resorts) vary from $8/hour (14ft sailboats and catamarans) to $57/hour (21ft pontoon boats). For reservations and information, call 407 939 7529.

There are several operators on the lakes around Orlando and Kissimmee, too, but some of them leave much to be desired, safety-wise. **Dave's Ski School** on Lake Bryan at Lake Buena Vista (right next to the Holiday Inn Sunspree Resort on SR 535) gets our recommendation for their safety-conscious approach and their virtual guarantee to get beginners up and water-skiing. Their **Watersports Adventure** includes an hour's water-ski lessons and rides, a tube ride and a wave-runner ride ($55 adult, $48 child), and lasts up to 3 hours, while an hour's water-ski school costs $40 and $36. You can also rent wave-runners at $35 for half an hour or try parasailing at $40/person. Many of the main tour operators also endorse this ski school and for more details, call 407 239 6939 (or look them up at www.bvwatersports.com).

For a more gentle experience and a close-up of the local wildlife try **Katie's Wekiva River Landing**. Here you can try up to a full day's canoeing on some of the most scenic waters of central Florida (take I4 east to Exit 51 and Highway 46 west for almost 5 miles, and Wekiva Park Drive is on your right). It's fairly leisurely, but does have its faster-flowing sections, and you can take time-outs for a picnic or to go fishing. The entire portion of the Wekiva River here has been designated a protected 'Scenic and Wild' area, while the neighbouring forest with its hiking trails is an official aquatic preserve. Thick cypress forest, clear, spring-fed waters, abundant water and wildlife, it's all here for nature-lovers. Katie's offers five different canoe trips, from a leisurely 2-hour, 6-mile paddle to a

19-mile overnight camping trip, all with a pick-up service at the end or transport up-river to start with. Prices range from $14.50 for a 2-hour paddle to $25 for all day (children 3–11 half-price), and the trips are suitable for beginners and more experienced canoeists alike. Katie's also offers trail bikes, camping, boating and fishing. For more details call 407 322 4470, or log on to www.ktland.com.

Horse riding

If horse riding takes your fancy (or your children's), you will want to know Orlando is home to one of the foremost equestrian centres in America. It is the **Grand Cypress Equestrian Center**, part of the 1,500-acre Grand Cypress Resort, and all its rides and facilities are open to non-residents. This stunningly equipped equine haven offers a dazzling array of opportunities for horse enthusiasts of all abilities.

A full range of clinics, lessons and other instructional programmes are available, from half-hour kids' sessions to all-summer academies, plus a variety of trail rides. Serious horse riders will note this was the first American equestrian centre to be approved by the British Horse Society, and it operates the BHS test programme. Inevitably, this five-star facility does not come cheap, but, especially for children, it is a worthwhile experience. Private lessons are $45 per half hour or $75 per hour, while a week's package of eight half-hour lessons is $270. Young Junior Lessons (15-minute supervised rides for under 12s) are $25, while the Western Trail Ride (an hour's excursion for novice riders) is $30 per person and the Advanced Trail Ride $45. The centre is open 8am–5pm daily and can be found by taking Exit 27 on I4 on to Route 535 north, turning left

after half a mile at the traffic lights and then following the road north for a mile (past the entrance to the Grand Cypress Hotel) until the equestrian centre is on your right (tel 407 239 1938).

On a smaller scale and none the less charming is the **Horse World Riding Stables** on Poinciana Boulevard, just 12 miles south of Highway 192. This gets you more out into the wilds and you can spend anything from an hour to a full day enjoying the rides and lessons on offer. The three main rides are the Nature Trail ($32), a walking-only tour for 45–50 minutes for beginners aged 6 and up through 750 acres of untouched Florida countryside, the Intermediate Trail (ages 10 and up) for nearly one hour ($36), and the Advanced Private Trail, a 75 to 90-minute trip for advanced riders with private guide ($49). There is also a picnic area with fishing pond, playing fields, pony rides for under 7s ($6) and farm animals to pet. Riding lessons are $25/hour with up to four in a group and $35/hour privately. The three-hour Children's Horse Camp (for 8 to 14-year-olds every Saturday at 9am) is $30 per child. There is no charge for just looking around, and the Stables are open 9am–5pm daily. Call 407 847 4343 or look up their website at www.horseworldstables.com for details and reservations.

Similarly out in the wilds (in the Rock Springs Run Wildlife Preserve in Seminole County, to be precise) are **Rock Springs Riding Stables**, another slice of native Florida, with rides varying from a 1-hour Turkey Trail to a full day's Wildlife Wander, all led by trained guides. The park's 6,000 acres guarantee plenty of wildlife, from otters and coyotes to the occasional wild boar and even bears, and the rides go out every day 9am–6pm, costing $25–$100, with $10 pony rides for under 8s. To find Rock Springs, take I4 to Exit 51

8

(Sanford-SR46) and go west 8 miles before turning left into the Preserve. Take the dirt road first left and follow all the way to the horse barn, or call 407 314 1000 for more info.

Spectator events

When it comes to spectator events, Orlando is not quite so well furnished as other big American cities, but there is always something on offer for the discerning sports fan who would like to sample the local version of the big match. There are no top-flight American Football or baseball teams, but there is an indoor version of gridiron, called Arena Football, plus a Minor League baseball team.

The main sport is **basketball** and the Orlando Magic of the NBA. The basketball season runs from November to May (with exhibition games in October), and the only drawback is the 16,000-seat TD Waterhouse Center where they play (on Amelia Street, Exit 41 off I4, turn left, then left again) is occasionally fully booked. The Center box office (407 649 3245) can always say if there are any tickets left, although you need to call in person to buy them (from $16 up in the gods to $60 courtside), or you can call Ticketmaster on 407 839 3900 for credit card bookings.

The Orlando Predators, one of America's top **Arena Football** teams, are also popular at the same venue (from May to August, ticket prices $10–$30) and you would need to call several days in advance to avoid missing one of their lively home games that feature some great entertainment as well as their fast, hard-hitting version of indoor gridiron in the magnificent Center.

For the Real Thing in gridiron terms, the nearest teams in the **National Football League** are the Tampa Bay Buccaneers, 75 miles to the west, the Miami Dolphins, some 3½ hours' drive to the south down the Florida Turnpike or the Jacksonville Jaguars way up the east coast past Daytona, a 3-hour drive up I4 and I95. Again, Ticketmaster can give you ticket prices ($25–$50) and availability (Sept–Dec).

Disney's Wide World of Sports Complex

The newest sports facility in the area is inevitably a Disney project to bring in some world-class events and competitors. *Disney's Wide World of Sports Complex* is a 200-acre, state-of-the-art complex, featuring more than 32 sports and is quite awesome to wander round even when no one is playing. A recent addition is a permanent version of the **NFL** (American Football) **Experience**, which gives you the chance to test your skills as a gridiron star in an interactive playground for adults and kids alike. The complex's main features are a 7,500-seater baseball stadium, a softball quadraplex, an 11-court tennis complex, beach volleyball and the **All Star Café** with a massive array of sports memorabilia and even themed food. The baseball stadium is home for spring training of the mighty **Atlanta Braves**, and the crowds positively flock in for their pre-season games. Once the season gets under way in April, the WWoS is home to the minor league **Orlando Rays** (the AA team of the Major League Tampa Bay Devil Rays), who play 70 games a season, and there are often games six or seven evenings in succession, with Disney putting on an excellent stage, with plenty of hoopla, for every one. In fact, with tickets only $5–$8 (and parking free), it is some of the best-value entertainment on offer as you check out America's future baseball stars in this family-orientated environment. There are games and competitions for kids between innings and the action is still intense and exciting (OK, I'll admit I'm a big baseball fan, but it is still a great slice of genuine Americana as both Spring Training and even minor league games are great sporting traditions).

Other prime events include the Harlem Globetrotters basketball and international beach volleyball. The facilities alone should inspire world-class performances in any athlete. Standard admission is $8, but it is one of your optional extras with a Park Hopper Plus Pass (although that does not cover special events), and *Disney's Wide World of Sports Complex* can be found off Osceola Parkway, on Victory Way. Call 407 939 4263 for events and prices.

The **Walt Disney World Marathon** is another major annual sporting event, which, in 2002, is scheduled for 6 January. Some 13,000 runners take part – including some of the world's leading athletes – but it also draws some huge crowds as the 26.2-mile route takes in all four theme parks. Be aware the parks face some serious disruption on the day, but, for anyone familiar with all the fun of the London Marathon, the Disney version also serves up a great spectacle. You can look up more details on their site at www.disneyworldsports.com.

Rodeo

For another all-American pursuit straight out of the Old West, go and see the twice-yearly **Silver Spurs Rodeo** at Osceola County Stadium. This is the biggest event of its kind in the south-east United States and is held the first week in October and the last week in February every year, but it sells out fast so you need to call at least a month in advance for tickets on 407 677 6336. The event features classic bronco and bull riding and attracts top rodeo competitors from as far away as Canada.

On a slightly smaller scale but still worth a visit, the **Kissimmee Rodeo** is held every Friday at 8pm (except when the Silver Spurs is on) at the Kissimmee Sports Arena, on Hoagland Boulevard 2 miles south of Highway 192. Events include calf roping, steer wrestling and bull riding, and admission is $10 for adults and $5 for children 12 and under. Children especially seem to enjoy the live action, which can be surprisingly rugged (not to mention dangerous), and there is even a kids' contest – grab the ribbon from the calf's tail! The Catch Pen Saloon lounge is open Friday and Saturday 8pm–2am, and Sunday 6pm–2am, with line dancing 6–8pm and $1 drinks. Call 407 933 0020 for more details.

Motor sport

For the guaranteed ultimate in high-speed thrills, *Walt Disney World Resort in Florida* has its own speedway oval which is home to the **Richard Petty Driving Experience**, taking you out in one of their 650bhp stock cars as either driver or passenger at up to 145mph. The programmes have been devised by top NASCAR driver Richard Petty and offer the three-lap **Ride-Along Experience**; a 3-hour **Rookie Experience** (with tuition and eight laps of the speedway); the **Kings Experience** (tuition plus 18 laps in two sessions); and the **Experience of a Lifetime** (an intense 30-lap programme in three sessions). The Ride-Along Experience will probably appeal to most, three laps of the 1.1-mile circuit with an experienced, race-proven driver lasting just 37 seconds a lap but an unbelievable blast all the way. Your initial take-off from the

8

Orlando Rays

pit-lane takes you 0–60mph in a couple of seconds and you are straight into Turn One with your brain some distance behind. It is a bit like flying at ground level, it is hot and noisy and you must wear sensible clothes (you have to climb in through the window), but it is definitely the Real Thing in ride terms and a huge thrill. You don't need to book for the Ride-Along Experience from mid-February to the end of September. There is also no admission fee, so you can come along just to watch. The three driving programmes all require reservations, while the track is occasionally closed for race testing from October to February. However, before you get carried away, wait for the prices: $89.99 for the Ride-Along Experience, $349.99 for the Rookie Experience, $699.99 for the Kings and $1,199.99 for the Lifetime Experience. For more details, or to book, call 407 939 0130 or visit www.1800bepetty.com.

Race fans will also want to check out **Daytona International Speedway** just up the road in Daytona (take I4 east, then I95 and Highway 92) for more big-league car and motorcycle thrills. It hosts 11 separate race weekends a year, including stock cars, sports cars, motorcycles, go-karts and trucks, and highlights are the Daytona 500 (17 February 2002), and Pepsi 400 (first Sunday in July). Call 386 253 7223 for full details or look up www.daytonainternationalspeedway. com). Also here year-round is **Daytona USA**, an interactive motorsport-themed attraction, boasting a series of hands-on exhibits to give you a taste of all the high-speed action. Change tyres in a timed pit-stop, design and video test a race car and experience The Daytona 500 film. New in 2001 were Acceleration Alley, with full-size NASCAR simulators combining motion, video and sound to capture the thrills of head-to-head racing at more than 200mph, and Daytona Dream Laps, another elaborate motion simulator to put riders inside the Daytona 500 itself! Race fan Alan Rogers of Chester rates the centre highly. 'Try the hands-on Pit Stop Live, the excellent Daytona 500 movie and the 30-minute tour of the track. It's a real thrill.' Hours are 9am–7pm daily (not Christmas) and adult admission is $16, children 6–12 $8 (under 6s free with a paying adult). Call 386 947 6800 or look up www.daytonausa.com. Finally, you can ride the **Richard Petty Driving Experience** here too, with the $99 fee for three laps of the world famous steeply-banked 2.5-mile tri-oval also including entrance to Daytona USA.

Okay, that's the full daytime scene, now let's check out all your night-time entertainment …

The Richard Petty Driving Experience

Orlando by Night
(or, Burning the Candle at Both Ends)

Hands up those who still have plenty of energy left! Right, this chapter is especially for you. If we can't wear you out at the theme parks and other attractions, we'll have to resort to a full-frontal assault on your sleep time – and take most of it away.

For, when it comes to night-time fun and frolics, Orlando again has a dazzling collection of possibilities, from its purpose-built entertainment complexes, through its range of evening dinner shows and on to a full array of bars and night-clubs. The choice is suitably widespread and almost always high in quality.

Unfortunately, the development that started the evening entertainment ball rolling has now closed down. A completely refurbished **Church Street Station**, in the heart of the downtown area, opened in 1974 with Rosie O'Grady's Goodtime Emporium and added six more clubs and restaurants to become the focal point of the city district. But a steady decline in attendance through the 1990s led to two ownership changes, the second of which, in May 2001, led to a drastic cut-back of the Station's clubs. Only the Country & Western style **Cheyenne Saloon** remained open, with no entrance fee and a new focus, returning to its live music and line dancing so popular with tourists and locals alike. The **Saloon's Barbeque Restaurant** and next-door **Crackers** seafood restaurant also continue, but everything else was closed pending a

new long-term strategy at the time of writing. However, with the range of attractions of the downtown area improving all the time (see the Night-clubs section at the end of the Chapter), this remains a great area to visit, and the Cheyenne Saloon is still a must-see venue for its amazing interior, which features masses of hand-carved golden oak panels and railings around its balconies and grand staircase, and chandeliers from the 1910 Philadelphia Mint. It is also worth visiting even if you are not a C&W fan as the sight of all the locals doing their line-dancing is thoroughly absorbing. The restaurant remains a great source of barbecued chicken, pork and ribs, while Crackers serves up some typically high-quality Floridian seafood fare.

Disney joined the big evening entertainment concept in 1987 with **Pleasure Island**, an imaginative range of clubs, discos and restaurants, and they continue to refine various elements all the time in order to keep it all fresh and

Downtown Disney Cirque du Soleil

© Disney

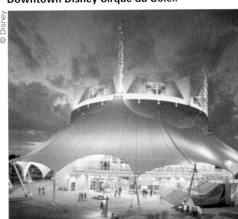

attractive. **Disney's BoardWalk**, which opened in 1996, added still further to their night-time amusement options.

International Drive caught up with this process in 1997 when **Pointe*Orlando** opened. Although its prime focus is shopping and restaurants, it has a strong evening entertainment component with the big Muvico 21-screen cinema centre, its bars and two new nightclubs, which replaced the original, failed concept in summer 2001. Finally, Universal Orlando got with the beat in late 1998 with the opening of **CityWalk**, possibly the most elaborate and sophisticated centre of the lot. They represent yet another slick opportunity to be dazzled and relieved of your cash in the name of holiday fun, but you should count on visiting at least one of them if your wallet can take the strain.

Downtown Disney

The large-scale development of what is now *Downtown Disney* (the old Village Marketplace and Pleasure Island) has evolved into a three-part complex (*Downtown Disney* Marketplace, Pleasure Island and West Side) doubling the size of the old site and providing two key evening entertainment sources.

Downtown Disney Pleasure Island: this is the traditional night-club zone which packs in the locals as well as the tourists and where every night is New Year's Eve. You must be 18 or above to enter (unless accompanied by a parent), while you must be at least 21 to enter two of the clubs (see below). The Island (which forms the centrepiece, or linking part, of *Downtown Disney*) comprises the **Rock 'n' Roll Beach Club**, a live music venue featuring 40 years of classic rock (and some outrageous DJs); the **Pleasure Island Jazz Company**, for excellent

modern jazz and blues in a 30s-style nightspot; **Mannequins Dance Palace** (21s and over only), a huge, popular disco featuring a revolving dance floor and live entertainment from the Explosion Dancers; **Comedy Warehouse**, improvised acts from up-and-coming comics and occasional big-name acts; **8Trax**, a homage to 70s music, dance and styles; the **West End Stage**, which hosts the Island's resident band and occasional big-name acts and is the focus for the street party and midnight fireworks; the unmissable **Adventurers' Club**, a multi-level live entertainment lounge where the place comes to life all round you (watch the animal heads and masks!) and the stars of the show are as likely to be next to you as on stage; **BET Soundstage Club**™, with an interactive VJ/DJ and featuring the best of R&B, soul and hip-hop sounds (again, 21 and over only); and **Motion** (formerly the Wildhorse Saloon), the newest venue, a pure dance club featuring everything from Top 40 sounds to Alternative.

> BRIT TIP: For the full run-down of Downtown Disney's Marketplace, see page 258 in the shopping chapter. Wallets beware!

As well as the clubs, the Island also has a range of shops, including **Reel Finds** for film memorabilia, **DTV**, an up-scale Disney fashion store and **Changing Attitudes**, offering some stylish men's and women's clothing. There is also a fine choice of eating outlets either on or next to the Island. **Planet Hollywood**® (the largest of this world-wide movie-themed chain) is the busiest restaurant in all *Walt Disney World Resort in Florida* and therefore draws big queues in the evening, while the **Portobello Yacht Club** offers excellent northern Italian cuisine in smart, lively surroundings. **Cap'n Jack's Restaurant** is another neat venue for great chowder, crabcakes, shrimp or the Captain's 'fishbowl' margaritas, while **Fulton's Crab House** serves up some of the best seafood in Orlando (although at a price – average $35 for a 3-course meal – and with serious queues from 6pm). Lunch is served from 11am–4pm and dinner from 5–11pm. As ever, to make a Priority Seating booking for a Disney restaurant, call 407 939 2648. *Downtown Disney* Pleasure Island is free before 7pm when the entertainment kicks off, then there is a $19.81 charge, with strict age restrictions (taking your passport as ID is a good idea even if you are the 'wrong' side of 30!). The seven shops here, plus the outstanding ice cream and coffee bar **D-Zertz**, are all open from 11am, and the 7pm admission fee is an option on your Park Hopper Plus Pass.

Downtown Disney West Side is the newest element of the Downtown expansion and incorporates the **AMC® Theater Complex**, which has been increased to 24 screens, with more than 6,000 seats in state-of-the-art cinema surroundings.

The most eye-catching part of West Side is home to the greatest show on earth (or at least, the greatest I've seen anywhere in the world), the **Cirque du Soleil** production *La Nouba*. Twice a day, five times a week, this purpose-built, eye-catching 1,671-seater theatre stages the most stupendous combination of dance, circus, acrobatics, comedy and live music that makes up this 90-minute show with more than 60 performers. Anyone familiar with the unique styling and outrageous costumes of the Cirque company will have an idea of what to expect, but even they will be left in awe by this multi-dimensional assault on the senses which includes trampolines, trapezes, balancing acts and even mountain bikes, interspersed with innovative dance routines and spell-binding music all with the most awesome staging. Words alone do not do it justice – go and see it. Even at $67 a ticket ($39 for children 3–9), it is worth every cent, but you often have to book in advance, and reservations can be made up to 6 months before your visit on 407 934 7719. Performances are at 6pm and 9pm Mon and Thu–Sat and 3pm and 6pm Sun (no performances Tue and Wed), but try to arrive at least 30 minutes early.

The other *Downtown Disney* elements are a fantastic mix of live music, fine dining, unique shopping and the ultimate in interactive game arcades, **DisneyQuest**. The cavernous **House of Blues®**, in backwoods Mississippi style, is a must for anyone even vaguely interested in blues, rock 'n' roll, R&B, gospel and jazz (call 407 934 2583 for info). Check out their magnificent **Gospel Brunch** on Sundays (8.30am, 1pm and 3.30pm), or the 500-seat restaurant next door to the stunning main hall for some fine food, including catfish, jambalaya and a host of other delicious Cajun dishes. The inevitable gift shop stocks some quality merchandise.

Similarly, **Bongos Cuban Café**™ (co-owned by Gloria and Emilio Estefan) brings the sights, sounds and tastes of Old Havana to another imaginative setting (check out the bongo-drum bar stools!), with red-hot Latin music and some of the best Cuban food in America. The **Wolfgang Puck® Café** also offers a rich experience from the renowned Californian chef, with no less than four dining options: Wolfgang Puck Café, gourmet food in a casual

Downtown Disney looks superb at night

setting; Wolfgang Puck Express, the fast-food version; B's Bar for sushi, seafood, pizzas and micro-brew beers; and the Dining Room, the up-scale restaurant (call 407 938 9653).

The shopping is also original and engaging, from the basic sweet shop **Candy Cauldron** that resembles a fairytale dungeon, through the one-off outlets like **Sosa Family Cigars, Celebrity Eyeworks' Studio** and the wonderfully stylish art, in both glass and ceramics, of **Hoypoloi**, to the more predictable souvenir stores and finally the truly mega **Virgin**™ **Megastore**, the largest music store in Florida, with 300 listening stations, a full-service café, hydraulic outdoor stage and a mean sound system!

The most unusual element opened in June 1998 and brought yet another novel idea to life. **DisneyQuest** is described variously as 'an immersive, interactive entertainment environment', the latest in arcade games, a series of state-of-the-art adventure rides or, as one Cast Member told me, 'a theme park in a box'. It houses 11 major adventures, like CyberSpace Mountain (design and ride your own roller-coaster), Invasion! An Alien Encounter (a fun VR rescue mission), Virtual Jungle Cruise (shooting the rapids, prehistoric style) and Aladdin's Magic Carpet (more virtual reality, riding in best cartoon fashion), a host of old-fashioned video games in the Replay Zone (do you remember Asteroids and Galaxian?), the latest sports games, a test of your imagination in Animation Academy and two futuristic cafés, one with computers and Internet tables, the other, Food Quest, straight out of a space-age comic book. Two new elements in 2000 were SongMaker (a computer-generated professional audio system that creates a CD with you as the star!) and Pirates of the Caribbean: Battle for Buccaneer Gold (an amazing 3-D immersion into a swashbuckling adventure as teams of four stage a battle for pirate treasure – don't miss it!). DisneyQuest is open 10.30am–midnight daily, but, if you want to avoid the queues (the building admits only 1,500), go during the day. A 1-day ticket costs $29 ($23 for 3–9s, although it is a bit

La Nouba show from Cirque du Soleil

too elaborate for most youngsters) and is an excellent way to keep teenagers in particular amused.

Finally, the whole of *Downtown Disney* West Side is characterised at night by outstanding lighting and special effects and a vibrant, thrilling atmosphere that is almost intoxicating. Words alone do not do it justice – go see it!

Disney's other big evening entertainment offering is **Disney's BoardWalk** resort, where the waterfront entertainment district contains several notable venues (not counting the excellent micro-brewery and restaurant of the Big River Grille and Brewing Works, the thrilling ESPN Club for sports fans and the five-star Flying Fish restaurant). **Jellyrolls** is another variation on the duelling piano bar, with the lively pianists conjuring up a raucous evening of audience participation songs (7pm–2am). The **Atlantic Dance Hall** underwent something of a transformation in 2001 and was due to reopen in October after a complete refurbishment as a Latin nightclub with live bands, DJs and a real salsa flavour (9pm–2am). Both have a $5 admission charge and you MUST be 21 or older to enter, so remember your passports for ID as they are strict. The Boardwalk also features some amusing stalls and live entertainers, which add to the fabulous night-time atmosphere here.

Universal's CityWalk

As part of the big Universal Orlando development – and in direct competition with *Downtown Disney* – comes this 30-acre spread of just about everything in the entertainment world. The resort's hub is a busy, bustling expanse of shops, restaurants, snack bars, open-air events and night-clubs. It offers a huge variety of cuisine, from fast food to fine dining, an unusual mix of speciality shops and a truly eclectic nightclub mix, from reggae to Motown to salsa and high-energy disco. Unlike Pleasure Island, there is no entry fee, but you do pay a cover charge ($4–$6) at the eight clubs. You can also buy a **CityWalk Party Pass** ($7.95) or Party Pass with Movie (one free film at the 20-screen Universal Cineplex; $11.95) for entry to all eight (except one-off concerts at Hard Rock Live), while the Orlando FlexTicket includes a Party Pass.

The area splits into three, with the main **Plaza** featuring shopping and restaurants. Among the most original (and entertaining) of the 13 main shops are **Endangered Species**, with merchandise designed to raise eco-awareness; **Quiet Flight**, a radical surf and beachwear emporium; the retro-American decor of **Fossil** for leather goods, watches and sunglasses; the wacky

DisneyQuest

Captain Crackers for toys, moving animals and outrageous T-shirts; the inevitable Universal Studios Store for character merchandise; and All Star Collectibles for (American) sports fans.

When it comes to eating, you have the NASCAR Café (a must for motor racing fans, 10am–10pm) with full-size stock cars and racing memorabilia, videos and interactive games while you dine on burgers, ribs, steaks and popcorn shrimp. Pastamore is a delightful al fresco Italian diner, with the choice of full-service dining (5pm–midnight) for pizza, pasta, grilled chicken and steaks or the Pastamore Café (8am–midnight) for sandwiches, pastries and ice cream. Emeril's restaurant is the five-star end of the range here, a sophisticated and vibrant journey into the cuisine of New Orleans master chef Emeril Lagasse. Fine wines and a cigar bar both add to Emeril's Creole-based gourmet creations, and if you don't try the Louisiana oyster stew here, you have missed a real treat (lunch 11.30am–2pm, dinner 5.30–10pm, 11pm Fri and Sat). It also books up well in advance at weekends, so try weekdays to avoid missing out. Jimmy Buffet's Margaritaville (11am–2am) is an island homage to Florida's laid-back musical hero, with 'Floribbean' cuisine (a mixture of Key West and Caribbean), live music and three bars, including the Volcano Bar which 'erupts' margarita mix (!) when the blender needs filling. There is a cover charge ($4) after 10pm when their live band hits the stage.

Across the CityWalk waterway is the Lagoon Front location of another huge dining experience, the two-storey NBA City which is sure to thrill basketball fans with its Cage dining area, interactive Playground area and Club lounge where you can watch live and classic games (all 11am–2am). Right next door is the

massive mock-Coliseum architecture of Hard Rock Live, a 2,500-seat concert venue with state-of-the-art staging and sound. Big-name bands and performers are on stage several times a week in this slightly retro rock 'n roll theatre; call 407 839 3900 for up-to-date details or check out the Universal Orlando website. Of course, you can't miss dining at the Hard Rock Café here, the world's largest example of this international chain, with its collection of rock 'n roll memorabilia (including a 1959 pink Cadillac). It remains hugely popular, so try to get in early for lunch or dinner (11am–2am) to sample their classic diner fare (notably the Pig Sandwich). Collectors of Hard Rock souvenirs will also find prices a little more to their liking here than the UK.

Finally, you come to the Promenade area, which offers the choice of night-clubs and some more fine dining (notably in the case of Latin Quarter). Motown Café (also with an entrance on Plaza level) is a homage to all the performers of the Motown record label, from the Four Tops and Jackson Five to modern artists, with a full-service restaurant, retro-style lounge and two revue stages featuring the Motown Moments, who emulate the likes of the Temptations and Supremes (cover charge $4, 5pm–midnight Sun–Thu, 5pm–2am Fri and Sat). Bob Marley – A Tribute to Freedom is a clever recreation of Marley's Jamaica home, turned into a courtyard live music venue, restaurant and bars. The bands are excellent, the atmosphere authentic and the place really comes alive at night (4pm–2am, 21 and over on Fri and Sat; cover charge $5 after 7pm).

Next up is Pat O'Brien's, a faithful reproduction of the famous New Orleans bar and restaurant, with its flaming fountains courtyard, duelling piano bar and main bar

(6pm–2am, cover charge $4 for the piano bar – you also need to be 21 or over, so remember your passport ID). Excellent Cajun food and world-famous Hurricane cocktails are also the order of the day, but don't drink too many and expect to walk home! **CityJazz** is a real contrast, a hip, up-market centre combining history, education and live music from a series of local and international musicians, with tapas-style food. Visually and in sound quality it is stunning and, if you're keen on the live music (8.30pm–1am, cover charge $6), you can easily spend all night here. For younger, club-minded visitors, **the groove** is the next generation in night-club entertainment, a vivid, pounding, high-energy dance venue designed like a Victorian theatre but with the latest in club music, lighting and special effects (9pm–2am, cover charge $6, 21 and over only).

Finally, completing the Promenade tour is the **Latin Quarter**, a truly sensational venue-cum-restaurant that serves up a genuine slice of Latin American style, in its atmosphere, music, dance, decor and cuisine. Quite simply, the food is outstanding – a combination of beef, fresh fish and poultry with tangy fruit sauces, spicy salsas and mouth-watering marinades (don't miss their version of rack of lamb) – the ambience is mesmerising and the sounds are so wonderfully vibrant and alive, you can't help dancing even in your seat. From Cuba to Chile, here is a great experience, with the live bands whipping up a samba and salsa storm. Drop in for dinner (5pm–2am) or just check out the music on Fri and Sat (cover charge $5 after 10pm).

Breathless yet? Well, there's still the **Universal Cineplex**, a 20-screen cinema complex with a 5,000 capacity and the latest in stadium seating, curved-screen visuals and high-tech sound systems. For all the attractions, you park in the big Universal multi-storey car park, and there is no charge after 6pm.

The Pointe*Orlando

This eye-catching development on International Drive, almost opposite the Convention Center, is a mix of unique shops, cinemas, restaurants, the WonderWorks science centre (with its magic-themed dinner show), a new arcade-style entertainment centre and two new nightclubs. It is open all day but has plenty of evening appeal, too.

The big-name stores (open 10am–11pm) are all up-scale and include some imaginative touches that make them stand out from the crowd. The collection of bars and restaurants strive to be different too, with **Lulu's Bait Shack** leading the way for New Orleans-style cuisine and entertainment (it looks like an old shack blown in from Bourbon Street), **Johnny Rockets** 50s-style diner, **Adobe Gila's**, a fine Mexican cantina featuring more than 70 tequilas (!), **Monty's Conch Harbor**, for fine seafood, the 'nearly world famous' wings, burgers and seafood of **Hooters** (with its equally famous 'Hooter Girl' waitresses) and **Dan Marino's Town Tavern**, sports-themed dining with the former American Football star. Lulu's and Adobe Gila's are popular with locals and are often packed at weekends as they stay open until 2am.

The 21-screen **Muvico** cinema, with its wonderfully vast and themed (inevitably) entrance foyer, boasts state-of-the-art stadium seating and sound systems, and you can often see a new-release film here several months before it is released back home. New entertainment venue **XS Orlando** (motto: Too much is not enough!) offers three floors of fun and games where you can 'dine,

Emeril's at CityWalk

Scheduled to open later in 2001 are the two nightclubs. **Metropolis** will be a high-energy club playing retro-top 40 music in a plush disco environment. It features billiards, TVs and an outdoor seating area, and guests MUST be 21 or older (no jeans or trainers; open 4pm–2am nightly). For the 18+ set, **Matrix** will feature top 40 and techno-alternative sounds, sophisticated

CityWalk

dance and defend the world.' An up-scale restaurant (try their excellent steaks or wood-fire grill pizzas among a really attractive California-style menu) occupies the ground floor, and you then ride the escalator up to the entertainment levels. Here, you will find more than 110 interactive games and attractions (including a virtual reality roller-coaster, rock-climbing challenge, several state-of-the-art shoot 'em up games, some arcade-style prize games and high-speed Internet access), fully stocked bars, live music with resident DJs and two roof terraces that enjoy views over I-Drive. XS Orlando is open 11am–1am (Sun–Wed), and 11am–2am (Thur–Sat), and is also an ideal venue for lunch here (visit www.xsorlando.com for more info).

light shows and a relaxed dress code (open 8pm–2am).

Pointe*Orlando is also in the process of developing another entertainment venue next door to XS Orlando, so check out their website at www.pointeorlanod.com for details or call 407 248 2838.

Dinner shows

After all the nightclub fun, another source of evening entertainment comes in the many and varied dinner-shows which are a major Orlando phenomenon. From

Hard Rock Café

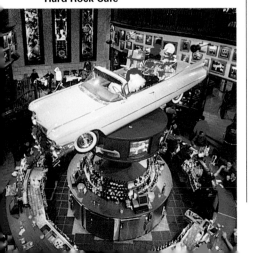

murder mysteries to magic shows, there is some wonderfully imaginative fun in store, even if the food element is usually distinctly ordinary. As the name suggests, it is live entertainment coupled with dinner in a fantasy-type environment where even the waiters dress in costume and act out roles, accompanied by unlimited free wine, beer and soft drinks.

There is always a strong family appeal and they nearly all seat you on large tables where you can get to know other folks, too, but, at an average of $35–$40 for adults, they are not cheap (especially when you add on the taxes and tips). Beware, too, the almost constant attempts to shake an extra few dollars out of you with photos, souvenirs, flags, etc.

Disney shows

Walt Disney World Resort in Florida's offerings here are often overlooked by visitors unless they are staying at one of the hotel resorts. For a night of South Seas entertainment, try the **Polynesian Luau Dinner Show** (at *Disney's Polynesian Resort*). It's a bit expensive at $38 for adults, and $19.50 for under 12s, but the entertainment is thrilling (fire jugglers, hula-drum dancers and clever musicians) even if the food, in keeping with most of Orlando's dinner shows, is nothing out of the ordinary. Beer, wine and soft drinks are all included. For reservations (usually necessary), call 407 939 3463, and shows are 5.15 and 8pm every Tue–Sat. The **Hoop-Dee-Doo Musical Revue** at *Disney's Fort Wilderness Resort and Campground* is an ever-popular nightly dinner show that carries on where the Diamond Horseshoe Saloon Revue in the *Magic Kingdom* Park leaves off, and has great food (all-you-can-eat ribs, fried chicken, corn on the cob, baked beans and strawberry

The Latin Quarter

shortcake). Especially loved by children, it features the amusing song and dance of the Pioneer Hall Players in a merry American hoedown-style show. Okay, it's corny and a tad embarrassing to find yourself singing along with the hammy action, but it is performed with great gusto, and you're on holiday, remember! The Revue plays three times a night (5pm, 7.15pm and 9.30pm) at the Pioneer Hall, $38 for adults, $19.50 for under 12s. Reservations are ALWAYS necessary but can be made up to two years in advance on 407 939 3463.

Another alternative is the nightly (and free!) **Electrical Water Pageant** on Bay Lake and the Seven Seas Lagoon in front of the *Magic Kingdom* Park. It lasts just 10 minutes (from around 9pm) so it is easy to miss, but it is almost a waterborne

Arabian Nights

version of the SpectroMagic parade in the *Magic Kingdom* Park itself, with thousands of twinkling lights on a floating cavalcade of boats and mock sea creatures. The best points from which to see it are outside the *Magic Kingdom* Park (in high season only), *Disney's Polynesian Resort* and the shores of *Disney's Fort Wilderness Resort & Campground*, but it can also be seen from *Disney's Contemporary Resort*, *Disney's Grand Floridian Resort and Spa* (notably Narcoosee's restaurant) and outside *Disney's Wilderness Lodge*.

Arabian Nights

This lovingly maintained, family-owned attraction is the largest-scale production and one of the most popular with locals as well as tourists. It's a real treat for horse lovers, but you don't need to be an equestrian expert to appreciate the spectacular stunts, horsemanship and marvellous costumes as some 60 highly trained horses perform a 25-act show, loosely based on the celebration of Princess Scheherezade's engagement to Prince Khalid, in the huge indoor Moorish-themed arena at the centre of this 1,200-seater Palace. The magnificent close-quarter drill of the Lipizzaner stallions, the daring riding and the thrilling chariot race all add up to a memorable show that kids, especially, adore. The recent addition of new characters (notably the great comic interlude provided by Gaylord Maynard and his horse Chief Bear Paw) costumes and special effects, plus the incorporation of a bumbling genie,

BRIT TIP: Take a sweater or jacket with you as Arabian Nights is kept particularly cool for the benefit of the horses.

have given Arabian Nights a real boost and helped to keep their appeal fresh.

The food (green salad, oven-roasted prime rib with new potatoes, and a dessert, vegetarian lasagne on request) is above average and decent value at $36.95 for adults and $23.95 for kids 3–11. Arabian Nights, which is located just half a mile east of I4 on Highway 192 (it's on the left, just to the side of the Parkway shopping plaza, or just past Water Mania if you are coming from the eastern end

BRIT TIP: NEVER pay full price for the dinner shows as there are always discounts to be had. Watch out for coupons among the tourist brochures, magazines and websites.

of 192), runs every evening at 7.30 or 8.30pm, with occasional matinees, lasting almost 2 hours, and tickets may be purchased at the box office between 10am and 6pm or by credit card if you phone 407 239 9223 (check out their website www.arabian-nights.com for a valuable money-off coupon).

Pirates Dinner Adventure

This show features one of the most spectacular settings, with the centrepiece Spanish galleon pirate ship being 150ft long, 60ft wide, 70ft tall and 'anchored' in a 300,000-gallon lagoon, and also delivers good value with its pre-show elements, plentiful (if ordinary) food and drink, after-show Buccaneer Bash disco (until 10.30pm) and the Pirate's Maritime Museum, which guests are free to wander around. The basic premise of the audience being 'hi-jacked' by the wicked eighteenth-century pirates is a clever one, even if the actual storyline is hard to follow. Chaos and mayhem ensue, some of it inaudible thanks to poor acoustics, but there is swashbuckling galore, sword-fights, acrobatics and boat races, and the goodies (inevitably) triumph over evil Captain Sebastian and his crew. There are plenty of stunts and special effects and ticket prices are $41.95 for adults and $22.50 for 3–11s (but watch out for discounts especially here). The show can be found on Carrier Drive between International Drive and Universal Boulevard daily from 6.30pm, with appetisers served until 7.45pm, when seating begins. Call 407 248 0590 for reservations (or visit them at www.orlandopirates.com).

Medieval Times

Eleventh-century Spain is the entertaining setting for this 2-hour extravaganza of medieval pageantry, sorcery and robust horseback jousts that culminate in furious hand-to-hand combat by the six knights. It is worth arriving early to appreciate the clever mock-castle design and costumes of all the staff as you are ushered into the pre-show hall and then taken into the arena itself with banks of bench-type seats flanking the huge indoor battleground. The weapons used are all quite real and there is a lot of skill, not to mention hard work, involved, plus some neat touches with indoor pyrotechnics and other special effects. You need to be in full audience participation mode as you cheer on your knight and boo the others, but kids (not to mention a few adults) get a huge kick out of it and they also love the fact eating is all done without cutlery – don't worry, there are handles on the soup bowls! The elaborate staging takes your mind off the fact the chicken dinner is only average,

but there is positively heaps of it and the serfs and wenches who serve you make it a fun experience. Prices (as of Dec 1, 2001), which also include Medieval Life, are $44 for adults and $28 for 3–11s (but check their website for discounts) and doors open 90 minutes prior to each show, the times of which vary according to the season, so call 1-800 229 8300 (or visit www.medievaltimes.com) for details. The castle is on Highway 192, 5 miles east of the junction with I4.

If you have 45 minutes to spare before the show, the adjoining **Medieval Life** exhibition makes an interesting diversion. This mock village re-enacts the life and times of 900 years ago, with artisans demonstrating pottery and tool-making, glass-blowing, spinning and weaving. There is also a Chamber of Horrors that might be a touch gruesome for small children.

Sleuth's Mystery Dinner Shows

Here's another fun variation, a real live version of Cluedo acted out before your eyes in hilarious fashion while you enjoy a substantial meal (with a main course choice of honey-glazed Cornish hen, prime rib or lasagne) and unlimited beer, wine and sodas. There are three theatres and eight different plot settings, including the new WKZY TV (a clever skit on trash television) that all add up to some elaborate murder mysteries, with the action taking place all around you and even with some cameo roles for various audience members. The quick-witted cast keep things moving well and keep you guessing during the 40-minute show, then you have the main part of dinner to formulate some questions to interrogate the cast (but be warned, the real murderer is allowed to lie!). If you solve the crime you win a prize, but that is pretty secondary to the overall enjoyment – and this is a show I do enjoy a lot. Prices are $40.95 for adults and $23.95 for children 3–11 and again show times vary, so call 407 363 1985 for details (or visit www.sleuths.com). Sleuth's Mystery Dinner Shows are located in Republic Square Plaza, on Universal Boulevard (half a mile north of its Sand Lake Road junction).

Wonderworks: Night of Wonder

On a smaller scale but no less fun is Night of Wonder at WonderWorks on International Drive (on one corner of Pointe*Orlando). This is a novel magical, musical comedy accompanied by all-you-can-eat hand-tossed pizza, beer, wine and Coca-Cola. Set in the intimate Shazam Theater, it features live music, special lighting effects and some slick, up-close magic tricks from illusionist Tony Brent. The storyline is pretty flimsy and the tricks are all fairly routine, but it is served up in style, it involves plenty

Sleuth's dinner shows

Pirates Dinner Adventure

of audience participation (which goes down particularly well with children) and it is still well-nigh impossible to spot all the clever sleight of hand involved. It definitely suits the family audience, and plays twice a night at 6 and 8pm at a well-priced $16.95 for adults and $13.95 for children and seniors. There is also a Magic Combo ticket for the show and unlimited use of WonderWorks afterwards (which stays open to midnight) for $29.95 and $24.95. For ticket information, call 407 351 8800 or visit them at www.wonderworksonline.com.

Masters of Magic

Brand new in summer 2001 was this new 90-minute Las Vegas-style magic review which, while it is not a dinner show as such, promises to be another major source of evening entertainment. The show's theme, *A Magical Journey Through Time & Space*, is designed to take guests through the different continents of the globe. The 272-seat theatre boasts a full surround-sound system, special effects and high-tech lighting to showcase the grand illusions prepared by Typhoon Lou (including a tour de force as he passes his body through a spinning industrial fan). Masters of Magic is performed at 6.30 and 9pm Wed–Mon (closed Tuesdays), with a 3.30pm matinee on Sundays, and it is located next to the Bahama Breeze restaurant on International Drive, just north of Pointe*Orlando. Prices are $29.95 for adults and $19.95 for children 4–12. Call the box office on 407 352 3456 or look up their website at www.mastersofmagic.net.

Night-clubs

Orlando is also blessed with a huge variety of other night-life, from common or garden discos to

BRIT TIP: Downtown Orlando is really the heart of the nightclub scene, with a host of clubs along Orange Avenue between Church Street and Jefferson Street.

elaborate live music clubs and no less then three 'duelling piano' bars. The majority are situated in the downtown area, i.e. away from the main tourist centres. The local paper, the Orlando Sentinel, has a regular Friday listing section called 'Calendar' which details every local nightspot worth knowing about as well as individual events and one-off concerts, and it is worth checking out as there is an amazing turnover rate of bars and discos. Don't be surprised if a nightclub suddenly undergoes a complete change of name and personality, as this is fairly common too. The basic distinctions tend to be **Live Music Clubs**, **Mainstream Night-clubs**, which also have the occasional live band, and **Bars** which specialise in evening entertainment.

Live Music

The following should give you a representative taste of the most popular venues (for those 21 and over only in most cases), starting with the Live Music clubs.

American radio

American radio stations come in a vast number of types and styles that conform to fairly narrow musical tastes. Here is a quick guide to finding the main ones in your car:

ADULT CONTEMPORARY
98.9 FM (WMMO)
99.3 FM (WLRQ)
105.1 FM (WOMX)
107.7 FM (WMGF)
POP
99.9 FM (WFKS)
106.7 FM (WXXL)
OLDIES
100.3 FM (WSHE)
790 AM (WLBE)
NEWS/TALK
90.7 FM (WMFE)
104.1 FM (WTKS)
SPORT
540 AM (WQTM)
CLASSICAL
90.7 FM (WMFE)
91.5 FM (WPRK)
JAZZ
89.9 FM (WUCF)
103.1 FM (WLOQ)
COUNTRY
92.3 FM (WWKA
97.5 FM (WPCV)
98.1 FM (WGNE)
102.7 FM (WHKR)
ROCK
91.5 FM (WPRK)
93.1 FM (WKRO)
96.5 FM (WHTQ)
101.1 FM (WJRR)
105.9 FM (O-ROCK)

9

The rock 'n roll piano bar idea was pioneered here in Orlando, by the wonderfully named **Howl at the Moon Saloon** on West Church Street and is equally popular there (6pm–2am Sun–Thu, and 5pm–2am Fri and Sat). Classic rock 'n roll, show tunes, current hits, the Saloon's duelling pianists play them all, with full audience involvement and non-stop banter. There is no cover charge Sun–Tues, while Wed–Thu it is $4 after 7.30pm, on Fri it's $6 after 6pm and Sat is $6 after 5.30pm, and the live piano action begins at 8pm every night (it also gets distinctly rowdy and even bawdy later on, so remember your sense of humour).

Then, of course, you will have already noted **Jellyrolls** at *Disney's BoardWalk Resort* and **Pat O'Brien's** (the original New Orleans version) at Universal's CityWalk, which are both popular with locals and tourists alike.

Live Music

Country music fans (and others in search of the 'in' crowd) will definitely need to check out **:08 Seconds**, a huge, multi-level entertainment centre. It earns its 'unique' tag by hosting live bull riding(!) and monster truck wars as well as having a huge dance hall with live bands, line dancing lessons, 12 bars (and bottled beer at $2, a real bargain), a pool hall, game room and classic country barbeque. The atmosphere is both authentic and infectious, right down to their well-stocked and excellently priced gift shop. This is one of my favourite clubs in town. On West Livingston Street in the heart of downtown, it has bags of style, but call 407 839 4800 for the latest details (usually, ladies' night Wed – ladies get in free all night and drink free until 11pm – monster trucks Fri, and bull riding

Sat). NB: The :08 Seconds refers to the average time a bull-rider manages to stay on his bull!

Blues, rock and jazz are the staples of **Sapphire**, at 54 North Orange Avenue, where resident DJs, a wide range of bands and special guest acts vary from week to week. Call for details on 407 246 1431. This has the reputation as one of the 'hippest' place to be seen, with its San Francisco-inspired decor.

The **Volcano** on South Orange Avenue is another curious mix of styles that promises something for everyone, with local bands performing on their Wednesday Night Live slot, hip-hop sounds on Thursday, dance music Friday and Saturday and the Latin music scene on Sunday (Wed–Sun, 9pm–3am). Call 407 999 0033 for the latest info.

As a complete alternative from the music scene, **Sak Comedy Club** (on West Amelia Avenue, in the Theatre Garage) is like a live version of the TV show *Whose Line Is It Anyway?* Fast-paced and funny (and with a 'no obscenity' rule for worried parents), the Sak performers do a mix of competitive improv comedy, with every show offering something different and the young performers living on their wits. On stage Tue–Sat, with two shows on Fri and three on Sat (the mid-evening one is usually packed), admission varies from $7–$12. Their LabRats show (Tue and Thur) features Sak's 'students' and costs just $3. Call 407 648 0001 for reservations and find out why Sak's has been consistently voted the best live comedy in Florida.

Nightclubs

In addition to the mainstream DJ dance centres at *Downtown Disney's* Pleasure Island and Universal's CityWalk, the new **Tabu** (formerly the Zuma Beach Club on North

Orange Avenue, just up from Church Street) appeals widely to the disco crowd with regular nightly line-ups, guest DJs and special events (usually of a fairly raucous nature!). Call 407 648 8363 for the latest details, and admission varies from $7–$10 (21 and over only). **Bar Orlando**, on South Orange Avenue, is another high-energy offering, with modern techno styles jostling with retro sounds from the 80s and 90s, while **Have A Nice Day Café** has become a happening venue for fans of the 70s, with their DJs pumping out the likes of the Bee Gees and Donna Summer until 2.30am Mon–Sat (also open for dinner from 4.30pm, on North Orange Avenue). **Cairo** has quickly become a haunt of the younger set on South Magnolia Avenue, with three rooms featuring dance music, reggae and out-and-out disco. House music also plays on Wednesday, and Friday is ladies night (no cover charge and free drink until 11.30pm for the ladies).

Barbarella, on Orange Avenue on the corner of Washington Street, offers alternative and new wave music 9pm–3am most nights. Again, it is more of a techno-dance sound, but with various retro-progressive, old wave and 'Bad Disco' nights. Friday is ladies' night, and the club has three contrasting levels, including an area with pool tables. Cover charge varies from $4 to $8, call 407 839 0457 for details. **The Club** is also hard to categorise but scores well with the alternative/ progressive crowd. It occasionally hosts rock and pop acts too big for Sapphire but otherwise ranges from mainstream disco to acid jazz lounge, with something different each night from Wed–Sat (including gay nights on Wed). Two venues – the Den and the Glass Chamber – feature dance, house, jungle and hip-hop, with their Latin night, El Club Caliente, usually on Fridays. About half a mile north of Church Street

on the corner of Orange Avenue and Concord Street, it is open 9pm–3am with cover charge ranging from $4 to $10. Call 407 426 0005 for night-by-night information (or visit www.theclub-online.com).

Bars

Bars of all types simply abound in Orlando, but there are again several which offer a particular tourist appeal, especially to newcomers to the scene. Live entertainment, extrovert barmen, sports-themed bars and raw bars (offering seafood, often by the bucket!), the choice is, as ever, wide-ranging.

The areas around Church Street are the core of this development (even since much of Church Street Station closed down), with a terrific range of restaurants and bars. Look out in particular for **Pebbles** and **Mulvaney's** (for a touch of the Emerald Isle, especially on St Patrick's Day) and **Chillers** (for an amazing range of daiquiris and frozen specialities). Upstairs is **Ybor's Martini Bar**, an up-scale cigar and cocktail emporium. Above Chillers is the highly recommended bar **Big Bellies**, which features its own micro-brewery and an impressive range of other beers (as well as an outrageous collection of wall art), and above that is the roof-top bar **Latitudes**.

Travel out past Church Street into Orange Avenue and you are into real locals' territory with the likes of **One-Eyed Jack's**, with its party pop atmosphere and live music sing-alongs, and its neighbouring connected bars the **Loaded Hog** and **Wall Street Cantina**, which get packed at weekends. Turn left on to West Central Boulevard and you find **Kate O'Brien's Irish Pub** for more lively bar entertainment (and a neat beer garden), the similarly Irish-themed **Scruffy Murphy's** is a block further north on Washington Street. Again, there is no cover charge and it boasts a real good-time atmosphere when it is busy (which is often). Heading south on Orange offers **Tanquerary's Bar and Grille** with live music on Fri and Sat.

The eclectic trio of the **Kit-Kat Club**, **Harold and Maud's** and **The Globe** (the latter an off-the-wall 24-hour diner) are also worth seeking out for a lively drink or three on Wall Street, just off Orange. The three are interconnected, which is mildly disconcerting, but boast a range of bars, a pool hall and live music, as well as The Globe's fun eating style.

Sports bars

Finally, with the multitude of sports bars that are another particularly American pastime, **Friday's Front Row Sports Grill** on International Drive (just south of the Sand Lake Road junction) really sticks out as a major tourist trap which even the locals enjoy. Here you can catch ALL the action (and, yes, they do show soccer as well) on 84 TV screens, plus enjoy some 100 beers from around the world (and bar features like $1 domestic 12oz drafts!), as well as try out their basketball nets, pool tables and shuffleboard, and rub shoulders with the local sports stars from time to time. The food is standard American diner fare and there is plenty to keep the kids amused, too (like crayons to colour in the paper tablecloths and a

huge range of video games). The atmosphere varies according to the time of day and the sports event (pretty rowdy for Orlando Magic basketball games), so call 407 363 1414 for up-to-the-minute info. There is never a cover charge, reservations are not accepted and it is open 11am–2am Mon–Sat, 11am–midnight Sun.

Other choices for the sports bar experience include the massive **Sports Dimension** on Curry Ford Road; 87 TV screens, with 12 big-screens, open 11am–2am every day (407 895 0807) and **Headlightz Sports Bar** on East Colonial Drive, which also offers live music (tel 407 273 9600). A personal favourite is the **Orlando Ale House** on Kirkman Road, just opposite Universal Studios (tel 407 248 0000). Boasting more than 30 TVs, a raw bar and some great seafood, it also carries an above-average range of beers. *Walt Disney World Resort in Florida* can boast the excellent **ESPN Club** at *Disney's BoardWalk Resort*, a full-service restaurant with sports broadcast facilities, video games, more than 70 TV monitors, giant scoreboards and even a Little League menu for kids. No sports fan should miss it. Equally, **NBA City** at Universal's CityWalk, and the **Cricketers' Arms** in the Mercado Center should not be overlooked as great sports venues, especially for TV/video addicts.

Now, you will also want to know a lot more about where, when and how to tackle that other holiday essential – FOOD. So, read on …

Night skyline

Eating Out
(or, Watching the Americans at Their National Sport)

Eating is a big deal in America. Consequently, eating out is a vital component in their entertainment business. Whether it be breakfast, lunch or dinner, the experience needs to be well-organised, filling and good value. To say Americans take meal times seriously would be the understatement of the year.

It is sometimes hard to dispel the notion that food is the be-all and end-all of some Americans' holiday experience, as the options for dining are omni-present and large-scale. However, this is all good news for us Joe Tourists.

Variety

As a consequence of the American love of all things edible, the variety, quantity and quality of restaurants, cafés, fast-food chains and hot-dog stalls is in keeping with this great tradition of eating as much as possible, as often as possible.

It is not out of the question to be able to eat 24 hours a day, and, at first glance, the full selection of food is rather overwhelming. Cruising along either International Drive or Highway 192 will quickly reveal a dazzling array of eateries, the choice of which can be quite bewildering.

As a general rule, food is plentiful, relatively cheap, readily available and nearly always appetising and filling. You will even encounter an increasing number of fine-dining possibilities, but the basic premise remains you will get good value for money and probably won't need to eat more than two full meals a day. Put simply, portions tend to be large, food of a heavily steak, chicken or pizza-based variety, service of an efficient, friendly character, and it is actually hard to come by a BAD meal. The one general exception (as pointed out by several readers) is if you like a good supply of fresh veg with your meals. The US diet often seems to overlook this staple, but if you look up the vegetarian options lower down or check out one of the outlets of **Chamberlin's**, notably at the Market Place on Dr Phillips Boulevard and in the new Winter Park Village shops, you will find a healthy, balanced choice.

Exceptional deals

In keeping with the climate, most restaurants tend towards the informal (T-shirts and shorts are usually acceptable) and cater readily for families. This also leads to two exceptional deals for budget-conscious tourists, especially those with a large tribe to keep happy. Many hotels and restaurants offer

The fabulous Planet Hollywood®

'kids eat free' deals, provided they eat with their parents. The age restrictions can vary from under 10s to under 14s, but it obviously represents good value for money and they are worth looking for. The second item of interest is the 'all-you-can-eat' buffet, another common feature of many of the large chain restaurants in particular. This means you can have a hearty meal for not too much and probably eat enough at, say, breakfast, to keep you going until dinner! A few establishments also offer 'early bird' specials, a dinner discount if you dine before 6pm.

> BRIT TIP: A buffet breakfast at Ponderosa, Sizzler or any other similar establishment will probably keep you going until tea-time and is a good way to start the day if you are tackling one of the theme parks.

Don't be afraid to ask for a doggy-bag if you have leftovers (even if you haven't brought the dog!). It is common practice to take away the half of that pizza you couldn't finish, or those chicken legs or salad. The locals do it all the time and, again, it is highly wallet-friendly. Just ask for the leftovers 'to go', (it's not usually a bag, either!).

Don't hesitate to tell your waiter or waitress if something isn't right with your meal. Americans will readily complain if they feel aggrieved, so restaurants are keen to make sure everything is to your satisfaction.

And, please, don't forget to tip. The basic wage for waiters and waitresses is low, so they rely heavily on tips to supplement their wages. Unless service really is shoddy, in which case you should mention it, the usual rate for tips is 10 per cent of your bill at buffet-style restaurants and 15 per cent at full-service restaurants. It is worth checking to see if service is added to your bill, although this is less common in the US than the UK.

With this being the world's favourite holiday destination, and with the city springing up from such eclectic roots, you will encounter a monumental array of food types. Florida is renowned for its seafood, which comes at a much more reasonable price than in the Mediterranean. Crab, lobster, shrimp (what we call king prawns), clams and oysters can all be had without fear of breaking the bank, as well as several dozen varieties of fish, many of which you won't have come across before (but don't worry about eating 'dolphin', it's actually dolphin fish or mahi-mahi).

Cuban, Cajun/Creole and Mexican are other more local types of cooking which are well represented here, and you'll also be spoiled for choice of Oriental fare, from the more common Chinese and Indian to Japanese, Thai and Vietnamese.

The big shopping complexes and malls also offer a good choice of eateries in their food courts, and, again, they often represent particularly good value. Cracker cooking is original Floridian fare, and the more adventurous will want

> BRIT TIP: Another way to save money given the large portions on offer is to share an entrée, or main course, between two. Your waiter/waitress will be happy to oblige (provided you keep their tip up to the full rate).

to try the local speciality – alligator meat. This can be stewed, barbecued, smoked, sautéed or braised. Fried gator tail 'nuggets' are an Orlando favourite. Of course, you can't leave Florida without trying the great speciality Key Lime Pie, a truly decadent dessert. Look for the stall in Pleasure Island selling it at $1 a slice – true heaven!

Ordering

Ordering your food can also be an adventure in itself. The choice for each item is often the cue for an inquisition of exam-type proportions from your waiter/waitress. You can never order just 'toast' – it has to be white, brown, wholegrain, rye, muffin or bagel; eggs and bacon come in a baffling variety of types; an order for tea or coffee usually provokes the response 'Regular or decaf? Iced, lemon or English?'; and salads have more dressings than the National Health Service. Whenever I've finished ordering I'm tempted to ask 'Have I passed?' after the barrage of questions. (NB: American bacon is always streaky and crisp-fried and sausages are chipolata-like.) Don't be afraid to ask to see a restaurant's menu if it isn't displayed. It is no big deal to Americans and the restaurant won't feel insulted if you decide to look elsewhere.

Vegetarian options

In a culinary country where beef is king, vegetarians often find themselves hard done by, and Orlando is little different to the general American rule. However, there are a couple of bright spots, plus a handy hint when all seems lost.

Firstly, there are two speciality vegetarian restaurants in Orlando, The **Lower East Side** at 3401 LB McLeod Road (tel 407 648 4830)

and the Chinese cuisine **Garden Café** on West Colonial Drive downtown (tel 407 999 9799), while the tapas-style **Café Tu-Tu Tango** on International Drive serves a number of veggie dishes.

Most of the up-scale restaurants should be able to offer a vegetarian option and will be happy for you to ask in advance. *Walt Disney World Resort in Florida* is slightly more enlightened in that the **California Grill** (in *Disney's Contemporary Resort*), **Seasons** (*Disney Institute*), **Citricos** (*Disney's Grand Floridian Resort and Spa*) and **Spoodles** (*Disney's BoardWalk*) feature vegetarian dishes, while all the full-service restaurants (notably Bongos Cuban Café™ and Wolfgang Puck's® Café in *Downtown Disney*), plus some of the counter-service ones are usually keen to try to cater for non-menu requests. It is always worth asking.

Worth looking out for on International Drive (by its Kirkman Road junction) is **Sweet Tomatoes**, a salad buffet restaurant with possibly the best meal deals in central Florida (and distinctly vegetarian-friendly). For just $6.69 at lunch ($7.49 at dinner, after 4pm), you get an astonishing all-you-can-eat choice that includes a vast salad spread, a choice of soups, pizza, pasta, bread and pastries, plus fruit and frozen yoghurt. Drinks are $1.49 (with free refills) and kids meals are $1.49 for under 6s and $4.49 for 6–12s. It is open from 11am–10pm and should be sought out by all value and health-conscious eaters! (Readers, Wendy Graham and Irene Bruce are among several to sing the praises of Sweet Tomatoes).

An excellent section of the Unofficial WDW Information Guide also lists special dietary requests, including vegetarian on www.wdwig.com/special.htm.

10

Race Rock

Drinking

The biggest complaint of Brits on holiday in the USA is of the beer. With the exception of a handful of English-style pubs (see page 243), American beer is always lager, either bottled or on draught, and ice-cold. It goes down great when it's really hot, but, as a general rule, it is weaker and fizzier than we're used to.

Of course, there are exceptions and they are worth seeking out (try Killian's Red, Michelob Amber Bock or Dos Equis for a fuller flavour), but if you are expecting a good, old-fashioned British pint, forget it. But I would suggest if you can't do without your pint of Tetley's, or whatever, for a couple of weeks, you're probably on the wrong kind of holiday! Spirits (always called 'liquor' by Americans) come in a typically huge variety, but beware ordering just 'whisky' as you'll get bourbon. Specify if you want Scotch or Irish whisky and demand it 'straight up' if you don't want it with

> BRIT TIP: If there are several of you, ordering a pitcher of beer will work out cheaper than by the glass.

a mountain of ice! If you fancy a cocktail, there is a massive choice and most bars and restaurants have lengthy happy hours where prices are very consumer-friendly (hic!). Californian wines also work out better value than imported European ones (and are usually of equally good quality). If you are sticking to soft drinks ('sodas') or coffee, most bars and restaurants give free refills. You can also run a tab in most bars and pay when you leave to avoid paying out for each round.

Another few words of warning. Florida licensing laws are stricter than ours and you need to be **21 or over** to enjoy an alcoholic beverage in a bar or lounge. Even if you are over 21 you will often be asked for proof of your age before you are served (or allowed in entertainment complexes like *Downtown Disney Pleasure Island*), and this means your passport, as it contains a picture of you (Americans use their driving licences as proof of ID because it also carries a photo of the owner). It's no good arguing or trying to reason with a reluctant barman. Licensing laws are strict and they can't afford to take chances. No photo ID, no beer! Anyone under 21 may not sit or stand near a bar either.

Right, that gives you the inside track on HOW to eat and drink like the locals, now you want to know WHERE to do it, so here's a handy guide to that veritable profusion of culinary variety. At the last count there were 3,600 restaurants in the metro Orlando area, with new ones being added and some biting the dust all the time, and, while it would be a tall order to list every one, the following section covers the main tourist areas and all the chain groups, as well as providing an insight into some specialist, one-off establishments.

Fast food

If you are a **McDonald's** fan you are coming to the right place as there are no less than 73 outlets in the greater Orlando area, varying from small drive-in types to the mega, 24-hour-a-day establishment on Sand Lake Road (near the junction with International Drive) that also has the biggest play area for kids of any McDonald's in the world and a number of differently themed eating areas. **Burger King** is also well represented, with 43 outlets, as is another familiar American franchise, **Wendy's**, which has 28 restaurants. If you're a burger freak and want to sample a variation on the theme, give **Checkers** (10 outlets) or **Hardees** (7) a try.

KFC has 22 restaurants around the area, but you might like to try the local variations on the chicken theme at **Popeye's Famous Fried Chicken & Biscuits** (12). If it's pizza you're after there is also a wide choice, from the well-known **Pizza Hut** (with 39 restaurants) to the local varieties of **Flipper's Pizza** (4) and **Domino's** (26), who all offer local delivery, even to your hotel room.

A particularly American form of take-away is the Sub, or torpedo-roll sandwich. This is what you will find at any one of the 48 local branches of **Subway**, or the 15 of **Sobik's** or eight of **Miami Subs**. They're a rather more healthy option than yet another burger, and offer some imaginative varieties. Two other variations on the fast-food theme are **Arby's** (with 13 outlets), which offers a particularly appetising roast beef sandwich and other beefy delicacies, and **Taco Bell** (17 outlets), which does for Mexican food what McDonald's does for the hamburger. If you've never had Mexican food before, this is probably not the place to start, but, for anyone familiar with their tacos, nachos and tortillas, it's a quick and cheap spicy meal.

Most of these establishments will have drive-through windows which are fun to try at least once on your Orlando visit. Simply drive around the side of the building where indicated and you will find their take-away menu with a voice box to take your order. Please, don't wait for the food to be produced from the voice box! Carry on around the building and your food will be served from a side window where the cashier also takes your money. You will probably find your car has a slide-out tray from the central dashboard area that will take your coffee or soda cup and you can drive along with your meal and pretend to be really American!

Family restaurants

This section may, at first, seem similar to the American Diner type,

BRIT TIP: Tourist brochures often include money-off coupons for many restaurants so you can find some useful savings.

but there are two major differences. First, they are only restaurants. You usually won't find a bar here. And second, they make a big effort for family groups in terms of kids' menus and activities (in many cases the kids' menu doubles up as a colouring and puzzle book) and budget-conscious prices. They also all serve breakfasts, and you will find the best of the all-you-can-eat buffet deals here. Nearly all are chain groups in the same way as you find Little Chef and Happy Eaters all over Britain, but there are one or two worthy individuals, too.

Leading the way in terms of popularity with British tourists are the **Ponderosa Steakhouse** group and **Sizzler**. Whether it's breakfast, lunch or dinner, you will find great value and good, reliable food. In terms of style they are almost indistinguishable: you order and pay for your meal as you enter and are then seated, before being unleashed on some of the biggest buffet and salad bars you will have seen. Ponderosa have the rather flashier style, but you'd be hard pushed to tell whose food was whose. Expect to pay about $4–$5 for their breakfast buffets and $6–$9 for lunch and dinner (there IS a difference in price depending on location, with the International Drive area tending to be a dollar or two dearer than elsewhere). Standard fare includes chicken wings, meatballs, chilli, ribs, steaks and fresh seafood, while their immense salad bars in particular represent major value for money. Both are open from 7am until late evening and are handily located in all the main tourist spots.

Reader Alastair Gillies says: 'We took your advice with Ponderosa (good value buffet breakfasts and dinners), but we also liked Shoney's for a slightly dearer but definitely superior buffet.'

A more homely touch can be found at the following selection, with equally good if not better value for money. **Bob Evans** restaurants (open 6am–10pm, or 6am–11.30pm Fri and Sat) specialise in American down-home breakfasts, with all manner of pancakes, omelettes and egg platters guaranteed to fill you up without breaking the bank. They also do the inevitable burgers and hot sandwiches and a special dish of the day that might be shepherd's pie, roast turkey or hickory-smoked ribs. Their restaurant on Canadian Court, just off International Drive, is entered through a delightful General Store where you can buy country crafts and some of the homestyle foods on their menu. For a hearty breakfast at any time of day, **International House of Pancakes** (otherwise known as IHOP) or the **Waffle House** will both appeal to you. You will struggle to spend more than $5 or $6 on a full meal, whether it be one of their huge breakfast platters or a hot sandwich with fries. Waffle Houses are also open 24 hours a day, while IHOPs open 6.30am–1.30am. Another traditional American 24-hour family diner is **Denny's Diner**, the nearest thing to our Little Chefs. Again, they make a traditional bacon and egg breakfast seem ordinary with their wide selection, and they do an excellent range of hot, toasted sandwiches and imaginative dinner meals, like grilled catfish, as well as a Senior Selections menu, featuring smaller portions at reduced prices for the over 55s. Similarly, **Perkins Family Restaurant** is open around the clock with a lookalike menu. For a really hearty breakfast try Perkins Eggs Benedict (two eggs and bacon on a toasted muffin with hash browns and fresh fruit), while their bread-bowl salads are equally satisfying. A new chain who impress for their clean, fresh style are **Golden Corral**, who have already chalked up a number of reader recommendations, and offer a delicious Carver's Choice of hand-carved meats plus the usual buffet deals and a terrific dessert bar.

If you are travelling on the major highways of Florida, one of the 34 branches of **Cracker Barrel** may catch your attention, in which case you should definitely check out their delightful Old Country Store style, with mountainous breakfasts, well-balanced lunch and dinner menus, Kid's Stuff choices and a real old-fashioned charm that is a nice change from the usual tourist frenzy.

Reader John Cartlidge says: 'While we agree with the recommendation for Sizzler and Ponderosa, one morning we found a huge line for their breakfast buffet, so we drove 200 yards down the road to the Black Angus – and the biggest buffet we saw all the time we were there. And no queue!'

Two new alternatives, worthy of note at any time but especially breakfast, are the mushrooming chains of **Panera Bread** (wonderful pastries, salads and sandwiches) and **First Watch** (all manner of egg dishes, plus great coffee and pastries, and all served double-quick!).

One of the most popular one-off restaurants for wide family appeal is **Captain Nemo's**, on Highway 192 opposite Fort Liberty. It serves breakfast 8am–noon, lunch until 3pm and dinner until 11pm, and its seafood and steak menu means mum and dad can try oysters, lobster, salmon, swordfish or grouper while the kids still get their burger fix. Prices are budget-orientated, with daily specials and Happy Hour 3–7pm.

For a real fun family treat (and the biggest crossover into the diner-type restaurant), take the clan to one of the two **Jungle Jim's** in the Orlando area (at Crossroads of Lake Buena Vista, and West Church Street). From the parrots that welcome you to the restaurant, you know you are in for an unusual dining experience, and sure enough you will eat in an entertaining jungle setting, with the menu promising 'An epic dining adventure of lost legends, forbidden pleasures and ancient rituals'. There are 63 (!) choices of burger, including the World Famous Headhunter, a 1lb burger with ham, bacon and cheese and a full 1lb of fries – polish off the lot and your next one is free! The alternatives are ribs, steak or chicken, but it would be a shame not to try at least one of the 63 varieties. The kids' menu is suitably varied, and a huge cocktail range is served by Dr S'Tiph Shotta Likker (ouch!). Open 11am–1.30am Sun–Thur, 11am–2am Fri–Sat.

British

To complete this section, it is appropriate to mention the handful of British pubs and diners which seek to attract the UK visitor. All offer a fairly predictable array of pub grub and a few imported British beers. You'll find the odd Brit or two working behind the bars, and you can happily take the kids into all of them, providing they don't sit at the bar. First and foremost is the **Cricketers' Arms** in The Mercado village on International Drive. This has become a favourite haunt for many British visitors due to the large selection of beers, appetising food, live evening entertainment and (soccer fans take note) live Premiership matches on their giant TV screen on a Saturday morning (from 10am – remember the time difference). It gets busy in the evenings, their live music is usually pretty good, and many of the staff are Chelsea fans, but we won't hold that against them! There is usually a cover charge for soccer matches.

Highway 192 in Kissimmee sports a number of fairly derivative pubs all keen to appeal to the home market. The best are **Harry Ramsbottom's** at Fort Liberty (between Markers 10 and 11), which also has its own fish 'n chippie, and the wonderfully

10

kept **Stage Door**, 6 miles west of the junction with I4 (and west of Marker 4, just past Lindfields Boulevard). This bar/ restaurant gets full marks from the locals, too.

American diners

This section is the one where it would be easiest to go OTT. Not surprisingly, there are so many American-style restaurants, it would be a full-time job just to keep track of them all. Therefore, I will limit this particular survey to the main tourist areas, plus a couple off the beaten track that are well worth finding. The $ price listings are intended only as a rough guide for a three-course meal:

$	=	$10–$15
$$	=	$15–$20
$$$	=	$20–$25
$$$$	=	$25–$30
$$$$$	=	$30 plus

Steak and Ale is a popular choice and can be found at six locations around Orlando (11.30am–10pm Mon–Thur, 11.30am–11pm Fri, noon–11.30pm Sat, noon–10pm Sun; $$). They do some great steaks and ribs, plus tempting seafood and chicken dishes, with early bird specials of a 3-course set meal 4–7pm (4–6pm Nov–Mar), and two-for-one drink specials at the same time. **TGI Friday's** will already be well-known from their outlets all over Britain and their fun style of lively meal-times is served up in the same way in their nine Orlando restaurants. (11am–1am; $$). They do a great range of burgers, plus Mexican dishes, pizza, pasta, steak, ribs and seafood.

The nationwide chain **Bennigan's** has five outlets in Orlando and is a particular personal favourite for their friendly, efficient service, smart decor and tempting menu, especially at lunchtime (11am–2am; $$). They make the ordinary seem appetising

and have a bar atmosphere straight out of the TV programme *Cheers!* Their Irish flavour really comes into its own on St Patrick's Day (17 March), and they have happy hours 2–7pm and 11pm–midnight.

Another enjoyable dining experience can be found at the two branches of **Darryl's** (one on International Drive, the other at Fort Liberty on Highway 192). Their weird and wonderful decor is totally original; they also have a great bar area and a nicely varied menu with some interesting choices, like Cajun-fried shrimp (11am–1am; $$). Thick, wood-fired steaks, delicious burgers and Southern-style dishes are their main fare, but they also offer tasty soups and quiches.

Hooters makes no bones about its style. 'Delightfully tacky yet unrefined' declares the menu proudly, and sure enough here is a relatively simple, lively establishment, especially popular with the younger crowd for its beach-party atmosphere – and the famous Hooter Girl waitresses (11am–midnight Mon–Thur, 11am–1am Fri–Sat, noon–11pm Sun; $). Their seven restaurants have a truly entertaining menu featuring great value seafood, salads, burgers and Hooters Nearly World Famous Chicken Wings in five strengths: mild, medium, hot, 3 Mile Island or Wild Wing. You have been warned!

By contrast, **Pebbles** (four outlets) goes for the casual but sophisticated style, with a genuinely imaginative menu that will appeal to the amateur gourmet and won't cost a fortune (11am–midnight; $$$). You can eat burgers or roast duck, salad or steak and be sure of an individual touch with every meal. Their pastas are particularly appetising and they offer a kids' menu, too.

Uno Chicago Pizzeria is the place to go if Pizza Hut has become passé. Their six outlets offer great deep-dish pizzas with the addition of pastas, chicken dishes, steaks and salads (11am–midnight; $$).

The Olive Garden restaurants (12 of them) are one of America's big success stories as they have brought Italian food into the budget, mass-market range (11am–10pm Sun–Thur, 11am–11pm Fri–Sat; $$). Their light, airy restaurants make for a relaxed meal and, while they don't offer a huge choice, what they do they do well and in generous portions. Pastas are their speciality, but they also offer chicken, veal, steak and seafood and some great salads, and there are unlimited refills of salad, garlic breadsticks and non-alcoholic drinks that add to their good value.

The two **Bahama Breeze** restaurants (one on International Drive, the other on SR 535 at Lake Buena Vista, next to the Holiday Inn Sunspree) are a must for their striking Caribbean styling – and popularity (the I-Drive one features an hour's wait at peak periods!). As the Bahamas are not strictly in the Caribbean, their theming is a little suspect, but we'll forgive them as it makes for a memorable experience with well above average food for a typical diner. Try West Indies Patties or Creole Baked Goat Cheese as a starter, while the main courses (primarily pastas, seafood, chicken, beef or pizza) feature outstanding items like Black Pepper Seared Tuna or the Cuban beef stew Ropa Vieja, with every dish coming up immaculately fresh. The plantation-room styling, delightful outside wooden deck for a pre- or post-dinner drink and live music most nights fully endorse their own slogan of: 'At Bahama Breeze there are no worries, just happy, friendly people and island hospitality!' (4pm–2am Mon–Sat, 4pm–midnight Sun; $$$.)

Hard to categorise but well worth visiting is the new **Cheesecake Factory** in Winter Park Village. While they make a feature of their

Hard Rock Café

desserts, the rest of the menu is pretty impressive, too, not to mention the high-tech, cavernous setting. Mexican dishes jostle with pizza, pasta, seafood, burgers, steaks and salads, and they also offer a great brunch selection (11am–11pm; $$$$).

Ribs

When it comes to steaks, ribs and barbecue food, Orlando has a magnificent array of restaurants that all proudly proclaim some kind of 'world famous' variety. In many instances they are right, and here's a good selection of the best on offer.

Lazy Bones Ribs (on Highway 192, just past the junction with State Road 535 going east), is an authentic barbeque diner that also has a kids' playroom. Baby back pork ribs, prime beef ribs, steaks, chicken and seafood are all succulent choices, plus there are gator ribs for the curious (4pm–11.30pm, with the Riverboat Bar and Lounge open until 2am; $$).

While in The Mercado, you may decide to try **Damon's**, which pronounces itself The Place for Ribs. While they also do salads, chicken, seafood and burgers, their rib platters are simply humongous (11am–10pm; $$$). Try their onion loaf as a starter as it is rightly 'famous', while their lunch selections are particularly good value and, they

10

BRIT TIP: Don't miss Wild Jack's jalapeño mashed potatoes, their dynamite chicken wings, cowboy baked beans and the Jack Daniels chocolate cake for dessert!

promise, served within 15 minutes with their 'express' label. Damon's new restaurant in Old Town is one of their sports-themed Clubhouse variety, with interactive sports and trivia games to add to their appeal (and is owned by former American Football star Fred Marion of the New England Patriots).

Cattleman's Steak House (on Vineland Road, at the intersection of SR 535 and Highway 192, and on International Drive south of The Mercado) goes for the cowboy approach once again, with a neat saloon bar, early bird specials 4–6pm and the Little Rustlers' Round-up menu for the kids. Steaks are again the order of the day, but you can also try chicken and seafood, while their Heavenly Duck is worth trying for something different (4–11pm, saloon open until 2am; $$$).

The up-market version of this type of establishment is **Wild Jack's** (on International Drive, just north of Sand Lake Road) where you are greeted by the most magnificent wood-smoked barbecue aroma as you walk in the door. The huge, western-themed interior features a big, open pit-barbecue where you can watch your food being cooked (11.30am–11pm; $$$). Steaks, ribs, chicken and turkey represent your main choices and they are all served up with bags of panache and a big helping of Wild West style. There is happy hour 4–7pm, kids eat free with a full-paying adult and you can even buy yourself a Wild Jack's souvenir boot-shaped beer mug.

Another good choice which also pulls in a lot of complimentary reader feedback is **Key W Kool's Open Pit Grill** on Highway 192 (just opposite Splendid China). Choice cuts of meat, mouth-watering steaks, prime rib, daily specials and a wonderfully succulent, inviting aroma add up to an outstanding dining choice, and at good prices (4–11pm; $$$).

I can also recommend any of the seven restaurants of **Tony Roma's**, which rightly pronounce themselves Famous for Ribs. The airy but relaxing decor and ambience, clever kids' menu (the Roma Rangers Round-up, full of puzzles and games), junior meals, and their melt-in-the-mouth ribs, try their Original Baby Backs, make a winning combination. You can still get chicken, burgers and steaks, but why ignore a dish when it's done this well? The Rib Sampler is a great platter, and there are chicken-rib and shrimp-rib combos (11am–midnight Sun–Thur, 11am–1am Fri and Sat; $$).

Tex-Mex

What the Olive Garden does for Italian cuisine, **Chili's** does for Mexican. Actually, it's an Americanised version of Mexican cooking originating in Texas (hence Tex-Mex), with the emphasis more on steak and ribs and less on tortillas and hot spices (11am–1am Mon–Sat, 11am–11pm Sun; $$). Service is frighteningly efficient, and, if you are looking for a quick meal, you'll be hard-pushed to find a quicker turnaround. Atmosphere is lively and bustling and they do a good kids' menu that is also a colouring/puzzle book. Similarly, the new **Chevy's** chain already has six restaurants in the area and offers a healthy slice of Mexicana.

The newest and most elaborate

Mexican offering is the cavernous **Don Pablo's**, next to the Visitor Center on I-Drive. Clever theming, lively atmosphere (especially around the Cantina bar!) and a classic, well-explained menu add up to a real fun experience (11.30am–10pm Sun–Thur, 11.30am–11pm Fri–Sat; $$).

Another one-off restaurant that has a lot of Brit appeal is **Café Tu Tu Tango** on International Drive, next to Vito's. The accent is artist-colony Spanish (whatever that means), with a really original menu, live entertainment and artwork all over the walls that changes daily. Vegetarians will find themselves well catered for here, while you can also try some particularly succulent pizzas, seafood, salads and paella. Mexican and Chinese dishes also make an appearance, and there is a thoughtful kids' menu (11.30am–midnight; $$). The overall style is based more on a tapas bar, so you order a number of different dishes rather than a starter and main course. Ultimately, it is as much an artistic experience as a meal, and the fun atmosphere perfectly complements the rich array of dishes.

Steakhouses

Serious steak-lovers will have to pay a visit to **Ruth's Chris Steak House** (with a new restaurants in the Winter Park Village and on West Sand Lake Road) where prime beef in a mouthwatering variety of choices is the order of the day. It isn't cheap, but you'll be hard-pushed to get a better steak (5–11pm Mon–Sat, 5–10pm Sun; $$$$$). 'Only the best', proclaims their slogan. 'Come judge for yourself, but come hungry.'

Similarly, the **Butcher Shop** (in the Mercado Center on International Drive) offers steaks, steaks and more steaks. Hugely impressive is the cold counter where

you can select your own piece of meat, and the hickory charcoal grill where you can actually cook your steak to the desired degree (of course, there is also a chef to do it for you or offer advice) (5–10pm Sun–Thur, 5–11pm Fri–Sat; $$$$).

Charley's Steak Houses (of which there are three, the biggest on International Drive just north of the Mercado Center) continue the theme of excellent steaks, cooked over a specially built pit woodfire. It's not cheap (although their Orange Blossom Trail location, 2 miles north of the Florida Mall, is noticeably cheaper than the other two), but the decor and bar area are splendidly furnished, and if you don't fancy steak, which you can watch being grilled on their large, hardwood grill, there are seafood choices as well (5–11pm; $$$$$).

Another new and imaginative choice is **Vito's Chop House** in front of the Castle Hotel on I-Drive. Their choice beef cuts are aged 4–6 weeks and cooked over wood fires, while they also offer trademark pork chops, seafood and pasta, as well as an extensive wine list (5–10.30pm Sun–Thur, 5–11pm Fri–Sat; $$$$). NB: check out the Tuscan T-Bone.

For more steak-induced hedonism, **Morton's** of Chicago (on the Market Place at Dr Phillips Boulevard) is hard to beat. Its rather more up-market (and sometimes pretty smoky) style is offset by a lively ambience that adds to the enjoyment of its trademark steaks, which you can watch being cooked on an open range. You are provided with a fully exhibited menu (they bring examples to the table!) and invited to enjoy some of the biggest, most succulent steaks it has been my pleasure to sample. The Porterhouse is an inspired choice, as is one of the principal alternatives, Shrimp Alexander. Needless to say, this does not come cheap, especially as your vegetables are extra, but it is a

10

Morton's Steakhouse

memorable experience
(5pm–midnight Mon–Sat,
5pm–11pm Sun; $$$$$).

Similarly, **Shula's Steak House** in
the *Walt Disney World* Dolphin
Hotel is both expansive (on your
waistline) and expensive. The
porterhouse and prime rib are
outstanding, and this restaurant (the
latest in a chain owned by famous
former American Football coach
Don Shula) is extremely popular
with locals (5–11pm; $$$$$).

Black Angus and **Western Steer**
complete the line-up of steakhouses
along more budget lines as they also
serve breakfasts and aim for the
family market. Black Angus (two
outlets on Highway 192) offers an
all-you-can-eat breakfast buffet as
well as a typical range of steaks, and
has a nightly karaoke session
(7am–11.30pm; $$). Western Steer
(on International Drive, opposite
Wet 'n Wild) offers a breakfast
buffet as well as a dinner buffet.
Steaks are the main fare, and with a
large tribe to feed, it's great value
(7am–11.30pm; $$).

Seafood

After that exhausting trek through
the steakhouses of Orlando, you
won't be surprised to learn the
choice of seafood eateries is equally
large. The **Crab House** (locations
on Goodings Plaza on International
Drive and Palm Parkway) should be

self-explanatory. Garlic crabs,
steamed crabs, snow crabs, Alaskan
king crabs, etc. Yes, this is THE
place for crab. You can always try
their prime rib, pasta or other
seafood, but it would be a shame to
ignore the house speciality when it's
this good (11.30am–11pm Mon–Sat,
noon–11pm Sun; $$$).

Red Lobster (10 restaurants) is
from the same company that has
made a success of the Olive Garden
chain. This is seafood for the family
market, with a varied menu, lively
atmosphere and one of the best kids'
menu/activity books. While lobster
is the speciality, their steaks, chicken,
salads and other seafood are equally
appetising, and they do a great
variety of combination platters
(11am–10pm Sun–Thur,
11am–11pm Fri–Sat; $$$).

Charlie's Lobster House (on
International Drive at the Mercado
Center) has a similar menu, with
nightly fresh fish specials and
reservations recommended. The bar
areas are immaculately furnished and
service has that extra charm
(4–10pm Sun–Thur, 4–11pm
Fri–Sat; $$$$).

Completing the chain restaurants
here are the three outlets of the
Boston Lobster Feast, with
elaborate nautical decor and an
unlimited lobster and seafood buffet
(hence the 'Feast'). They have early
bird specials from 4.30–6pm
Mon–Fri, 2–4.30pm Sat–Sun (and
that represents excellent value),
while their 40-item Lobster Feasts
are guaranteed to stretch the
stomach (4.30–10pm Mon–Fri,
2–10pm Sat–Sun; $$$$).

Of the one-off restaurants, **Ocean
Grill** (on I-Drive, just north of the
Sand Lake Road junction) offers
great seafood at moderate prices.
Daily specials, including the early-
bird variety from 4–6pm, jostle with
the likes of fried clams, south-
western swordfish, fried catfish,
shrimp creole and seafood lasagne.

Fulton's Crab House

Their fish and chips would put most British chippies to shame and, for the really hearty appetite, they do a magnificent surf 'n turf (lobster or shrimp and steak), although at a hearty price (4–11pm; $$$).

The **Atlantic Bay Seafood Grill** (on Highway 192, just east of I4) surprisingly offers a breakfast buffet on top of its well-priced seafood dishes, early-bird specials (4.30–6.30pm) and steaks, ribs and pasta. It's not gourmet but it is hearty and good value, especially their all-you-can-eat seafood bar (4–11pm; $$).

Inside the new Omni Rosen hotel on International Drive is the **Everglades Restaurant**, an up-market seafood and steak choice which again combines unusual decor (an environmental look at the Everglades, complete with manatee, swamp scenery, tropical music and a 12ft aquarium) with fine cuisine. Daily seafood specials jostle with wild boar, venison and buffalo steak, while the gator chowder is a must-try starter. There is a relaxing adjacent bar area in this cavernous hotel, and diners at the Everglades also enjoy complimentary valet parking (5.30–11pm 7 days a week; $$$$).

Along at Pointe*Orlando is **Monty's Conch Harbor**, where Key West is the relaxed, casual theme and the specialities include conch chowder, clams, oysters, stone crabs and Cajun-spiced tuna. Their fresh fried seafood baskets are also a real treat and key lime pie is a must for dessert (11.30am–11pm; $$$$).

However, my vote for the most memorable seafood dining experience in town is **Fulton's Crab House** in *Downtown Disney's Marketplace*. This mock riverboat has six differently themed dining rooms (albeit with the same menu), plus the Stone Crab Lounge which features a complete raw bar (and always seems to be busy). Nautical props, photos and lithographs fill the interior, giving it a wonderfully eclectic, period atmosphere, but the real attraction is the food – some of the freshest and most tempting fish, crab and lobster dishes in Florida. The Alaskan king crab is a rare treat, as is tuna filet mignon, but there are fresh specials every day (the air shipping bills for which are posted in the main hall), as well as a children's menu. Fulton's also features an extensive wine list, micro-brewed

Planet Hollywood® at Downtown Disney

beers and its own specialities, but the restaurants often have a queue as early as 6pm, so it is advisable to book (407 394 2628). The Stone Crab Lounge serves lunch and dinner 11.30am–midnight, while the restaurant is open for dinner (5–11pm. $$$$).

The Fab Four

There are four other restaurants that sort of fit into the Diner category but are really delightful, one-off restaurants in their own right. All four provide a genuinely exciting dining experience in novel settings that will linger long in the memory, and without costing you a fortune.

Planet Hollywood®: the largest restaurant in the recently troubled world-wide chain of this glitzy, showbiz-style venture is next door to *Downtown Disney Pleasure Island* and is a pure fun entertainment venue. The food is fairly predictable diner fare, although everything is served up with pizazz, but the cavernous interior lends itself to a party atmosphere, complete with numerous film clips and a stunning array of movie memorabilia. Some memorable house cocktails, too, but visit either mid-morning or mid-afternoon to avoid the serious queues! (11am–2am; $$$).

B-line Diner: inside the Peabody Hotel on International Drive lurks an amazing art deco homage to the traditional 50s-style diner, faithful to every detail, including the outfits of the staff. You sit at a magnificent long counter or in one of several booths, with a good view of the chefs at work, and with a rolling menu that changes four times a day (which isn't bad when it is open around the clock). The food is way above usual diner standard, but the prices aren't, so you can munch away on catfish in a papaya-tartare sauce or pork chops with apple-sage chutney, as well as the traditional favourites of burgers, steaks and ribs, happy in the knowledge you won't break the bank. Their desserts are displayed in a huge glass counter and I defy you to ignore them! (Open 24 hours; $$.)

Rainforest Café: The two versions of this eco-aware jungle-themed restaurant chain are adjacent to *Disney's Animal Kingdom* Theme Park and in the heart of *Downtown Disney Marketplace*, one with a huge waterfall exterior and the other topped by an active, smoking volcano, and they have to be seen to be believed. You don't dine, you go on a 'safari adventure' in a rainforest setting amid audio-animatronic animals (including elephants and gorillas), thunderstorms, tropical birds, waterfalls, aquariums and some of the cleverest lighting effects I have seen. It is an amazing experience, especially for children, and the food is well above average. Try the Rasta Pasta or Mo' Bones ribs, but the menu alone will take a while to negotiate. Unless you arrive before midday, you'll have to wait for a table, but that's no hardship given their locations. Beware the huge gift shop! (11am–11pm; $$$.)

Another unmistakable landmark on International Drive is the super-charged, super-large restaurant of **Race Rock**, packed with rare motor-racing memorabilia and eye-catching machines of all kinds. This does for motor sport what the Hard Rock does for music, and how! Two giant car transporters line the entrance, which also boasts a giant-wheeled buggy, two dragsters and a hydroplane speedboat, welcoming you in to the circular, 20,000-sq-ft restaurant itself. Giant TV screens and a host of regular TVs, video games, virtual-reality racing machines and loud, loud music and chequered flag tables complete the atmosphere, while the central bar sports an upside-down racing car circulating as the world's biggest ceiling fan! The food is traditional diner fare given a few tweaks like Start Your Engines (the starter selections), Circle Tracks (pizza), Stock and Modified (burgers and sandwiches), Pole Position Pastas and The Main Event (ribs, chops, chicken and salmon). I rate the Road Runner chicken, marinated in lime juice, olive oil and garlic and char-grilled. There is a Quarter Midget menu at $4.99 for children 12 and under (11.30am–midnight; $$).

Chinese

Chinese food is well established in America and well represented in Orlando, although many outlets are pretty uninspired, not to mention downright insipid.

Ming Court on International Drive, just south of King Henry's Feast, is the Rolls Royce of local Chinese restaurants. With the magnificent setting and live entertainment you can easily convince yourself you have been transported to China itself. The menu is extensive and many dishes can be had as a side order rather than a full main course to give you the chance to try more (11am–2.30pm and 4.30pm–midnight; $$$).

Bill Wong's Famous Super Buffet (yes, they really do call it that) on International Drive offers a cross between Chinese and diner-type fare. Their all-you-can-eat buffet features jumbo shrimp (and they mean Jumbo!), as well as crabs, prime rib, fresh fruit and salad (11am–10pm; $$). A rather classier version of this style is the new **China Garden Buffet** at The Mercado. The elegant surroundings are the perfect complement to the extraordinary buffet choice, with more than 50 items – from spring rolls to chilled crab claws – on offer at any one time. There is also a full à

la carte selection, but the buffet price of $14.95 for adults and $6.95 for 3–10s ($7.59 and $3.95 at lunch) make this one of the best deals I've seen (10am–11pm; $$).

Similarly, the **Sizzling Wok**, on Sand Lake Road, just across from the Florida Mall, offers an opportunity to get stuck into a massive Chinese buffet at a very reasonable price (11am–10pm Sun–Thur, 11am–10.30pm Fri–Sat; $$).

The new **China Café** on International Drive (at the corner of Kirkman Road) is also above average, with a lunch buffet from 11am–3pm and a well presented array of dishes (Crispy Duck is outstanding). Daily specials also feature (11am–11pm; $$).

Reader Penny Parker says: 'We tried Jungle Jim's at the Crossroads plaza at your recommendation and loved it but we also found a Chinese there tucked behind the IHOP, called Dragon Court – great food, great service and a fantastic price!'

Japanese

The more adventurous (and those already familiar with their cuisine) will want to try one of the fine Japanese restaurants with which Orlando is blessed. **Shogun Steakhouse**, on International Drive under the Rodeway Inn, is ideal for those who can't quite go the whole hog and get stuck into sushi (raw fish). If you decide to 'chicken' out, you can still order a no-nonsense steak or chicken, but their full Japanese menu is well explained and vividly demonstrated by their chefs in front of you at long, bench-like tables (6–10pm Mon–Thur, 6–10.30pm Fri–Sun; $$).

Kobe brings a touch of Americana to its dining content. With four locations around the area, Kobe go for the mass market but still achieve individual style with the chef

10

preparing your food at your table in a style that is as much showmanship as culinary expertise (11.30am–11pm; $$).

Ran-Getsu, on I-Drive opposite the Mercado Center, does for Japanese cuisine what the Ming Court does for Chinese – it's stylish, authentic and as much an experience as a meal, and still reasonably priced. The setting is simple and efficient, and you can choose to sit at conventional tables or their long, S-shaped sushi bar (5pm–midnight; $$$).

Benihana completes a formidable quartet of outlets, situated in the Hilton Hotel at *Walt Disney World Village*, Lake Buena Vista. Again, it's a memorable experience, with everything cooked in front of you by their expert chefs, and their steaks are among the most tender you will ever taste (5–10.30pm; $$$).

Indian

If you have come all this way and still fancy a curry, believe it or not you will be able to get one as good as any you have tried back home. There are already more than a dozen Indian restaurants around the Orlando area and they all maintain a pretty fair standard, from the up-market **Far Pavilion**, at the

Inside Race Rock

intersection of International Drive and Kirkman Road, to the budget-price **New Punjab** at the upper end of International Drive and on West Vine Street, Kissimmee, with its excellent lunch and dinner specials. For a medium-range restaurant, **Passage to India** (also on International Drive) gets the locals' vote as best Indian restaurant and is a cut above the average, with unusual and exotic chicken dishes and vegetarian Sabzi Dal Bahar (11.30am–midnight; $$$). It is a particular personal favourite for its attentive service and relaxed atmosphere, and you'll probably find yourself dining with a few fellow Brits.

Thai and more

For other types of Oriental cooking, the **Siam Orchid** (on Universal Boulevard, round the corner from

Sunday brunch at the Rennaissance Orlando Resort

Palm Restaurant

Wet 'n Wild) offers exceptional Thai food in a picturesque setting overlooking Sandy Lake (5–11pm; $$). If you'd like to try another variation, **Little Saigon** (on East Colonial Drive) will introduce you to Vietnamese cuisine and a whole new array of soups, barbecue dishes, fried rice variations and other interesting treats that take up where Chinese food leaves off (10am–9pm; $).

Possibly the best amalgam of all the Asian cuisine styles is offered by **Haifeng**, inside the Renaissance Orlando Resort near SeaWorld. Here, in a suitably elegant setting, the fusion of Japanese and Chinese offerings is superb, with the service matching the high quality of the food. Their speciality tea is also a cut above (5–11pm, Tue–Sun only; $$$$).

Cuban

Cuban food is a Floridian speciality and you will find some of the best examples at **Rolando's** (on Semoran Boulevard, in the suburb of Casselberry, head east from I4 exit 48). Try the red snapper or pork chunks and find out why the Orlando Sentinel rates this the best Cuban food north of Havana (11am–9pm Tue–Thur, 11am–10pm Fri–Sat, 1–8pm Sun; $).

However, the new **Samba Room** on West Sand Lake Road is the five-star experience hereabouts, an elegant lakefront restaurant full of Latin verve and ambience. The menu exhibits a wonderfully exotic touch, with the likes of mango barbecued ribs, cachaca smoked boneless chicken and sugar cane beef tenderloin (with chipotle mashed potatoes and mushroom sofrito), and their range of cocktails is suitably Cuban-tinged (i.e. with lots of rum and martini). Definitely worthy of investigation, but also extremely popular, so reservations are advised (407 266 0550). (11am–midnight Mon–Sat; noon–10pm Sun; $$$$).

Italian

No survey of Orlando's restaurants would be complete without mention of its fine tradition of Italian cooking. **Pacino's** on Highway 192, opposite Old Town, goes for the family market and scores a big hit with value, a friendly atmosphere and Sicilian style, with clever animated puppet operettas, a fountain that occasionally spouts flame and a relaxing open-air feel that is enhanced by the clever use of the differently arranged seating areas (4pm–midnight; $$$).

Bergamo's, in the Mercado Center, is actually German-owned but nonetheless authentic for all that. Don't be surprised if your waiter suddenly bursts into song – it's all part of the unique charm of this extremely tempting and highly entertaining restaurant (5–10pm Sun–Thur, 5–11pm Fri–Sat; $$$$).

Jiko at Disney's Animal Kingdom Lodge

© Disney

10

Italianni's (on International Drive just south of its Sand Lake Road junction) won't hurt your wallet quite so much and does a great pizza among a typical selection of Italian fare. Don't miss their home-made cheesecake (11am–11pm; $$$).

The five-star version of Italian cuisine here belongs to two contrasting restaurants, Christini's on Dr Phillips Boulevard, and Michaelangelo on Kirkman Road. Strolling musicians, elegant surroundings and a 40-year history of award-winning cuisine characterise **Christini's**, where their home-made pasta and filet mignon are as good as anything you will find in Italy (5–11pm; $$$$$).

Michaelangelo, just north of Universal Studios in Turkey Lake Village, promotes a candlelit atmosphere with live music in the cocktail lounge, formal, dinner-jacketed staff and a northern Italian cuisine that features delicious veal, snapper and pasta delicacies. Their pasta, bread and desserts are all home-made and it is all presented in an old-world style that is a million miles away from the tourist hurly-burly of the theme parks (6–11pm, 6pm–2am in the bar; $$$$$).

German

A recent and highly worthwhile discovery of mine is **Gain's German Restaurant** on the South Orange Blossom Trail (just past Oakridge Road going north), both for their food and their excellent selection of bottled and draught beers. The friendly welcome, authentic Bavarian decor and tempting menu come as a real surprise in the heart of tourist Orlando, but owners Hans and Kessy Gain have lavished much care and attention on building up their trade here. A tasty ragout is an ideal appetiser, while there are sausage specialities (naturally),

wiener schnitzel (of course), and rotisserie chicken and pan-fried rainbow trout (for something different). Apple strudel and Black Forest cake are the ideal desserts, while the Diebels amber ale is a fine choice for beer connoisseurs. Call 407 438 8997 for reservations (11.30am–2.30pm and 4.30–10pm Tue–Thur, 4.30–11pm Fri and Sat, 4.30–10pm Sun; $$–$$$).

Splashing out

Finally, if you fancy really splashing out, here are some notable suggestions where both the food and ambience are way above average (albeit with the price tag to match). This fine dining aspect has become a real growth area in Orlando's culinary panorama, and long may it continue! Their popularity also requires that you book well in advance if possible.

The **Park Plaza Gardens** is part of the Park Plaza Hotel on Park Avenue, Winter Park and this beautiful courtyard restaurant gives you the feel of outdoor dining with the air-conditioned comfort of being indoors. Attentive service is coupled with an elegant, versatile menu that offers the choice of a relatively inexpensive lunch or a three-course adventure featuring escargot, pasta with salmon, medallions of beef or one of several tempting fish dishes. Cuisine is distinctly nouvelle rather than American, but nonetheless satisfying for all that. Its setting becomes even more intimate and charming in the evening with lights scattered among the foliage. Enjoy happy hour in the lounge (5–7pm, with complimentary buffet Thur and Fri), while their popular three-course Sunday brunch features unlimited champagne and live jazz (11.30am–3pm Mon–Sat and 11am–3pm for Sunday brunch, 6–10pm Mon–Thur, 6–11pm

Fri–Sat, 6–9pm Sun; $$$$$). Tel 407 645 2475.

Another highlight of the Renaissance Orlando Resort is their **Atlantis** seafood signature restaurant. This wonderfully elegant and quite intimate corner of an equally smart hotel offers fine dining in the normal course of events, but also offers a scintillating range of daily fresh Floridian seafood specials that just demand to be sampled. A fine wine list complements the full à la carte dinner menu (5–10.30pm; $$$$$). For another meal with a difference check out the **Renaissance's Sunday Brunch**, which is something of an Orlando tradition. Not so much a buffet as a 100-item banquet, it costs $30.95 for adults, $15.95 for children 4–12. Try this and brunch will never be the same again (10.30am–2.30pm). Tel 407 351 5555.

A recent arrival in The Mercado and a pleasant surprise for their up-scale style in this largely mass-market location is **DiVino's**, a rural themed Italian restaurant with the full essence of Tuscany. Relatively simple pastas jostle with wood-grilled swordfish, braised chicken and the trademark Osso Buco (roast veal shank), plus some excellent daily specials (seafood especially) to offer a genuine slice of Italiana. It is not a cheap exercise (main courses run from $20–$30) but the deep flavours, allied with excellent service, make for a thoroughly memorable meal. Reservations are advisable as it gets pretty busy most evenings around 8pm, on 407 345 0883 (5–11pm daily; $$$$$).

The opening of Universal's Hard Rock Hotel brought with it the **Palm Restaurant**, the latest in an up-scale nationwide chain which has a big film-star and celebrity following. Founded in New York in 1926, it is famous for prime-aged steaks and jumbo lobsters, all served in spacious, elegant surroundings and with personable, knowledgeable service. And, I have to say, the house speciality Jumbo Nova Scotia Lobster is truly spectacular, with a succulence and depth of flavour that justifies its reputation. Of course, their steaks are a bit special, too (check out the Double Steak, a 36oz New York strip for two at $60), while they also feature crab, swordfish and salmon, pork, veal and pasta. All this decadence is, however, reflected in the prices, and the vegetable dishes are extra, but the lunch menu shows a more modest touch while maintaining the quality (11am–11pm Mon–Sat; noon–10pm Sun; $$$$$). Tel 407 503 7256.

Sticking with the hotel theme, **Jiko** in *Disney's Animal Kingdom Lodge* is possibly their most imaginative and impressive culinary offering to date. Maintaining the hotel's African theming with its décor and lighting, Jiko ('The Cooking Place') features twin wood-burning ovens, a masterful menu and an exclusive selection of South African wines sure to please any connoisseur. The menu reflects influences from India and Asia as well as Africa and offers dishes like banana-leaf steamed sea bass, whole roast papaya stuffed with spicy minced beef and oven-baked garlic chicken tagine with grapefruit, olives and herbs. The personal level of service and ethnic ambience underline the adventure of any meal here and make it a real highlight of this amazing hotel (5–11pm; $$$$$). Tel 407 939 3463.

Now on to another of my favourite topics. As already mentioned, and in keeping with the area's great diversity of attractions, the other main way in which Orlando will seek to separate you from your hard-earned money is in shopping. The choice is suitably wide-ranging …

10

11 | Shopping

(or, How to Send Your Credit Card into Meltdown)

As well as being a theme park wonderland, the vast area that constitutes metropolitan Orlando is a shopper's paradise, with a dazzling array of specialist outlets, malls, flea markets and discount retailers. It is also a vigorous growth market, with new centres springing up seemingly all the time, from the smartest of malls to the cheapest of gift shop plazas (and you can hardly go a few yards in the main tourist areas without a shop insisting it has the best tourist bargains of one sort or another).

You will be bombarded by shopping opportunities every way you turn, and the only hard part is avoiding the temptation to fill an extra suitcase or two with the sort of goods that would cost twice as much back home. As a general rule, you can expect to pay in dollars what you would pay in pounds for items like clothes, books and CDs, and there are real bargains to be had in jeans, trainers, shoes, sports equipment,

T-shirts and cosmetics.

But beware! Your duty-free allowance in the catch-all duty category of 'gifts' is still only £145 per person, and it is perfectly possible to exceed that sum by some distance. Paying the duty and VAT is still often cheaper than buying the same items at home, however, so it is worth splashing out, but remember to keep all your receipts and go back through the red 'goods to declare' channel on your return. You will pay duty (which varies depending on the item) on the total purchase price (i.e. inclusive of Florida sales tax, see below) once you have exceeded your £145 allowance, plus VAT at 17.5 per cent. Unfortunately, you can no longer pool your allowances to cover one item that exceeds a single allowance. Hence, if you buy a camera, say, that costs £200, you have to pay the duty on the full £200, taking the total to £213.20, and then the VAT on that figure. However, if you have a number of items that add up to £145, and then another which exceeds that, you pay the duty and VAT only on the excess (and the customs officers will usually give you the benefit of the lowest rate on what you pay for). Duty rates are up-dated regularly and can be as little as 2.7 per cent (golf clubs) or 15 per cent (mountain bikes). If you have any queries, consult the Customs and Excise office before you leave your home airport.

Your ordinary duty-free allowances from America include 200 cigarettes and 1 litre of spirits or 2 litres of sparkling wine and 2 litres of still

Shopping in Old Town

KEY TO ORLANDO – SHOPPING CENTRES

A Mall at Millenia
B Old Town
C Kissimmee Historic District
D Seminole Towne Center
E Orlando Premium Outlets
F Oviedo Marketplace
G Downtown Disney Marketplace
H Mercado Center
I Goodings International Plaza
J Crossroads Of Lake Buena Vista
K Belz Factory Outlet World
L Festival Bay
M Kissimmee Manufacturers' Outlet Mall

N Flea World
O Osceola Flea And Farmers' Market
P Florida Mall
Q Altamonte Mall
R Osceola Square Mall
S Colonial Plaza Mall
T Orlando Fashion Square Mall
U Winter Park Village
V Lake Buena Vista Factory Shops
W The Marketplace at Dr Phillips
X The Pointe*Orlando
Y Park Avenue
Z Belz International Outlet Center

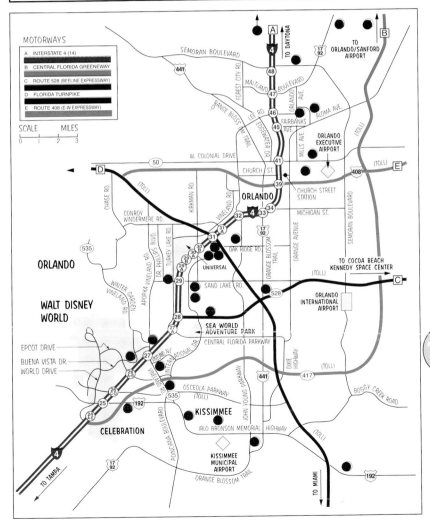

wine. Alligator products, which constitute an endangered species, require a special import licence, and you should consult the Department of the Environment first.

Be aware, also, of the hidden 'extras' of shopping costs. Unlike our VAT, the local version in Orlando, the Florida State sales tax, is NOT added to the displayed purchase price, so you should add 6 or 7 per cent (depending on which county you are in) to arrive at the 'real' price. This frequently catches visitors out. The sales tax is added to everything you buy in Orlando, from your theme park tickets to a beer at the hotel and all meals (but not supermarket groceries).

BRIT TIP: If you are tempted to use 'doctored' receipts to show a lesser value – don't, it is illegal. Your goods will be confiscated and there are heavy fines. Also, you can't escape the duty by saying the items have been used (in the case of golf clubs, for example) or that they are gifts for someone else.

Here is a rundown of the main shopping attractions and the sort of fun and bargains that can be had, divided into four categories. First, the purpose-built speciality shopping complexes, specifically out to catch the tourist's eye; second, Orlando's speciality flea markets and discount outlets; third, the large shopping malls; and finally a few shops for the bargain-hunter.

The best examples of the first category are all in the main tourist areas, starting, of course, with Disney.

Downtown Disney

The heart of *Walt Disney World Resort in Florida* in many ways is their Downtown Disney development. And the **Downtown Disney Marketplace** is typical Disney, a beautiful location, imaginative building and landscaping and a host of one-off elements that make shopping here a pleasure. Don't miss the awesome **World of Disney** store, the largest of its kind in the world, the **Lego Imagination Center** (an interactive playground and shop), **Discover Garden Shop** for unique gifts and gardening accessories with an environmental awareness theme, the amazing **Art of Disney** and **Team Mickey's Athletic Club**. Dancing fountains and squirt pools (where kids tend to get seriously wet), the lakeside setting and boating opportunities all add to the appeal. Restaurants include the superbly themed **Rainforest Café** and the first on-site **McDonald's**. Once you have taken in *Downtown Disney Marketplace*, stroll over to **Downtown Disney West Side** and see a film or visit the world's largest **Virgin Megastore**. The **Hoypoloi Gallery** is one of my favourites for a wonderfully eclectic range or artwork, from metal to glass. The whole complex is open 9.30am–11pm every day. It is off exit 26A of I4 and is well signposted (avoid exit 27 for the increasing traffic congestion).

International Drive

This core tourist area boasts two cleverly-built developments which offer some unique shopping attractions, starting with **The Mercado**, the original speciality complex, in the heart of the I-Drive corridor just south of Sand Lake Road. This Mediterranean-style 'village' boasts 34 speciality shops, six superb restaurants (including **Bergamo's, Charlie's Lobster House, China Garden Buffet, Divino's** and the **Butcher Shop**), the **Cricketers' Arms** pub, live evening entertainment (Wed–Sun in the courtyard) and an impressive international food court (especially for the budget-conscious). The wonderful Spanish architecture encourages browsing along the 'streets', lined with one-off shops. The Mercado is open 10am–10pm daily (longer at the bars and restaurants), and will amuse you and your wallet for several hours. Shops like **Kandlestix, Andean Manna, Swings 'n Things** and **American Cola Company** are all good for a variety of unusual gifts, while hand-carts and artists also enliven the scene. Look out for The Mercado's distinctive free shopping shuttle, which operates daily from various hotels in the area for non-drivers.

The second standout complex on I-Drive is 17-acre **Pointe*Orlando** (already discussed in Orlando by Night in Chapter 9), which is as much an evening adventure as mere shopping. The 60-plus stores here are all more up-market than usual tourist fare, and you can indulge your passion for fashion at places like **Gap** and **Gap Kids, Banana Republic, Armani Exchange, Image Leather, Tommy Hilfiger, Abercrombie & Fitch** and the **Everything But Water** swim-wear store, or stock up on gifts and souvenirs at **Disney Worldport, Bath & Body Works, Yankee Candle, Glow** and **Magnetville USA**. If nothing else, you should let the kids loose in the huge interactive toy shop **FAO Schwarz,** go to the state-of-the-art **Muvico** cinema complex, and finish up with a meal at lively **Johnny Rockets** American diner, where the staff all join in with various jukebox favourites.

Kissimmee's version of the purpose-built tourist shopping centre is **Old Town**, an antique-style offering in the heart of Highway 192, with a tourist-friendly mix of shops, restaurants, bars and fairground attractions, all set out along brick-built streets. The shops – some 75 of them – range from standard souvenirs, novel T-shirt outlets and Disney merchandise to sportswear, motorbike fashions and other collectables (check out the **General Store** for a step back in time, too, or the **Old Town Portrait Gallery** for more period style). Then there are 13 restaurants or snack bars, The Haunted House ($7 for adults, $5 for children), and a host of rides, including the 60ft-tall Century Wheel, the Windstorm roller-coaster, go-karts, a **Kids' Town** area of junior rides and the Skycoaster mega-ride. Allow up to four hours here and try at all costs to take in the weekly **Saturday Nite Cruise** at 8.30pm, a drive-past of 300-plus vintage and collector cars from all over America which has become a real Old Town trademark (and a new **Friday Nite Cruise** featuring cars built from 1973–85, plus live music and prizes). Parking is free and Old Town is open 10am–11pm 7 days a week (amusement rides open from 4pm Mon–Fri, from noon Sat–Sun). **Damon's Clubhouse** restaurant is the stand-out dining choice, with great ribs, burgers and salads (and the chance to play various Trivia games and watch every kind of sport on their big screens) but the **Cadillac Diner** is a fun alternative. The whole place really comes alive in the evening, too.

New in 2002 should be **Festival Bay**, a 25-acre spread of shops, restaurants and entertainment, with a Cinemark 20-screen cinema complex, at the top of International Drive. This has been on-going since late 1999, with only the cinemas and the amazing Bass Outdoor World store open by the original completion date of summer 2001.

11

The Mercado

However, all the signs were the project will eventually be completed as planned, with major outlets of Ron Jon's Surf Shop and Vans (a trendy sports footwear specialist who will open a 'skate park'), plus a host of fashion and designer label stores, plus an array of themed restaurants.

Sadly, **Church Street Station**, for so long one of the main purpose-built venues (a mix of shops, restaurants and nightclubs in Downtown Orlando), has closed its shopping center while it tries to reinvent itself.

Discount outlets

Belz Factory Outlet World is by far the most impressive of the

Belz Factory Outlet

second category of shops, the 'factory' or discount outlet, and is a positive Mecca for all serious shoppers. Actually, it almost defies description as it is too widespread to be a full shopping mall, too elaborate to be a flea market and too down-to-earth to be a straightforward tourist trap (the locals do a lot of shopping here, too). Belz can be found on West Oak Ridge Road at the top of International Drive and consists of more than 160 shops arranged in two indoor malls (both with lively food courts and one with a vintage carousel to amuse the kids), plus four separate annexes that all require a separate journey by car (unless you want to wear out a lot of shoe leather!). Avoid Belz at weekends, if you want to beat the crowds. The aim is to sell name brands at factory-

> BRIT TIP: For the best value genuine Disney merchandise, try the Character Warehouse in Belz Mall 2 and Character Premiere in Mall 1.

direct prices and, while you may have to wade through a fair amount of stuff you wouldn't want if they were giving it away, you will find shoes, clothes, books, jewellery, electronics, sporting goods, crockery and more at bargain rates. Check out the Calvin Klein outlet (Annex 2), Reebok footwear (Annex 4), the Van Heusen factory store (Malls 1 & 2), Oshkosh B'gosh kidswear, the Umbro store and Guess Jeans (all Mall 2). Serious shoppers will want to spend several hours here, and Belz is open 10am–9pm Mon-Sat and 10am–6pm Sun.

Quality Outlet Center (9.30am–9pm Mon–Sat, 11am–6pm Sun) further down International Drive offers much of the same, although

Lake Buena Vista Factory Stores

not in the same quantity (Disney Gifts for heavily discounted Disney merchandise is worth a look).

For a classier version, the **Belz Designer Outlet Center**, just south of Belz on I-Drive has a more up-market range of shops, including Donna Karan, Bose, Fossil, Fila and Polo Ralph Lauren (10am–9pm Mon–Sat, 11am–6pm Sun). For a full listing of ALL Belz stores, look up www.belz.com/factory/index.html.

Kissimmee's version of the discount outlet is the **Kissimmee Manufacturers' Outlet Mall** on Old Vineland Road (just off the central drag of Highway 192, between Markers 13 and 14). Again featuring name brands like Nike, Levis and Van Heusen, plus **Publishers Outlet** for discounted books, it is open 10am–9pm Mon–Sat, 11am–5pm Sun.

The newly expanded **Lake Buena Vista Factory Stores** offer another range of big-name products at discount prices, from Adidas, Calvin Klein, Reebok and Casio to a budget-priced Disney Character Corner, OshKosh B'Gosh and (the better-priced) Carter's Childrenswear, plus a lively food court and a kids' playground. A 1999 expansion added Gap and Liz Claiborne stores, and it all has the bonus of being one of the closest outlet centres to Disney's attractions. They can be found on SR 535 (2 miles south off Exit 27 of I4) and are

open 10am–9pm Mon–Sat, 10am–6pm Sun. They also have a daily shuttle service that picks up at various hotels and timeshare units in a 10-mile radius (call 407 238 9301 for info or visit www.lbvfs.com).

Possibly the best of the lot, though, are the **Orlando Premium Outlets**, which were an instant hit with UK shopping devotees when they opened in 2000. Offering a fresh look and style, and with a legion of big-name designers (from

Orlando Premium Outlets

Burberry to Hugo Boss and Ermenegildo Zegna) they can be found between International Drive and I4 (just south of SeaWorld; Exit 27 off I4). In all, they offer 110 stores of well-known brand names (like Timberland, Adidas, Reebok, Banana Republic, Ralph Lauren and Calvin Klein) spread out through four themed areas, with easy

11

BRIT TIP: As with parks and restaurants, there are special coupons and discounts in the various tourist hand-outs for some of the shops. A few are worth keeping but the majority are pretty tacky.

BRIT TIP: American video tapes are NOT compatible with European VCRs, so you will be wasting your money unless the video is marked PAL, which signifies European use.

parking, a good food court and the convenience of being at the southern end of the I-Ride Trolley (Blue Route). Watch out also for big Disney bargains at the Character Premiere store. Opening hours are 10am–11pm (Mon–Sat) and 10am–9pm (Sun). Call 407 238 7787 or see www.premiumoutlets.com. Highly recommended.

Flea markets

Flea World boasts America's largest covered market, with 1,700 stalls spread out over 104 acres, including three massive, themed buildings, plus a 7-acre amusement park, **Fun World**, to keep the kids amused for a good hour or two (rides cost about $2 each). It is open Fri, Sat and Sun only 9am–6pm and can be found a 20-minute drive away on Highway 17-92 (best picked up from exit 47 of I4) between Orlando and Sanford (to the north). The stalls include all manner of market goods (nearly all new or slight seconds), from fresh

BRIT TIP: Despite the attractive prices, avoid the temptation to collect a house-load of electrical goods as they are geared to run on American 110-120 volt supplies and not our 220, and you would have to buy special adapters to use them back home.

produce to antiques and jewellery (leather lingerie, anyone?!) and a whole range of arts and crafts (try Rag Shoppe USA for some real bargains in materials and lace), while there is a full-scale food court and a 300-seat pizza and burger eatery, the **Carousel Restaurant**, plus free entertainment on the Fun World Pavilion stage. Call 407 330 1792 for more details.

On a slightly smaller scale is the **Osceola Flea and Farmers' Market** at the eastern end of the tourist area of Highway 192 in Kissimmee (Fri–Sun, 8am–5pm), offering food, clothing, household and kitchen supplies, electronics, sporting goods, collectables and handicrafts (call 407 846 2811 for more details). Similarly the **192 Flea Market**, on the central Vine Street stretch of Highway 192, has some 400 booths, plus a food court, in four bright-blue buildings under big oak trees, selling everything from Nintendo games to Florida souvenirs (open 7 days a week, call 407 396 4555).

Malls

The area's big indoor malls tend to run a touch more expensive than the outlets already mentioned, but they do boast a huge range of pretty stylish shops. The outstanding **Florida Mall** features more than 250 shops, with six large department stores (seven by autumn 2002, when the fashion-conscious Nordstrom store should be open) and an excellent food court offering a choice of 17 outlets, plus the lively bar-restaurant **Ruby Tuesday**, the excellent **California Café Bar & Grill** and the chic little **Pebbles** in Saks Fifth Avenue. It is located on the South Orange Blossom Trail, on the corner of Sand Lake Road, and is open 10am–9.30pm Mon–Sat, 11am–6pm Sun. Highlights of this

BRIT TIP: Need a good book? Make a beeline for Barnes & Noble by the Florida Mall or opposite the Colonial Plaza for a magnificent array of titles (especially travel) and a wonderful coffee shop.

spacious and quite stylish Mall are the up-market (but expensive) Saks Fifth Avenue, Burdine's (Florida's oldest – and biggest – department store) and JC Penney.

The huge two-storey **Altamonte Mall**, on Altamonte Avenue in the suburb of Altamonte Springs (take exit 48 on I4 and head east for half a mile on Route 436 and it is on the left), is also well above average and slightly off the beaten tourist track. It is one of the largest in America, featuring 175 speciality shops, four major department stores – Burdines, Dillard's, JC Penney and Sears – a choice of 15 eating outlets in Treats food court, plus another four restaurants, including Ruby Tuesday and the Orlando Ale House, and an elegant overall design with marble floors that makes visiting a pleasure. You can also get away from the usual tourist frenzy here to do some serious shopping from 10am–9pm Mon–Sat and from 11am–6pm Sun (weekdays are best, though).

One of the most extensive mall developments is **Seminole Towne Center** just off I4 to the north of Orlando on the outskirts of Sanford. This vast complex (opened in 1997) offers another two-storey wonderland of 100 designer shops and boutiques and 5 department stores (like Burdines and JC Penney) as well as craft stalls, a wide-ranging food court and six full-service restaurants (including Orlando Ale House, Olive Garden and Red Lobster). Turn right off exit 51 of I4

and you are there, and it makes a handy place to while away your last few hours if you have an afternoon flight from the nearby Orlando-Sanford Airport. The Towne Center is open 10am–9pm Mon–Sat, and noon–6pm Sun.

Another recent Seminole County addition is the **Oviedo Marketplace**, an impressive development of almost 100 shops just off the Central Florida Greeneway at Red Bug Lake Road (exit 41, head west and then right into Oviedo Marketplace Boulevard). With three main department stores (Sears, Burdines and Dillard's), a well-planned food court with children's play area, plus four restaurants and the ultra-smart 22-screen Regal Cinema complex ($5.50 before 6pm, $7.75 after, tel. 407 977 1107), the Marketplace has yet to be discovered by the masses and is open 10am–9pm Mon–Sat and noon–6pm Sun. In particular, Cha Cha Coconuts (a taste of the Caribbean) and Chamberlin's Market & Café (for a more health-conscious choice) are highly worthwhile eateries.

The spacious **Osceola Square Mall** (where Highway 192 mysteriously becomes Vine Street along its central stretch) is the only enclosed mall in Kissimmee, with 54 shops and a 12-screen cinema complex (open 10am–9pm Mon–Sat, noon–6pm Sun), including the local outlet of the retail store **Ross**, which deals in end-of-line items from big-name manufacturers like Calvin Klein, Gap and Tommy Hilfiger. If you are prepared for a good rummage through their packed racks, you can collect some real bargains. *'Ross should be on every Brit's shopping list,'* advises reader Mrs B Mair of Stockport.

Orlando Fashion Square Mall just out of the city center has undergone a major redevelopment and now offers a 165-shop spread, four restaurants, a 14-counter food court and an 8-screen AMC cinema

11

complex. Four department stores – JC Penney, Dillard's, Sears and Burdines – anchor a typically broad range of outlets, including Gap, Everything But Water, Bath & Body Works, Zales and The Disney Store. Open from 10am–9pm (Mon–Sat) and noon–6pm (Sun), Fashion Square Mall is located on East Colonial Drive (Route 50), take Exit 41 off I4 and head east 3 miles to Maguire Boulevard.

The big mall news, though, is the building of the most up-scale development to date, the **Mall at Millenia**, just off I4 to the north of Universal Orlando. Scheduled to open in October 2002, it will feature New York's most famous department stores, Bloomingdale's, Neiman Marcus and Macy's, among an expected list of top-name boutiques. These latter had yet to be announced at the time of writing, but the Mall design suggests there will be some innovative and extremely eye-catching elements, all right by Exit 31A of I4. The main entrance will feature a 60ft glass rotunda with a water garden theme, there will be marble and terrazzo floors, a 14-café food court (with orangery garden theming) and two restaurants. It promises to be a breathtaking centre, taking the shopping experience to a new level in Florida.

The Pointe*Orlando

Traditional shopping

The attractions and possibilities of Winter Park's **Park Avenue** have already been detailed in Chapter 8, but the area also boasts the new **Winter Park Village**, a small, up-scale, open-plan development of boutique shops, larger speciality stores like Borders Books, and some fine restaurants. The Village replaced the old Winter Park Mall and is on North Orlando Avenue (exit 45 off I4, head east on Fairbanks Avenue and then north on Highway 17-92, North Orange Avenue, for 2 miles, and it is on the right). It has proved immensely popular with the locals and offers a nice change from the usual malls and plazas – as well as some excellent dining. Check out **PF Chang's Chinese Bistro** (their spicy Szechuan chicken is to die for), **Brio Tuscan Grille** (fine Italian fare) and the amazing (not to mention cavernous) new **Cheesecake Factory**.

More traditional shopping can also be found in the recently revamped **Historical District of Kissimmee** on Broadway, which can be found two blocks south of Highway 192 on Route 17-92, along Main Street and Broadway. These are a number of restored turn-of-the-century buildings featuring craft and gift shops, a children's boutique, country store and seven restaurants (including **Azteca's** for fine Mexican fare), plus antiques, western and sports wear. Every Thursday, the Downtown Farmers Market displays its wares here, too. The Historical District shops are open 10am–5pm (10am–3pm on Sat). Computer

BRIT TIP: You can also take advantage of free e-mail services at main public libraries (*says reader Ann Tootell of Leicester*).

addicts may want to check out the **netkaffee** for the chance to send and receive e-mail (9am–9pm). Look up www.kissimmeecra.com for more information.

Another recent development (and worth a look because they are off the beaten tourist path) are the shops and restaurants of Disney's town of **Celebration**, a unique collection of speciality stores, an ice cream and candy shop, restaurants, cinemas, lakeside dining and Saturday Farmers' Market, plus boat and bike rentals and the superb Celebration Hotel. Follow the signs to downtown Celebration down Celebration Avenue, just off Highway 192 ¼ mile east of its junction with I4. The shops are open 10am–9pm Mon–Sat, noon–6pm Sun. The whole area is worth a look for this recreation of the 'ideal' 1950s-style town, complete with white picket fences, while there are some lovely walks around the main lake.

Park Avenue, Winter Park

Supermarkets

Apart from the big chemist chain stores, **Eckerd** and **Walgreens**, already mentioned, there are a few more typical large-group stores. The main supermarkets you will find are **Publix** and **Goodings**, which are comparable with Asda, Safeway or (in the case of Goodings) Marks and Spencer, while for clothes, DIY, home furnishings, souvenirs, toys, electrical goods and other household items the big discount stores are **K-Mart**, **Wal-Mart** (open 24 hours for serious shopaholics!) or **Target** (like a big version of Tesco's, but without the food department, if that makes sense). If there is anything you've forgotten, the chances are you can get it at the **Wal-Mart Supercenters**, one on Highway 192 next to Medieval Times, another at the junction of Sand Lake Road and John Young Parkway and a new one

towards the east end of Osceola Parkway in the Buenaventura Lakes area. For photographic supplies and film processing, you should try one of the many branches of **Eckerd Express Photo** (although they charge a few dollars more in the main tourist areas).

Specialist shops

Finally, a few worth making a note of for specific items are the various outlets of **World of Denim** (no explanation necessary), **The Sports Authority** and **Sports Dominator**, the former on Sand Lake Road and the latter north of Sand Lake Road, on International Drive, which both offer all manner of sporting goods and apparel, while serious sportsmen and women will also want to visit the magnificent range of the five **Edwin Watts Golf** shops, including their national clearance centre on International Drive, or any of the five **Special Tee Golf & Tennis** shops. On golf clubs in particular you can pick up some great deals and save a lot on the same equipment back home. The **:08 Seconds** store (on Highway 192 opposite Medieval Times) offers the chance to get yourself fully kitted out in the latest cowboy fashions.

11

12 Going Home

(or, Where Did The Last Two Weeks Go?)

And so, dog-tired, financially crippled but (hopefully) blissfully happy and with enough memories to last a lifetime, it is time to deal with that bane of all holidays – the journey home.

If you have come through the last week or two relatively unscathed in terms of the calamities that can befall the uninformed or the plain unlucky, there are still one or two more little pitfalls that can catch you out.

The car

First and foremost is the hire car. It has to be returned to Alamo, or whoever, and that can take a little time if you had to use an off-airport car depot. It is usually a lot easier and quicker to return the car and complete any outstanding paperwork (rare) than to get mobile in the first place, but it is wise to allow half an hour, just in case. The process tends to be even slicker with the firms who operate directly from the two airports.

Orlando International Airport

For reference purposes, the International Airport is 46 miles from Cocoa Beach and 54 from Daytona Beach on the east coast, 84 miles from Tampa and 110 from Clearwater and St Petersburg to the west, 25 from *Walt Disney World* and 10 from Universal Studios; so always allow plenty of time for the journey.

Once negotiated, you are now back where you started in terms of your Orlando adventure, and probably with some time to kill, so here is a full guide to the two main airports.

This modern airport is the 24th largest in the world, one of the fastest-growing and one of the most widely acclaimed for its overall passenger satisfaction values (No. 1 in America and second only to Singapore world-wide in 1999). It topped 30 million passengers in 2000 for the first time (some 80,000 a day on average), putting it level with Gatwick and Hong Kong, and with half the traffic of Heathrow (which has four terminals to Orlando's one). It can, therefore, get busy at peak times, but its 854-acre terminal complex usually handles the crowds with ease, and this is one of the most comfortable and relaxing airports you will find. It boasts a great range of facilities, and its wide, airy concourses feel more like an elegant hotel than an airport (perhaps not too surprising when one end of the terminal is taken up by the airport-run Hyatt Hotel).

Ramps, restrooms, wide lifts and large open areas ensure easy access for wheelchairs, and there are special features like TDD and amplified telephones, wheelchair-height drinking fountains, braille lift controls and companion-care restrooms to assist travellers with disabilities.

You will also find plenty to do here to while away that final hour or two, and, should you have more than a couple of hours to spare, it is worth knowing you can leave your hand luggage at the Baggage Checkroom and take the 15-minute taxi ride to the Florida Mall or take in a film at the big cinema complex just to the north of the airport (a 5-minute journey by taxi). The airport's two information desks (on Level Three) keep all the cinema timetables, so if you think you have time, consult them and hail a cab!

In keeping with the Orlando area, the International Airport is always engaged in staying a step ahead, and a good example is the addition of the **Shipyard Pub and Brewery** in the centre of the terminal, which has bags of Brit appeal. Real beer (albeit still a little on the cold side), excellent bar meals and the option of a tour of their micro-brewery add up to an above-average airport experience. A fourth (and ultra-smart) satellite arm to the main terminal was added in 2000, and a multi-billion dollar project to add a complete new terminal, runway, taxiway and control tower is underway, with the first phase due for completion in 2003.

Landside

As with all international airports, you have a division between **LANDSIDE** (for all visitors to the airport) and **AIRSIDE** (beyond which you need to have a ticket). Orlando's **LANDSIDE** is divided into three levels: **One** is the greatly enhanced area for ground transportation, tour operator desks, parking, buses and the car rental agencies; **Two** is for Baggage Claim (which you negotiated on the way in) and for any private vehicles meeting passengers; **Three** is where you should enter the airport on your

return journey as it holds all the check-in desks, plus shops, restaurants, lockers, bank and information desks. Level Three is effectively sub-divided into four sections: **Landside 'A'** is the check-in section for **Gates 1–29** and **102–126**. Here you will find American Airlines, ATA (American TransAir), Britannia, Continental, TWA, Southwest, JetBlue and AirTran. **Landside 'B'** is home to the check-in desks for **Gates 30–99** and other main airlines, including Northwest, United, USAirways, BA, Delta and Virgin.

Then, once you have checked in, you can choose to explore the **East** and **West** sections of the main concourse which occupies the centre of Level Three. The West end houses the Great Hall, around which are the main shopping and eating areas. Inevitably, Disney & Co. make one last attempt to part you from what's left of your money, so here you will find some more highly impressive gift shops for *Walt Disney World*, SeaWorld and Universal (and there is no airport mark-up either). Other outlets include Bunch-A-Books, Tie Rack, Sunglass International, the Golf Gallery, two newsagents and a highly varied food court (including Burger King, Pizza Hut and Nathan's Famous Hot Dogs). Up the escalators in the centre of the hall is a restaurant of the lively Chili's chain, a Tex-Mex diner and bar.

The **East** end of Level Three tends to be quieter and more picturesque as it is dominated by the eight-storey Hyatt Hotel atrium, featuring palm trees and a large fountain, and there are fewer shops. Universal and SeaWorld both have secondary (and different!) shops, while the Paradise Shop is a newsagent and gift store. For food and drink, there is a **Starbuck's** coffee shop and the **Shipyard Pub**.

12

ORLANDO INTERNATIONAL

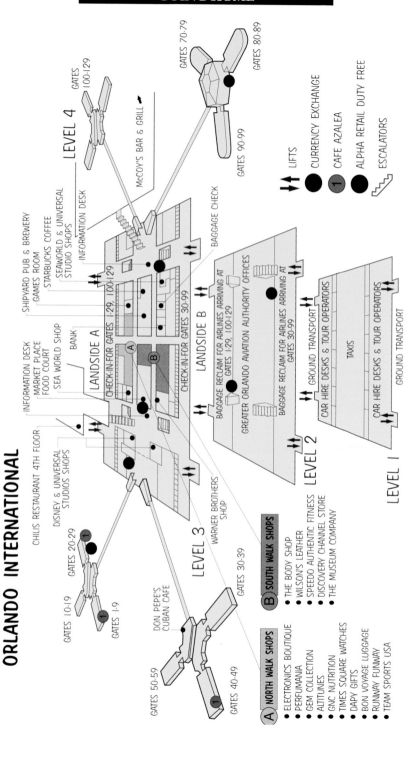

LEVEL 4

GATES 70-79
GATES 80-89
GATES 90-99
GATES 100-129

McCOY'S BAR & GRILL

LIFTS
CURRENCY EXCHANGE
CAFE AZALEA
ALPHA RETAIL DUTY FREE
ESCALATORS

CHILIS RESTAURANT 4TH FLOOR

SHIPYARD PUB & BREWERY
GAMES ROOM
STARBUCKS COFFEE
SEAWORLD & UNIVERSAL STUDIOS SHOPS
INFORMATION DESK
BAGGAGE CHECK

INFORMATION DESK
MARKET PLACE
FOOD COURT
SEA WORLD SHOP
BANK

LANDSIDE A
CHECK-IN FOR GATES 1-29, 100-129

LANDSIDE B
CHECK-IN FOR GATES 30-99

BAGGAGE RECLAIM FOR AIRLINES ARRIVING AT GATES 1-29, 100-129

GREATER ORLANDO AVIATION AUTHORITY OFFICES

BAGGAGE RECLAIM FOR AIRLINES ARRIVING AT GATES 30-99

GROUND TRANSPORT
CAR HIRE DESKS & TOUR OPERATORS
TAXIS
CAR HIRE DESKS & TOUR OPERATORS
GROUND TRANSPORT

LEVEL 2
LEVEL 1

DISNEY & UNIVERSAL STUDIOS SHOPS

WARNER BROTHERS SHOP

LEVEL 3

GATES 20-29
GATES 10-19
GATES 1-9
DON PEPE'S CUBAN CAFE
GATES 30-39
GATES 40-49
GATES 50-59

A NORTH WALK SHOPS
- ELECTRONICS BOUTIQUE
- PERFUMANIA
- GEM COLLECTION
- ALTITUNES
- GNC NUTRITION
- TIMES SQUARE WATCHES
- DAPY GIFTS
- BON VOYAGE LUGGAGE
- RUNWAY FUNWAY
- TEAM SPORTS USA

B SOUTH WALK SHOPS
- THE BODY SHOP
- WILSON'S LEATHER
- SPEEDO AUTHENTIC FITNESS
- DISCOVERY CHANNEL STORE
- THE MUSEUM COMPANY

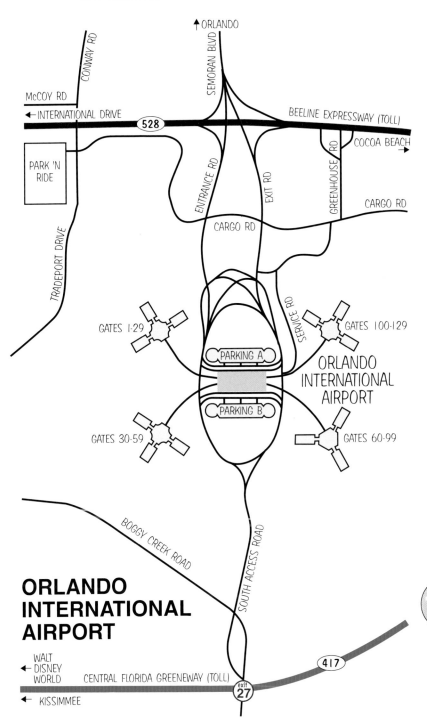

ORLANDO INTERNATIONAL AIRPORT

There is also, up the escalator, the entrance to the Hyatt Airport Hotel if you fancy seeing out your visit in style. **McCoy's Bar and Grill** (up and turn right) is a suitably smart bar-restaurant and has the bonus of a grandstand view of the airport runways to watch all the comings and goings (good for kids). The surroundings are immensely stylish and a long way removed from the average airport lounge. If you want to go really up-market, go up the escalator, turn left and take the lift to the ninth floor and **Hemisphere Restaurant**. Not only do you have an even more impressive view of the runways, its northern Italian cuisine provides some of the best fare in the city. It's slightly on the pricey side, but the service and food are five-star.

> BRIT TIP: Overlooked by many, McCoy's Bar and Grill in the Hyatt Hotel is the perfect little sanctuary to while away that final hour or two.

The central access corridors between the East and West ends house a bank, travel agent, post office, the baggage checkroom and a hair salon, as well as more shopping with the likes of Body Shop, Perfumania, Electronics Boutique, Discovery Channel store and a well-equipped video arcade and playroom for the youngsters.

If you still have time to kill after visiting all these establishments and buying those final gift items, wander round the concourse and examine some of the airport's magnificent art collection or view the large aquarium next to the SeaWorld shop at the East end.

Airside

Once it is time to move on to your departure gate, you have to be aware of the four satellite arms that make up the airport's **AIRSIDE**.

These are divided into **Gates 1–29** and **30–59** at the West end of the terminal, and **60–99** and **102–126** (American domestic flights only) at the **East** end. ALL the departure gates are here, plus duty-free shops, more restaurants and lockers.

The airport's four satellites are each connected to the main building by a shuttle service (as exists between the North and South terminals at Gatwick), so you need to be alert when it comes to finding your departure gate. There are no tannoy announcements for flights, so it's wise to check your departure gate and time when you check in. However, there are large, new monitors in the main terminal which display all the necessary departure information. As a general rule, British Airways and Virgin use Gates 60-99, as do Delta. NorthWest, United and USAir usually use Gates 30-59, while Britannia and ATA depart from Gates 1-29, along with American, Continental and TWA. Airlines using the new Gates 102-126 include low-cost carriers Southwest, JetBlue and AirTran.

In most airports, once you have moved Airside it is not possible to return to the Landside area again. However, that is not the case here, and, if you find the crowds milling around your departure gate too much to bear, you can always return to one of the terminal hostelries, for a bit of peace and quiet.

Having said all that, you should find the Airside areas just as clean and efficient as the main terminal, with the added bonus of three duty-free shops just in case your credit card hasn't already gone into meltdown.

As you pass through the ticket and baggage check at the West end of the terminal you will find the Alpha Retail Duty Free immediately on your right. This is the biggest of their three shops and is open only to departing international passengers, so you will need to have your boarding card handy. Unlike other duty-free shops, you don't walk out with your purchases. Instead, they are delivered to the departure gate for collection as you board the plane. This is because international flights are mixed in with domestic ones and, of course, duty-free shopping does not apply to internal flights.

At **Gates 1–29**, you will find another duty-free shop, plus a newsagents (the Keys Group News and Gifts), two bar-lounges of the Café Azalea, a kids' play area and a mini food court, featuring **Burger King, Cinnabon** and **TCBY** (which stands for The Country's Best Yoghurt). **Gates 30–59** do not to have a duty-free shop, so remember to bag your duty-frees back at the Airside ticket check. However, you will still find a **Café Azalea** lounge bar, **Don Pepe's Cuban Café**, a food court (with **Miami Subs, Villa Pizza** and **Freshens Yogurt**) and a WH Smith's.

Travelling from **Gates 60–99** gives you another duty-free shop, Disney's Flight Fantastic stores, a Stellar Partners newsagents and food court containing **Burger King** (inevitably – it's always the busiest, too), **Nathan's Famous Hot Dogs**, and the **Shipyard Brewport** for that final beverage. As a bonus for parents with young children, there is a sea-themed play area here.

Gates 102-126 offer two outlets of the **Johnny Rivers Smokehouse Express**, a food court with **The Coco Oasis Bar & Lounge, McDonalds** and **Sbarro Pizza**, and two more shops.

For more detail on Orlando International Airport, visit their website at www.fcn.state.fl.us/goaa, which also features 'live' departure and arrival information.

Orlando Sanford Airport

Returning to what is now the main Orlando gateway for British charter flights should be a relatively simple experience, providing you retrace your route on the Central Florida Greeneway and come off at Exit 49. You go across one set of traffic lights, then turn right at the second set on to Lake Mary Boulevard and follow it all the way back into the Airport. New signs have been posted along all the main routes to make the return journey straightforward, and the efficiency of the Alamo and Dollar car-rental return adds to this simplicity.

By way of a little more explanation, Orlando-Sanford was created as a full international airport only in the spring of 1996 as an initiative between the airport authorities and several of the main British tour operators. And so Airtours, jmc airlines, Monarch and Air 2000 all now go for the cheaper and simpler (in operating terms) option of Orlando-Sanford. With its small, uncomplicated design (straight off the plane into Immigration, one baggage carousel and then a walk across the road into the Dollar or Alamo offices) it can get you mobile appreciably quicker. Of course, you are that much further to the north to start with, so your journey time is a

BRIT TIP: By all means stay in the Sanford area for a day or two to check out their natural attractions, but it is not a great base for visiting the theme parks because of morning congestion along I4.

12

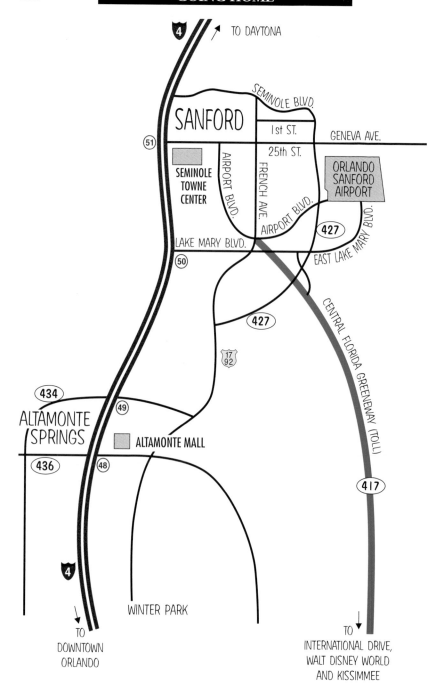

ORLANDO/SANFORD AIRPORT

good 35–40 minutes longer and you have to pay an extra $4–5 in tolls, but, providing you follow the simple directions to the main tourist areas, you can save as much as an hour in overall time taken.

However, while this new charter gateway is a much simpler operation, it stands to reason that you lose out on the extra facilities of the International Airport, which can be a drawback if there is a delay in the flight home for any reason.

The one departure gate access can also create a bit of a bottleneck, but the airport is in the process of expanding and adapting to ease these growing pains, completing its new terminal complex in March 2001. And, when the airport is not at full capacity or subject to unforeseen delays, its facilities are perfectly adequate for a comfortable stay, with a British-style pub and restaurant, snack bar, cafeteria and ice cream shop, a video games room, a well-stocked duty-free shop and a fully supervised (free) childcare centre. More facilities are being added all the time, notably a children's shop, a larger outdoor smoking deck (smoking is severely restricted inside) and a VIP travel lounge for customers of Airtours' Premiair service and other up-graded cabin options. The addition of the extra departure gates has alleviated much of the pressure of sheer numbers, and helped to make Orlando-Sanford as smooth a proposition on the way out as it is on your arrival.

After all that, you can expect your return flight to be somewhat shorter than the journey out thanks to the Atlantic jetstreams that provide handy tail-winds to high-level flights. Differences of more than an hour in the two journey times are not uncommon.

Finally, you will land back at Heathrow, Manchester, Glasgow, etc., rather more jet-lagged than on the trip out. This is because the time difference is more noticeable on eastward flights, and it may take a good day or two to get your body's time-clock back on to local time. It is therefore even more important not to indulge in alcoholic beverages on the flight if you are driving home.

And, much as it may seem like a good idea, the best way to beat Florida jet-lag is NOT to go straight out and book another holiday to Orlando!

But, believe me, the lure of this theme park wonderland is almost impossible to resist once sampled – you WILL want to return.

Now give something back

After hopefully having the holiday of a lifetime, you might like to know about a charity helping children with terminal illnesses to have a memorable time here, too. **Give Kids The World** is a unique, amazing organisation in Kissimmee which provides a week's fantasy holiday for terminally ill children who wish to visit the central Florida attractions. GKTW works with other wish-granting foundations around the world and basically provides all the local facilities for the child – and their family – to find some joy in their lives. It is set up as a village resort and includes all meals, accommodation, transport, attractions, tickets, use of video camera and many other thoughtful touches in a magical setting. It is a truly wonderful charity, one I am happy to support myself, and I hope you will help, too. You can make a donation on their website – www.gktw.org – or send it to: Give Kids The World, 210 South Bass Road, Kissimmee, Florida 34746, USA. Thank you.

12

13 Your Holiday Planner

You can design your own holiday schedule on pages 278–79 with the aid of the theme park Busy Day guide on page 280.

Example 1: with 5-day Park Hopper Plus Pass

DAY	ATTRACTION		NOTES
SUN	DAY		
	EVE		
MON	DAY		
	EVE		
TUE	DAY		
	EVE		
WED	DAY		
	EVE		
THUR	DAY	Arrive 2.40pm local time Orlando-Sanford Airport	*NB: 55 mins to drive to hotel*
	EVE	Check out local shops and restaurants	
FRI	DAY	Welcome meeting/UNIVERSAL STUDIOS	
	EVE		
SAT	DAY	DISNEY'S ANIMAL KINGDOM THEME PARK	*(8am start)*
	EVE	Medieval Times Dinner Show	
SUN	DAY	THE MAGIC KINGDOM PARK	*(Open until 10pm today)*
	EVE		
MON	DAY	SEAWORLD	
	EVE		
TUE	DAY	BUSCH GARDENS	
	EVE		
WED	DAY	KENNEDY SPACE CENTER	
	EVE	Skull Kingdom/WonderWorks/Pointe*Orlando	

Disney's 5-Day Park Hopper Plus Pass gives 5 days at the main theme parks, plus TWO of Blizzard Beach, Typhoon Lagoon, River Country, Pleasure Island and Disney's Wide World of Sports; there may be a separate charge for big events at Wide World of Sports.

DAY		ATTRACTION	NOTES
THUR	DAY	DISNEY-MGM STUDIOS	
	EVE		
FRI	DAY	ISLANDS OF ADVENTURE	
	EVE	Universal Orlando's CityWalk	*(until late!)*
SAT	DAY	Winter Park Lakes/shopping/museums	
	EVE		
SUN	DAY	EPCOT	*(open until 9pm)*
	EVE		
MON	DAY	Fantasy of Flight and Splendid China	
	EVE	Pleasure Island	
TUE	DAY	Aquatic Wonders Tours/Warbird Air Museum	
	EVE	Arabian Nights	
WED	DAY	Blizzard Beach/EPCOT	*(Arrive late this time)*
	EVE		
THUR	DAY	Gatorland/Back to airport	
	EVE		*Flight 6pm; return car at 3.30pm*
FRI	DAY	Return Gatwick 7am	
	EVE		
SAT	DAY		
	EVE		
SUN	DAY		
	EVE		

14

Example 2: with 7-day Park Hopper Plus Pass

Disney's 7-Day Park Hopper Plus Pass gives 7 days at the main theme parks, plus FOUR of Blizzard Beach, Typhoon Lagoon, River Country, Pleasure Island and Disney's Wide World of Sports; there may be a separate charge for big events at Disney's Wide World of Sports.

DAY		ATTRACTION	NOTES
SUN	DAY		
	EVE		
MON	DAY		
	EVE		
TUE	DAY		
	EVE		
WED	DAY		
	EVE		
THUR	DAY	Arrive 2.40pm local time Orlando-Sanford Airport	*NB: 55 mins to drive to hotel*
	EVE	Check out local shops and restaurants	
FRI	DAY	Welcome Meeting + UNIVERSAL STUDIOS	*(Open until 8pm)*
	EVE		
SAT	DAY	DISNEY-MGM STUDIOS	
	EVE		
SUN	DAY	THE MAGIC KINGDOM PARK	*(Open until 11pm today)*
	EVE		
MON	DAY	KENNEDY SPACE CENTER	
	EVE	Medieval Times Dinner Show	
TUE	DAY	DISNEY-MGM STUDIOS	
	EVE	Evening at Fun Spot with kids	
WED	DAY	Disney's Blizzard Beach/EPCOT	*Late afternoon at Epcot*
	EVE		

DAY		ATTRACTION	NOTES
THUR	DAY	SEAWORLD	
	EVE	Hoop-Dee-Doo Revue	*(9pm show)*
FRI	DAY	THE MAGIC KINGDOM PARK/River Country	*(Open until 10pm; go to River Country for an afternoon break)*
	EVE		
SAT	DAY	Winter Park Lakes or Silver Springs	
	EVE	Relax!	
SUN	DAY	ANIMAL KINGDOM	*(8am start)*
	EVE	Pleasure Island	*(Open until late!)*
MON	DAY	BUSCH GARDENS	
	EVE		
TUE	DAY	ISLANDS OF ADVENTURE	
	EVE	Wet 'n Wild	*(Open until 11pm)*
WED	DAY	Typhoon Lagoon/EPCOT	
	EVE	Universal Orlando's CityWalk	*(Final fling!)*
THUR	DAY	Gatorland/Back to Airport	*Check-out by midday*
	EVE		*Flight 6pm; return car at 3.30pm*
FRI	DAY	Return Gatwick 7am	
	EVE		
SAT	DAY		
	EVE		
SUN	DAY		
	EVE		

14

Blank form: your holiday!

DAY	ATTRACTION	NOTES
SUN	DAY ——————————— EVE	
MON	DAY ——————————— EVE	
TUE	DAY ——————————— EVE	
WED	DAY ——————————— EVE	
THUR	DAY ——————————— EVE	
FRI	DAY ——————————— EVE	
SAT	DAY ——————————— EVE	
SUN	DAY ——————————— EVE	
MON	DAY ——————————— EVE	
TUE	DAY ——————————— EVE	
WED	DAY ——————————— EVE	

DAY	ATTRACTION	NOTES
THUR	DAY	
	EVE	
FRI	DAY	
	EVE	
SAT	DAY	
	EVE	
SUN	DAY	
	EVE	
MON	DAY	
	EVE	
TUE	DAY	
	EVE	
WED	DAY	
	EVE	
THUR	DAY	
	EVE	
FRI	DAY	
	EVE	
SAT	DAY	
	EVE	
SUN	DAY	
	EVE	

14

BUSY DAY GUIDE

	BUSIEST	AVERAGE	LIGHTEST
MON	EPCOT MAGIC KINGDOM DISNEY'S ANIMAL KINGDOM THEME PARK ISLANDS OF ADVENTURE	DISNEY-MGM STUDIOS UNIVERSAL STUDIOS	BUSCH GARDENS SEAWORLD KENNEDY SPACE CENTER WATER PARKS
TUE	EPCOT UNIVERSAL STUDIOS DISNEY'S ANIMAL KINGDOM THEME PARK	MAGIC KINGDOM DISNEY-MGM STUDIOS	BUSCH GARDENS SEAWORLD KENNEDY SPACE CENTER ISLANDS OF ADVENTURE WATER PARKS
WED	DISNEY-MGM STUDIOS DISNEY'S ANIMAL KINGDOM THEME PARK	ISLANDS OF ADVENTURE MAGIC KINGDOM WATER PARKS	UNIVERSAL STUDIOS SEAWORLD KENNEDY SPACE CENTER BUSCH GARDENS EPCOT
THUR	MAGIC KINGDOM UNIVERSAL STUDIOS	EPCOT WATER PARKS DISNEY'S ANIMAL KINGDOM THEME PARK BUSCH GARDENS SEAWORLD	DISNEY-MGM STUDIOS KENNEDY SPACE CENTER ISLANDS OF ADVENTURE
FRI	WATER PARKS EPCOT SEAWORLD	ISLANDS OF ADVENTURE BUSCH GARDENS KENNEDY SPACE CENTER DISNEY-MGM STUDIOS	MAGIC KINGDOM UNIVERSAL STUDIOS DISNEY'S ANIMAL KINGDOM THEME PARK
SAT	MAGIC KINGDOM UNIVERSAL/IOA BUSCH GARDENS SEAWORLD KENNEDY SPACE CENTER WATER PARKS	DISNEY-MGM STUDIOS	DISNEY'S ANIMAL KINGDOM THEME PARK EPCOT
SUN	DISNEY-MGM STUDIOS BUSCH GARDENS SEAWORLD KENNEDY SPACE CENTER WATER PARKS UNIVERSAL STUDIOS ISLANDS OF ADVENTURE	DISNEY'S ANIMAL KINGDOM THEME PARK	MAGIC KINGDOM EPCOT

14 Index

The author wishes to acknowledge the help of the following in the production of this book:

The Orlando Tourism Bureau in London, The Orlando/Orange County Convention & Visitors' Bureau, Visit Florida, The Kissimmee/St Cloud Convention & Visitors' Bureau in London and Kissimmee, Walt Disney Attractions Inc., Universal Orlando, The Greater Orlando Aviation Authority, Orlando-Sanford International Airport, The Busch Entertainment Corporation, The Orange County Sheriff's Office, Seminole County Convention & Visitors' Bureau, Visit USA Association, St Petersburg/Clearwater Area Convention & Visitors' Bureau, Daytona Beach Area Convention & Visitors' Bureau, Winter Park Chamber of Commerce, The Orlando Sentinel, Alamo Rent A Car, Grand Theme Hotels Group, HM Customs and Excise Office, Airwave Communications.

In person, Oonagh McCullagh (Orlando Tourism Bureau) and Zoe Ward (Icas PR), Jason Bevan, Margaret Melia, Paula Cressey, Jason Lasecki (Walt Disney), Danielle Courtenay, Rick Gregory (Orlando CVB), Larry White, Geo Morales (Kissimmee CVB), Wit Tuttell (St Petersburg/Clearwater CVB), Sherman Briscoe, Susan McLain (Daytona Beach CVB), Linda Buckley, Michael McLane (Universal), Kate Burgess (Visit Florida), Carolyn Fennell (Orlando Aviation Authority), Mike Moran (Airwave), Susan Flower, Kjerstin Dillon (SeaWorld), Glenn Haddad (Discovery Cove), Honoria Nadeau, Will Darnall (Busch Gardens), Anthea Yabsley, Sarah Bolam (Synergy PR), Jack West (Seminole county CVB), Laura Richeson (Bennett & Company), Mary Kenny (Grand Theme Hotels), Michelle Salyer, Heather Strickland (Kennedy Space Center), Al Riley (Splendid China), Robyn DeRidder (Cypress Gardens), Steve Specht (Silver Springs), Pamela Peterson (Fantasy of Flight), Pashen Black (US Astronaut Hall of Fame), Angel Bencivenga (Wet 'n Wild), Michael Caires (Orlando-Sanford Airport), Suzanne McGovern (Yesawich, Pepperdine & Brown), Allan Oakley (Alexander & Associates), Nigel Worral (Florida Leisure), Wrenda Goodwyn, Zina Talsma International Drive/I-Ride), Todd Hansen (Ripley's), Loretta Shaffer (Old Town), Melissa Kranz (Orange County History Center), Jeff Stanford (Orlando Science Center), Donna Turner (Medieval Times), Michele Plant (Disney's Wide World of Sports), Phillip Jaffe (Pro Gold Guides of Orlando), Lisa Klemme (Pointe*Orlando), Kyle Eshliman (Fun Spot), Lisa Christian (Church Street Station), KT Budde Jones (Warbird Museum), Tom Richard (Warbird Adventures), Mella Jacobs (Forever Florida), Brian Wettstein (Winter Park Chamber of Commerce), Margie Long (Boggy Creek Airboats) and Naomi Lewis (Virgin Holidays), plus my research 'assistants' Michele Carpenter, Marcia Harris and Matt Heffernan, and travel writer Karen Marchbank. Thank you all.

Very special thanks to Pete Werner and all at DIS – you know who you are!

Got a red-hot Brit Tip to pass on? The latest info on how to beat the queues or the best new restaurant in town? We want to hear from YOU to keep improving the guide each year. Drop us a line at: Brit's Guides (Orlando), W. Foulsham & Co. Ltd, The Publishing House, Bennetts Close, Cippenham, Slough, Berkshire SL1 5AP. Or e-mail: simonveness.orlando1@virgin.net

Reader tips from: Les Willans, Shirley Ahmed and family, Edward Lipinski Baltrop, John Knights, Paul Monagham, Mark Henderson, Tom burton, Paul Lang, Fiona Chapman, Lisa Gill, Mindy Gittoes, Charles Scholes, Matt Rentell and Liz Shaw, John Cartlidge, Wendy Graham, Alastair Gilliees, Penny Barker, Denise Buckley and ave Anderson (via e-mail); Mrs B Mair, Stockport; Mrs A Tootell, Leicester; Mr R. Williams, Stafford; Miss Irene Bruce (Montrose); Caroline Green (West Molesey); and Pat Crouzieres (Staffs).